The Frontier Complex

Kyle J. Gardner reveals the transformation of the historical Himalayan entrepôt of Ladakh into a modern, disputed borderland through an examination of rare British, Indian, Ladakhi, and Kashmiri archival sources. In so doing, he provides both a history of the rise of geopolitics and the first comprehensive history of Ladakh's encounter with the British Empire. He examines how colonial border-making practices transformed geography into a political science and established principles that a network of imperial frontier experts would apply throughout the empire and bequeath to an independent India. Through analyzing the complex of imperial policies and practices, *The Frontier Complex* reveals how the colonial state transformed, and was transformed by, new ways of conceiving of territory. Yet, despite a century of attempts to craft a suitable border, the British failed. The result is an imperial legacy still playing out across the Himalayas.

Kyle J. Gardner is a nonresident scholar at the Sigur Center for Asian Studies at the George Washington University.

The Frontier Complex

Geopolitics and the Making of the India–China Border, 1846–1962

Kyle J. Gardner

George Washington University

CAMBRIDGE
UNIVERSITY PRESS

CAMBRIDGE
UNIVERSITY PRESS

University Printing House, Cambridge CB2 8BS, United Kingdom

One Liberty Plaza, 20th Floor, New York, NY 10006, USA

477 Williamstown Road, Port Melbourne, VIC 3207, Australia

314–321, 3rd Floor, Plot 3, Splendor Forum, Jasola District Centre, New Delhi – 110025, India

79 Anson Road, #06–04/06, Singapore 079906

Cambridge University Press is part of the University of Cambridge.

It furthers the University's mission by disseminating knowledge in the pursuit of education, learning, and research at the highest international levels of excellence.

www.cambridge.org
Information on this title: www.cambridge.org/9781108840590
DOI: 10.1017/9781108886444

© Kyle J. Gardner 2021

First published 2021

A catalogue record for this publication is available from the British Library.

ISBN 978-1-108-84059-0 Hardback

For Amanda

Contents

Figures

Maps

Tables

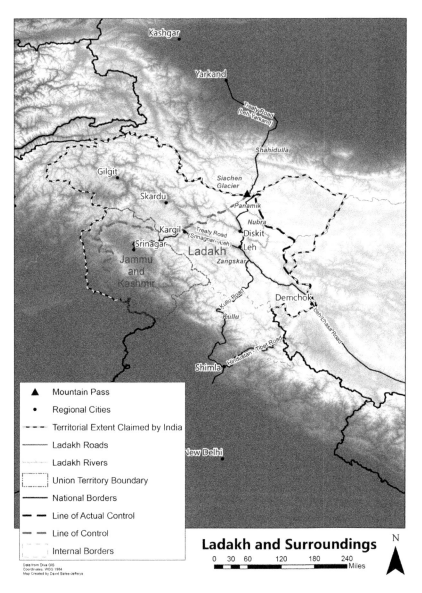

Map 0.1 Ladakh and its surroundings. © David Bates-Jeffreys.

Preface

Our interest's on the dangerous edge of things.[1]

— Robert Browning, 1855

In a dark corner of the main reading room at the National Archives of India in New Delhi hangs an unusual map. Rendered in the standard colors of political maps of the late British Empire, this 1950 Survey of India production contains one peculiar feature. In a large segment of its northern extreme, there is no sign of a border. Instead, the ubiquitous pink wash signaling territorial control gradually fades into the empty white space of northwestern Tibet. In this Switzerland-sized high-altitude region, now generally referred to as the Aksai Chin, the map shows no borderline and no stark color contrast to delimit territorial control – nothing but an official acknowledgment of absence. For the colonial and early postcolonial governments of India, the northwestern Himalayan border was a "known unknown," to evoke a hierarchy of ignorance from a more recent moment of geopolitical hubris.[2] Numerous maps produced by the Survey of India, from the late nineteenth century through (and shortly after) independence and Partition in 1947, include similar details (Maps 0.2 and 0.3).

Not all political maps of the newly independent state were as revealing as Map 0.2 or the 1950 Survey of India map that hangs in the National Archives of India. But whether represented on maps or not, the ambiguity of the northwestern border proved intolerable to the young nation-state in the decades after its independence. This imperial legacy of an undemarcated boundary culminated in a deadly face-off across the desolate Aksai

---

[1] Robert Browning, "Bishop Blougram's Apology," in *Browning's Men and Women, 1855* (Oxford: Clarendon Press, 1911), 141. The "dangerous edge" Browning describes is moral ambiguity. As this book will argue, ambiguous edges are equally applicable to the history of border making.

[2] Though earlier instances of the phrase exist, it was made famous by US president George W. Bush's secretary of defense, Donald Rumsfeld, during a Department of Defense news briefing on February 12, 2002. Rumsfeld used the term to defend evidence (later debunked) linking the Iraqi government's alleged weapons of mass destruction to terrorist groups.

Map 0.2 "India: Projects in Hand" (August 1947). Survey of India.
PAHAR/Mountains of Central Asia Digital Dataset.

Chin in 1962.[3] The brief Sino-Indian War imposed the first effective
borderline in the region, referred to in India as the Line of Actual
Control (LAC) – though that line has yet to be demarcated by actual
boundary commissions from either side.[4] The vast territory of this virtually uninhabited region remains a bone of contention between the world's
two most populous nations. Not unexpectedly, its cartographic representation has thus become a major concern for the Indian state. In 2015,
the Indian government banned Al Jazeera from television airways for
five days in response to that network's failure to label as a part of

---

[3] The 1962 war also witnessed fighting in the northeastern Himalaya, in the region now
known as the Indian state of Arunachal Pradesh – but referred to by the Chinese government as Zàngnán (South Tibet).
[4] Shaurya Karanbir Gurung, "India and China Need to Demarcate LAC," *The Economic
Times*, September 6, 2017.

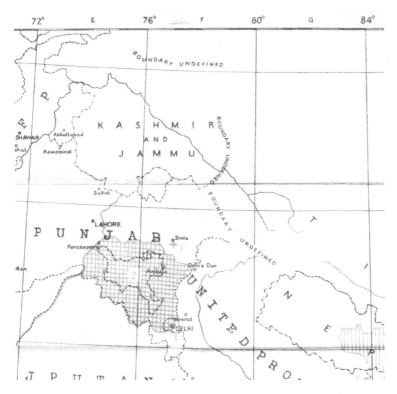

Map 0.3 Detail of Map 0.2, showing "boundary undefined."

India certain territories now occupied by Pakistan and China in the northwestern Himalaya. The government labeled this failure a "cartographic aggression."[5] A year later, legislation was introduced in India's Parliament to strengthen existing laws that criminalized maps for failing to represent India's claimed border.[6] In responding to these "aggressions," the government of India was also confronting a legacy of colonial border making and the inheritance of an imperial frontier.

The history of the undefined border in the Aksai Chin also reveals a more pronounced fault line: the temporal divide between empire and nation-state. The British Empire had long tolerated a degree of vagueness in its frontiers and borders. Its management of these spaces involved practices that varied according to economic interests, proximity of rival

[5] Avaneesh Pandey, "India Bans Al Jazeera for 5 Days over 'Incorrect' Kashmir Map," *International Business Times*, April 23, 2015.
[6] Officially titled the Geospatial Information Bill of 2016, which failed to pass the Lok Sabha.

powers, and apparent threats posed by indigenous peoples. Though often cause for administrative anxiety, territorial ambiguity could be accepted. But the new Indian nation-state could not accept this ambiguity. This intolerance was in no way lessened by the fact that much of the land surrounding the western Himalayan borders in question was uninhabited: a barren, high-altitude plateau "where not even a blade of grass grows," according to India's first prime minister, Jawaharlal Nehru.[7] For India, the border possessed existential significance, reflecting the limit of what Thongchai Winichakul has aptly called the "geo-body" of a nation.[8]

But besides this dramatic shift in how frontiers and borders were viewed by empires and nation-states, the imperial legacy of border making reveals a global shift in how states view their territory. This book contends that the twentieth-century global preoccupation with borders was not simply a by-product of decolonization and the proliferation of nation-states. Rather, this preoccupation resulted from a new way of envisioning political space, one that bound the abstract notion of sovereignty to the concrete practices of geographical science. It is the purpose of this book to show how colonial border-making practices, rooted in changing conceptions of geography, actively shaped conceptions of territory and produced postcolonial borderlands. The coeval development of border-making practices, geographical science, and imperial security reveals a new means of envisioning space: geopolitics.

---

[7] Nehru made this comment in the Rajya Sabha on September 10, 1959, during a discussion of growing tensions with China. Madhavan K. Palat, ed., *Selected Works of Jawaharlal Nehru*, vol. 52 (1959), Second Series (New Delhi: Jawaharlal Nehru Memorial Fund, 1984), 186.

[8] Thongchai Winichakul, *Siam Mapped: A History of the Geo-Body of a Nation* (Honolulu: University of Hawai'i Press, 1994).

Acknowledgments

This book emerged from a decades-long fascination with the Himalaya. Its genesis had no central research question or problem, no guiding hypothesis, and certainly no awareness of what archival records might exist to give it life. But it has emerged, nonetheless, thanks in no small part to mentors, colleagues, and friends who have advised, challenged, and helped me to refine my ideas along the way.

I first visited Ladakh in 2005, toward the end of the School for International Training's Tibetan Studies semester program during my junior year at Wesleyan University. I returned to spend one very long winter in Sabu village, helping the Ladakhi scholar Nawang Tsering Shakspo compile his *Cultural History of Ladakh*. The hospitality of Nawang's family made the winter much warmer. After leaving Ladakh to start graduate school at the University of Chicago, I was able to return to Ladakh with some regularity between extended archival trips to Jammu and Shimla and, of course, lots of time in Delhi. Nawang and his family have made Sabu feel like a second home, and I am deeply grateful to them all: *Ama-le* (Yangchan Dolma), *Meme* Phuntsok, Rinchen, Dhondup, Stanzin, Kuney, and, of course, Chondrol. Sonam Wangchuk Shakspo, Rinchen, and Norbu have been wonderful hosts in Delhi, and thanks are also owed to Sonam for giving me access to Bakula Rinpoche's unpublished autobiography.

This book first took shape at the University of Chicago. Thanks there are owed to many but, above all, to my dissertation committee: James Hevia, Dipesh Chakrabarty, Fredrik Albritton Jonsson, and Ken Pomeranz. Their insights, feedback, and encouragement helped me to transform my fascination with the Himalaya, empire, and borders into the book before you. Muzaffar Alam, Elena Bashir, C. M. Naim, and Karma Ngodup guided me through the hurdles and intricacies of studying Urdu and Tibetan. Irving Birkner and the staff of the Committee on Southern Asian Studies helped me navigate the byzantine administrative structures of the University of Chicago. The South Asia bibliographers Jim Nye and Laura Ring were invaluable fonts of historical resources. And the former

Department of South Asian Languages and Civilizations administrator and "Foster [Hall] mother" Alicia Czaplewski was always the epitome of kindness and institutional wisdom, even to students like me from other departments. Finally, Mark Philip Bradley was an exceedingly generous teacher, mentor, and guide to navigating graduate school – a trait that stood out all the more in a department not known for its friendliness.

Directly and indirectly, a number of friends have also contributed to this project. Thanks to Nick Abbott, Sam Allison, Robin Bates, Dan Haines, Kate Hartmann, Jaewoong Jeon, Elisabeth Leake, Zak Leonard, Elizabeth Lhost, Naveena Naqvi, Hasan Siddiqui, Tom Simpson, Lauren Stokes, and Jesse Watson for offering invaluable feedback on various chapter drafts. Thanks also to David Ansari, Lee Bagan, David Bates-Jeffreys (whose wonderful map has made this book's subject more legible), Davi Bernstein, Josh Bryant, Louis Caditz-Peck, Cathleen Chopra-McGowan, John Cropper, Eugene Dizenko, Liz Fretwell, Namrata Kotwani, Nabanjan Maitra, Alison Davis Ricketts, Will Ricketts, Mike Riggio, Colin Rydell, the (growing) Strayer–Turado–Gutkotvich clan, and Mathurin Tia. And to the members of the Wednesday writing group who let me crash their party – Liz Chatterjee, Tyler Williams, and Faridah Zaman – thank you (and thank you all for being consistently late, as it saved me a lot of money in unbought rounds of coffee).

My archive friends helped turned solitary spaces into friendly places – not to mention helping to ward off rogue monkeys, wait out power outages, and commiserate over obstructive archivists: Tanja Buehrer, Adhitya Dhanapal, Francesca Fuoli, Bérénice Guyot-Réchard, James Hall, Rajbir Singh Judge, Shahin Kachwala, Raphaëlle Khan, and Padma Maitland. In Delhi, thanks above all to Nick Abbott for showing me the ropes at the archives and kebab stands alike.

I also thank scholars and mentors farther afield who have been guides at various stages of research, writing, and thinking about Himalayan borders: the late Chris Bayly, Mona Bhan, John Bray, Swati Chawla, Salman Haider, Ben Hopkins, Dan Jantzen, Vijay Pinch, Tashi Rabgyas, Mahesh Rangarajan, Janet Rizvi, Jim Scott, Arjun Sharma, Gary Shaw, and Sonal Singh.

Thanks to Daniel Morgan for helping me decipher challenging hand-written documents in Persian and Urdu – and in some cases completely translating them for me. Suzanne Bratt and James Bratt are owed a tremendous debt of gratitude for their painstaking editing to help get the manuscript of this book fit to print. And Lucy Rhymer and Emily Sharp at CUP have been wonderful shepherds through the publication process. Above all, thanks to my tenth-grade English teacher, Richard White, for his meticulous comments on first drafts and his liberal use of red pen. Together with his former colleagues, Tom Kelly and John Knudsen, Mr. White proves that our best teachers (though he would prefer "one's") always remain teachers. Happily, he has become a good friend as well. The best parts of these chapters are most likely thanks to them, while the remaining typos or errors are mine.

Funding for much of my research was made possible by a Junior Fellowship from the American Institute of Indian Studies, two Foreign Language Area Studies Fellowships to study Urdu, the University of Chicago's Committee on Southern Asian Studies and Nicholson Center for British Studies, and a William Rainey Harper/Provost Fellowship from the Social Science Division at the University of Chicago.

Thanks are also owed to several journals and their editors for kindly allowing me to reproduce portions of previously published work. An earlier version of chapter 2 appeared in *The Historical Journal* in 2019.[1] Sections of my 2013 *HIMALAYA* article, "The Ready Materials for Another World," appear in chapters 1 and 3.[2] And many thanks to Shah Mahmoud Hanifi and Hurst & Co. for permission to reproduce portions of the chapter I contributed to his edited volume, *Mountstuart Elphinstone in South Asia*.[3]

The final stages of this book were completed while working at McLarty Associates in Washington, DC. I could not have asked for a better team to introduce me to the South Asia policy world, nor a friendlier or more distinguished group of experts: Alyssa Ayres, Bob Blake, Safiya Ghori-Ahmad, Rick Rossow, Tezi Schaffer, and Balinder Singh.

My family might not have instilled in me the practical skills to push me toward a profitable career, but they always indulged my intellectual curiosity. This book takes that indulgence to its logical extreme. Thanks to Mom, Diane, and Ed for their love and support over the years. My father, the one family member who would have actually enjoyed reading this book, did not live to see me go to graduate school. But I can still probably thank or blame him more than anyone else for my academic pursuits.

Most of all, I owe thanks to Amanda. I have graduate school to thank for our happy chance meeting during math camp. I didn't sharpen my math skills, but I did find a partner with whom to explore the world.

---

[1] Kyle Gardner, "Moving Watersheds, Borderless Maps, and Imperial Geography in India's Northwestern Himalaya," *The Historical Journal* 62, no. 1 (2019): 149–70.

[2] Kyle Gardner, "The Ready Materials for Another World: Frontier, Security, and the Hindustan–Tibet Road in the Nineteenth Century Northwestern Himalaya," *Himalaya, the Journal of the Association for Nepal and Himalayan Studies* 33, nos. 1–2 (2013): 71–84.

[3] Kyle Gardner, "Elphinstone, Geography, and the Specter of Afghanistan in the Himalaya," in *Mountstuart Elphinstone in South Asia: Pioneer of British Colonial Rule*, ed. Shah Mahmoud Hanifi, 205–21 (London: Hurst, 2019).

A Note on the Text

Tibetan Script

At least on paper, standard Tibetan and Ladakhi are the same language. As spoken languages, however, they are not mutually intelligible. Spoken Ladakhi pronounces many of the prefixes, suffixes, and superscripts that fall silent in most modern Tibetan dialects. Debates in Ladakh have simmered for decades over whether to reflect these differences by employing a simplified script better suited to colloquial Ladakhi pronunciation. Fortunately, I do not need to wade into this fraught territory for the purposes of transliteration.

For Tibetan and Ladakhi, I have generally followed the American Library Association–Library of Congress (ALA-LC) romanization of Tibetan letters derived from the Wylie transliteration system. To reflect the Tibetan/Ladakhi use of a mark (*tsheg*) to separate syllables (regardless of whether it falls within or between words), I have inserted periods to mark multisyllabic terms (i.e., *rgyal.po* [king] rather than the Wylie version, *rgyal po*). For readers unaccustomed to Tibetan, I hope this will render these terms slightly more readable.[1] For proper nouns without common romanized versions, I have capitalized the first pronounced letter. I have used common spelling conventions for those words commonly known in English (yak, as opposed to *g.yag*, or Lhasa, as opposed to Lha.sa). Finally, I have used the modern English spellings for commonly known place-names, for instance, Ladakh instead of its Ladakhi and Tibetan transliteration (La.dwags), its common Urdu transliteration (Ladākh or Laddākh), or the many colonial-era English renderings (Ladak, Latac, Ladag, Ladec, and so on).

---

[1] The complicating exception to this practice will be to follow Wiley in using a period to distinguish between a small number of subscribed letters and prefixes. For instance, I transliterate "yak" as *g.yag*, to distinguish the prefix *g* from the conjoined letter formed with *g* and *y*.

Arabic and Devanagari Scripts

Transliteration is more straightforward for Urdu, Persian, and Hindi. I have generally followed ALA-LC rules, except for commonly romanized words. For instance, I have simplified transliterations of the nasalization mark in Devanagari (known as Anusvāra), utilizing "ṉ" (the ALA-LC's transliteration of Urdu's nūn g̣unnā) instead of the six variations preferred by the ALA-LC for Hindi romanization.

Introduction

Whether or not we acknowledge them, the territorial borders of our modern world still shape the narratives historians write. These ubiquitous lines of political control have become "global uniformities," emerging with what C. A. Bayly termed the "birth of the modern world."[1] Many of today's borders embody linear legacies of empire, reflecting the territorialization of the globe in the nineteenth century as European empires reached the zeniths of their power. And while many historians have recently attempted to transcend the national borders of the present by turning (or returning) to global scales of analysis, persistent questions of state formation at the core of even the most global histories resist the boundary-dissolving tendencies of transnational history – though the history of modern border making is itself a decidedly transnational one.

For all their continued relevance, however, territorial borders are rarely examined through the historical practices and ideas that actually produced them.[2] Analyzing border making has mostly fallen to political theorists interested in examining issues of sovereignty and the rise of border infrastructures relating to globalization, migration, security, and capital flow.[3] For historians, territorial borders are too often assumed to be diplomatic or cartographic byproducts of imperial rivalries and state

---

[1] C. A. Bayly, *The Birth of the Modern World, 1780–1914* (Oxford: Blackwell, 2004).

[2] Recent work in political geography, however, has given rise to a number of "border biographies" that examine the histories of individual borders. The term "boundary biography" was proposed by Nick Megoran, *Nationalism in Central Asia: A Biography of the Uzbekistan–Kyrgyzstan Boundary* (Pittsburgh, PA: University of Pittsburgh Press, 2017). Other notable examples at varying geographical scales include Peter Sahlins, *Boundaries: The Making of France and Spain in the Pyrenees* (Berkeley: University of California Press, 1989); Wim van Spengen, *Tibetan Border Worlds: A Geohistorical Analysis of Trade and Traders* (London: Kegan Paul International, 2000); Willem van Schendel, *The Bengal Borderland: Beyond State and Nation in South Asia* (London: Anthem Press, 2003); and Madeleine Reeves, *Border Work: Spatial Lives of the State in Rural Central Asia* (Ithaca, NY: Cornell University Press, 2014). Thanks to Claire Kaiser for this last recommendation and others on Central Asian borderlands.

[3] Recent examples in political theory and philosophy include Wendy Brown, *Walled States, Waning Sovereignty* (New York: Zone Books, 2010); Sandro Mezzadra and Brett Neilson,

formation, ignored on the ground until walls were built and guards were deployed.[4] But borders and borderlands, whether real or imagined, are spaces and ideas produced over time through particular practices. Though these practices may result in built structures – what the philosopher Thomas Nail has recently called "border regimes" – these structures are rooted in much more significant changes in conceptions of space, geography, territory, and the concept of the border itself.[5] Similarly, acknowledging the mutable quality of borderlands should not imply a neat, progressive trajectory within a given border's history. This teleological tendency has been too often asserted or assumed in scholarship on borderlands.[6] Rather, as this book will show, the creation of borders and borderlands is far from linear in practice. The transformation of regions into borderlands is not simply about the making of a particular kind of space. Instead, the history of colonial border making reveals new ways of thinking about geography, politics, and power. For the British in the Himalaya,[7] the process of transforming a historical crossroads into a frontier also transformed the colonial, and eventually the postcolonial, state.

Border as Method; or, The Multiplication of Labor (Durham, NC: Duke University Press, 2013); Walter Mignolo, *Local Histories/Global Designs: Coloniality, Subaltern Knowledges, and Border Thinking* (Princeton, NJ: Princeton University Press, 2012); and Thomas Nail, *Theory of the Border* (Oxford: Oxford University Press, 2016). Those works that do take into account the historical *longue durée* of borders tend to focus on European conceptions of borders (Stuart Elden, *The Birth of Territory* [Chicago: University of Chicago Press, 2015]), though sometimes in an imperial context (Charles Maier, *Once within Borders: Territories of Power, Wealth, and Belonging since 1500* (Cambridge, MA: Harvard University Press, 2016).

[4] There are some exceptions. Notable historical works on specific borders include Sahlins, *Boundaries*; and Alexander C. Diener and Joshua Hagen, eds., *Borderlines and Borderlands: Political Oddities at the Edge of the Nation-State* (Plymouth, UK: Rowman and Littlefield, 2010). In South Asia, Partition has received intense historical scrutiny, although, as Joya Chatterji and others have shown, the process of partitioning India actually reflected very little concern over the lines of partition as borders. See Joya Chatterji, "The Fashioning of a Frontier: The Radcliffe Line and Bengal's Border Landscape, 1947–52," *Modern Asian Studies* 33, no. 1 (1999): 185–242; Ritu Menon, *Borders and Boundaries: Women in India's Partition* (New Delhi: Kali for Women, 1998); Lucy Chester, "The 1947 Partition: Drawing the Indo-Pakistani Boundary," *American Diplomacy* 7, no. 1 (2002); and Willem van Schendel, "Stateless in South Asia: The Making of the India-Bangladesh Enclaves," *The Journal of Asian Studies* 61, no. 1 (2002): 115–47.

[5] Nail, *Theory of the Border.*

[6] This tendency is reflected in Michiel Baud and Willem van Schendel's pathbreaking essay, "Toward a Comparative History of Borderlands," *Journal of World History* 8, no. 2 (1997): 211–42, often considered to have inaugurated borderland history beyond North America. In their essay, Baud and van Schendel propose a "life cycle" of borders: moving from "infant" and "adolescent" stages to "adult," "declining," and "defunct" ones.

[7] I use the term "Himalaya" to refer to the broader cultural region and "Himalayas" to refer to the complex of mountain ranges stretching from Afghanistan to Burma.

This book reveals this transformation by examining ongoing tensions between precolonial understandings of space and territory and colonial ones, embedded in archival records from British India. Similar tensions are also revealed between the practices of surveyors in situ and the ideal conception of borders formulated by administrators and geographers far afield. More significantly, this book shows how the colonial state's use of geography became intimately tied to the particular demands of security and to the general process of making legible political territory. This increasingly close relationship between geography and the state reveals a major spatial reorientation of the modern period: a geopolitical vision that conceived of the world as a set of coterminous territories tied to, and dependent upon, geographical features. While the British Empire would ultimately fail to define its territorial borders in the northwestern Himalaya, it bequeathed to its successor nation-states a conception of political space that made borders objects of existential significance.

To explore this transformation, this book focuses on the history of the northwestern Himalaya centered on Ladakh – now a fragmented part of India that long served as a gateway to the plains of India and Central Asia. It examines the colonial-era border-making practices that transformed a once central "exchange market" – the "crossroads of High Asia" – into a fractured and disputed borderland.[8] Central to this transformation was the deployment of geography in the service of the imperial state. The British Government of India attempted to rationalize its territory through geographical science and, in so doing, tried to work toward what James C. Scott has described as "the complete elimination of nonstate spaces."[9] Ironically, the failure to achieve a suitable border in the remote northwestern Himalaya became one of the most durable legacies of the British Empire in South Asia.

---

[8] The phrase "crossroads of High Asia" comes from Janet Rizvi, *Ladakh: Crossroads of High Asia* (New Delhi: Oxford University Press, 1999). Rizvi credits Pinto Narboo in her acknowledgments with the title. Others before and after Rizvi have made similar observations. Hashmatullah Khan Lakhnavi, the Dogra-appointed *wazīr-i-wazārat* (district administrator) of Ladakh in the early twentieth century, and a classic example of the "administrator-scholar," made similar observations on Ladakh's position as a nexus of trade between Central Asia and the plains of India. "Ladakh's city [Leh]," he wrote, "is an exchange market for traded goods from the plains of India and the mountainous regions of Chinese Turkistan and Lhasa" (*Ladākh kā shaher turkistān chīnī aur lhāsa ke māl tajārat ke mamālik Hind ke medānī aur ma'tdil darjah ke kohistanī 'laqah jāt ke sāmān tijārat ke sāth tibādilah kī maṇḍī he*). My translation. Hashmatulah Khan Lakhnavi, *Tārīkh-i-Jammūṇ* (Anarkali, Lahore: Maktaba Asha't Adab [publishing house for the dissemination of literature], 1968), 380.

[9] James C. Scott, *The Art of Not Being Governed: An Anarchist History of Upland Southeast Asia* (New Haven, CT: Yale University Press, 2009), 10–11.

Part of the British failure to establish a suitable borderline through Ladakh rested in the processes of border making itself. This transformation of space into territory involved the development of surveying techniques, cartography, and boundary-making principles, all of which became political practices as well. Indigenous landscapes, long understood in multiple and noncontiguous ways, were rationalized through the development of principles that employed systematized natural objects – mountains, rivers, and, most importantly, watersheds (which combined the two). The surveying process rendered land and water onto increasingly authoritative maps that, in turn, became political instruments. These maps also shaped the systematic organization of geographical information about territory and borders into manuals of governance – most noticeably in the imperial and district-level gazetteers produced by the government of India, beginning in the latter half of the nineteenth century. As more precise geographical information about the frontier was collected, greater efforts were employed to control the flow of goods and people across it – most directly by regulating all forms of communication through a network of frontier roads. Finally, the increased volume of intelligence on the regions beyond the ideal border, gathered by a growing number of experts, induced the British to expend more resources to establish and regulate the border itself. In this process, a new geopolitical approach to global territory, security, and geography emerged. This complex of practices and ideas about borders and border space was inherited by the Indian state at its independence.

But in the case of the northwestern Himalaya – as in much of South Asia's borderland[10] – imperial border-making practices failed to achieve their desired territorial legibility. The apparently fixed "water-parting" limits of the "Indus watershed system" that were used to determine the northern boundaries of India had a suspicious tendency to move. As British surveyors examined more and more of the Himalayas and Tibetan Plateau, their neat assumption that the highest mountain ranges and the major watersheds were coterminous broke down. Changing rationales in frontier road building, and in regulating the movement of people and goods along them, also challenged the imperial state's ability to demarcate its border. This challenge grew more potent as security concerns gradually replaced commercial aspirations. In fact, the desire

---

[10] For the history of ambiguous or nonexistent borders in the northeastern Himalaya, see Bérénice Guyot-Réchard, *Shadow States: India, China and the Himalayas, 1910–1962* (Cambridge: Cambridge University Press, 2017). For the history of the Indo-Afghan and Afghan-Pakistan borderlands, see B. D. Hopkins, *The Making of Modern Afghanistan* (New York: Palgrave Macmillan, 2008), and Elisabeth Leake, *The Defiant Border: The Afghan-Pakistan Borderlands in the Era of Decolonization, 1936–1965* (New York: Cambridge University Press, 2017).

to open up trade and communication with Central Asia paradoxically helped produce the security concerns that pushed the state to define, secure, and "close" its border. And all this while preexisting historical relations among so-called trans-frontier peoples frequently eroded the political meaning of the imposed imperial border, resisting its authority.

These failures troubled the Raj. But it was only with Indian independence that this legacy of failure became intolerable. India and China went to war over not only the Aksai Chin, but also an ambiguous territorial claim in northeastern India: now known as the state of Arunachal Pradesh but claimed by China as South Tibet. Today, India and China remain locked in a political and military standoff over these two borders. While much of the legacy of the British in India has receded in the decades since 1947, this inheritance of ambiguity remains.

To examine this legacy, this book begins with a survey of precolonial understandings of space in Ladakh. By examining an array of Ladakhi, Tibetan, Urdu, and English sources, the book first reveals how local cosmologies, seasonal trade, and pastoralism shaped indigenous conceptions of territory that failed to adhere to a standardized, mappable image of political space. It then analyzes the strategies that the British administrators, engineers, and strategists deployed to bound the region: boundary commissions, surveying and mapping, road building, trade regulation, and the production and restriction of "trans-frontier" information. Finally, it illustrates the problems produced by these processes, exposing the troubled inheritance of imperial frontiers for the modern Indian nation-state.

In doing so, this book brings together macro-level historical studies of imperial frontiers, and regional work on the northwestern Himalaya, to examine how multiple modes of seeing space can cohabitate and conflict with each other, producing borderlands that simultaneously reflect the hegemony of the nation-state and the historical forces that have undermined the state's power. It also challenges the work of political theorists and historians that discounts the role of geographical science in general, and border-making practices in particular. Instead, this book shows how geography played an intimate role in imperial state formation and, when coupled with growing security concerns, gave birth to a new, geopolitical way of envisioning space. Geographical science not only rationalized natural objects like rivers and mountains, but also turned them into political tools. It also suggests an alternative approach to borderland studies, one focused on the production of the border itself. Finally, this book offers a new approach to the global history of frontiers: one that reveals the colonial practices and ideas that helped to shape postcolonial borders. By treating the history of borders and frontiers as a complex of practices and ideas – a *frontier complex* – we can better understand the active legacies of empires in today's postcolonial nation-states. The following sections discuss each of these interventions in greater detail.

I.1   Space

Unlike the many social scientists seeking to identify laws independent of space and time, historians have long acknowledged the heterogeneity of time as one of the distinguishing features of historical approaches to socio-political phenomena.[11] Less explicitly articulated are historical investigations into the heterogeneity of space. While many scholars have explored what Edward Said called "the extraordinary constitutive role of space in human affairs," historians, with some notable exceptions, have shied away from applying theories of space and place to the fluctuating temporality of their subjects.[12]

Philosophical engagement with the often unwieldy concept of space has led to an array of understandings of the term itself.[13] Michel de Certeau chose to define space in contrast to place: place was stable and specific, while space existed "when one takes into consideration vectors of direction, velocities, and time variables."[14] Other philosophers have described

---

[11] William H. Sewell, *The Logics of History* (Chicago: Chicago University Press, 2005), 9–10.

[12] Edward W. Said, "Invention, Memory, and Place," in *Landscape and Power*, ed. W. J. T. Mitchell (Chicago: University of Chicago Press, 2005). Notable exceptions among historians to this tendency to ignore concepts of space include Rhys Isaac, *The Transformation of Virginia, 1740–1790* (Williamsburg, VA: University of North Carolina Press, 1982); Daniel Lord Smail, *Imaginary Cartographies: Possession and Identity in Late Medieval Marseille* (Ithaca, NY: Cornell University Press, 1999); André Wink, "From the Mediterranean to the Indian Ocean: Medieval History in Geographic Perspective," *Comparative Studies in Society and History* 44 (2002): 416–45; Lauren A. Benton, *A Search for Sovereignty: Law and Geography in European Empires, 1400–1900* (Cambridge: Cambridge University Press, 2010); and Sara Shneiderman, "Are the Central Himalayas in Zomia? Some Scholarly and Political Considerations across Time and Space," *Journal of Global History* 5 (2010): 289–312.

[13] For an overview of philosophical perspectives on space and place in the Western tradition, see Edward S. Casey, *The Fate of Place: A Philosophical History* (Berkeley: University of California Press, 2013). Other notable works of philosophy on space include Michel Foucault, *Security, Territory, Population: Lectures at the Collège de France, 1977–78*, trans. Graham Burchell (New York: Picador, 2007); the posthumously published Foucault, "Des Espaces Autres [Of Other Spaces]," *Architecture, Mouvement, Continuité* 5 (1984): 46–49; Martin Heidegger, "Building, Dwelling, Thinking," in *Basic Writings: From Being and Time (1927) to The Task of Thinking (1964)* (San Francisco: Harper, 1993); Raymond Williams, *The Country and the City* (New York: Oxford University Press, 1975); Michel de Certeau, *The Practice of Everyday Life* (Berkeley: University of California Press, 1984), and numerous scholarly writings on memory and place ushered in by the "cultural turn."

[14] Certeau, *The Practice of Everyday Life*, 117.

an inverse relation: space is uniform and static, while place is a far more fluid concept.[15] Michel Foucault further abstracted the binary by positing a distinction between utopias and heterotopias: the former being "no place," while the latter being places where "all the other real sites that can be found within the culture, are simultaneously represented, contested, and inverted."[16] But regardless of the particular aspects of differentiation, across the Western philosophical tradition "space" – particularly since the seventeenth century – has been uniformly privileged over "place."[17]

The modern discipline of geography contains this philosophical place/space distinction, particularly with regard to the scholarly traditions associated with Carl O. Sauer and Yi-Fu Tuan (cultural and human geography, respectively). However, drawing too sharp a division obscures the inherent instability of ideas of place and space over time.[18] "Place," for instance, often reflects tensions between localizing and universalizing forces within complex traditions. One need only examine the history of pilgrimage sites to see how many conceptions of place have existed and co-existed at the same locale over time.[19] Place and space should, I suggest, be viewed as co-constitutive categories, reflecting both scalar difference and the perspective of the viewer.

Without itemizing all the differences found in this vast body of scholarship, we may conclude that most contemporary scholars addressing the concepts of space and place broadly agree on a point put most succinctly by Lefebvre: "If space is produced, then we are dealing with *history*."[20] But missing from much of this philosophical literature is a sense of space in historical time. Over the last few decades, however, different scholars have begun to interrogate the construction of space in

---

[15] For instance, Pierre Gassendi (1592–1633), whose articulations of the place/space distinction, according to Edward Casey, "emboldened Newton to make his own, still more decisive formulations" of space. Casey, *The Fate of Place*, 139.

[16] Foucault, "Des Espace Autres [Of Other Spaces]," and Michel Foucault, *Les Mots et les choses: une archeology des sciences humaines* (Paris: Gallimard, 1966), 9.

[17] This is the argument of Edward S. Casey in *The Fate of Place*.

[18] Carl O. Sauer, "The Morphology of Landscape," *University of California Publications in Geography* 2, no. 2 (1925): 19–53. The two most prominent works of Yi-Fu Tuan are *Topophilia: A Study of Environmental Perception, Attitudes, and Values* (Englewood Cliffs, NJ: Prentice Hall, 1974), and *Space and Place: The Perspective of Experience* (Minneapolis: University of Minnesota Press, 1977).

[19] On the history of sites of Indian and Tibetan pilgrimage, see, for instance, Toni Huber, *The Holy Land Reborn: Pilgrimage and the Tibetan Buddhist Reinvention of Buddhist India* (Chicago: University of Chicago Press, 2008); Diana L. Eck, *India: A Sacred Geography* (New York: Harmony Books, 2012); and Alex McKay, *Kailas Histories: Renunciate Traditions and the Construction of Himalayan Sacred Geography* (Leiden: Brill, 2015).

[20] Henri Lefebvre, *The Production of Space*, trans. Donald Nicholson-Smith (Oxford: Blackwell, 1991), 46. Lefebvre's emphasis.

historical context – particularly in terms of the modern state, the rise of nationalism, and the processes through which the state comes to "see" its population and territory. Scholars such as the historian Thongchai Winichakul (1994), the political scientist and anthropologist James C. Scott (1998, 2009), the historical sociologist Patrick Carroll (2006), and the political theorist and geographer Stuart Elden (2013) have illustrated the role of various geographical, technological, and political practices in the standardizing visions of the modern state.[21] James Hevia, in his *Imperial Security State* (2012), has described how imperial military intelligence, surveying, and expertise combined to "[discipline] the space of Asia" in the late nineteenth and early twentieth centuries.[22] This growing interdisciplinary body of literature illuminates the evolution of techniques with which the state (imperial or otherwise) has attempted to make its population and territory legible.[23]

In contrast, scholarship in the fields of Ladakhi, Tibetan, and Himalayan studies has highlighted the deep influence of locality – or place – on Himalayan societies.[24] It establishes a crucial perspective "from below," exploring the varied and complex means by which locality shapes conceptions of social, political, and spiritual space. This is particularly true of notions of locality that are separate from political visions of territory controlled by a central state or nonlocal government. At the same time, this scholarship has tended toward synchronic studies of culture and environment, due in part to the dearth of traditional historical records and in part to the academic domination of anthropologists in studying a region long relegated to the antiquated categories of "primitive" and "remote." As Arik Moran and Catherine Warner recently put it, historians of the Himalaya have often been "fundamentally dependent on the ethnographic studies that have defined the field [of Himalayan studies] since the 1950s."[25] Some of these regionally focused scholars have also employed compelling conceptual frames to explore and critique

---

[21] Winichakul, *Siam Mapped*; James C. Scott, *Seeing Like a State: How Certain Schemes to Improve the Human Condition Have Failed* (New Haven, CT: Yale University Press, 1998); Scott, *The Art of Not Being Governed*; Patrick Carroll, *Science, Culture and Modern State Formation* (Berkeley: University of California Press, 2006); and Elden, *The Birth of Territory*.

[22] James Hevia, *Imperial Security State: British Colonial Knowledge and Empire-Building in Asia* (Cambridge: Cambridge University Press, 2012).

[23] I use "legible" in the sense of the term "legibility" employed by James C. Scott in *Seeing Like a State*.

[24] See, for example, Joëlle Smadja, ed., *Reading Himalayan Landscapes over Time: Environmental Perception, Knowledge and Practice in Nepal and Ladakh* (Paris: Centre National de la Recherche Scientifique, 2003).

[25] Arik Moran and Catherine Warner, 32–40 "Charting Himalayan Histories," *Himalaya, the Journal of the Association for Nepal and Himalayan Studies* 35, no. 2 (2016).

tendencies within their own field. Ravina Aggarwal, for instance, used Foucault's concept of heterotopia to discuss how anthropological studies of Ladakh tended to use excessively "Tibetan," static, and homogenous images of Himalayan space.[26] Echoing earlier critiques by Arjun Appadurai and Margaret Rodman, Aggarwal showed that much of the regional literature, while producing valuable insights with deeply local textures, reinforced a purely synchronic genre centered on a supposedly timeless relationship between culture and environment.

Despite the potential complementarity of these macro- and micro-spatial approaches, there exists to date little historical scholarship analyzing multiple, cohabitating visions of a single region. Perhaps more significantly, few scholars have asked how these visions might change over time. Yet such an approach could effectively challenge the inevitability of the modern political mode of envisioning space as territory. There is much to be gleaned from a sustained focus on the pluralistic precursors to modern, statist visions of organized social space. In other words, I suggest, we should invert James C. Scott's phrase – "seeing like a state" – to make the state a political object, not just a subject. But we should also extend this exercise historically. In doing so we may recover alternative spatial configurations: modes of seeing space that are simultaneously social, physical, and imagined.[27]

Ideas of space, I will show throughout this book, are historical, multiple, and often rooted in their localities. To support this argument, in the first chapter I focus on how the space of precolonial Ladakh was envisioned by its inhabitants over time.

One of the central concerns of modern South Asian historiography – and imperial historiographies more broadly – has been to ascertain the degree to which colonial rule affected and transformed the societies it encountered. Studying the continued existence, modification, or erasure of concepts of space can therefore reveal how colonial practices impacted indigenous modes of seeing space. This study can also reveal the converse: how colonial ideas of space might have been challenged by indigenous conceptions. Recent work on the historical production of South Asian sacred spaces by Chitralekha Zutshi and others have shown how ideas of space were transformed

---

[26] Ravina Aggarwal, "From Mixed Strains of Barley Grain: Person and Place in a Ladakhi Village" (PhD dissertation, Indiana University, 1994), and "From Utopia to Heterotopia: Toward an Anthropology of Ladakh," in *Recent Research on Ladakh 6*, ed. Henry Osmaston and Nawang Tsering (Bristol, UK: University of Bristol, 1997).

[27] I use "imagined" in the sense employed by Benedict Anderson in his *Imagined Communities: Reflections on the Origin and Spread of Nationalism* (London: Verso, 1983), namely, spaces that exist beyond the immediate community experienced in everyday life.

by the colonial encounter.[28] I seek to build on this literature by extending it beyond the too-often segregated realm of "sacred space." In doing so, I uncover significant transformations occurring in the last two centuries across a wider range of modes of seeing, modes that included historically distinct ways of ordering past worlds. In other words, the colonial history of the northwestern Himalaya graphically illustrates a broader *structural change in spatiality*.[29] This structural shift in seeing space was enacted through specific spatial practices – surveying, road building, map making – and through the development of scientific theories, fears, and fantasies about spatial limits and the peoples who lay beyond and moved across them. It is most graphically represented in the development of concepts of territory and changing geographical *epistemes* manifest in increasingly restricted "trans-frontier" maps, expansive boundary commissions, and the compilation of gazetteers and other manuals of governance – subjects discussed throughout this book.[30]

I.2   Geography and Territory

Few geological events in the earth's 4.54 billion-year-old history have produced such dramatic physical results as the slow collision of the Indian Plate with the Eurasian Plate some 50–55 million years ago. The result – the Himalayas – is one of the great corporeal features of the planet: "a rod taking the Earth's whole measure," as the Sanskrit poet Kālidāsa wrote in the fourth or fifth century CE.[31] This complex of the highest mountain ranges in the world – the Karakoram, the Pamir, the Hindu Kush, and the

---

[28] Chitralekha Zutshi focuses on Kashmiri Islamic sacred space in *Kashmir's Contested Pasts: Narratives, Sacred Geographies, and the Historical Imagination* (New Delhi: Oxford University Press, 2014). See also Huber, *The Holy Land Reborn*; Eck, *India: A Sacred Geography*; and McKay, *Kailas Histories*.

[29] This is a rough paraphrase of Reinhardt Koselleck's observation on temporality in modern history. In *Futures Past*, Koselleck argues that modern history reflects a structural "shift in temporality." *Futures Past: On the Semantics of Historical Time* (New York: Columbia University Press, 2004), 12.

[30] Here I borrow Foucault's definition of *episteme*: "the totality of relations that can be discovered, for a given period, between the sciences when one analyses them at the level of discursive regularities." In his rather rambling definition, he elaborates that *epistemes* are "the total set of relations that unite, at a given period, the discursive practices that give rise to epistemological figures, sciences, and possibly formalized systems." Michel Foucault, *The Archaeology of Knowledge* (New York: Harper Torchbooks, 1972), 191. I use Foucault's term here in a very general sense, given that the "discursive regularities" and "orders of things" I am focused on are distinct from the subjects Foucault actually examines in his work.

[31] "Kumārasambhavam" in Chandra Rajan, trans., *The Complete Works of Kālidāsa: Poems*, vol. 1 (New Delhi: Sahitya Akademi, 2005).

Great Himalayas – shapes the Indian subcontinent in dramatic ways. It contains the sources of the largest rivers of South Asia, as well as a vast array of glaciers that act as critical, and shrinking, water reserves.[32] It slows and holds in place the monsoon rains, and with them the agricultural cycles of the subcontinent. Unique animal and plant species climb its upper reaches and dwell in its valleys.[33] At its edges lie the few gaps that have allowed conquering armies to enter the subcontinent. The range also holds the loci of sites sacred to millions of people across the region, most notably Shiva's temporal abode at Mount Kailash, a mountain also sacred to Buddhists, *Bon.po*, and Jains for connected yet distinct mythological reasons.[34] And among this mass of mountains live diverse groups of people who have incorporated the region's great physical variety into particular lifestyle elements that have awed, revolted, and perplexed visitors for millennia.

In the timescale of human concern, "Himalaya" has come to act as one of the most potent geographical imaginaries in the world: at once tied to Western "Shangri-la" narratives (associated with Tibet and the Himalaya), and to older worldwide fascinations with mountains (whether to climb, to worship, or to use as boundaries for lifeworlds).[35] This region has also been used by Euro-American scholars and policy makers to demarcate regional divisions within the category of "Asia" itself. South, East, Southeast, and Central Asia are frequently marked by reference to the greater complex of mountain chains collectively referred to as the Himalayas, and to the Tibetan Plateau which that complex supports. But

---

[32] "Ten of the region's largest and longest rivers (the Amu Darya, Brahmaputra, Ganges, Indus, Irrawaddy, Mekong, Salween, Tarim, Yangtze, and Yellow) originate in the Himalayas. These rivers help provide water, food, and energy for nearly 4 billion people in China and across South and Southeast Asia – nearly half of the world's population." Kenneth Pomeranz, "Asia's Unstable Water Tower: The Politics, Economics, and Ecology of Himalayan Water Projects," *Asia Policy* 16 (July 2013): 1–10.

[33] The Himalayas are home to between 18,000 and 21,000 plant species. Varieties originating in this region, such as rhododendron, peony, and azalea, have become ubiquitous fixtures in gardens the world over. This was in no small part thanks to the botanical fieldwork of Joseph Hooker and others, with the Gardens at Kew as their entrepôt of seeds. Kew now serves as a home to the Millennium Seed Bank, tasked with preserving seeds from around the world.

[34] See McKay, *Kailas Histories*. For a critique of McKay's work, see Kyle Gardner, "Review of Kailas Histories: Renunciate Traditions and the Construction of Himalayan Sacred Geography, by Alex McKay," *Bulletin of the School of Oriental and African Studies* 79, no. 3 (2016): 677–79.

[35] For the Western construction of "Shangri-la," see Peter Bishop, *The Myth of Shangri-La: Tibet, Travel Writing and the Western Creation of Sacred Landscape* (Berkeley: University of California Press, 1989). For a recent global history of different social and political significances of mountains, see Bernard Debarbieux and Gilles Rudaz, *The Mountain: A Political History from the Enlightenment to the Present* (Chicago: University of Chicago Press, 2015).

long before area studies existed in the academy, the Himalayan region, as with many mountainous regions across the globe, functioned as a limit for those who lived far from it.

Though many in India in the nineteenth and twentieth centuries would have echoed Iqbal's ode to the Himalayas – "at first glance you are a mere mountain range / [But in reality] you are our guardian, you are India's wall" – for those who lived within its valleys and for those who regularly traversed its mountain passes, it was anything but a wall.[36] Rather, its vast array of exchange routes produced one of the largest high-altitude economic and cultural networks on earth.[37] The very name "Ladakh" (*la.dwags*) refers to a "land of passes," signaling the centrality of routes and movement in constituting the historical region.[38] With Ladakh at its center, the northwestern Himalaya, was in the words of Janet Rizvi, a "crossroads of high Asia." Economically, culturally, and politically, the region long resisted the boundaries that its imposing heights evoked in the imaginations of those who never traversed its paths. The Himalayan region, in other words, was not a "natural" political border until it was configured as such.

As a region long assumed to be a natural barrier by the Mughals, the British, the Qing, and the Russians, the Himalayan terrain played a unique role in the history of modern border making – a role that reveals tensions in the interactions of geography and state formation.[39] Generally, these tensions became more pronounced as the concept of territory became more precisely tied to the state. Stuart Elden's recent

---

[36] Muhammad Iqbal, "Hamāla," 1901, http://iqbalurdu.blogspot.com/2011/02/hamala-bang-e-dra-1.html. "*imtihān-i-dīdah-i-zāhir mein kohistān hai tu/ pāsbān āpnā hai tu, dīwār-i-hindustān hai tu.*" My translation.

[37] These networks stretched from Xinjiang to the Punjab and from Kashmir to central Tibet. Traders moved from Yarkand through Ladakh to the plains of India, selling Chinese tea, Central Asian opium, and hashish/*charas*. The semi-nomadic Changpa sold precious pashmina wool to Ladakhi (both Buddhist and Muslim) and Kashmiri traders, some of whom resided in Lhasa so as to better oversee one end of this trade network. Muslim pilgrims from Kashgar and other parts of Central Asia travelled via Ladakh en route to Mecca. Buddhists from Ladakh, Spiti, and Zanskar made regular pilgrimages to Mount Kailash in western Tibet (Guge), and sent young monks (and a small number of nuns) to the monasteries of central Tibet.

[38] Similarly, the name of the northwestern Himalayan hill state Spiti – directly south of Ladakh – refers to the "middle land" between India and Tibet. Harish Kapadia, *Spiti: Adventures in the Trans-Himalaya* (New Delhi: Indus, 1996), 9.

[39] For the Qing conceptions of the Himalayas, and India in general, see Matthew Mosca, *From Frontier Policy to Foreign Policy: The Question of India and the Transformation of Geopolitics in Qing China* (Stanford, CA: Stanford University Press, 2013), and Mosca, "Kashmiri Merchants and Qing Intelligence Networks in the Himalayas: The Ahmed Ali Case of 1830," in *Asia Inside Out: Connected Places*, ed. Peter C. Perdue and Helen F. Siu (Cambridge, MA: Harvard University Press, 2015). For the Mughal conceptions of the same areas, see Abu'l Fasl's *Ain-i-Akbari* and my discussion of it in Chapter 4.

study of territory within Western political thought provides a working definition to test in the British imperial context in South Asia.

For Elden, the territorial notion of space is, broadly speaking, "a bounded space under the control of a group of people, usually a state" that is historically produced.[40] The concept of territory is a conflation of a juridico-political idea and geographical space.[41] In a similar vein, territoriality constitutes "the properties, including power, provided by the control of bordered political space."[42] Thus territory is an idea of space that requires some notion of limits to bound it and a political power to exert control within it. A border therefore becomes the *sine qua non* of territory.[43] Unlike "frontier," a term that so often references a certain kind of zonal space, "border" (or "boundary," the preferred British term) represents a starting point. As Heidegger poetically put it, "the boundary is that from which *something begins its essential unfolding*."[44] As such, border making is the necessary prerequisite for "territorialization": a term that can be defined broadly as the processes of conceptualizing, defining, and regulating territory.

Yet political theorists typically treat territory like sovereignty, a philosophical concept untethered from physical space. While scholars such as Charles Maier do acknowledge the physical dimension of the concept, they often assert that the history of territory "excludes necessarily the histories of landscape and the natural environment."[45] By making territory a purely political space without content, these scholars assume that political conceptions cannot be rooted in natural ones. But natural

---

[40] Elden, *Birth of Territory*, 322.

[41] My thanks to Daniel Haines for helping me to refine this point.

[42] Charles Maier, "Consigning the Twentieth Century to History: Alternative Narratives for the Modern Era," *The American Historical Review* 105 (June 2000): 808.

[43] Elsewhere, Elden questions the proposition that territory requires borders. Stuart Elden, "Territory without Borders," *Harvard International Review* (2011). Elden writes that territory, in the "modern sense, should not be understood as defined by borders, in that putting a border around something is sufficient to demarcate it as a territory. Rather, territory is a multi-faceted concept and practice, one which encompasses economic, strategic, legal and technical aspects, and can perhaps better be understood as the political counterpart of the homogeneous, measured and mathematicized notion of space that emerged with the scientific revolution." But he quickly backtracks, noting that the "modern notion of territory is certainly partly about boundaries and impermeability." While his point that borders are not necessarily sufficient to define territory is an instructive one, it is impossible to think about territory without reference first to a limit. No political conception of space, short of one spanning the entire globe, could dispense with an articulation of its borders and still retain its coherence.

[44] Heidegger, "Building, Dwelling, Thinking," 356. This quote is also found as the epigraph of Homi Bhabha's introduction to his *Locations of Culture* (1994), with a slightly different translation ("presencing" instead of "essential unfolding"). Heidegger's emphasis.

[45] Maier, *Once within Borders*, 6.

objects – rivers, mountains, deserts, and seas – have long served to demarcate political influence. The nineteenth century witnessed the territorialization of the globe in large part through the slow process of surveying land and water, conceiving of nature as sets of systematized objects, mapping the results of that process, and using that information, in turn, to redefine the degree to which the state "saw" the space it attempted to control.[46] Across the nineteenth century and into the twentieth, geography not only transformed into a science, but also became a political science. This transformation reflected the broader rise of the statistical sciences and colonial technocratic governance, documented by C. A. Bayly, Timothy Mitchell, and others.[47]

Finally, to further complicate the history of territorialization in the nineteenth century, it is worth noting that, like concepts of sovereignty, concepts of territory can be multilayered, ambiguous, or incomplete.[48] Beyond the Westphalian model of "perfectly equal" states – one that dominates the modern world system as a byproduct of European imperialism – there have existed numerous multilayered conceptions of interstate relations that were neither perfectly equal nor strictly connected to the idea of exclusive control over a bounded space.[49] Even within those states apparently following the Westphalian model, sovereignty was often not clearly delimited. In her recent work on law and geography in the *longue durée* of European empires, Lauren Benton has noted that European empires often produced "uneven legal geographies."[50] Although Benton's work largely focuses on maritime examples of sovereignty, law, and geography, she acknowledges that these "uneven" geographies could

---

[46] Patrick Carroll has referred to this process as "technoterritorialization." Carroll, *Science, Culture and Modern State Formation*.

[47] See Timothy Mitchell, *Colonizing Egypt* (Berkeley: University of California Press, 1991), and C. A. Bayly, *Empire and Information: Intelligence Gathering and Social Communication in India, 1780–1870* (Cambridge: Cambridge University Press, 1996).

[48] F. H. Hinsley, *Sovereignty* (New York: Cambridge University Press, 1966), and Benton, *Search for Sovereignty*.

[49] The degree to which the Westphalian model can lay claim to a modern form of sovereignty, superseding premodern models like tributary systems, has been a source of debate among historians – most notably, historians of Qing China. James Hevia's *Cherishing Men from Afar: Qing Guest Ritual and the Macartney Embassy of 1793* (Durham, NC: Duke University Press, 1995) called into question John Fairbank's Chinese "tributary system" by illustrating the degree to which Qing "guest ritual" during the Macartney Embassy (1793) constituted a Qing conception of sovereignty that was neither solely a guise for trade, nor merely the isolationist and sinocentric behavior that the British read it to be. Hevia argued that the Macartney Embassy represented two competing views of sovereignty articulated by two expanding empires. Elsewhere, Hevia has also called attention to ways in which the British themselves employed tributary systems within their own empire. See Hevia, "Tributary Systems," in *The Encyclopedia of Empire* (Hoboken, NJ: John Wiley, 2016).

[50] Benton, *Search for Sovereignty*, xii.

include undefined land borders and ambiguous designations for particular spaces (enclaves, corridors, etc.). On land, imperial frontiers often produced uneven and exceptional legal spaces – a global phenomenon that B. D. Hopkins has termed "frontier governmentality."[51] While it is less surprising that maritime sovereignty and territory should be rather fluid in legal definition, it is worth underscoring the distinction between the formal articulation of political space and the result of practices employed to produce that space. Nineteenth-century geographical science was employed to determine territory by attempting to rationalize and standardize boundary-making principles and practices. But the resulting frontiers and borders were simultaneously physical spaces and spatial ideals that reflected a host of aspirations and anxieties of the state.

I.3   Frontiers, Borders, and Borderlands

Few terms are as intimately tied to the history of empire as is the term "frontier." In a certain sense – from the imperialist's perspective at least – frontier is synecdoche for empire, since it so often connotes the expansion of territory, the violence associated with clashes of asymmetric power, and the spatial limits of imperial control. For imperial administrators and geographers, the term served more generally as an epistemic defense against unknowns, and more specifically as a concrete category of spatial organization that could denote the extent of settlement, the limit of political influence, a strategic military position, or a particular ecological change.[52] But as the historian Lucien Febvre noted, the English term "frontier," like its French cousin whose history he details, has a particular history tied to the Anglophone world.[53] Tellingly, there is no comparable distinction between the English "frontier" and "border" (or "boundary") in the two most widely spoken language families of the northwestern Himalaya. The Ladakhi/Tibetan *mtshams*, and the Urdu/Hindi *sarhad* or *sīmā*, possess many distinct and varied meanings, but are most commonly utilized to refer to both precise spatial points and vague

---

[51] B. D. Hopkins, *Ruling the "Savage" Periphery: Frontier Governance and the Making of the Modern World* (Cambridge, MA: Harvard University Press, 2020).

[52] Frederick Jackson Turner, "The Significance of the Frontier in American History," in *The Frontier in American History* (New York: Henry Holt, 1920). The vague nature of the term frontier and its implied directionality (a frontier requires a center) is instructive for the study of imperial territoriality. The relatively recent rise of borderland studies has signaled a shift toward recentering peripheral spaces, while also shifting away from the geopolitical and environmental foci long associated with frontier history toward social and cultural approaches.

[53] Lucien Febvre, "Frontière: The Word and the Concept," in *A New Kind of History: From the Writings of Lucien Febvre*, ed. Peter Burke (New York: Harper Torchbooks, 1973).

spatial limits.[54] The polysemic quality of the English term frontier reflects its long-standing utility among the historical agents of empire.

In historical studies, the definitional ambiguity of the term "frontier" goes back to the "father" of modern frontier history, Frederick Jackson Turner. In his famous 1893 address to the American Historical Association in Chicago, "The Significance of the Frontier in American History," Turner noted that "the term is an elastic one, and for our purposes does not need sharp definition."[55] For Turner, a frontier embodied the idea of a "nationalizing force," just as much as it did a vague and changing space on a map. It was capable of moving westward, and it was also capable of "closing." Lucien Febvre elaborated on the polysemic quality of frontiers by exploring the etymological paths of the closely related French terms, *frontière* and *limite*. *Frontières*, Febvre concluded, can really only be studied in relation to the development of the state, because different states necessarily produced different frontiers.[56] While empires and other polities have long used variations of the term to designate peripheral spaces, the practices associated with one frontier often do not apply to those of another. Alex McKay's application of Turner's Frontier Thesis to the Indo-Tibetan borderlands is a case in point.[57] The absence of settler expansion and the imposition of the Himalayas between the two established and distinct political and cultural spheres of India and Tibet makes McKay's creative hypothesis highly implausible.

In the British imperial context in India, "frontier" took on a zonal meaning employed to designate ambiguous or violent spaces and the limits of political control. Alfred Lyall defined a frontier as "the outmost political boundary projected, as one might say, beyond the administrative border."[58] Yet Lyall also spoke of a vague "influence" associated with the frontier.

Our political influence radiates out beyond the line of our actual possession, spreading its skirts widely and loosely over the adjacent country. ... The true frontier of the British dominion in Asia, the line which we are more or less pledged

---

[54] The Tibetan term *mtshams* has a wide range of meanings that can include "border," "boundary," "retreat," and "intermediate direction." A *sa.mtshams* is, more specifically, a land border. But there is no oppositional pairing of terms analogous to the border/ frontier pairing in English – a long, historical absence of distinction, according to Matthew Kapstein.

[55] Turner, "The Significance of the Frontier in American History," 3.

[56] Febvre, "Frontière," 213.

[57] Alex McKay, "'Tracing Lines upon the Unknown Areas of the Earth': Reflections on Frederick Jackson Turner and the Indo-Tibetan Frontier," in *Fringes of Empire*, ed. Sameetah Agha and Elizabeth Kolsky (New Delhi: Oxford University Press, 2009).

[58] Alfred Lyall, "Frontiers and Protectorates," *Nineteenth Century: A Monthly Review* 30, no. 174 (1891): 315.

to guard, from which we have warned off trespassers, does not by any means tally with the outer edge of the immense territory over which we exercise administrative jurisdiction, in which all the people are British subjects for whom our governments make laws.[59]

This ambiguous formulation also subtly reflected the inherent violence of the frontier. Lord Robert Bulwer-Lytton, viceroy of India from 1876 to 1880, made this violence more explicit when he wrote, with considerable understatement, that the word "frontier" was always a synonym for "quarrel."[60]

In contrast, a border could reflect the resolution of tension, by eliminating the friction caused by the indeterminate space of a "no-man's land." By the end of the nineteenth century this rhetoric of reduced friction was articulated by a number of prominent frontier experts who worked to demarcate precise borderlines based on a set of boundary-making principles. For instance, a 1917 review in the Royal Geographical Society's *The Geographical Journal* observed that, for the preeminent British frontier expert, Thomas Holdich, "the first and greatest object of an international frontier [was] to ensure peace and good-will between contiguous people by *putting a definite edge to the national political horizon*, so as to limit unauthorized expansion and trespass."[61] In other words, a frontier was made peaceful by the successful definition of a borderline. But tellingly, this review also revealed the frequent semantic slippage between the terms frontier and border (or boundary).

While scholars from the historian Frederick Jackson Turner to the economist Edward Barbier have acknowledged the role played by natural resources and environmental factors on the edges of expanding territories, few historians of South Asia have adequately examined the environmental and geographical aspects of frontier formation – particularly in the most understudied of Indian frontiers, the northwestern Himalaya.[62] Instead, historians have tended to emphasize "Great Game"[63] narratives and the adventurous nature of a few enterprising British men who espoused a "forward" view of British

---

[59] Ibid., 313–14.
[60] G. J. Alder, *British India's Northern Frontier: A Study of Imperial Policy* (London: Longmans, Green, 1963), 4.
[61] "Frontiers in Theory and Practice," *The Geographical Journal* 49, no. 1 (1917): 58. Emphasis given by the anonymous author of the review.
[62] Edward B. Barbier, *Scarcity and Frontiers: How Economies Have Developed through Natural Resource Exploitation* (Cambridge: Cambridge University Press, 2011).
[63] For the anachronistic and misleading history of the term "Great Game," see Malcolm Yapp, "The Legend of the Great Game," *Proceedings of the British Academy* 111 (2001): 179–98; Hopkins, *Modern Afghanistan*; and the introduction to Hevia's *Imperial Security State*.

regional expansion.[64] In the imperial semantic play that turned serious international rivalries into an understated "game," European explorers covertly penetrated the *terra incognita* of the mountainous regions surrounding India. Those "boys with digestions" became imperial celebrities and best-selling authors.[65]

This perspective minimizes the role of the actual inhabitants of these regions, whose preexisting trade and cultural networks made these "unknown lands" anything but. The "Great Game" narrative also assumes that the only major imperial concern in gathering information beyond the frontier was diplomatic and strategic. In truth, the work of imperial administrators, explorers, and surveyors along the frontier reflected their need to bring these spaces into accord with internal and international territorializing practices, while increasingly restricting access to this "trans-frontier" information. By drawing on recent scholarship on technology and state formation, and on environmental histories that emphasize the intimate connections between trade, politics, and environment, I aim to paint a more complex and dynamic picture of frontier formation by highlighting the crucial, co-constitutive roles played by geographical science, imperial politics, and security concerns.

While the term "frontier" might be polysemic, by the beginning of the twentieth century it had become, generally speaking, distinct from "boundary" or "border." As noted above, if a frontier roughly signaled the slow dissolution (or formation) of a certain kind of political space, a border marked a definite transition: one where a single kind of political space stopped, and another began.[66] For the experts I will describe in the fourth, fifth, and sixth chapters, borders are distinguished from frontiers by the degree of precise geographical and cartographical information known about them. As the frontier expert Henry McMahon noted in 1935, a "frontier *often* has a wider and more general meaning than a boundary, and a frontier *sometimes* refers to a wide tract of border country, or to hinterlands or buffer states, undefined by any external

---

[64] Alastair Lamb, Alex McKay, Parshotam Mehra, Owen Lattimore, and others have painted a picture of the broader Himalayan region that views British interest as driven almost exclusively by security concerns, pushed "forward" by a small cadre of adventurous men.

[65] For a history that reflects this approach, see Peter Hopkirk, *The Great Game: On Secret Service in High Asia* (Oxford: Oxford University Press, 1991). In his short story "Pig," Kipling wrote that "the boys with digestions hope to write their names large on the Frontier, and struggle for dreary places like Bannu and Kohat [on the Afghan frontier]." Rudyard Kipling, *Plain Tales from the Hills* [1888] (Oxford: Oxford University Press, 2001), 162.

[66] Though I will use the more common term "border" throughout this book, instead of the term "boundary" preferred by empire-era sources, both terms are generally interchangeable.

boundary line."[67] McMahon's qualifying "often" and "sometimes" acknowledged the ambiguity that lingered between the two terms. And, indeed, the ambiguity in the term "frontier" often served a strategic purpose. Borders, in contrast, had come to unambiguously refer to a linear limit to a given territory by the turn of the twentieth century.

The ambiguous qualities present in the term frontier – a vague frontline facing outward from a safe center toward a "barbaric" periphery – have generated doubts among scholars as to the utility of the term as an analytic category.[68] Yet the indispensability of the "centrality of the margins" to what David Ludden described as the "process of empire" make it imperative that we interrogate the meanings of "frontier" and "border" in tandem.[69] In recent decades, a new focus on the periphery, coupled with critiques of the dominance of state-centered and interstate politics, has helped drive the rise of borderland studies. This interdisciplinary approach to historically peripheral spaces has moved to recenter the periphery by replacing the diplomatic and geopolitical focus of frontier history with more localized social and cultural approaches. Yet though the border has now become a "method" as much as an object to be studied, it remains susceptible to the problem of the "objective" region first raised by Bernard Cohn.[70] Baud and van Schendel's "Toward a Comparative History of Borderlands" suggested that within border-lands lie "heartland zones," "intermediate zones," and "outer zones" – with the preestablished border working to center the whole.[71] Against this idea of a neatly demarcated space, Cohn worked to disaggregate the various factors that could differentiate a single, "objective" region: language, history, social structure, cuisine, or culture. By illustrating how multiple regions cohabitate and overlap in the same spaces, Cohn cast doubt on the possibility of a fully coherent, objective region. Applying Cohn's critique to the borderland studies inaugurated by Baud and van

---

[67] A. H. McMahon, "International Boundaries," *Journal of the Royal Society of Arts* 84, no. 4330 (1935): 3. McMahon gave this lecture at his November 6, 1935, inaugural as Chairman of the Council of the Royal Society of Arts. That society subsequently published the address in its *Proceedings*. My emphasis.

[68] For critiques of the frontier as a category of analysis, see, for instance, Baud and van Schendel, "Toward a Comparative History of Borderlands"; and Manan Ahmed, "Adam's Mirror: The Frontier in the Imperial Imagination," *Economic and Political Weekly* 46, no. 13 (2011): 60–65.

[69] David Ludden, "The Process of Empire: Frontiers and Borderlands," in *Tributary Empires in Global History*, ed. C. A. Bayly and P. F. Bang (London: Palgrave Macmillan, 2011), 132–50.

[70] Bernard S. Cohn, "Regions Subjective and Objective: Their Relation to the Study of Modern Indian History and Society," in *An Anthropologist among the Historians and Other Essays* (New Delhi: Oxford University Press, 1987), 100–135. For the theorization of the border as a "method," see Mezzadra and Neilson, *Border as Method*.

[71] Baud and van Schendel, "Toward a Comparative History of Borderlands," 221.

Schendel therefore suggests that the border may be the only "objective" feature of a borderland.

It is also doubtful whether a general recentering on the borderland does much to actually diminish the "traditional view from the center"[72] if the center is still the state that imposed the border in the first place. A critical approach to the categories of frontier and borderland must not only dispense with antiquated notions of "civilization" versus "barbarity," or "settled" versus "empty" space, but also account for changing understandings of space and territory over time. By analyzing the practices and ideas that produced (or attempted to produce) borders throughout the Himalaya over time, this book seeks to focus borderland studies more closely on the one object that can actually define a borderland: the border itself.

I.4   The Frontier Complex

This book thus examines the two sides of colonial frontiers and borders. The one side features concrete practices of exploring, defining, and, above all, conceptualizing territory through the emerging science of geography. The abstract obverse of those practices encompasses fears, fantasies, and changing geographical and political rationales. Besides analyzing the factors behind the transformation of the northwestern Himalaya, from a crossroads of commerce and cultural exchange to a disputed and isolated borderland, the more ambitious task of this book is to make the now-remote region of Ladakh central to the histories of modern South Asia and the British Empire. As one of the first regions on what James Mill called "the most desirable frontier" of India to be surveyed and mapped (repeatedly and unsuccessfully, as it turns out, for over a century), the northwestern Himalaya offers a crucial, early example of the imperial frontier laboratory.[73] Ladakh serves as a focal point for technical and epistemological frontier "problems" and practices, both of which extended across British India, the British Empire, and the globe. Britain's imperial administrators' preoccupation with defining peripheral territory, and their desire to cultivate commercial and political connections in the space beyond that periphery, also highlight the psychological fears and fantasies that permeated British imperial history. This book also casts doubt on the supposedly historical claims of modern-day India and China to a space which was never "effectively occupied" by either of their imperial predecessors, but which has continued to be a major source of

---

[72] Baud and van Schendel, "Toward a Comparative History of Borderlands," 212.
[73] "Evidence of James Mill," February 16, 1832: *Parliamentary Papers, 1831–2*, vol. xiv, p. 8, Qu. 49.

tension.[74] Finally, it underscores the perhaps obvious point that India's territory – its international borderlands and its internal national space – remains an assemblage of contested ideas. This was the case at Partition and continues to be so seven decades later, despite waves of state dissolution and formation, forcible annexations, and continued calls for internal partitions. This book explores these tensions by introducing the idea of the *frontier complex*: a set of practices that included surveying, mapping, road building, information gathering, border demarcation, and the regulation of people, animals, and goods in motion. Rather than replicating colonial terminology, or insisting on a definition derived from a particular historical case as Turner's or Febvre's definitions require, by approaching "frontier" as a complex of practices and ideas, I aim to acknowledge both the features particular to the northwestern Himalayan frontier and the ad hoc nature of the term itself.

This approach also emphasizes how empires experienced the frontier in the second sense of the term "complex," namely, emotionally charged ideas that often lead to abnormal behavior. In this sense, this work examines not only the shaping of the landscape of British imperial frontiers, but also – to employ Ashis Nandy's felicitous phrase – the "mindscape of British colonialism."[75] If the frontier was a near constant concern for the imperial state, for the Indian nation-state after 1947 it became an object of existential importance. The undefined border that British India bequeathed in 1947 to India and, less directly, to China, highlights the supposedly clear temporal border that divides empire and nation-state. If the empire's frontier was managed with anxiety but an acceptance of ambiguity, the nation's borders became objects for which soldiers gave their lives. In the aftermath of the Sino-Indian War in 1962, the acclaimed Indian playback singer Lata Mangeshkar brought Jawaharlal Nehru and countless Indians to tears, singing, "*jo k̲h̲ūn gīrā parvat par, wah k̲h̲ūn thā Hindustānī* [that blood shed on the mountains, that blood was Indian]."[76]

---

[74] "Effective occupation" became one of the military rationales that combined with "natural frontiers" to justify claims to so-called no-man's lands like the Aksai Chin (see Chapter 2). It has been a foundational – and undeniably colonial – pillar of international legal theory, from the days of Queen Victoria to the present.

[75] Ashis Nandy, *The Intimate Enemy: Loss and Recovery of Self under Colonialism* (New Delhi: Oxford University Press, 2005), 63.

[76] On Republic Day 1963, Lata Mangeshkar first sang "Aye Mere Watan Ke Lōgon" ("Oh, People of My Country"): "*jab g̲h̲āyal huā himālaya, k̲h̲atre men̄ paḍī āzādī, Jab tak thī sāns laḍe woh, phir apnī lāsh bichhā dī, . . . koī Sikh koī Jāṭ Maraṭha, koi Gurkha koī Madarāsī, sarḥad par marnevāla har vīr thā bhāratvāsī, jo k̲h̲ūn gīrā parvat par, wah k̲h̲ūn thā Hindustānī.* [When the Himalaya was injured and our freedom was threatened, they fought right to the end and then they laid down their bodies . . . some were Sikh, some Jath, and some Maratha, some were Gurkhas and some Madrasi. But each brave man

But while the nation-state demanded a more concrete, consecrated territorial limit than its imperial predecessor, the desire for that precise border – tied as it was to a complex of supposedly rational border-making practices – was over a century in the making.

To recount this transformation, the first chapter draws on Ladakhi and trans-Himalayan sources to examine precolonial understandings of space, boundaries, and frontiers in Ladakh and the broader northwestern Himalayan region. Sources surveyed range from the earliest available records of the tenth and eleventh centuries to the beginning of British rule in 1846. This chapter provides both a historical background to the region and an exploration of four major facets of indigenous Himalayan space: *matter, cosmology, politics,* and *language.* In illustrating multiple historical modes of seeing by indigenous historical actors, I suggest that the single, bounded entity called Ladakh was primarily a product of imperial possession in the nineteenth century. I am not arguing that there was not an earlier political entity known as Ladakh, but rather that indigenous conceptions of its space were more pluralistic than the subsequent territory envisioned by its imperial rulers. The commingling of material, cosmological, political, and linguistic ways of seeing, I argue, produced identities that failed to map neatly. This chapter draws not only on the limited extant precolonial Ladakhi sources, but also on an array of anthropological, linguistic, and archeological sources.

The second chapter draws on material from numerous colonial archives to examine the rationale behind initial British attempts to create a borderline through the northwestern Himalaya. These attempts, taking place as they did in a region where only border points had previously existed, were rooted in efforts to systematically read the landscape and transcribe it onto paper using generalized principles – principles that came to symbolize a growing sense that, for the empire, geography was destiny. The watershed, in particular, emerged as the ideal border-making object. In theory, these general border-making principles were meant to mitigate territorial disputes and to establish clear lines of sovereignty for the empire. But as this chapter shows, the determining and drawing of boundary lines was a task fraught with unexpected divisions and contradictions, both geographical and political. Despite surveys that revealed shifting limits of the Indus watershed, British administrators sought to apply the "water-parting principle" to their desired border through Ladakh and across most of the 1,500-mile long Himalayan range. Their ongoing failure to successfully "border" the Himalaya was

who died on the border was an Indian, the blood shed on the mountains, that blood was Indian]." My translation.

primarily the result of ongoing tensions between ideas of natural frontiers and strategic ones – two frontiers ostensibly unified by the logic of the so-called scientific frontier.

The third chapter examines the sharp rise of security concerns in the late nineteenth century and the changing role of roads: from conduits of trade to instruments of imperial security. In particular, it focuses on the two central examples of road building in the northwestern Himalaya: the Hindustan–Tibet Road and the Indo-Yarkand Treaty Road. Roads, I show, were conduits that became synonymous with communication. By examining the vast and detailed journals kept by the British Joint Commissioners stationed in Ladakh, beginning in 1870, I reveal how commercial potential beyond the frontier eventually led to the paradoxical desire to "close" the frontier in order to better secure it. As the commissioners were responsible for supervising the Indo-Yarkand and Indo-Tibetan trade routes, their primary tasks were to regulate the movement of people on these routes, and to ensure the roads were in good working order. But they were also concerned with gathering intelligence from Central Asia and Tibet. The records of the British Joint Commissioners highlight the simultaneous production and circulation of frontier expertise and the increased restrictions that the imperial state imposed on the movement of "trans-frontier" people and materials. Here we see the interplay of technology, commercial expansion, and security, and the limits placed on each by the Himalayan environment. Road building, I show, became a central piece of the larger complex of border making.

The fourth chapter focuses on two different ways of "reading" the landscape of the northwestern Himalaya. The first evolved from the surveying and road-building practices discussed in chapters two and three: practices which resulted in an increasingly standardized body of environmental knowledge that was widely circulated through gazetteers, route books, and intelligence reports. This way of reading the landscape reflected the broader development of a new geographical episteme – an increasingly technocratic and systematic mode of seeing territory, which in turn crafted an image of a unified territory of India. But there is also a second way of reading the Himalayan landscape; one that emerged from earlier precolonial modes of seeing, discussed in Chapter 1. Jurisdictional problems between the imperial state and its Himalayan frontier – including disputes over taxation, water rights, territory, and grazing rights – produced deep uncertainty about the limits of frontier locales. In fact, the main challenge to the imperial vision of the would-be border came from an unlikely source: pashmina goats. These animals, taken from the high altitudes of Ladakh and given to the British as tribute from the Maharaja of Jammu and Kashmir, illustrated the often hypocritical stance imperial officials took on the subjects of tribute and sovereignty. On the one hand, the British were quick to minimize traditional trans-frontier relationships that compromised any sense of absolute sovereignty. On the other, the British insisted that tribute continue to be paid to them, even when, year after year, the goats sent down from the Tibetan Plateau failed to survive their transplantation. By illustrating the emergence of a geographical episteme illustrated in gazetteers and other official publications, I show how information about borders, terrain, and geographical features became a necessary prerequisite for understanding political territory. This episteme, I argue, reveals the slow emergence of geopolitical thinking. But the utility of this form of thinking was consistently undermined by the multiple modes through which indigenous groups conceived of the space around them.

The fifth chapter reexamines boundaries, roads, and changing geographical epistemes in the context of the multiple categories of "trans-frontier men" that emerged in the late nineteenth century. These multiple categories – groups threatening the security of empire or those protecting it – reveal the anxieties and aspirations tied to the frontier and to the imperial policy surrounding it. Growing security concerns pushed imperial administrators to better define and "close" the frontier, in large part by restricting access to information about it.

The sixth chapter reexamines the work of boundary commissions in the context of the emergence of frontier experts such as Thomas Holdich. These experts, who became increasingly central to imperial policy, reflect the increasingly intimate relationship between geography and the state and reveal the networks through which geographical information fused with political and military policy. The chapter also examines the engagement of the frontier experts with the Royal Geographical Society and *The Geographical Journal*. The co-habitation of geographical studies and international political concerns, I argue, reflected a new *geo*political mode of seeing the region and the world that was in turn bequeathed to India at independence.

The final chapter evaluates the state of the region before the Sino-Indian War of 1962, and illustrates how colonial practices produced a disputed postcolonial borderland in independent India. It reexamines local perspectives and the political rearticulation of Ladakh as a crucial frontier of India against threats from China and Pakistan. Finally, it highlights the enduring legacy of imperial border making: the inherited complex of practices and ideas about territory, borders, and security, magnified by the significance of a nation-state for which its citizens were willing to die.

By revealing the transformation of a historical entrepôt into a modern borderland, this book provides both the first comprehensive history of Ladakh's encounter with the British Empire and a history of the birth of geopolitics. Focusing on this complex of practices and ideas, which slowly fused geography and politics, reveals a dramatic shift in how modern states conceive of territory. But in the case of Ladakh, a century of employing an increasingly broad array of techniques failed to produce an acceptable international border. For the newly independent Indian nation-state, like many postcolonial states, the managed colonial frontier came to embody the limit of the nation. It had to be defended to the death – an imperative tragically enacted across the desolate Aksai Chin during the Sino-Indian War of 1962. The history of failed border making in a remote corner of the Himalaya proved central to a global transformation of political space.

1 Territory before Borderlines
Trade, Cosmology, and Modes of Seeing in Precolonial Ladakh

Ladakh traces its politico-geographical birth to the mid-tenth century, when sKyid.lde Nyi.ma.mgon established himself as ruler of the western Tibetan region known as mNga'.ris skor.gsum.[1] Nyi.ma.mgon was descended from the Tibetan emperor Langdarma (gLang.dar.ma), whose assassination in c. 842 CE – allegedly by a Buddhist monk in retaliation for Langdarma's persecution of Buddhists – triggered the collapse of the Tibetan Empire. On his death, Nyi.ma.mgon's territorial authority, tenuous as it may have been, was divided among his three sons.[2] The eldest, dPal.gyi.mgon, inherited (or perhaps conquered) Mar.yul, a region roughly corresponding to the portion of today's Ladakh centered on the upper Indus River.

The Ladakhi historian dGe.rgan bSod.nams Ts'e.brtan, whose supplement to the composite *La.dwags rGyal.rabs*[3] (The royal chronicles of Ladakh) synthesizes many now-lost documents, offers one of the earliest articulations of the dimensions of Mar.yul:[4]

[Nyi.ma.mgon] gave to his eldest son, dPal.gyi.mgon, Mar.yul, where they possess black bows. The borders [*mtshams*] of Mar.yul are as follows: in the east bDe. mchog dkar.po and the red range as far as the Yi.mig boulder (the size of a yak); in

---

[1] Prior to the tenth century, scant archeological and written evidence suggests that at least lower Ladakh was part of the Kusana Empire (from the second century BCE to the fourth century CE) and that it was certainly a part of the Tibetan Empire from the seventh or early eighth century through Langdarma's assassination in 842 CE.

[2] Luciano Petech suggests that this was a theoretical right to rule. Petech, *Kingdom of Ladakh: c. 950–1842 A.D.*, Serie Orientale Roma 51 (Rome: Istituto italiano per il Medio ed Estremo Oriente, 1977).

[3] The most literal translation of *rGyal.rabs* is "royal succession." There are at least seven versions of the *La.dwags rGyal.rabs*. For a description of each of these manuscripts, see Petech, *Kingdom of Ladakh*. More generally, see Dan Martin's *Tibetan Histories: A Bibliography of Tibetan-Language Historical Works* (London: Serindia, 1997) for a taxonomy of the genres of historical writing in Tibet.

[4] Mar.yul is often translated as "low country," a description that makes sense only when the region is compared to the even more elevated Tibetan Plateau (Byang.thang).

the west, the stone with a big hole [i.e., cave] at the foot of the Kha.che pass;[5] in the north, as far as gSer.kha mGon.po. This is the extent of the [Mar.yul] lands.[6]

These royal records describe a series of localities that constituted boundaries, according the chroniclers of the *rgyal.po* – the Ladakhi ruler. The eastern and northern border points are specific places: Demchok and gSer.kha mGon.po.[7] The western border point is a definite feature: a cave at the foot of the Zoji Pass (*la*) to the Kashmir Valley. No southern border marker is given.[8]

These physical points were merely referents for a series of dynamic, overlapping, and sometimes competing understandings of space across the northwestern Himalaya. There existed, in short, multiple *modes of seeing* space for the precolonial inhabitants of Ladakh and its surroundings. In this chapter I provide both a historical background to the making and eventual demise of independent Ladakh[9] and an exploration of four indigenous modes of envisioning its space: *material, cosmological, political,* and *linguistic.* Although I make generalizations about certain sociocultural practices, often without being able to locate their precise temporal origins or the pace at which they changed, I do not intend to suggest timeless practices of a "premodern" society. Rather, I seek to identify a dynamic assortment of ways in which indigenous historical actors perceived the space(s) they inhabited and to document these ways through a combination of cautious generalizations and particular historical examples.

Furthermore, the limited precolonial sources on Ladakhi history do not allow for a detailed excavation of many first-person accounts of "seeing" space. Few historical sources are kind enough to mediate themselves in

---

[5] This geographical marker was also known as the Zoji-*la*: the pass on the main road connecting the Kashmir Valley to the upper Indus.

[6] dGe.rgan bSod.nams Ts'e.brtan, *bLa.dwags rGyal.rabs 'Chi.med gTer* [The immortal treasury of the royal chronicles of Ladakh], ed. sKyabs.ldan dGe.rgan (New Delhi, 1976), 181. The author's alternative spelling of Ladakh (i.e., bLa.dwags instead of La.dwags) suggests that he may have followed early Western visitors in describing it as the "land of lamas" (*bla.ma*) instead of the "land of passes" (*la*).

[7] The names of both of these border villages suggest associations with two major protective deities. Tibetan *bDe.mchog* = Sanskrit *Chakrasambara*, and Tib. *mGon.po* = Sans. *Mahakala.*

[8] This suggests, perhaps, that the mountains to the south of the Indus valley were self-evident physical boundaries.

[9] While many scholars describe the period between the collapse of the Tibetan Empire and the Dogra invasion as one of Ladakhi independence, that same independence was relative due to the fact that the political integrity of the region frequently changed. Sometimes Ladakh expanded or contracted under a single ruler; at other times, it existed as a loose territorial expression, subjected to external political and economic pressures that fragmented its rulers and left it beholden to the imperial machinations of its neighbors. In this last sense, Ladakh has long been a transimperial territory, situated both temporally and spatially across and between numerous empires.

this way. To recover this sense of historical understandings of space, we must work backward from "seen" objects and institutions to the subjects who did the seeing. By drawing on insights from anthropologists, linguists, and historical records, I assert in this chapter that indigenous conceptions of space were more pluralistic than the subsequent political territory envisioned by Ladakh's imperial rulers in the nineteenth century. The complex amalgamation of cosmological, political, linguistic, and material factors produced spatial configurations that failed to map neatly onto, as it were, maps.

The chapter begins by exploring what I have termed the cosmological, political, linguistic, and material modes of seeing in independent Ladakh. These categories are themselves palimpsestic and interwoven. In this chapter I disaggregate these four categories in order to reveal the complexity of indigenous conceptions of space, not to suggest that Ladakh's past inhabitants did not see what a modern visitor might see when viewing a similar object (a mountain, for instance). I do this by identifying a number of broad cultural, economic, religious, and social developments over a period ranging from dPal.gyi.mgon's "founding" of Ladakh in the tenth century to the present.

Drawing on the limited historical records from the seventeenth century to the early nineteenth century, I then survey the region's economic and political interactions with its neighbors. By highlighting Ladakh's position as a religious, commercial, and political nexus, this chapter also illustrates how Ladakh had long been the central crossroads of a larger regional network of commerce and politics – and not the peripheral and isolated borderland that it would later become. Finally, the chapter recounts early British encounters with the broader northwestern Himalayan region, the first sustained British interest in Ladakh, and the impact of the 1834 Dogra invasion on Ladakhi society.[10]

By mapping the economic, cultural, and religious networks that encircled Ladakh and, more broadly, the northwestern Himalaya at the time of the Dogra and British conquests in the 1830s and 1840s, this chapter sets the scene for the region's colonial encounter. I assert that Ladakh only became a peripheral space through this encounter – or, at the risk of tautology, that Ladakh only became a borderland when its rulers became preoccupied with making its borders.

---

[10] The Dogras, an ethno-linguistic group primarily found in northern India and Pakistan, gave their name to the Hindu Rajput dynasty founded by Gulab Singh in the early nineteenth century. Gulab Singh, a vassal of the Sikh Maharaja Ranjit Singh, was made the first maharaja of the princely state of Jammu and Kashmir by the British, as a result of the treaties of Lahore and Amritsar in 1846.

1.1   Modes of Seeing

Long after the tectonic upheaval and ensuing erosion that formed the Himalayas, the valleys of the upper Indus became home to humans. These humans and their settlements depended on the seasonal fluctuations of snow and glacial melt. The springtime swell of streams irrigated high-altitude crops, while the melting away of snowpack in the region's many passes often cleared the way for crucial travel and trade. These inhabitants of the upper Indus moved from valley to valley and up to the Tibetan Plateau (*byang.thang*).[11] In addition to providing for subsistence agriculturalists, this seasonal movement led to the trade of wool, salt, barley, livestock, other foodstuffs, and scarcer commodities among the region's agrarian and pastoralist communities. Villages arose along glacier-fed streams or just beyond the flood range of rivers and were often located en route to passes leading to neighboring valleys.

The ruler dPal.gyi.mgon gained authority over the region referred to as Mar.yul in the tenth century. By then, many of the region's settlements had likely established aspects of the social hierarchies, localized cosmologies, and complex irrigation and trade networks that would flourish for the next millennium.[12]

1.1.1   Material

From at least the tenth century, the region began to see networks emerge through the interactions of transhumant herders, traders, pilgrims, and the agriculturists of the upper Indus. Agrarian settlements grew along glacier-fed streams, developing complex forms of irrigation to account for variable water flow during the relatively short growing season that loosely coincided with the opening of passes into neighboring valleys.[13] Trade

[11] The Tibetan Plateau is often referred to as the Changthang, literally "northern plateau." In terms of the uncertainty of snow melt on mountain passes, there were occasionally years when late snows, colder-than-average temperatures, or unusually high snowpack prevented the passes from opening in time for the necessary trade. Similarly, the death of pack animals near the passes often resulted in the near total loss of caravan loads of goods. Janet Rizvi, *Trans-Himalayan Caravans: Merchant Princes and Peasant Traders in Ladakh* (New Delhi: Oxford University Press, 1999).

[12] For an example of how irrigation systems constructed perhaps a millennium ago have endured the historical processes of settlement and social change in Ladakh (though with modifications), see Corinne Wacker, "Can Irrigation Systems Disclose the History of the Villages of Ladakh? The Example of Tagmachig," in *Recent Research on Ladakh 2007*, ed. John Bray and Nawang Tsering Shakspo (Leh: J&K Academy of Art, Culture, and Languages, 2007), 205–16.

[13] The *La.dwags rGyal.rabs* attributes the development of irrigation in the outlaying valleys of the broader Tibetan region to the reign of Khri.sngan.bzung.btsan, who ruled in central Tibet four generations before Srong.btsan sgam.po (600–650 CE): "During his

routes, "webs of water" that irrigated the high-desert terrain,[14] and seasonally shifting grazing patterns inscribed the region's many landscapes. These paths of migration and lines of material connection spread over vast, desolate, and uninhabited distances. Movement across this space was typically measured in time, not in distance. A day's walk was a common unit of measurement, reflecting the widespread enmeshing of time and space that existed before standardized units.

Over subsequent centuries, trans-Himalayan trade routes grew in number and importance. These brought an array of peoples into the region, shaping Ladakh into an entrepôt that connected various far-flung places: the Silk Road oases of Kashgar and Yarkand, the Kashmir Valley, Baltistan, the area of present-day Afghanistan, the many polities of the western Himalaya, western and central Tibet, the Punjab, and the plains of northern India. Tibetan traders regularly crisscrossed Western Tibet, trading goods with communities in Nepal and the western Himalaya.[15] Muslim traders known as the Lhasa Khaché (discussed below) oversaw an even broader trade network stretching from Lhasa through Ladakh to Kashmir. The region became a conduit for luxury goods like *pashm* wool (used for pashmina),[16] brick tea, silk, precious stones, and, eventually, opium and hashish. As early as the sixteenth century, villages situated closest to neighboring polities or adjoining the region's eastern and northern uninhabited spaces became established border points. They signaled to traders, travelers, and pilgrims the jurisdictions of established authorities: typically monasteries (*dgon.pa*), local chiefs (*jo.bo*), or ministers (*blon.po* or *bka'.blon*) of the king (*rgyal.po*).[17] dGe.rgan bSod.nams Ts'e.brtan's map (Map 1.1), based on numerous precolonial Ladakhi

---

lifetime the outlying valleys were brought under notice and cleared for fields. / 'The lakes were furnished with gates, / And drawn into irrigation canals. / The glacier-water was collected in ponds, / And the water collected overnight was used for irrigation during the day.'/ Such like things were done in his time." August Hermann Francke, trans. and ed., "La.dwags rGyal.rabs," in *Antiquities of Indian Tibet*, vol. 2 (Calcutta: Superintendent Government Printing, India, 1914).

[14] Kim Gutschow refers to the systems of irrigation common throughout the western Tibetan region and Ladakh as "webs of water," in her "'Lords of the Forth,' 'Lords of the Water,' and 'No Lords at All': The Politics of Irrigation in Three Tibetan Societies," in *Recent Research on Ladakh 6* (Bristol, UK: University of Bristol, 1997).

[15] van Spengen, *Tibetan Border Worlds*.

[16] Properly speaking, pashmina is the material woven from *pashm*, the downy undercoat of the Tibetan goat (*byang.ra*: "north[ern] goat").

[17] Janet Rizvi makes a similar point when she notes that "[perhaps] the most vibrant of the trading stations were the towns roughly at the border between inhabited and uninhabited portions of [Indian and Central Asian trade routes], where cultivation gave way to desert or mountain range. Here the merchants and caravan staff would pause to recruit [porters] and equip themselves for the rigours of the journey, or recover from its hardships." Rizvi, *Trans-Himalayan Caravans*, 11.

sources, marks the two most prominent border points using the Ladakhi/ Tibetan term *sa.mtshams*, or "land border,"[18] while, significantly, omitting any actual borderlines. These two border points are at the Zoji Pass on the main route to Kashmir and near Demchok on the Leh–Lhasa route (Map 1.1). As I will illustrate in the second and third sections of this chapter, controlling the flow of traded goods was a pivotal strategy for the imperial aspirations of Ladakh's neighbors. This aggressive interest spurred both the Dogra invasion of 1834 and subsequent British designs on the region.

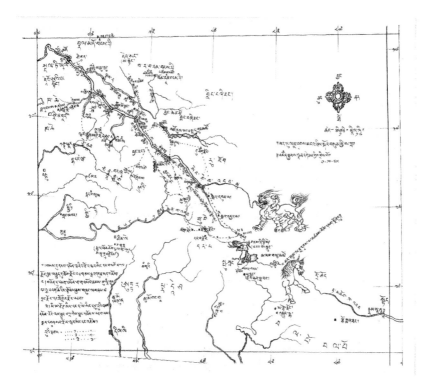

Map 1.1 dGe.rgan bSod.nams Ts'e.brtan's map based on the *La.dwags rGyal.rabs* marks the two most prominent border points (see Map 1.2 for detail). These two borders, marked with "X," are at the Zoji Pass on the main route to Kashmir and near Demchok, on the Leh–Lhasa route.[19]

---

[18] Interestingly, the term *mtshams* has a wide range of meanings, including "border," "boundary," "retreat," and "intermediate direction."
[19] Ts'e.brtan, *bLa.dwags rGyal.rabs 'Chi.Med gTer [The Immortal Treasury of the Royal Chronicles of Ladakh]*.

(a)

(b)

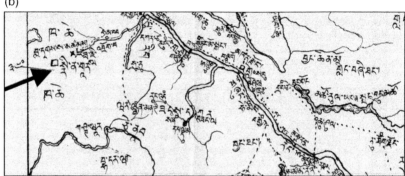

(c)

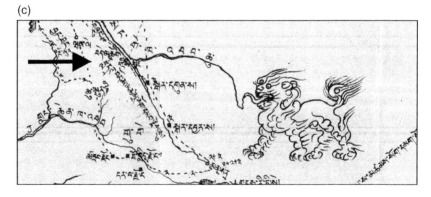

Map 1.2 Details of Map 1.1. In Map 1.2a, an "X" marks the location of
the border (*sa.tshams*). The text besides the "X" reads "In Mar.yul, the
border of Ladakh before the war with Mongolia" [i.e., the Tibet–
Ladakh–Mughal War of 1679–84 in which the Tibetans were assisted
by Mongolian troops]. In Map 1.2b, an "X" marks the border of Ladakh
at the Zoji Pass to Kashmir. In Map 1.2c, the X marks the border at the
Lha.ri stream near Demchok "after the Mongolian war."

1.1.2   Cosmological

A patchwork of highly localized spiritual spaces overlaid these material paths of trade, webs of irrigation, and pastoral migration routes. This patchwork was a part of the vast cosmogeography of Tibetan Buddhism that spread in the ninth and tenth centuries across the Tibetan Plateau.

1.1.2.1 Local Cosmogeographies

The worship of deities (*lha*) and other spirits (*klu, btsan,* etc.) associated with specific regions, mountains, streams, lakes, rivers, and trees reflected spiritual ties to local landscapes. These ties were in place, for the most part, before the arrival of Buddhism. Natural features – particularly mountains and streams – were focal points that attracted and shaped communities. By the time of dPal.gyi.mgon, villages in the upper Indus had formed patrifamilial groupings (*pha.spun*) that connected families at a subvillage level to a single deity (*pha.lha*) and to a single location of worship (the *pha.lha lha.tho*[20]). While local monasteries would eventually come to be seen as the religious centers of villages – analogous to the Hindu *mandir* or Muslim mosque – the sites of *lha* worship were distinct from the local monasteries in several significant ways.

First, they lacked the political dimensions that had arisen in the monastic institution by the middle of the second millennium CE. These sites were often tied to village agriculture. *Lha.tho*, which to this day are regarded as indicators of crop success for the coming year, were constructed and maintained by villagers, who nurtured them with prayers (*sangs*) and material offerings to the *lha*. Over time, local monasteries became involved in these rites. Nowadays, as in centuries past, it is the role of a local monk to oversee these prayers at the *lha.tho*.[21] While the involvement of local monasteries in these rites may have been tied to village-level patronage and politics, the role of the *lha.tho* themselves primarily concerned the agricultural and spiritual well-being of the particular locality.

Second, these sites of worship gained significance by virtue of the particular deity's or spirit's relationship to the natural feature with which it was associated (a mountain, stream, lake, or tree). A *lha.tho* thus physically connected people to a village deity, to a subvillage deity, or, in some cases, to a villager's own family deity (Figure 1.1).[22]

---

[20] *Pha.lha lha.tho* may be translated as the *pha.lha*'s "deity residence."

[21] Martin Mills, "The Religion of Locality: Local Area Gods and the Characterisation of Tibetan Buddhism," in *Recent Research on Ladakh 7*, ed. Thierry Dodin and Hans Rather (Bonn: Ulmer Kulturanthroplogische Schriften, 1997), 309–28.

[22] Nawang Tsering Shakspo, *A Cultural History of Ladakh*, ed. Kyle Gardner (New Delhi: Centre for Research on Ladakh, 2010); and Kyle Gardner, unpublished research paper for Tibetan Studies Program, School for International Training, 2005: "*Lha*: Deity Worship in Family, Village and Monastery in Sabu, Ladakh."

Figure 1.1 *lha.tho* ("deity-residence") above the village of Basgo. The ruins of Basgo's medieval fort are visible in the background. Photograph by the author.

Last, these sites reflected an array of deities that were unique to the place they inhabited, though they were often considered members of categories that existed throughout the Tibetan Buddhist world.[23] The name of a deity in Ladakh, for instance, was often associated with a particular patrifamilial communal grouping (*pha.spun*), hamlet, or village.

A rough hierarchy exists within the ranks of these so-called mundane deities.[24] While scholars have been unable to date the practices associated

---

[23] These categories were not uniform across that world. For additional details, and for a somewhat antiquated typology of the (mostly higher-ranking) protective deities, see Rene de Nebesky-Wojkowitz, *Oracles and Demons of Tibet: The Cult and Iconography of the Tibetan Protective Deities* (Delhi: Book Faith India, 1996), and Mills, "Religion of Locality."

[24] That is, those deities still trapped within *samsara*, the Buddhist (and Hindu) cycle of death and rebirth for nonenlightened beings. The supramundane deities would be those who, like buddhas, bodhisattvas, and some dharmapala (protective deities), have achieved freedom from *samsara*.

with these deities with any precision, they certainly predate the arrival of Buddhism in Ladakh. They continue, albeit with less widespread veneration, today.

A *yul.lha*[25] wields power over a particular region. This may be a single hamlet or, as in the case of the *yul.lha* Chenrezig, all of Tibet.[26] In Ladakh, *yul.lha* are usually associated with specific mountains and regarded as wrathful or peaceful. Villages may require additional spatial "protection" from them in the form of *mchod.rten* (Sanskrit: *stupa*, "heap") – reliquary structures often venerated by circumambulation (Figure 1.2).[27] Many locals believe that these deities live inside of the same *lha.tho* that are built by villagers and offered monthly prayers on auspicious days.[28] *Rtse.lha*, or *khim.lha*, are family gods – more localized than the *pha.lha* mentioned above – and are worshiped at *lha.tho* within certain family compounds.

Klu, or water spirits, reside in streams, springs, or marshes,[29] bringing clean water if properly appeased.[30] *Klu.stor* – offerings to *klu* – are occasionally performed near the *klu*'s residence, a *klu.bang*. Despite the

---

[25] "Yul" is typically translated as country, or, in a loose sense, "territory." See Mills, "Religion of Locality." For the Bhutanese context of this term, see Françoise Pommaret, "Yul and Yul Lha: The Territory and Its Deity in Bhutan," *Bulletin of Tibetology* 40, no. 1 (2004): 39–67.

[26] *Spyan.ras.gzigs*, or Avalokitesvara, a bodhisattva, is also considered to be a *yul.lha* because of his status as Tibet's patron deity. See Gardner, "*Lha*: Deity Worship."

[27] Only seven kilometers by road east of Leh, the upper limit of the village of Sabu is surrounded by the Ladakh Range. At the head of the village stand the peaks known as *Srin.mo.gan.rkyal*: the "sleeping demons" (or "supine demon"). Both of these peaks, Nawang Tsering Shakspo writes, have been considered inauspicious by the villagers, and have had their influence countered by a number of *chorten* known as *rigs.gsum.mgon.po*. The latter term translates as "the Three Reverences," referring to Avalokitesvara, Manjusri, and Vajrapani – the Bodhisattvas of Compassion, Wisdom, and Strength, respectively. Centre for Research on Ladakh (CRL), unpublished notes by Nawang Tsering Shakspo titled, "Historical Perspectives of Saboo."

[28] Once a year, during the *lha.tho po.ches*, their contents are changed. At this event, representatives of each family, along with several lamas, gather at the site of the *lha.tho* and dismantle it. A mud vessel filled with grain and butter is kept inside the structure; when the *lha.tho* is dismantled, the vessel is examined. Predictions are made based on the state of the contents (e.g., If the butter is melted it will be a warmer season; if the amount of grain inside has risen, there will be a good crop; if it is sunken, the crop will fail. If there are seeds other than wheat [i.e., barley], it will be a bad season). The vessel is then emptied and refilled with grain and butter, covered in cloth, and sealed with mud. It is replaced in the *lha.tho* and covered with rocks. Juniper branches are tied to the top of the *lha.tho* and are decorated with prayer flags, a purification mantra is chanted by a monk, and incense is burned.

[29] These spirits are sometimes referred to as the nāgas of broader Indic Hindu and Buddhist traditions, but their worship has notable local inflections.

[30] For descriptions of *klu* see Patrick Kaplanian, "L'homme Dans Le Monde Surnaturel Du Ladakh," in *Recent Research on Ladakh 4 & 5* (Delhi: Motilal Banarsidas, 1995); and Sonam Phuntsog, "Sacrificial Offerings to Local Deities in Ladakh," in *Recent Research on Ladakh 6*, ed. Henry Osmaston and Nawang Tsering (Bristol, UK: University of Bristol, 1997).

Figure 1.2 An array of old *mchod.rten* in Nubra Valley, northern Ladakh. The soldier on the bridge marks the last point to which nonlocals are allowed to travel before the disputed border with Pakistan. Permits to visit Nubra are required for all nonlocal residents. Photograph by the author.

seemingly low status of *klu* in the spirit world, treatises have been written about them. They even merited inclusion in the *La.dwags rGyal.rabs*, which relates an event connected to the *klu*'s ability to heal skin diseases. King Jams.yang rNam.rgyal (who reigned from 1595 to 1616) was apparently afflicted with leprosy. A lama from Mount Kailash came to perform a *klu.stor* for the king's sake. The success of this ceremony apparently convinced the king to invite Gelukpa monks to establish themselves in Ladakh.[31]

Other categories of spirits include *gzhi.bdag* (lord of the place/locality), *sa.bdag* (lord of the ground/earth/soil), *lha.lcang* (deity-trees), and *btsan*, spirits inhabiting the netherworld.[32] *Btsan* are warded off by *btsan.dos*, small clay markers painted red and installed throughout villages. This final category of spirit, rarely spoken of today, also reflects temporal dimensions at work in local cosmologies. As ghosts, failing to be reborn, *btsan* often haunt the villages where they once lived.

---

[31] Francke, "La.dwags rGyal.rabs."
[32] Shakspo, *Cultural History of Ladakh*, 237–43. Tucci, McKay, and Nebesky-Wojkowitz suggest that in Tibet, *btsan* are more commonly viewed either as demons or as powerful local gods.

Together, these spatial markers – *lha.tho, mchod.rten, btsan.dos, klu. bang* – have connected individuals, families, subvillage groupings, villages, and whole regions to an array of deities. The geographic ranges of these deities may vary significantly, yet they possess one characteristic in common: they have little correlation to political categories of space.

1.1.2.2 The Worlds of Tibetan Buddhism   By the seventeenth century, as a result of both sustained cultural interactions with the region's neighbors and the regular movement of traders and pilgrims through its valleys, Islam and Buddhism were cohabitating in Ladakh. While both religions originally entered the region from Kashmir in the west, Ladakh's Buddhist majority would be shaped more profoundly by eastern influences – from central and Western Tibet, the western Himalayan kingdoms, and even Bhutan and Sikkim.[33] Although Buddhism may have been introduced there as early as the first or second century CE, it was only by the twelfth or thirteenth century that *Vajrayāna*, the Tibetan variant of Buddhism, became the dominant institutional religion in the upper Indus.[34]

According to the revealed textual tradition (*gter.ma*) that emerged in the Nyingmapa (old school) tradition of Buddhism in Tibet, the abbot of the Indian Buddhist university of Nalanda, Śāntarakṣita (725–88 CE), summoned the Tantric master Padmasambhava from the Swat Valley to Tibet. Śāntarakṣita had, in turn, been summoned to Tibet by Emperor Khri.srong sDe.btsan (755–c. 800 CE). Padmasambhava's first major act was to subdue Srin.mo, the "supine demoness" whose wrathful power was said to have spread over the whole of Tibet (Figure 1.3).[35] By erecting a series of temples and fortifications at geospatial points corresponding to vulnerable body points of the demoness, the Buddhist master geomantically restrained her. Srin.mo was not vanquished entirely but rather pinned down by Padmasambhava's use of political and religious – or miraculous – control. Nor did this localized control vanish into myth. Lhasa's Jokhang, Tibetan Buddhism's most revered site, was believed to be constructed over Srin.mo's heart. By exercising spiritual (and masculine) authority over a preexisting world of regional deities, Padmasambhava laid the patriarchal foundation of Buddhism in

---

[33] Rizvi, *Ladakh: Crossroads of High Asia*, 56.

[34] This variant is often referred to as *Vajrayāna* ("the lightning bolt vehicle") to distinguish it from other variants: *Hīnayāna* ("the lesser vehicle" – typically given the less derogatory name *Theravada*) and *Mahāyāna* ("the great(er) vehicle"). Vajrayāna, "the lightning bolt vehicle," is an amalgamation of *Mahāyāna*, Kashmiri Shaivism, and animist practices predating Buddhism. See Rizvi, *Ladakh: Crossroads of High Asia*, 56–61; and Petech, *Kingdom of Ladakh*, 10.

[35] Janet Gyatso, "Down with the Demoness: Reflections on a Feminine Ground in Tibet," *Tibet Journal* 12, no. 4 (1987): 38–53.

Figure 1.3 Srin.mo, the "supine demoness." Rubin Museum. *The Demoness of Tibet.* Tibet, late nineteenth/early twentieth century. Rubin Museum of Art. C2006.1.1 (HAR 65719).

Tibet.[36] In doing so, he conscripted, rather than rejected, a vast pantheon of local deities, channeling their power into a reconstructed Tibetan political cosmology. A similar founding mythology lies at the heart of the *hbo.yig*, the earliest and now fragmentary chronicles that recount the history of Zangskar.[37]

Another spiritual-spatial tradition attributed to Padmasambhava is that of the *beyul* (*sbas.yul*): hidden valleys revealed by masters known as tertön

[36] The gendered element of this subjugation and geomancy is worth noting. Gyatso makes this point forcefully in the case of Tibet (see Gyatso, "Down with the Demoness," 1987). The subjugation of numerous demonesses in Bhutan by the Buddhist master, Drukpa Kunley, exemplifies an even more graphic narrative of masculine Buddhist power exerted over pre-Buddhistic feminine forces. Drukpa Kunley wandered the Bhutanese country-side violently subduing demonesses with his "flaming thunderbolt of wisdom." Though his exploits are typically recounted in a comic mode, they could also be read as sexually assaulting unruly spirits into submission. These stories account for the nearly ubiquitous presence of phalluses painted on the sides of houses in Bhutan and rendered in wood for popular plays. See Keith Dowman and Sonam Paljor, trans., *The Divine Madman: The Sublime Life and Songs of Drukpa Kunley* (Varanasi: Pilgrims, 2000).

[37] Zangskar, a region to the south of the upper Indus, existed under varying degrees of Ladakhi political influence after being ruled by dPal.gyi.mgon's brother in the tenth century. See John H. Crook, "The History of Zangskar," in *Himalayan Buddhist Villages* (Bristol, UK: University of Bristol, 1994).

(*gter.ston*). Their locations – ranging across present-day Pakistan, the northwestern Himalaya in India, Nepal Bhutan, Sikkim, Tibet, and China – attest to the widely held belief in spaces that can only be seen or accessed by spiritual achievement and faith. Like the mountains and streams of local worship, these valleys are associated with and guarded by particular deities. The greatest of these *beyul*, common to Hindu, Tibetan Buddhist, and Bon traditions, is Shambhala, mentioned in both the *Kalacakra Tantra* and ancient texts from Western Tibet (Zhangzhung). But Shambhala, often considered an ethereal "pure land" abode of buddhas and bodhisattvas, formed an exception rather than the rule. Most *beyuls* are regarded as earthly realms that can be accessed by humans.

This spiritual territorialization connected Ladakh and Tibet through a network of sacred sites across the Himalaya and Tibetan Plateau, and through shared histories and mythologies of heroic founding figures and peripatetic Buddhist masters. Besides the deep political connections between Tibetan and Ladakhi monasteries that emerged by at least the middle of the second millennium, the growing prominence of the sacred mountain Kailash in Western Tibet provided a cosmogeographical focal point connecting the two regions.[38] On a still larger scale, Buddhism connected Ladakh to China and Mongolia in the east, and, in the south, to the plains of northern India, birthplace of Buddhism and home to its most sacred sites.[39]

These connections undermined any limited political visions of Ladakh's territory by enmeshing the region within the larger Tibetan Buddhist world and eventually subordinating Ladakhi religious institutions to various powerful Buddhist sects within central Tibet. Of particular significance for this book, the Treaty of Tingmosgang gave the king of Ladakh the right to property near Mount Kailash in order to establish a pilgrimage station for Ladakhis traveling to the sacred mountain and its lakes. As the British later attempted to solidify territorial boundaries in Ladakh in the nineteenth century, the status of this enclave (called *Men.ser*) became one of several problems that complicated their imperial notions of sovereignty, territory, and legal jurisdiction.

Finally, it is worth noting that the legitimacy of the *rgyal.po* stemmed from his role as a "dharma king" (*chos.rgyal*), asserting descent from the early Buddhist kings of Tibet.[40] Thus, the very foundation of political

---

[38] The extent to which Kailash can claim authority as the region's preeminent sacred geographical center has recently been disputed by McKay, *Kailas Histories*.

[39] See Huber, *The Holy Land Reborn*.

[40] John Bray, "The Lapchak Mission from Leh to Lhasa in British Indian Foreign Policy," *Tibet Journal* 15, no. 4 (1990): 75–96; Peter Schwieger, "Power and Territory in the Kingdom of Ladakh," in *Recent Research on Ladakh*, ed. Thierry Dodin and Heinz Rather (Ulm: Universität Ulm, 1997), 427–34; and John Bray, "Ladakh's Lopchak Missions to Lhasa: Gift Exchange, Diplomatic Ritual, and the Politics of Ambiguity," in *Commerce*

power in independent Ladakh was rooted in a spiritual connection to the historical lineages that had ruled in central Tibet. But the historical connections to Tibetan Buddhist institutions within Tibet also revealed sectarian tensions. In the early seventeenth century, thanks to the influence of the famous translator, sTag.tsang.Ras.pa, the royal family of Ladakh became patrons of the Drukpa Kagyupa sect. Concurrently, in central Tibet, the Gelukpa-led Ganden Phodrang (dGa'.ldan Pho. brang) consolidated its power under the rule of the fifth Dalai Lama, Ngag.dbang bLo.bzang rGya.mtsho. While each sect was expected to treat the other with respect, tensions erupted sporadically. However, Ladakh and Tibet remained connected through formalized political, religious, and economic ties.

1.1.2.3 Islam   By the seventeenth century, significant Islamic networks stretched throughout Ladakh, often producing villages and families where the region's two principal religions cohabitated. It was not uncommon to find Muslims utilizing spiritual resources – such as local oracles[41] – that were typically associated with Buddhism.

Regular trade carried on by Tibetan Muslims between the Kashmir Valley and Lhasa, as well as the presence of Central Asian Muslims – traders and *Haj*-goers alike – passing through Ladakh, signaled hybrid Islamic identities distinct from those of Kashmir and Central Asia. The Tibetan term for Muslim, *kha.che*, is also a Tibetan term for Kashmir. By the seventeenth century, it came to refer to a group of Muslim traders – the Lhasa Khaché – from Kashmir and Ladakh, who often resided in Lhasa to oversee their trade network.[42]

Besides the Lhasa Khaché, numerous long-established trade networks connected northern India with Central Asia. The vast webs of commerce and pilgrimage connecting the subcontinent to Central Asia facilitated a robust trade in everything from textiles to slaves.[43] As Muzaffar Alam has shown, the long-held view of the Mughal Empire and Uzbek khanates as hostile to interregion trade is largely unsupported by the historical

---

and Communities: Social Status and the Exchange of Goods in Tibetan Societies, ed. Jeannine Bischoff and Alice Travers (Berlin: EB, 2018).

[41] These oracles are known as *lha.mo* when the possessed is female and *lha.ba* when male.

[42] The network was also known as the Lhasa Khaché (Kha.che), or, more simply, Khaché. David G. Atwill, *Islamic Shangri-La: Inter-Asian Relations and Lhasa's Muslim Communities, 1600 to 1960* (Oakland: University of California Press, 2018). Details on the Khaché in Lhasa may also be found in an account of a trip made to Lhasa from Kathmandu in 1882–83, by Ghulam Muhammad, a Kashmiri residing in Kathmandu. See Ghulam Muhammad, *Récit d'un Voyageur Musulman Au Tibet*, trans. M. Gaborieau (Paris: Librairie C. Klincksieck, 1973).

[43] Arup Banerji, *Old Routes: North Indian Nomads and Bankers in Afghan, Uzbek and Russian Lands* (Gurgaon: Three Essays Collective, 2011).

records of the mid-sixteenth to mid-eighteenth centuries.[44] These networks sometimes used Islamic pilgrimage networks connecting Sufi *dargāh*s (shrines). In some cases, Sufi orders engaged in trade actively facilitated that same use. While there appear to have been no dargāhs in Ladakh, the Nurbakhshiyya Sufis had a sustained presence in the region from at least the early fifteenth century up to the nineteenth century.[45] Whether Buddhist, Muslim, Bön.po, Hindu, Sikh, or animist, the networks spread across the western Himalaya – and across northern South Asia – were vast and multidirectional.

It thus seems fair to conclude that a typical Ladakhi of the independence period (the mid-tenth through early nineteenth centuries) – whether a trader, a herder, an agriculturalist tied to a village, or an occasional pilgrim – had the visible and spatial dimensions of his or her world profoundly shaped by both local and distant cosmologies. Furthermore, these varied cosmologies remained distinct from, if often related to, political conceptions of space.

1.1.3 Political

Coexisting with the material and cosmological modes of seeing space were political visions formed by the growing power of monasteries and by regional allegiances to ruling families. Kings functioned as religiously ordained temporal rulers. However, the taxation systems that developed in much of the western Himalaya and Tibet in the second millennium CE were imposed by increasingly powerful monasteries and local chiefs. Taxation typically demanded *corvée* labor (Tibetan: *'u.lag*; Urdu/ Persian: *begār*), military service, or varying percentages of crop yields.

Rivalries among Buddhist sects – particularly between the Drukpa Kagyupa (*'brug.pa bka'.brgyud.pa*) and Gelukpa (*dge.lugs.pa*) – signaled the political hold of the monasteries and the often-tenuous authority of the king (or, at times, competing kings).[46] These rivalries also indicated affiliations with, and allegiances to, various monastic institutions in far-off

---

[44] Muzaffar Alam, "Trade, State Policy and Regional Change: Aspects of Mughal-Uzbek Commercial Relations, C. 1550–1750," *Journal of the Economic and Social History of the Orient* 37, no. 3 (1994): 202–27.

[45] Abdul Ghani Sheikh, "The Traditions of Sufism in Ladakh," in Abdul Ghani Sheikh, *Reflections on Ladakh, Tibet and Central Asia* (Leh, Ladakh: Yasmin House, 2010).

[46] As John Bray has noted, "in the thirteenth and fourteenth centuries the kings' closest links were with the 'Bri.gung.pa school. By the mid-fifteenth century, the dGe.lugs.pa had gained influence. However, from the seventeenth century onwards the royal family's closest relationship was with the 'Brug.pa bKa'.brgyud.pa sect." John Bray, "Introduction: Locating Ladakhi History," in *Ladakhi Histories: Local and Regional Perspectives*, ed. John Bray, Brill's Tibetan Studies Library 9 (Leiden: Brill, 2005), 1–30.

central Tibet. The practice of sending novice monks to central Tibet's monasteries began, according to the *La. dwags rGyal.rabs*, during the reign of Lha.chen dNgos.grub (c. 1290–1320).[47] Also around this time likely began the similar practice of each Buddhist family sending a son to the local monastery for training. These practices strengthened ties between local monasteries, villages, and families, even as they established degrees of loyalty to particular sects.

While the *rgyal.po* of Ladakh may have exerted primary political control over his vassals, monasteries and local chiefs complicated notions of unitary allegiance. This was a society where, as the historian John Bray has noted, "political structures [were] centred on personal allegiances to ruling families rather than on 'nations' defined by clearly marked boundaries."[48] The kings expended vast resources as patrons of monasteries in Ladakh and Western Tibet, underscoring that their legitimacy was contingent upon their support of Buddhism.[49]

In this political mode, control of space was contested by allegiances to monastic networks, local rulers, and the king – all of whom sought to regulate territory for the purpose of extracting revenue, labor, and military service. In contrast to how they were viewed cosmologically and materially, streams, rivers, and mountains were viewed politically as objects used to delineate ranges of taxation and demarcate local political influence. Intervillage political affiliations were not contiguous. Rather, villages differed depending on their sectarian affiliation and on the political allegiances of their respective ruling classes. By the time of the Treaty of Tingmosgang in 1684, hierarchies of political power had arisen that resisted any formal and absolute notion of sovereignty tied to territory. For instance, the *rgyal.po* of Zangskar offered tribute to the *rgyal.po* of Ladakh. The Ladakhi *rgyal.po*, in turn, offered occasional tribute to the Mughal emperor and triennial tribute to the Dalai Lama (though no tribute at all, it is worth noting, to the Qing emperor). This chain of tribute reveals a multilayered notion of sovereignty distinct from the form that would later be imposed on the region by the British.

The close and often indistinguishable ties between the monastic establishment, local rulers, and the *rgyal.po*s, resist attempts to draw too neat a distinction between political and religious spheres. The *La.dwags rGyal. rabs* offers numerous instances of kings and local chiefs building temples, as well as numerous *mchod.rten*, *ma.ni* walls, and prayer wheels, all of which cemented direct ties to the monastic establishments. *Mchod.rten*, prayer wheels, and *ma.ni* walls also bridged the gap between cosmological

---

[47] Francke, "La.dwags rGyal.rabs," 98.

[48] Bray, "Introduction: Locating Ladakhi History," 7.   [49] Bray, 10.

and political modes of seeing. *Mchod.rten* construction, in particular, was a way for rulers to interact with the cosmogeographies of specific villages. By covering the construction cost of these reliquaries, these same rulers could please the monastic establishment and the village populace simultaneously, and also placate the sometimes-wrathful local deities. Often the products of royal or monastic patronage, or tied to historical figures like the tenth-century translator Rinchen Zangpo, these reliquaries profoundly shaped local space and movement. As objects designed to be circumambulated clockwise for the accrual of merit, *ma.ṇi* walls, *mchod. rten*, and prayer wheels guided people through village and town space. *Ma.ṇi* walls (long rectangular raised earthworks covered with stones with mantras[50]) were often built between villages. They also served a practical role in offering shelter to weary travelers.[51] Like the fortresses often perched on ridges above villages, these monasteries, temples, *mchod. rten*, *ma.ṇi* walls and prayer wheels were physical objects that shaped village space while also – less visibly perhaps – asserting the authority of a local or distant political power.

The coordinated looting and destruction of many monasteries by the Dogra invaders from Jammu in the 1830s was a testament to the widely perceived political and economic power of monastic institutions, and to the monasteries' often-substantial wealth. Zorawar Singh, the Dogra general who oversaw most of the conquest, decreed that the surviving monasteries increase their local taxes. This began a period of hardship that was partially relieved, decades later, by the British Joint Commissioners, who saw the high taxation as hindering the stimulation of trade with Central Asia and Tibet.

1.1.4   Linguistic

Finally, as numerous scholars have discussed, language provided another means of shaping Ladakhi space. Local linguistic variations divided that space, while various lingua francas worked to connect certain communities. As Michel Neyroud notes in regard to the organization of space in Zangskar, "When the Zanskarpa divided their territory, it was most often to signal a difference in the spoken language."[52] These linguistic

---

[50] A mantra is a word or sound, usually with a sacred connotation, that is repeated silently or aloud to aid focus in meditation.

[51] Shakspo, *Cultural History of Ladakh.*

[52] Michel Neyroud, "Organisation de l'espace, Isolement et Changement Dans Le Domaine Transhimalayen: Le Zanskar," in *Ladakh Himalaya Occidental Ethnologie, Écologie: Recherches Récentes Sur Le Ladakh No. 2A*, 2nd ed. (Université de Pau: Centre de biologie des Écosystèmes d'altitude, 1985), 25. My translation.

variations were often associated with specific valleys. A more pronounced example of language dividing space is that of Tibet's historical regions (i.e., Kham, Amdo, U-Tsang), each of which has a dialect distinct enough to hinder mutual intelligibility. When geologist Frederic Drew compiled a series of maps of Jammu and Kashmir in the 1870s, his "Language Map" tellingly illustrated the variety of major languages in the broader region. It overlooked, however, the subtler shifts in dialect from valley to valley in Ladakh, by classifying the whole territory as "Tibetan" speaking.

Besides dialects within the Ladakhi language, numerous lingua francas were used throughout the region. Most of the traders and caravan leaders who plied the Leh-Yarkand and Leh–Lhasa trade routes were multilingual, often speaking Urdu and Uighur in addition to their native tongues. The *kiraiyakash* – local Ladakhi transporters in Dras, Kargil, Leh, and Nubra – often encouraged their children to learn Uighur, to better communicate with Yarkandi traders and caravan leaders.[53] According to numerous sources, it was common throughout the nineteenth century to hear Ladakhi, Tibetan, Urdu, Uighur, Kashmiri, Persian, Pashto, and Punjabi spoken in the market at Leh in trading season.

1.1.5   From Seen to Seeing

In sum, a person residing in the upper Indus prior to the Dogra invasion of 1834 would be unlikely to look over this high-altitude landscape and simply envision a homogenous political entity called Ladakh. Rather, when she cast her eyes up at the mountains over her village, she would perceive a barrier and conduit, a source of water and food, and a deity's presence. When she looked across the valley to a distant neighboring village, she would see a natural and human landscape shaped by various dialects, traded commodities, and local hierarchies. These political, cosmological, linguistic, and material spaces did not neatly align. Those living in the region prior to Dogra and British rule had scant awareness of a contiguous, sovereign, and bounded territory – let alone a hegemonic state with jurisdiction over that territory. Political identity was tied to local rulers and monasteries; as such, it was often pluralistic. Cosmological identities varied by family, village, and subvillage community. Conceptions of the material physicality of daily life, whether based on seasonal trade, transhumance, or local agriculture, connected valleys to each other and villages to the glaciers whose snowmelt supported them. These interweavings of life produced a tapestry of multiple, cohabiting spaces.

---

[53] Bray, "Introduction: Locating Ladakhi History," 19–20.

Any society, of course, has multiple ways of conceiving physical, social, cosmological, and political spaces. Imperial encounters are frequently moments that render these spatial conceptions most visible, particularly when one vision conflicts with another. When the British first attempted to determine Ladakh's boundaries in the late 1840s, they did so assuming that the best way of understanding and organizing Ladakh was to consider it a bounded, uniform physical space to be mapped – that is, primarily, in a political mode of seeing. Secondarily, in the material mode of seeing, the British endeavored to promote the expansion of trade with Central Asia, often viewing Ladakh as a conduit to untapped markets throughout the continent. These two modes of seeing, as I will illustrate throughout this book, competed over the course of the nineteenth century. The desire to "open" trade with Central Asia conflicted with the implicitly "closed" nature of a settled border. By the early twentieth century, the political mode of seeing a territorialized state had become preeminent. It was with this mode's ascendance that the British had begun to "see" a different Ladakh: one surrounded by a solid border and governed by uniform regulations for those seeking to cross it.

The other modes of seeing did not disappear. *Lha.tho, ma.ṇi* walls, *mchod.rten,* are still visible in Ladakh today, though they perhaps command less respect, and certainly less interest, than they did in past centuries. But the kind of space they continue to shape is one that is far less prominent than the political spaces generated by strictly regulated (and disputed) political borders. As I will show in Chapter 2, geography – the preeminent "imperial science" – profoundly reconfigured Himalayan space.

1.2   Ladakh: Crossroads of High Asia

We know relatively little about Ladakh in the period prior to the seventeenth century. A mixture of archeological evidence, along with Tibetan Buddhist hagiographies called *rnam.thar,* various fragmentary versions of the *La.dwags rGyal.rabs,* a few foreign travelers' accounts begun by 1603,[54] and the histories of neighboring and invading countries, collectively sketch a mountainous polity with growing economic and cultural ties to Central Asia, Tibet, and Kashmir. At the height of the rNam.rgyal dynasty in the seventeenth century, the rulers of Ladakh asserted various degrees of control over neighboring regions, such as Zangskar, Nubra, Purig, Rudok, Guge, Purang, Lahoul, and Spiti.

---

[54] Some early scholars, including Alexander Cunningham, attempted to find references to Ladakh in the writings of the peripatetic Chinese monk, Xuanzang (602–64 CE). The references are dubious.

This political expansion of Ladakh provoked tensions with Tibet in the east and Kashmir in the west. In the first instance, these tensions manifested in the struggles of various sects of Tibetan Buddhism to establish dominance in the region. In the second instance, rising tensions led to occasional invasions, and to Kashmiri and Mughal attempts to secure access to Ladakh's valuable trade routes. During periods of attack by external powers, the rulers of the upper Indus also contended with internal tensions: the oscillating powers of local rulers whose political machinations could challenge their dominance.

With the rise of Islam in the Kashmir Valley in the fourteenth century, some newly converted rulers sought to wage jihad on their mountain-bound neighbors. Sultan Zain ul-Abidin (1420–70), according to the *Rajatarangini*, personally led an expedition that "plundered the country and massacred the people" of Ladakh and Western Tibet.[55] Another sultan of Kashmir, Hasan Shah (1472–84), sent a military expedition to Ladakh that was apparently destroyed.[56] And Mirza Muhammad Haider Dughlat – a Chagatai general, adventurer, and cousin to the first Mughal emperor, Babur – waged an unsuccessful jihad through Ladakh to Tibet beginning in 1532.[57] Returning to Ladakh as the ruler of Kashmir in 1545, Mirza Haidar established a short-lived nominal governorship over Ladakh and Baltistan that likely dissolved on his death in 1551.[58] But with the rise of the rNam.rgyal dynasty (a branch of the earlier royal family), political power became more centralized. The chronicles make no mention of multiple rulers after the reign of bKra.shis rNam.rgyal (c. 1555–75).

On the Turkic front, Ladakh repelled an invasion from *Hor.yul* – in this instance likely the region of Yarkand and Kashgar – in the late sixteenth century.[59] When Tse.dbang rNam.rgyal became king in 1575, he was dissuaded from reprisal by the "entreaties of the Nubra people," who argued that attacking the people of Hor "would have seriously damaged the trade through the passes, which was of vital importance to Nubra."[60] On the eastern front, sectarian disputes fostered ongoing tensions

---

[55] Petech, *Kingdom of Ladakh*, 22–23.   [56] Petech, 26.

[57] Ney Elias, ed., *The Tarikh-i-Rashidi of Mirza Muhammad Haider, Dughlát, A History of the Moghuls of Central Asia*, trans. E. Denison Ross (London: Sampson Low, Marston, 1895), 407. In the tradition of his ancestor Timur, Mirza Haider besieged the chief fortification of the Nubra valley, north of Ladakh's central Indus valley. He eventually killed all the defenders. "[Their] heads formed a lofty minaret – and the vapour from the brains of the infidels of that country ascended to the heavens" (p. 418). Haider was forced to retreat to Kashmir, due to the effects of altitude, the brutal cold of winter, and the lack of supply. See also Jigar Mohammed, "Mughal Sources on Medieval Ladakh, Baltistan and Western Tibet," in *Ladakhi Histories: Local and Regional Perspectives*, ed. John Bray (Leiden: Brill, 2005), 147–60.

[58] Petech, *Kingdom of Ladakh*, 27–28.   [59] Petech, 30.   [60] Petech, 32.

between Ladakh and the central Tibetan authorities, as well as the often-autonomous western Tibetan local rulers.

Historians generally agree that King Seng.ge rNam.rgyal's 1630 annexation of Rudok, Guge, and Purang marked the apogee of Ladakh's political power.[61] The terms of this annexation were brokered by the famous Buddhist translator, sTag.tsang.Ras.pa.[62] After this success, Seng.ge rNam.rgyal then attempted to conquer Baltistan. Although the *La.dwags rGyal.rabs* records a great victory over the combined Mughal-Balti Muslim forces, the episode is omitted from the more reliable contemporary account found in sTag.tsang.Ras.pa's biography. Mughal sources in turn claim the Ladakhis were defeated. In response, according to the French traveler François Bernier who visited the region in 1663, Seng.ge "entirely closed the route and permitted no one to enter his country from Kashmir."[63] Instead, according to Bernier, the caravans coming from India would travel to Patna and from there cross the mountains to Lhasa.

This proved foolish. As Rizvi notes, "it surely indicates a total failure to grasp economic realities, for to close any one important route obviously cost Ladakh its position at the center of a network of routes, and so a large part of its revenue."[64] Indeed, the decline of Ladakh's commercial fortunes that set in after his death in 1642 may be attributed to, in Luciano Petech's words, Seng.ge's "economic suicide."[65]

bDe.ldan, Seng.ge's successor, made the mistake of granting the Drukpa Kagyupa sect royal favor at a time when the fifth Dalai Lama was ruthlessly ensuring the domination of the Gelukpa sect. Following the rout of Tibetan forces by Drukpa-dominated Bhutan, bDe.ldan decided to provoke a fight with Tibet. The Tibetans, in response, promptly began a campaign against Ladakh. This forced bDe.ldan to seek the assistance of the Mughal emperor, Aurangzeb, to whom he had

---

[61] Bray, "Introduction: Locating Ladakhi History," 11.

[62] Petech, *Kingdom of Ladakh*, 40.

[63] François Bernier, *Voyages de François Bernier, Contenant La Description Des États Du Grand Mogol, de l'Indoustan, Du Royaume de Cachemire, Etc.* (Paris: Imprimé aux frais du gouvernement, 1830), 294. The relevant passage reads, *"Mais depuis cette entreprise que fit Chah-Jehan de ce côté-là, le roi du grand Thibet a entièrement fermé le chemin, et ne permet que personne du côté de Cachemire entre dans son pays; et c'est pour cela que les caravanes partent à présent de Patna sur le Gange pour ne point passer par-dessus ses terres, les laissant à la gauche, et gagnant droit le royaume de Lassa.* [but since the venture made by Shah-Jehan on that side, the king of Great Thibet (i.e., Ladakh) has entirely closed the route, and permits no one from Kashmir to enter his country; and it is for this reason that the caravans now depart from Patna on the Ganges in order to avoid passing through his lands, leaving them to the left, and gaining access to the Kingdom of Lhasa]." My translation.

[64] Rizvi, *Ladakh: Crossroads of High Asia*, 69.   [65] Petech, *Kingdom of Ladakh*.

pledged nominal allegiance decades earlier. Aurangzeb's Kashmiri troops eventually arrived and pushed the Tibetans back.

Having already agreed to convert to Islam and build a mosque in Leh, bDe.ldan signed a treaty with the Kashmiri-led Mughal forces. Soon after the Kashmiri soldiers left, however, the Tibetans returned with Mongol assistance and concluded a separate treaty with Ladakh at Tingmosgang. This treaty fixed the border between the two countries at the Lha.ri stream, which flows into the Indus five miles southwest of Demchok.[66] Though no original text of the treaty survives, its outcome is described in the *La.dwags rGyal.rabs*. The treaty marked the Lha.ri stream near Demchok as a border point at the edge of Ladakhi territory (Map 1.2c).[67] It included monopoly concessions on significant trade goods: giving the Ladakhis a trading monopoly over the shawl wool produced in Western Tibet and the Tibetans a monopoly over the brick tea trade with Ladakh. It also established two complementary tribute missions: the triennial *Lopchak* (*lo.phyag*) from Ladakh to Lhasa, and the reciprocal *Chaba* (*La.dwags gzhung.tshong*), undertaken annually.

These aspects of the treaty are significant for three reasons. First, as mentioned earlier in reference to Gergan's map (Map 1.1), they stipulate not a border*line*, but rather a border*point*: the segment of the Lha.ri stream near the village of Demchok. Second, the reciprocity of the Lopchak and Chaba missions[68] symbolized the easy coexistence of religion, trade, and politics in regional relationships. The treaty also suggested that sovereignty and territory were not necessarily neat and absolute concepts, and that the political space of the northwestern Himalaya itself was envisioned in plural, overlapping, and noncontiguous ways. Finally, the treaty indicates that trade had become essential to the political and social order of the region at least as early as the seventeenth century. For a high-altitude region with immense mountainous obstacles, this trade was remarkably complex and wide-ranging. As Rizvi writes, "By the mid-1680s, the trade in 'shawl wool' had become a matter of such importance as to be the subject of the most significant clause of the Treaty of Tingmosgang, which was to define Ladakh's relations with Tibet on the one hand, and Kashmir on the other, for the next century and a half."[69]

---

[66] Demchok is the southeasternmost settlement in Ladakh. Its name suggests a connection to the deity Chakrasambara and, by extension, to Mount Kailash, where Chakrasambara is said to dwell.

[67] The relevant line of the *La.dwags rGyal.rabs* reads, "*Mtshams bde.mchog lha.ri chu nas byas* [The border is made at the Lha.ri [literally 'sacred mountain'] stream [near] Demchok]." My translation. Francke, "La.dwags rGyal.rabs," 42.

[68] The *La.dwags gzhung.tshong* was also called the *ja.ba* ("Chaba") because of the tea (*ja*) that was typically traded during the mission.

[69] Rizvi, *Trans-Himalayan Caravans*, 53.

The tension between trade and consolidated political power that had marked the century leading up to Tingmosgang was resolved, to an extent, by the granting of monopolies, the establishment of border points, and the creation of reciprocal tribute missions. But the treaty concerned only one of many significant trade networks that stretched through Ladakh. While this text might be taken as a sign of a dominant political vision of Ladakh, it also overlooks a vast array of smaller material networks omitted in the royal chronicles.

As was the case in much of the periphery of South Asia, complex networks of movement had long crisscrossed Ladakh. The very name "Ladakh" (*la.dwags*: "expanse/land of passes") reflects the significance of its transportation routes in forming its historical identity. In her synthesis of historical trans-Himalayan trade networks, Rizvi employs a host of historical documents and an extensive array of oral histories to paint a detailed and multifaceted picture of the centuries-old networks traversing what she aptly terms the "crossroads of high Asia." While the volume of trade ebbed and flowed over the many centuries that trans-Himalayan trade existed, the phenomenon itself maintained a remarkable continuity, persisting until the mid-twentieth century. Much of this continuity can be attributed to the relative lack of interference by regional political actors, and to the durability of networks of mobile peoples – two key features James C. Scott and Willem van Schendel have attributed to the regions they each describe as "Zomia."[70] The occasional dips and rises in trade statistics also assert that trade was intimately tied to regional politics and to economies of various scales, as well as to seasonal climatic conditions that affected the flow of people over passes and rivers and through high-desert valleys. Ladakhi trade statistics, collected regularly from the 1860s till 1946, show that trade volume was affected by a variety of factors: from sporadic heavy snowfall on the Karakoram Pass to the Russian Revolution of 1917.[71]

Unlike Rizvi, most scholars who have examined Ladakh's trade history have focused on the glamorous and global pashmina trade, thus overlooking the great variety of items flowing throughout the region. Some of these items were luxury goods: precious stones, charas, opium, brocades, silk, and ponies. Others were local necessities: salt, coarse wool, butter, and borax. Access to many of these resources was highly variable and dependent on seasonal flux. Pashmina wool, for instance, came from goats that moved from the high-summer grazing lands of the Tibetan Plateau to the

---

[70] Van Schendel coined the term, and included the Himalayan region in it, while Scott used the term to refer more exclusively to the highland regions of Southeast Asia.
[71] For nineteenth-century trade statistics, see Table 3.1.

lower altitudes of Ladakh, Spiti, and Lahaul in the winter months, herded by the transhumant Changpa (*byang.pa*). Likewise, the flow of traded items – brick tea, charas, opium, borax, and wool – depended on when and whether the annual accumulation of snow would allow access over mountain passes.

This commercial activity continued through much of the colonial period. Hashmatullah Khan, both historian and Dogra Administrator of Ladakh, remarked in his *Tārīkh-i-Jammūn* [The History of Jammu] that "Ladakh's capital [was] an exchange market for traded goods from the temperate plains of India to the mountainous regions of Chinese Turkistan and Lhasa."[72] While these terminal points – Amritsar in the plains of the Punjab, Lhasa in Tibet, and Yarkand in Turkestan – marked the longest and most lucrative routes, there were numerous shorter routes that traversed the mountainous region. Collectively, these local and long-distance routes meant that Ladakh remained the critical hub connecting Central Asia to the plains of India and the Tibetan Plateau to Kashmir. In contrast to foreign perceptions of the region as isolated and remote, those regularly moving across Ladakh knew its routes to be both vast and intricate.

1.3   Where Traders, Mountains, and Empires Meet: William Moorcroft to Zorawar Singh

The British East India Company (or EIC) first initiated formal contact with the broader Himalayan region in 1774, when Warren Hastings speculated on its significance for India's defense and for the expansion of British trade with Tibet (and, relatedly, China).[73] That year he sent George Bogle to Bhutan and Tibet (which Hastings initially believed to be one state) in a first attempt to establish trans-Himalayan diplomatic and commercial relations. In a way similar to the East India Company's exploration of the northeastern Himalaya, Ladakh, and the western Himalaya were initially approached as potential avenues for trade with the regions that lay beyond.[74]

A few Western travelers had ventured into the Himalaya before the EIC arrived – notably the Tuscan Jesuit, Ippoliti Desideri, and the aforementioned François Bernier.[75] But it was only after the Anglo-Nepalese War

---

[72] Khan Lakhnavi, *Tārīkh-i-Jammūn*, 380.

[73] Kate Teltscher, *The High Road to China: George Bogle, the Panchen Lama and the First British Expedition to Tibet* (London: Bloomsbury, 2006), 49–50.

[74] For the early history of British engagement with the northeastern Himalaya, see Gunnel Cederlof, *Founding an Empire on India's North-Eastern Frontiers, 1790–1840: Climate, Commerce, Polity* (Oxford: Oxford University Press, 2014).

[75] For an example of the writings that followed such ventures, see Ippolito Desideri, *An Account of Tibet: The Travels of Ippolito Desideri of Pistoia*, ed. Filippo de Filippi (London: George Routledge, 1937).

(1814–15), and ensuing territorial concessions, that the British made direct contact with the western Himalayan regions of Garwhal and Kumaon. It was a gradual contact, however, and, to use Aniket Alam's phrase, "non-cataclysmic." The regions' terrain made standard British administrative practices difficult to establish and apply.[76]

The fifty years following Bogle's mission witnessed a consolidation of numerous small Himalayan states by a series of imperial aspirants: first the Gorkha ruler Prithvi Narayan Shah who unified Nepal (r. 1743–75), followed by the Sikh Empire (1799–1849) of Maharaja Ranjit Singh (d. 1839), the Dogra Raja Gulab Singh of Jammu (1846–57), and finally the British East India Company and its formal imperial successor, the British government of India.

After 1803, when the EIC took over Delhi and its territories, the Calcutta-based Company's attention gradually turned northward. In 1808, they sent their first official expedition to reconnoiter the territories under Gorkha rule. Sponsored by the Asiatic Society of Bengal, this mission was charged with exploring the upper reaches of the Ganges.[77] The published report of the expedition indicates a threefold additional goal: to investigate the region's economy (specifically, trade with the region known as Chinese Turkestan), its socio-political condition, and the nature of Gorkha rule. As a result, the report includes the nature of agricultural production, natural resources, and geography in the region, as well as organizational details of Gorkha administration.

In 1818, the British sent a team under the leadership of Alexander Gerard to explore the Sutlej and investigate the possibility of trade across its mountains. This team eventually crossed into Western Tibet along the route that would later become the Hindustan–Tibet Road.[78] By the 1820s, British media reported sporadic accounts of western Himalayan commercial goods arriving in British-held towns (particularly Rampur, in Bashahr) along this route.[79] Slowly, the British started to recognize these preexisting trade routes, and thus began to appreciate the region's commercial potential.

William Moorcroft, one of the most enterprising English travelers in the service of the East India Company, reached Ladakh's capital in

---

[76] Aniket Alam, *Becoming India: Western Himalayas under British Rule* (Delhi: Foundation Books, 2008).

[77] Alam, *Becoming India*, 99–102.

[78] J. D. Herbert, "An Account of a Tour Made to Lay Down the Course and Levels of the River Sutlej or Satudra, as Far as Traceable within the Limits of the British Authority, Performed in 1819," *Asiatic Researches* 18 (1819): 227–58. For a more detailed discussion of the Hindustan–Tibet Road, see Chapter 3.

[79] Cf. *Calcutta Gazette*, March 13, 1828, and *The Morning Chronicle* (London), September 22, 1828, which detail the arrival of Ladakhi grain in the Punjab.

September 1820 while en route to Central Asia.[80] The first officially practicing veterinarian in the Company – who styled himself "Superintendent of the Hon'ble Company's stud" – Moorcroft sought more robust horse breeds to improve the EIC's stock. He was also tasked with exploring the possibilities of opening the trans-Himalayan region to British commerce. G. J. Alder, C. A. Bayly, B. D. Hopkins, and others have shown that Moorcroft's activities constituted an early form of intelligence gathering.[81] But the term "intelligence" was, at this point, an undeniably vague category: a catch-all that included geographical, ethnographic, botanical, and commercial information, as well as the more specific details of commercial penetration by Russia in the region and the likely demand for British goods. To facilitate his information gathering, Moorcroft was furnished with certificates of introduction in English, Russian, Persian, and Chinese, all stamped with the Company's seal.

Although distrusted and sometimes stymied by the Ladakhi officials in Leh, Moorcroft managed to make a number of useful friends there. These included the peripatetic Hungarian linguist, Sándor Kőrösi Csoma,[82] who Moorcroft convinced to write the first English-Tibetan dictionary.[83] During his stay in Ladakh, Moorcroft wrote detailed letters to the

---

[80] For Moorcroft's story, I have drawn on the published accounts of his travels: William Moorcroft and George Trebeck, *Travels in the Himalayan Provinces of Hindustan and the Panjab; in Ladakh and Kashmir; in Peshawar, Kabul, Kunduz, and Bokhara; from 1819 to 1825*, ed. Horace Hayman Wilson, 2 vols. (London: John Murray, 1841). I have also benefited from the biographical work done by G. J. Alder, "Standing Alone: William Moorcroft Plays the Great Game, 1808–1825," *International History Review* 2, no. 2 (1980): 172–215. See also the 51-volume Moorcroft papers at the British Library (Mss Eur K307-64; J 823–24).

[81] For a view on his role as intelligence gatherer, see C. A. Bayly, *Empire and Information: Intelligence Gathering and Social Communication in India, 1780–1870* (Cambridge: Cambridge University Press, 1996), 135–40. For an analysis that plays up the Russian specter, see Hopkirk, *The Great Game: On Secret Service in High Asia*, 90–91. For the purported correspondence between the Russian tsar and Ranjit Singh, which Moorcroft intercepted, see Hopkins, *Modern Afghanistan*.

[82] Known to most English speakers as Alexander Csomo de Koros.

[83] Csoma's dictionary is considered by many to have "founded" Tibetan studies. Moorcroft's encounter with Csoma de Kőrös highlights a curious spatial disposition within the field, namely, that much of the early formal study of Tibet and the Tibetan cultural world transpired at the region's edges. Ladakh and the western Himalaya, India, Nepal, Sikkim, and Bhutan have played particularly prominent roles as sites of Tibetology. Csoma de Kőrös' story also highlights, in a modest way, a prominent theme in Tibetan Studies particularly, and in historical writing about South Asia more generally: the relationship between scholarship and politics. When Csoma de Kőrös met William Moorcroft near the Zoji-*la*, two sets of interests became one. The first century of Western attempts to gather systematic information about Tibet's culture, religions, language, and history was guided by this relationship between colonial interests and scholarly ones. See, for instance, Dipesh Chakrabarty, "The Birth of Academic Historical Writing in India," in *The Oxford History of Historical Writing: Vol. 4. 1800–1945* (Oxford: Oxford University Press, 2011), 520–36.

governor-general (Lord Hastings) in Calcutta, highlighting the commercial and strategic importance of Ladakh. He observed that British control over the region would facilitate the project of tapping the shawl wool trade from Western Tibet, and that Ladakh would serve as a key for opening up the potentially "vast markets of Chinese Turkestan" and other Central Asian regions.[84] Moorcroft estimated that the Company's monthly expenditure for maintaining peace in the region would not exceed a thousand rupees.[85] Furthermore, he asserted, Ladakh could serve as a base for operations against China should it become necessary. Influence of the region could also keep Maharaja Ranjit Singh and the distant yet ambitious Russians at bay.[86] Moorcroft used fantastical and dramatic language to depict the "prize" of British trade with the region.

Whether [Tibetans and Central Asians] shall be clothed with the broadcloth of Russia or of England ... with hardware of every description from Petersburgh [i.e., St. Petersburg] or Birmingham, is entirely in the decision of the Government of British India. At present there is little doubt to which the prize will be awarded, for enterprise and vigour mark the measure of Russia towards the nations of Central Asia, whilst ours are characterised by misplaced squeamishness and unnecessary timidity.[87]

In May 1821, Moorcroft exceeded his mandate by signing a commercial agreement with Ladakh's rulers. The EIC's merchants were thereby "permitted to trade with Ladakh and through it with the Chinese and Western Turkestan."[88]

Moorcroft's stay in Ladakh aroused the suspicions of Maharaja Ranjit Singh, who sent envoys to inquire after his activities in Leh. Moorcroft openly replied to the envoys in a letter, saying that if the rumors of a Sikh military force being assembled were true, the pashmina industry of Kashmir would suffer. According to Moorcroft himself, his letter was written to alarm the Sikh ruler and to forestall an invasion of Ladakh until

---

[84] Moorcroft and Trebeck, *Travels*, 151–54.

[85] National Archives of India (hereafter NAI), Foreign Political Proceedings, September 20, 1823, no. 63 (207).

[86] Moorcroft and Trebeck, *Travels*, 154.

[87] Moorcroft and Trebeck, 154. This quotation would later be used by the principal engineer on the Hindustan–Tibet Road, Lieutenant David Briggs, supervisor of much of the Hindustan–Tibet Road's construction, as an unheeded warning (c. 1820), House of Commons United Kingdom, "Minutes and Correspondence in Reference to the Project of the Hindostan and Thibet Road, with Reports of Major Kennedy and Lieutenant Briggs Relating Thereto; and, an Account of the Expenditure Incurred in the Construction of the New Road between Kalha and Dugshai," Sessional Papers, 1857 East India (roads), February 2, 1857, 73.

[88] Nisith Ranjan Ray, *Himalaya Frontier in Historical Perspective* (Calcutta: Institute of Historical Studies, 1986), 198.

the British governor-general, Lord Hastings, decided whether to accept the Ladakhi ruler's request for aid.

The letter did not have the intended effect. Ranjit Singh's agent in Delhi passed the letter on to the "white Mughal" Sir David Ochterlony, British Resident at Delhi, demanding an explanation.[89] In response, the governor-general wrote to the Maharaja explaining that Moorcroft had acted on his own, and that the British would ignore the request from Ladakh. Concern for an overextended territory, plus high costs incurred in the Anglo-Nepalese War, no doubt contributed to British reluctance to extend their imperial holdings in South Asia.

Moorcroft's actions exacerbated the tensions that would drive the Sikh invasion of Ladakh in the following decade. The desire to maintain control over the lucrative pashmina trade was central to Maharaja Ranjit Singh's logic of invasion.[90] When the time came, despite many Ladakhi pleas to the British, no help arrived. Similar waves of disorder, invasion, and political consolidation also struck several of Ladakh's neighboring states.[91] Moorcroft's visit signals the first instance, in this history, of commercial expansion and imperial security concerns causing tension between the "man on the spot" and administrators in Calcutta.

1.4   Enter the Dogras

In 1834, a century and a half after the conclusion of the Tibet–Ladakh– Mughal War of 1679–84, Ladakh was invaded again. This time it was by the Raja of Jammu, Gulab Singh, a Dogra vassal of Ranjit Singh's short-lived

---

[89] William Dalrymple, *White Mughals: Love and Betrayal in Eighteenth-Century India* (London: Viking, 2002), 183–84. Ochterlony was knighted for his role in the Anglo-Nepalese War.

[90] K. M. Panikkar, *The Founding of the Kashmir State: A Biography of Maharajah Gulab Singh, 1792–1858* (London: George Allen & Unwin, 1953).

[91] In 1820, the people of Kullu invaded Spiti through the Losar Valley. As Trebeck described in his 1821 visit, they "destroyed several houses by lighting large fires in the rooms. The Gompa of Kih was much injured. The property taken off consisted chiefly of yaks, horses, and other livestock." The raid was caused by the suzerain Sikhs' heavy taxation of the people of Kullu. Similarly, circa 1825, the ruler of Chamba invaded Zanskar and made it a tributary district. In 1821, a strong Balti force entered Ladakh, plundered several villages and took off with a hefty amount of booty. Ladakh's relations with Bashahr state also deteriorated. Bashahr, one of the most important of the Hill States, had come under EIC control in 1816 and had been a friendly trade partner to Ladakh prior to Tse.pal rNam.gyal's erratic and damaging reign (1802–37). Captain C. P. Kennedy, Assistant Deputy Superintendent, Sikh and Hill Sates, wrote in 1824 that the aggressions between Ladakh and Bashahr "resembled those that formerly occurred in Scotland in feudal times, consisting of forays and assaults on the borders the seizure of cattle and firing of villages." Moorcroft, *Travels*, 60–63.

Sikh Empire. Gulab Singh's principal concern in invading Ladakh was to ensure a monopoly over the pashmina trade routes.[92]

Gulab Singh's general, Zorawar Singh, crossed the Zoji Pass in 1834. Over the following years, the general pressed on toward Tibet to further consolidate control over the trade routes and subdue a resisting Ladakhi populace.[93] As he was marching toward Lhasa, his supply lines were stretched by severe winter conditions. Then, after Zorawar Singh was killed in an attack in Western Tibet, his army was forced to retreat to Ladakh.[94] But Zorawar Singh's incursion did lead to a tripartite treaty, signed in 1842, between the Raja of Jammu, the Emperor of China, and the "Lama Guru of Lhasa" (the Dalai Lama). The treaty reaffirmed the "boundaries of Ladakh and its surroundings as fixed from ancient times."[95] Although most of the upper Indus had been swiftly conquered in 1834, it was not until 1842 that the Dogras formally annexed Ladakh.

This annexation led to major economic and political changes. The *rgyal.po* was exiled from Leh Palace, and Ladakh was divided into five districts: Ladakh (referring to the central district around Leh); Zangskar, Kargil, Dras, and Nubra. Each of these districts was placed under a *thanadar,* who exercised both military and civil authority and was accountable only to Raja Gulab Singh.[96] The Raja also imposed a tax on the monasteries, and instituted a death penalty for those convicted of slaughtering cows.[97] Prior to the Dogra conquest, taxation varied depending on size of home and profession, and the monasteries were entirely exempt.[98] Following the Dogra conquest, the first *thanadar* of

---

[92] Rizvi, *Trans-Himalayan Caravans*, 19, 61–62.

[93] Sukhdev Singh Charak, trans., *Gulabnama of Diwan Kirpa Ram: A History of Maharaja Gulab Singh of Jammu and Kashmir* (New Delhi: Light and Life, 1977), 206–33.

[94] *The Examiner* (London), February 12, 1842: "Thibet: it at one time appeared probable that Zorawar Sing would succeed in wrestling from the Chinese some portion of their Thibetian territory. Our celestial friends, however, have now entered the field against the enemy; and the Seikh forces have given way, and are retreating on Ladakh, quite discomfited."

[95] J&K State Archives, Jammu (JKSA-J). "Treaty between Ladakh and Tibet: 1920, 276/R. P-4."

[96] C. L. Datta, *Ladakh and Western Himalayan Politics: 1819–1848. The Dogra Conquest of Ladakh, Baltistan and West Tibet and Reactions of Other Powers* (New Delhi: Mushiram Manoharlal, 1973), 39.

[97] Alexander Cunningham, *Ladák, Physical, Statistical, and Historical; With Notices of the Surrounding Countries* (London: W. H. Allen, 1854), 268, 272. The tax amounted to Rs. 6,300 each year, and, according to Cunningham, the death toll from cow-related executions totaled eight.

[98] This is according to an 1887 report on the Revenue Assessment in Ladakh by the British official stationed there. He noted that his principal informant was the Dogra-appointed governor of Ladakh, the *wazīr-i-wazārat.* Large-sized houses paid twelve seers [roughly 1.25 kg] of grain annually, while medium-sized houses paid eight, and small ones paid six. In addition to this, each village was expected to work the *rgyal.po*'s land held in every

Ladakh (later referred to as the *wazīr-i-wazārat*), Basti Ram, implemented a land tax that was quite severe and generated substantial complaints from Ladakhis.[99] He was succeeded as *thanadar* by his son, Mehter Mangal (also known as Mangalju) who revised the land taxes in 1864 to be in closer accordance to the *rgyal.po*'s earlier rates on houses. The resulting system assumed that larger houses were to have one "*zamīn*" (literally "land"), which was defined as the amount of land one could sow with thirty to forty "khals" of seed. (A khal was "a sheep's load" of twenty-four pounds). Medium- and small-sized houses were expected to pay the equivalent of one-half and one-quarter of a *zamīn*, respectively. Later still, in 1884, the *wazīr* would again change the tax system by extending the uniform tax rate to the monasteries. Those monasteries greatly resented this development and appealed to the Maharaja of Jammu and Kashmir. The Maharaja in turn magnanimously allowed them to push their share of taxes onto Ladakhi peasants, some of whom could not afford the added 25 percent and were forced to flee their land.[100]

Although the British largely ignored these internal changes, they took control of Ladakh in 1846 as a part of the larger princely state of Jammu and Kashmir. They obtained this control relatively efficiently. In 1845, the Sikhs crossed the Sutlej: the disputed boundary marker between Sikh and British territories. This gave the British an excuse to start what became known as the First Anglo-Sikh War.[101] After a British victory in March 1846, Ranjit Singh's successor signed the Treaty of Amritsar – under which Gulab Singh, the Dogra ruler of the suzerain state of Jammu,[102] was appointed the Maharaja of Jammu, Kashmir, Ladakh, Baltistan, and Hazara. In exchange for this title, he acknowledged the supremacy of the British and agreed to a joint frontier commission to officially establish his state's borders. He also agreed to pay the British an annual tribute of "one horse, twelve perfect shawl goats of approved breed ... and three pair of Kashmir shawls," a tribute that the British insisted would continue into the twentieth century.[103]

village and collectively pay him forty-eight seers annually. Any owners of substantial flocks paid an annual tax of one animal for every thirty, though the seminomadic Changpa were expected to pay two sheep and one sheep's load of wool and salt for every hundred sheep in the caravan, in addition to a seer of wool, ten seers of salt, and one sheep per caravan "irrespective of its size." There were also taxes on "shops, brokers, and trade passing through Ladakh," but the details of these rates are not known.

[99] Francke, "La.dwags rGyal.rabs," 133–34.
[100] NAI, Foreign, Frontier Part B, July 1890, no. 157.
[101] Byron Farwell, *Queen Victoria's Little Wars* (New York: Harper & Row, 1972), 37–38.
[102] Gulab Singh had earlier helped the British against the Sikhs.
[103] Frederic Drew, *The Jummoo and Kashmir Territories: A Geographical Account* (E. Stanford, 1875), 547.

When the British finally achieved apparent regional hegemony at the close of the Second Anglo-Sikh War (1848–49), they began to appreciate just how diverse and active Ladakh was. Alexander Cunningham, an enterprising EIC captain soon to become one of the most prominent British experts on Ladakh, noted that the results of the 1842 Treaty left a monopoly in the hands of the Dogra Raja of Jammu. British attention, he wrote, "might also with great advantage be directed to the removal of abuses which considerably impede the trade of their frontier through Ladak."[104] Cunningham was tasked with determining the borders of Ladakh, and was assigned to inquire about trade opportunities with Tibet and Central Asia. The first two British boundary commissions, in which Cunningham played a major role, form the basis of the next chapter.

1.5   Conclusion

In the late 1830s, toward the end of his long reign, it is said that Maharaja Ranjit Singh was shown a map that depicted in large swathes the extent of British-controlled territory on the subcontinent. The aging ruler is said to have responded ominously, "*sab lāl ho jāyegā* [all will become red]."[105] From his position in Lahore, Ranjit Singh had witnessed the rapid expansion of the East India Company's military-fiscal machinery over its ever-widening territory. The British had taken their first territorial steps into the Himalayan region with the defeat of the recently unified Gorkha kingdom of Nepal in 1816. By the end of the 1840s, they had achieved,

[104] Erskine, Superintendent for Hill States, to Ellit, Secretary to the Government with the Governor-General, July 19, 1847. NAI, Foreign, S.C. No 101 "Mission to Thibet of Cunningham, Captain A. Result of."

[105] The episode may be apocryphal. Majumdar in his *Advanced History of India* (p. 741) mentions the remark but fails to give a source, date, or location. Was it originally spoken in the given Hindustani or in the maharaja's native Punjabi ("*sabh lal ho javega*")? More context is given in a less authoritative chapter by S. K. Pachauri: "British Perceptions of Relations with Maharaja Ranjit Singh," in *Maharaja Ranjit Singh: Ruler and Warrior*, ed. T. R. Sharma (Chandigarh: Panjab University Publication Bureau, 2005). Jasbir Singh Ahluwalia and Parm Bakhshish Singh's *An Overview of Maharaja Ranjit Singh and His Times* (Patiala: Punjabi University, 2001) contains no mention of the remark; nor does Bikrama Jit Hasrat's expansive *Life and Times of Ranjit Singh: A Saga of Benevolent Despotism* (Hoshiarpur: V. V. Research Institute Book Agency, 1977). Despite the questionable nature of this story's origin, it is instructive to note that Ranjit Singh has recently reemerged as a major historical political figure. Recent literature focusing on him argues that his short-lived empire, because of its defeat by Britain, has wrongfully been consigned to a peripheral position – especially given the more central role played by the declining Mughal empire in the main narrative arc of South Asian political history. For an example of this type of literature, see Patwant Singh and Jyoti M. Rai, *Empire of the Sikhs: The Life and Times of Maharaja Ranjit Singh* (London: Peter Owen, 2008).

either by direct or indirect rule, substantial progress toward controlling what James Mill had called "the most desirable frontier" of India.[106] But a series of major problems soon arose for them. As I will show in the next chapter, the contradictory view they held of the northwestern Himalaya – a simultaneous natural boundary and commercial conduit – produced a complicated frontier for the British. The prospect of accessing the region's high-value trade networks would tempt generations of British administrators – and a few private adventurers – to pin down its exact contours. Yet the more time the British spent surveying this "most desirable frontier," the less clear that frontier became.

This political mode of seeing distinctly reflected imperial concerns. It understood Ladakh to be first and foremost a territory to be controlled for economic, political, and strategic gain. The political landscape of Ladakh had long been contested by aspiring conquerors and home-grown rulers alike – but it was only with the conquests of the 1830s and 1840s that its new rulers found it necessary to enclose Ladakh, with a borderline symbolizing unambiguous sovereignty. That the attempts at enclosure could fail, and the borderline remain shadowy, did not enter into considerations in the political mode.

Complicating this static, territorial vision of political space imposed by the region's latest conquerors were long-established networks of economic, linguistic, and cultural exchange. Seasonal oscillations led to uncertainties in all spheres of daily life in Ladakh, from trade and pilgrimage to crop yields and the survival of animal herds. Flooding, precipitation, and unusual temperature fluctuations impacted pashmina prices in the far-off plains of India and beyond, while these climatic variables impacted even more profoundly the staples consumed closer to home. The crucial role played by the transhumant Changpa in the wool and salt trades illustrates how critical migration was to the economic livelihoods of many Ladakhis. And lingua francas blended together with local dialects to reflect Ladakh's connections with regions far beyond it. These material and linguistic connections to the landscape did not neatly transpose onto a political vision of territory.

Similarly, the Himalayan landscape was imbued with cosmological significance: the result of deep dependence on the land itself and an intermingling of spiritual traditions at this "crossroads of high Asia." Acknowledging this cosmological aspect of northwestern Himalayan space leads to a multidimensional image of Ladakh that again complicates a strictly political conception of space. Mountains, rivers, streams, and

---

[106] "Evidence of James Mill," February 16, 1832: *Parliamentary Papers, 1831–2*, Vol. xiv, p. 8, Qu. 49.

trees were associated with particular deities, many of whom were worshiped through subvillage and village-level social groupings. This further connected Ladakhis to their local environments by means of a variety of spiritual-spatial beliefs and practices. Through these connections, natural features like mountains would, in many cases, become "centering" objects that tied the landscape together rather than divided it.

The bounding of village-level geography, reflected in walls, irrigation systems, and other structures, was quite precise; the bounding of the larger polity of Ladakh, much less so. Instead, larger-scale distances reflected the space between certain points, such as a particular mountain pass, stream, village, or pilgrimage site. As I will show in Chapter 2, a novel kind of geography would soon arise to transform the spatial conception of Ladakh. A region that had long been a central hub would be increasingly sidelined: moved to a newfound geographic periphery.

2 Surveys
Boundary-Making Principles, Mapping, and the Problem with Watersheds

> The whole of the intervening country between India and China is a blank.
>
> – H. H. Wilson, *Travels in the Himalayan Provinces of Hindustan and the Panjab*, 1841

By the mid-nineteenth century Ladakh found itself increasingly close to the point where the empires of Britain, China, and Russia would eventually meet. But while the massive Himalayas might have seemed an ideal candidate to represent the solidified lines of British India's political borders, in reality, their candidacy provided endless problems in the mapping process. When India gained independence in 1947, it also gained a largely borderless northern frontier. But this borderlessness was not for lack of trying.

Beginning in the 1840s, and inspired by the geographical principles espoused by Alexander von Humboldt, a century of surveys using ever more sophisticated technologies attempted again and again to define a border in the Himalaya based on the idea of the limit of a watershed: the so-called water-parting principle.[1] These efforts yielded maps of staggering technological sophistication and personal daring, all attempting to put nature to work for the imperial state. But the scientific precision of utilizing the watershed produced unintended complications, as it slowly became apparent that the edge of the Indus River watershed and the highest range of the Himalayas did not always align. This was particularly true in the high-altitude Aksai Chin, where the absence of a single mountain range to act as a clear "water-parting line" challenged the wisdom of using the Indus watershed as a boundary-making object.

A version of this chapter previously appeared in *The Historical Journal*. See Kyle Gardner, "Moving Watersheds, Borderless Maps, and Imperial Geography in India's Northwestern Himalaya," *The Historical Journal* 62, no. 1 (2019): 149–70.

[1] The term "watershed" first appeared in English just after the turn of the nineteenth century, and perhaps slightly earlier in German (*Wasserscheide*). The rapid increase in use of the term suggests that it filled a lacuna in the technical vocabularies of geography and hydrology.

This geographical incongruity laid the groundwork for a conflict between the two most populous nations of the twenty-first century; ironically, over one of the least populous spaces on earth. The complex ecological system of the Himalayas did not lend itself to neat political solutions.

The causes of the long-running borderlessness in much of the Himalaya have long been ascribed by historians to "top-down" diplomatic failures.[2] Historians interested in explaining the causes of the Sino-India War of 1962 have pointed to the absence of a single accepted borderline between China and India as a potential catalyst. But they have rarely questioned the problems produced by the geographical principles that generated those lines in the first place. By the second half of the nineteenth century, colonial geography had organized the world into natural systems. This view of systematized natural objects was reflected in the development of the water-parting principle, wherein the edge of a watershed was used to establish a border. In the Himalaya, this principle was used to impose a border*line* in a region that had previously possessed only established notions of border *points*, as noted in the previous chapter. Border points were practical solutions in a mountainous region with a limited number of routes traversing it; they functioned as effective points at which to extract customs. But they did not satisfy the imperial need to map, claim, and control territory.

While historians have fruitfully explored the technological and political roles that surveying and mapping played in crafting colonial borders, few have examined the crucial geographical concepts resting beneath these border-making practices.[3] In focusing on the development of these

---

[2] Alastair Lamb's extensive writings offer in-depth detail about the geopolitical rivalries on British India's northern frontiers. See Alastair Lamb, *Britain and Chinese Central Asia* (London: Routledge & Kegan Paul, 1960); *The China–India Border: The Origins of the Disputed Boundaries* (London: Oxford University Press, 1964); and *The Sino-Indian Border in Ladakh* (Canberra: Australian National University Press, 1973). Other works include Alder, *British India's Northern Frontier*; Margaret W. Fisher, Leo E. Rose, and Robert A. Huttenback, *Himalayan Battleground: Sino-Indian Rivalry in Ladakh* (New York: Praeger, 1963); Dorothy Woodman, *Himalayan Frontiers: A Political Review of British, Chinese, Indian, and Russian Rivalries* (London: Barrie & Rockliff, 1969); Neville Maxwell, *India's China War* (New York: Pantheon Books, 1970). Parshotam Mehra, in *An "Agreed" Frontier: Ladakh and India's Northernmost Borders, 1846–1947* (New Delhi: Oxford University Press, 1992), also deals with this topic. However, this last work is so riddled with factual errors, and so redolent of pervasive and pernicious bias against all things Chinese, that I am reluctant to even cite it. Furthermore, Mehra, a well-respected historian from Panjab University, plagiarizes certain documents that he purports to analyze. (See, for example, page 31, when he takes Governor-General Hardinge's language as his own without citing the NAI sources.)

[3] Matthew H. Edney's *Mapping an Empire* perhaps comes closest. However, as it ends in 1843, his work stops short of examining the late Victorian period – when boundary demarcation, mapping, and the underlying geographical propositions connecting the two became increasingly important to the configuration of the imperial state. See Matthew H. Edney, *Mapping an Empire: The Geographical Construction of British India,*

practices and concepts, this chapter contributes to a diverse body of historical scholarship at the nexus of two academic endeavors: the study of imperial statecraft, and that of the history of science.[4] At the heart of imperial border making was the deployment of geography in the service of the state. As the *sine qua non* of territory, borders and frontiers became of existential importance to the imperial state – "the razor's edge on which hang suspended the modern issues of war or peace, of life or death to nations."[5]

By examining the assumptions and contradictions at work in their theorizing, configuring, and mapping, this chapter delves into the geographical thinking that produced frontiers and borders. It also explores and details an example of imperial statecraft becoming tied to changing scientific practices and ideas. The development of the water-parting principle reveals how natural features were systematized and generalized for both cartographical and political ends. As this chapter will show, this process of systematization becomes visible through two interrelated developments. First, it was revealed through *cartographical thinking* – making maps that reflected both the concrete location and abstract representation of natural features. Mountains became more abstractly linear objects on maps, just as their dimensions were being more precisely recorded. Along with this transformation in cartography, tensions between ideas of natural frontiers and strategic began to reveal the increasingly intimate relationship between geography and the imperial state. This tension resulted in the repeated failure to craft a suitable border through the northwestern Himalaya in the century before Indian independence in 1947. These two different categories of frontiers – natural and strategic – were unified by the

---

1765–1843 (Chicago: University of Chicago Press, 1997). Ian J. Barrow's *Making History, Drawing Territory* studies the Survey of India through the year 1905 and the end of Curzon's tenure as viceroy: a point often seen as the high-water mark of British imperialism in South Asia. See Ian J. Barrow, *Making History, Drawing Territory: British Mapping in India, c. 1756 – 1905* (New Delhi: Oxford University Press, 2003). Yet, unlike Edney's focus on the cartographic construction of modern India, Barrow is more interested in how British imperial identity was shaped by the "idea" of India. Other works that explore colonial surveying include D. Graham Burnett, *Masters of All They Surveyed: Exploration, Geography, and a British El Dorado* (Chicago: University of Chicago Press, 2000); and Kapil Raj, *Relocating Modern Science: Circulation and the Construction of Knowledge in South Asia and Europe, 1650–1900* (New York: Palgrave Macmillan, 2007).
[4] As examples of the literature found at this nexus, see Timothy Mitchell, *Colonizing Egypt* (Berkeley: University of California Press, 1991); David Arnold, *Colonizing the Body* (Berkeley: University of California Press, 1993); Bayly, *Empire and Information*; Hevia, *Imperial Security State*; and, most recently, the work of Tom Simpson, especially Thomas Simpson, "Modern Mountains from the Enlightenment to the Anthropocene," *The Historical Journal* 62, no. 2 (2018): 553–81. For the concept of territoriality and its relation to practices of the state, see Maier, "Consigning the Twentieth Century to History."
[5] George N. Curzon, *Frontiers* (Oxford: Clarendon Press, 1908), 7.

logic of the so-called *scientific frontier*[6] – a second phenomenon throwing into greater relief the systematization and generalization of natural features. The tension between natural and strategic frontiers was also illustrated by tensions between central colonial administrators, who desired maps that reflected broad strategic concerns, and frontier experts, who appreciated the technical requirements of boundary demarcation. Together, the scientific frontier and cartographical thinking reflected attempts both to standardize colonial frontier practices and to optimize the frontier's visibility to the colonial state. By the mid-nineteenth century, this frontier terrain was, in mountainous regions at least, organized through the idea of the watershed, which emerged as a natural *and* political unit capable of being precisely surveyed, mapped, and utilized for border making.[7]

Although some scholars have viewed the surveying of British India as a triumph of state-sponsored scientific practice, this triumph did not extend across much of the Himalaya.[8] Rather, surveying was a slow and uneven process of attempting to stitch together distinct frontier segments – not only on increasingly restricted maps, but also under increasingly unified frontier policy. Needless to say, a shift in policy does not always correlate with direct or consistent increases in information. Frontiers were often integrated at the central government level, using maps that presumed an authority over those peripheral spaces. In defining imperial territorial limits, the British were also testing the limits of their geographical knowledge. But the repeated attempts by the British to configure a scientific frontier across northern India failed: in part because surveying revealed fluctuating locations for the Indus watershed and in part because political and military rationales for border locations changed in response to Russian and Chinese encroachment upon India. These concrete challenges to border making also reflected a more abstract notion in play: that of incongruity, in which the idea of the colonial state and its claimed territory failed to neatly overlap.

This ambiguity often stemmed from maps and their political use. One of the great hidden powers of maps is their capacity to obscure the

---

[6] Curzon, 26.

[7] This chapter draws inspiration from recent work by Bernard Debarbieux and Gilles Rudaz exploring the ways in which mountains are socially constructed objects. See Bernard Debarbieux and Gilles Rudaz, *The Mountain: A Political History from the Enlightenment to the Present* (Chicago: University of Chicago Press, 2015).

[8] For the history of the ambiguities of the northeastern Himalayan frontier, see, most recently, Guyot-Réchard, *Shadow States*. For a comparative study of the failures of mid-nineteenth century frontier making in the northeastern and northwestern extremities of the British Empire, see Thomas Simpson, "Bordering and Frontier-Making in Nineteenth-Century British India," *The Historical Journal* 58, no. 2 (2015): 513–42.

processes and "propositional logic" that produce them – particularly the assumptions and conventions that simplify, obscure, or enhance the natural features used to define territory.[9] In the nineteenth century, as advances in surveying techniques yielded maps with greater degrees of detail, maps came to hold increased political authority. But despite the claims of recent critical interventions in the history of cartography, maps were "technologies of power" only in so far as they could achieve the state's desired degree of territorial legibility.[10]

The notions of territorial legibility and territorial inviolability emerged and developed in tandem. In other words, the clearer the territory appeared on the map, the greater the assertion of – or the need for – political control. By the end of the nineteenth century *terra incognita* had almost completely disappeared. As the whole world became mapped, "geopolitics" emerged: a theory of interdependent parts constituting that whole world, dependent on geography. The intimate relationship between geography and state was reflected in publications like *The Geographical Journal* of the Royal Geographical Society, which provided a forum for recent discoveries, evolving surveying technologies, new maps, and newly discovered routes across imperial frontiers. Crucially, it also provided a platform for former imperial frontier experts and scholars, like Oxford's first Professor of Geography, Halford Mackinder, to articulate theories of geography's determining effect on human societies and states.[11] Geographical science had become political science; watersheds had become political instruments.

This chapter begins with a brief history of the idea of the watershed, which grew out of earlier notions of water and mountain systems, Humboldtian geography, and international legal theory. It then explores the first British boundary commissions in Ladakh (1846–48) and their employment of the water-parting principle, which would form the basis of increasingly authoritative and restricted trans-frontier maps. The third section shifts to the 1870s and 1880s, when revisions to these initial demarcation attempts asserted that the "Indus watershed system" should be the natural boundary of northern India. Late nineteenth-century

---

[9] Denis Wood and John Fels, *The Natures of Maps: Cartographic Constructions of the Natural World* (Chicago: University of Chicago Press, 2008), 26.

[10] J. B. Harley, "Deconstructing the Map," in *The New Nature of Maps: Essays in the History of Cartography*, ed. Paul Laxton (Baltimore: Johns Hopkins University Press, 2001), 150–68; Denis Wood, *The Power of Maps* (New York: Guilford Press, 1992); and Scott, *Seeing Like a State.*

[11] On January 25, 1904, Halford Mackinder presented to the Royal Geographical Society his influential paper "The Geographical Pivot of History." The Society subsequently published that paper in *The Geographical Journal*. See Halford J. Mackinder, "The Geographical Pivot of History," *The Geographical Journal* 23, no. 4 (1904): 421–37.

colonial administrators, as well as international legal theorists, statesmen, and surveyors around the world, understood this watershed system to be the land through which the Indus and its tributaries drained, up to the water-parting ranges that separated the Indus from its neighboring water-shed systems. However, the application of these principles also reflected tensions between the surveyors, who sought to identify natural markers to map, and administrators, who appreciated the elegance of a single bound-ary principle even if its mapped reality failed to correspond to a line on the ground. The chapter concludes by demonstrating how the production of borderless maps in the decades leading up to 1947 resulted from the continued insistence on use of the water-parting principle and the assumed authority of earlier survey maps of the region. The eventual omission of a northwestern Himalayan boundary line on successive Survey of India maps was not simply the result of a diplomatic failure to determine an acceptable international border. Rather, it was the result of competing and contradictory ideas about how best to use natural features as a means to achieve political ends.

2.1   Bounds of Nature: Water, Law, and Humboldt's New Geography

Bodies of water have long demarcated regions. Across the world one finds many examples of names of regions shaped, literally, by water: Mesopotamia ("between rivers"), the Doab ("two waters"), the Punjab ("five waters"), Sichuan ("four rivers"), Hebei ("to the north of the [Yellow] River"), or Henan ("to the south of the [Yellow] River"). The significance of the hydrographical networks of the Indus and Ganges is well documented in the major texts of precolonial India, from ancient Sanskrit Ayurvedic texts to the Mughal *Akbarnama*.[12] In his *Ai'n-i-Akbari* ("the Regulations of Akbar"), Emperor Akbar's vizier Abu'l Fazl Allami (1551–1602) described Hindustan as a land bordered by oceans: oceans that included the mountains separating the Mughal territories from Central Asia and Tibet. Thus water – actual and metaphorical – has flowed through human history to shape definitions of territories and to serve as natural boundaries. Yet water was never a fixed element. As understandings of water's nature changed, so too did boundaries.

In the European colonial context, connected bodies of water such as rivers, lakes, and bays have been associated with territorial claims since at

---

[12] On the former, see Francis Zimmerman, *The Jungle and the Aroma of Meats: An Ecological Theme in Hindu Medicine* (Berkeley: University of California Press, 1987), particularly chapters 1 and 3.

least the seventeenth century.[13] But only in the eighteenth and early nineteenth centuries did the study of water and earth systems become increasingly schematized within the study of geography and geology. In the minds of political actors, these newly systemic visions of the natural world combined with older notions of mountains and rivers as boundaries, to manifest in so-called natural divisions marking the edges of territories being put to political use. While mountains had long been natural dividers, the combination of mountains and water into "water-partings" was a product of eighteenth-century knowledge formation and colonial claims to territories – the latter first conquered in North America and later elsewhere across the globe.[14] The increased frequency of river exploration that accompanied European imperial expansion also enhanced the political importance of waterways as useful conduits and potential boundaries, simultaneously.[15] These developments were largely ignored by the natural philosophers of the seventeenth and eighteenth centuries who studied changes in the land and water networks.

Although James Hutton (1726–97), the "father" of modern geology, had discussed "the system of the earth" in the context of geological time, his consideration of the role of water was largely relegated to questions of fluvial decay.[16] It was another Scottish natural philosopher, John Playfair (1748–1819), whose *Illustrations of the Huttonian Theory of the Earth* (1802) first detailed the theory that came to be known as Playfair's law of accordant junctions: "Every river appears to consist of a main trunk, fed from variety of branches, each running a valley proportioned to its size, and all of them together forming a system of vallies [*sic*]."[17] While acknowledging the connected, systemic nature of rivers and streams, Playfair – like Hutton – was principally concerned with the apparent relationship between river and valley size as indicators of the eroding force of water.

In contrast, Alexander von Humboldt (1769–1859) was arguably one of the earliest geographers whose theories were regularly employed by political actors. As he was concerned with not just geological time, but also historical time, Humboldt combined growing geological and hydrological understandings of water networks and mountain ranges with the increased

[13] See, for instance, the Royal Charter of the Hudson's Bay Company: www.hbcheritage.ca /hbcheritage/collections/archival/charter/charter.asp.
[14] On the role of mountains in shaping early modern borders, see Sahlins, *Boundaries*; and, more recently, Debarbieux and Rudaz, *The Mountain*.
[15] See, for example, Noboru Ishikawa, *Between Frontiers: Nation and Identity in a Southeast Asian Borderland* (Athens: Ohio University Press, 2010).
[16] Keith J. Tinkler, *A Short History of Geomorphology* (Totowa, NJ: Barnes and Noble Books, 1985), 49.
[17] Tinkler, 58–59.

authority of maps. Humboldt sought to establish general principles that, by accurately defining and visually rendering the world's regions, would lead to better understanding of the "unity of nature": the deep and intimate connections between the various branches of science, and between human society and its varied environments. Like Montesquieu and others before him, Humboldt also sought to explain human culture through the lens of climate. Colonial explorers, boundary commissioners, and legal jurists all regularly cited Humboldt, eschewing the earlier natural philosophers like Hutton and Playfair. "Invoking Humboldt," Burnett notes, "suggested that the explorer was working within what many thought the most reliable and measurement-centered geographical science of the day."[18] Critically, Humboldt's work followed several decades of notable advances in the expanding fields of geography, geology, and cartography, each of which also exerted increased political influence. Through the medium of maps in particular, watersheds emerged as territorial objects assembling systems of mountains, valleys, plains, and bodies of water.

By the 1840s, European and American legal scholars were citing Humboldt's writings. This suggest both his widespread influence and the ex post facto colonial concern with legal justification for territorial conquest and ensuing demarcation. The prominent English jurist, Sir Travers Twiss (1809–97), writing about legal disputes over the Oregon territory, frequently utilized examples from Humboldt's *Political Essay on the Kingdom of New Spain* (1811) – a geographical and cartographical description of Mexico. In his *The Oregon Question Examined, in respect to the Facts and the Law of Nations* (1846), Twiss employed Humboldt's work to articulate a theory of discovery. He used the example of disputes over the Columbia River between Britain and the United States in the 1820s to illustrate a growing principle of "progressive discovery." Against British protests, the US government maintained that, in the words of one American diplomat, "a nation discovering a country, by entering the mouth of its principal river at the sea coast, must necessarily be allowed to claim and hold as great an extent of the interior country as was described by the course of such principal river, and its tributary streams."[19] Twiss thus concluded that the American discovery of the Columbia River gave, "by the acknowledged law and usage of nations, a right to the whole country drained by that river and its tributary streams."[20] This type of claim departed from previous riparian principles, such as those articulated by international legal theorists like Emer de

---

[18] Burnett, *Masters of All They Surveyed*, 15.
[19] Travers Twiss, *The Oregon Question Examined, in Respect to the Facts and the Law of Nations* (London: Longman, Brown, Green, and Longmans, 1846).
[20] Twiss, 148–49.

Vattel (1714–67) and Henry Wheaton (1785–1848) – who both favored the use of rivers as boundaries.[21] However, it became increasingly apparent to colonial officials that rivers rarely divided politically distinct peoples. Viceroy George Curzon would note this salient detail in his 1907 discussion of the history of natural frontiers. In his words, a river was a better "means of access to a country than a line of division between races," a category of increasing importance to the definition of nations.[22]

Twiss's work on the "Oregon question," and his well-known later work, *The Law of Nations Considered as Independent Political Communities* (1884), articulated the advantages of using watersheds and boundary limits. By the second half of the nineteenth century, the term "watershed" was regularly invoked to assert a principle of territorial organization and border making.[23] Twiss's early reliance on Humboldt and other "scientific travellers" highlights the powerful confluence of geography, cartography, colonial expansion, and international law; a confluence existing by the mid-nineteenth century.

Numerous European travelers in the western Himalaya in the first half of the nineteenth century also cited Humboldt's work.[24] Although the Prussian Humboldt gained permission from the Russian government to travel through Central Asia, British authorities refused him access to the Himalaya.[25] His principal work on the geography of Asia, *Asie Centrale*, was thus a compilation of travelers' accounts, his own observations from traveling through Russian Central Asia, and older material from European, classical Greek and Roman, and Chinese geographers. In it, he applied theoretical insights from his earlier works to construct a geography of mountain and water systems, glaciers, and climates that

---

[21] Emer de Vattel, *Droit des gens; ou, Principes de la loi naturelle appliqués à la conduite et aux affaires des nations et des souverains* (Washington: Carnegie Institution of Washington, 1916); and Henry Wheaton, *Elements of International Law*, 3rd ed. (Philadelphia: Lea and Blanchard, 1846).

[22] Curzon, *Frontiers*, 12.

[23] See, for instance, Legislative Assembly, *The Proceedings before the Judicial Committee of Her Majesty's Imperial Privy Council on the Special Case Respecting the Westerly Boundary of Ontario . . .* (Toronto: Warwick, 1889).

[24] Examples include Victor Jacquemont, *Letters from India; Describing a Journey in the British Dominions of India, Tibet, Lahore, and Cashmeer, during the Years 1828, 1829, 1830, 1831. Undertaken by Order of the French Government*, 2 vols. (London: Edward Churton, 1834); and William Lloyd and Alexander Gerard, *Narrative of a Journey from Caunpoor to the Boorendo Pass in the Himalaya Mountains*, 2 vols. (London: J. Madden, 1840).

[25] Richard Stratchey, "On the Snow-Line in the Himalaya," *Journal of the Asiatic Society*, April 1849, 287. In a recent biography of Humboldt, Andrea Wulf suggests that it was owing to Humboldt's well-known anticolonial opinions that the British refused to allow him to conduct his scientific travels in the Himalaya. Andrea Wulf, *The Invention of Nature: Alexander von Humboldt's New World* (New York: Vintage, 2015), 192–95. As thanks for the Russian government's assistance, Humboldt dedicated *Asie Centrale* to the Tsar Nicholas I.

shaped the region. He begins the first of three volumes by outlining his process and general theory:

I have reviewed the current state of our knowledge, the foundations of our maps, and the directions assigned to unevenness in the surface of a vast continent. It is in the uprising of the masses, in the extent and orientation of mountain systems in their relative positions, dominant traits that from ancient times have exerted influence on the state of human societies and determined the trends of their migration.[26]

As in his earlier work on Europe and the Americas, in *Asie Centrale* Humboldt sought to identify the sources and major courses of rivers, and to determine dominant mountain systems. He did so in order to develop principles for what constituted a naturally demarcated region, and to show, in the process, the environmental foundations of human societies. This association of "natural" regions and race was a common feature of nineteenth-century geographies. The English geologist Frederic Drew, for instance, wrote of the inhabitants of the northwestern Himalaya: "of the four races of men who inhabit the country on the northeast of the main chain of mountains – *the country which drains into the Indus* – whose names are Champa, Ladakhi, Balti, and Dard, the first three belong to the Tibetan race."[27]

Foremost among Humboldt's observations on the great mountain systems of the world was the strong tendency toward "parallelism" – that is, the tendency of mountains to form in linear, parallel chains. The Himalayan boundary commissioner Alexander Cunningham remarked in his *Ladák* (1854), that "the general parallelism of the principal mountain-ranges of the world – of the Himalayas and the Altai, in Asia – of the Atlas, in Africa – and of the Alps and Apennines, the Pyrenees and Carpathians, in Europe – has already been noticed by Humboldt and others."[28] But Humboldt also acknowledged a crucial divide within the Himalayas and the Tibetan Plateau, thanks largely to the writings of the explorer William Moorcroft and other scientific travelers' accounts, published in the *Transactions of the Royal Asiatic Society of Great Britain and Ireland* and the *Journal of the Royal Geographical Society of London* (later renamed *The Geographical Journal*). Humboldt wrote that east of the sacred lakes of Manasarovar and Rakshastal in Western Tibet there was a "transverse uprising"[29] that signaled the "water-parting" ("formant le partage d'eau

---

[26] Alexander von Humboldt, *Asie Centrale: Recherches sur les Chaines des Montagnes et la Climatologie Comparée*, 3 vols. (Paris: Gide, 1843), 1:xi.

[27] Drew, *Jummoo and Kashmir Territories*, 238. My emphasis.

[28] Cunningham, *Ladák*, 42.

[29] That is, a mountain range running perpendicular to the main axis of the mountain range.

[divortia aquarum] à l'est des lacs sacrés") between the Indus and the Yarlung Tsangpo/Brahmaputra, the origins of which still remained a mystery to these geographers. Humboldt further noted these rivers divided the Tibetan Plateau into two great parts and that "the part of the plateau the least interrupted" by "the system of mountains of the Himalayas" was in Western Tibet, situated "between Ladakh, Gartok [a town in Western Tibet], and the arid shores of Lake Manasarovar."[30] While he stops short of using the term "watershed," Humboldt's insistence on the water-parting as a key object of dividing natural units of land reflected a shift in geographical thinking toward a territorial unit that could be determined by water and mountain systems, and, most importantly, mapped.

More than sixty years later, the Swedish explorer Sven Hedin would assert that the amalgamation of Asian sources and traveler's accounts in *Asie Centrale*, combined with Humboldt's own peripatetic observations, produced a "more reliable" description of the region than had ever existed previously. But Hedin went on to criticize Humboldt for his excessively mechanistic description of the region. "Humboldt considers the mountain skeleton of Asia very simple and regular," wrote Hedin, "and on his map the various systems were drawn with the greatest geometrical preciseness."[31] Hedin noted that most mid-nineteenth-century maps of Central Asia relied on "Humboldt's four systems, the Altai, Tian-Shan, Kwen-lun, and Himalayas," while omitting smaller, nonparallel ranges.[32] The omission of complicating perpendicular ranges and "spurs" reflected the practice, seen on many large-scale maps, of rendering the Himalayas as a neat, thin line of mountains. Hedin's "discovery" of the "Trans-Himalaya" during his travels in 1907–9 would complicate the notion that the Himalayan range and the Indus water-parting line were roughly co-terminus – a central assumption of the first Himalayan boundary commissions.[33]

A century after the first Himalayan boundary commissioners applied Humboldt's theories to their survey of the northwestern Himalaya, the "water-parting principle" would be an established ideal in international border making. Applying this principle, however, required surveyors to first locate the water-parting line.

---

[30] Humboldt, *Asie Centrale*, 1:13–15.
[31] Sven Hedin, *Trans-Himalaya: Discoveries and Adventures in Tibet* (New York: Macmillan, 1909), 3:139.
[32] Hedin, 142. Humboldt describes the four mountains in volume two of *Asie Centrale*.
[33] In fact, several "Trans-Himalayas" would be discovered over the course of the nineteenth and early twentieth centuries.

2.2   From Valley to Ridge: The First Boundary Commissions and the "Water-Parting Principle"

When the two Himalayan boundary commissions were established in 1846–48, the British had already presided over a violent and rapid expansion that required extensive definition of its territorial limits. In many places throughout its South Asian empire, Britain readily adopted historical boundaries – particularly for those districts that utilized older political divisions from the Mughal period. But in places where boundaries were unknown or unsatisfactory, commissioners frequently resorted to utilizing nearby rivers and streams. The "Thalweg Principle" – measuring a boundary from the lowest point of a riverbed – was frequently used in relatively flat riverine regions, such as the Indo-Nepalese plains. Rivers, however, proved less than ideal boundary markers. This was because, to quote a British Resident in Kathmandu, Charles Girdlestone, "their tortuous, shifting and erratic character" made them less suitable than boundary pillars and mountain peaks, which formed "straight lines from conspicuous point to point."[34] Straight lines, unlike "erratic" rivers, are rarely found in nature, but they work very well on maps.

Boundary pillars (typically neat stone piles or stone markers) were often used in the plains, allowing for precise geodetic points to be determined and plotted on maps. "Should the boundary marks themselves vanish," the frontier expert Thomas Holdich noted, "there should always remain a record of their position on the map, and a repetition of the same survey process will show precisely where the original site may have been."[35] But it was the "water-parting principle" that gained preeminence in the mountainous frontiers; by the century's end, it would be the undisputed ideal of boundary demarcation. "The best and most recognizable natural boundary," asserted Holdich in 1896, "is a well-defined watershed."[36] By 1945, the water-parting principle had become a key tenet of international boundary making. In his *Boundary-Making: A Handbook for Statesmen, Treaty Editors and Boundary Commissioners*, the American geographer Stephen B. Jones observed that "the virtues of waterparting [*sic*] boundaries are that ... they are precise and unique and that they separate drainage basins, which for many purposes are best treated as units under a single government."[37] The development of this international

---

[34] NAI, Foreign, A Pol E, 187–196, May 83. "Alluvial Streams (Nipal). Permanent land line Boundaries to be adopted in supersession of Boundaries."
[35] NAI, Foreign, Secret, no. 41, October 1896.   [36] NAI.
[37] Stephen B. Jones, *Boundary-Making: A Handbook for Statesmen, Treaty Editors and Boundary Commissioners* (Washington, DC: Carnegie Endowment for International Peace, 1945), 101–2.

border-making principle reflected a transformation in how borders were first envisioned and then represented.

Unlike borderlines, border points had long existed – and had been long accepted – in the Himalayan region. Typically located on established trade and pilgrimage routes, these points often signaled seasonal customs duties to be paid. They could also signal *corvée* labor to be given for the triennial tribute mission to Lhasa and the reciprocal biennial mission from Lhasa, established by treaty in 1684.[38] These border points acknowledged the transition of jurisdictions at the edges of populated regions. Most of the region to the north and east of Ladakh – now referred to as the Aksai Chin – had no permanent population, though it was regularly traversed by traders, pilgrims, and seminomadic herders. While rarely explicitly referenced in indigenous accounts, these border points continued to function as political markers for centuries.

In 1842, eight years after the Dogra-led invasion of Ladakh, representatives of the Dogra Raja of Jammu,[39] the Emperor of China, and the Dalai Lama, signed a treaty that reaffirmed the "boundaries of Ladakh and its surroundings as fixed from ancient times," though without acknowledging the location of those boundaries.[40] Four years later, the first British boundary commission arrived to survey its newly acquired dependent princely state, Jammu and Kashmir.

In November 1846, Sir John Davis, governor of British Hong Kong, wrote to the Governor-General of Liang-Guang, Qiying, urging that the two governments ascertain "the exact boundaries which divide the Thibetan territory from that pertaining to Great Britain, and from that also which has been conferred on [Gulab] Singh," the newly aggrandized Maharaja of Jammu and Kashmir – and that they so ascertain "with the aid of the best maps."[41] Qiying replied that, "the borders of those territories have been

---

[38] As discussed in Chapter 1, these were respectively called the *lo.phyag* and the *gzhung. tshong*. See also John Bray, "Corvée Transport Labour in 19th and Early 20th Century Ladakh: A Study in Continuity and Change," in *Modern Ladakh: Anthropological Perspectives on Continuity and Change*, ed. Martijn van Beek and Fernanda Pirie, Brill's Tibetan Studies Library 20 (Leiden: Brill, 2008), 43–66.

[39] After its conquest and eventual annexation by the Sikhs in 1816, the northern principality of Jammu, ruled by a dynasty of Dogra Rajputs, became a tributary of the Sikh Empire. Gulab Singh, the Raja of Jammu (1822–57), invaded Ladakh in 1834. He did so – likely at the behest of the Sikh Maharaja Ranjit Singh – in order to secure access to the valuable pashmina trade routes threatened by British expansion further south. Following the defeat of the Sikh Empire in the First Anglo-Sikh War of 1845–46, and in thanks for his tacit assistance them during the war, the East India Company granted Gulab Singh the title of Maharaja of Jammu and Kashmir. This inaugurated the Dogra dynasty, which would rule the princely state of Jammu and Kashmir until 1947.

[40] JKSA-J, "Treaty between Ladakh and Tibet: 1920, 276/R. P-4."

[41] NAI, Foreign, Secret, nos. 139–42, August 28, 1847, "Result of Captain A. Cunningham's Mission to Thibet."

sufficiently and distinctly fixed so that it will be best to adhere to this ancient arrangement, and it will prove far more convenient to abstain from any additional measures for fixing them." But it was unclear whether the Qing officials themselves knew what exactly this "ancient arrangement" was.

In 1846, the East India Company's governor-general, Henry Hardinge, appointed two successive commissions to determine a permanent boundary in the northwestern Himalaya, on the easternmost edge of the newly conjoined and politically subordinate state of Jammu and Kashmir. The commissions comprised the future founder of the Archaeological Survey of India, Alexander Cunningham, and a celebrated Himalayan explorer, Henry Strachey. They also involved a botanist, Thomas Thomson, whose inclusion reflected the growing practice of including natural scientists as members of boundary commissions. The governor-general wanted a "clear and well defined boundary [that would] prevent the possibility of dispute."[42] The commissioners were told by those in charge to seek out as boundaries "such mountain ranges as form water-shed lines between the drainages of different rivers." For their published contributions to the study of Himalayan geography, both Strachey and Thomson would receive the Royal Geographical Society's highest prizes.

When the British requested that the Qing Government send representatives to the northwestern Himalaya to jointly demarcate a border between the two empires in 1846, Qiying refused. Qiying cited a long historical understanding of the boundary, reaffirmed in an 1842 treaty, which could be traced back to at least the seventeenth century and the Treaty of Tingmosgang.[43]

Once the British determined that no Chinese boundary commissioners would participate in the demarcation, the three boundary commissioners, Cunningham, Strachey, and Thomson, were given orders to begin. This established the precedent for unilateral boundary making in the region that would continue for more than a century.[44] Again, the commissioners were given instructions to make use of the region's natural features for the purposes of deriving a paper boundary:

[42] NAI, Foreign, nos. 162–64, August 28, 1847. "Instructions for [Cunningham's] guidance on his approaching Mission to the Thibetan Frontier."

[43] In 1684, following five years of Tibetan incursions fueled by sectarian disputes between the Drukpa Kagyu of Ladakh and Gelukpa-dominated Government of Tibet, the Ladakhi king had enlisted the aid of the Mughals and expelled the Tibetans from his kingdom. The king, having agreed nominally to convert to Islam and to build a mosque in Leh, signed a treaty with the Kashmiri-led Mughal forces. He then had concluded a separate treaty with the Tibetan government at Tingmosgang, fixing a border point between the two countries at the *Lha.ri* stream, high up on the Changtang Plateau on the main Leh-Lhasa route. Francke, "La.dwags rGyal.rabs," 101.

[44] NAI, Foreign, nos. 162–64, August 28, 1847. "Instructions."

Boundary marks are neither requisite nor probably possible, you will find plenty of mountains ready to your hand. And these natural pillars should not only be carefully mapped for registry with the British Government, but their appearance and bearings should be fully and distinctly recorded in writing, and a copy furnished to the representations of each of the three contracting parties. The experience acquired in your last trip should enable you to accommodate your route to the seasons, i.e. to finish your work in the higher tracts before snow falls and cuts off your retreat.[45]

Thomson set about testing Humboldt's general principles. "The whole of Tibet," he wrote, "appears to be characterized by great uniformity of climate and productions and perhaps also of natural features, on which account it appears convenient to retain the name for the whole country, which however as has already been pointed out by Baron Humboldt, is naturally separable into two grand divisions."[46] The first of these divisions was the watershed of the Tsangpo, which in India becomes the Brahmaputra; the second was the Indus.

But Thomson also began to see complications in these divisions. In his report to the East India Company, he noted that if all of Western Tibet were a single, "extensive plain bounded on the South by the great chain of the Himalaya and on the north by the lofty mountains of Kunenlun [sic] it would be an easy task to define its boundaries."[47] However, in reality, he noted:

A line of high snowy peaks may doubtless be traced in a direction nearly parallel to the plains of India, but these are separated from one another by deep ravines along which flow large and rapid rivers, and *therefore afford no tangible line of demarcation between the two countries.* Between the river Indus and the plains of N.W. India is interposed a mountain tract which has a breadth of about 150 miles in line as distance.[48]

Thomson thus acknowledged that the geographical reality of the supposedly systemic, parallel Himalayas was much more complicated than had earlier been assumed, and that deriving a clear, natural line of demarcation would be no simple task. This complication also highlighted a critical topographical irony of much of the history of surveying in the region. The Himalayas were long seen as a barrier – what the poet Muhammad Iqbal would later call the "dīwār-i-Hindustān" ("wall of India")[49] – that separated India from the land beyond. But, as most topographical maps drawn since 1800 illustrate, Ladakh is beyond, or within that "wall." When Thomson wrote of a mountain tract 150 miles wide, he effectively

---

[45] NAI.
[46] NAI, Foreign, December 29, 1849, 332–34, F.C. "Thomson, Asstt.-Surgeon T. Report on Western Thibet."
[47] NAI.
[48] NAI, Foreign, December 29, 1849, 332–34, F.C. "Thomson, Asstt.-Surgeon T. Report on Western Thibet." My emphasis.
[49] Muhammad Iqbal, "Hamāla," 1901.

acknowledged that Britain's frontiers could not end at a clear wall of mountains, but instead, would stretch somewhere deep within them. But Thomson also recognized that the main rivers running through this complex of mountains could offer a path out of this topographical tangle. "If [the rivers] be taken as a guide, the mountains will be found to resolve themselves into two great systems, connected to the eastward but otherwise independent of, though nearly parallel to one another." Thus, the watersheds of the Indus and the Tsangpo/Brahmaputra became two central objects of demarcation. The "Indus watershed system," as it came to be known, would soon become the understood frontier of northern India.

The map generated by the second commission satisfied colonial officials in charge, asserting that a natural boundary had been found and that a principle had been established (Map 2.1). But more pressing problems of governance soon drew the attention of the East India Company back to the plains of India.

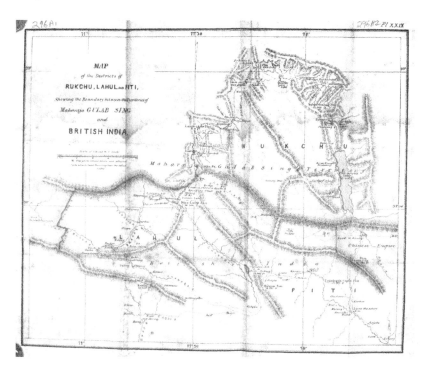

Map 2.1 "Map of the Districts of Rukchu, Lahul and Piti, Showing the Boundary between the Territories of Maharaja Gulab Sing and British India" (1848). This map is the result of the sketch included with Alexander Cunningham's report. PAHAR/Mountains of Central Asia Digital Dataset.

2.3   Securing the Perimeter: Scientific Frontiers and the Indus Watershed System

The Rebellion of 1857 marks a critical moment in South Asia's political history. In the face of widespread violence, political upheaval, and brutal retribution, problems pertaining to mapping mountains and rivers at the edges of the empire became a decidedly peripheral concern. But as the British refashioned their rule of the subcontinent in the wake of internal rebellion, they also grew concerned by the external threats posed by the approach of the Russian and Chinese empires to their still vague northern frontiers. From this moment forward, security suffused all political and commercial considerations for British administrators in India – and guided the production of maps. As the government of India grew alarmed by Russian encroachment, more precise techniques and extensive boundary commissions were established to detail India's frontier. This frontier in turn became an increasingly restricted and "classified" space.

By the early 1850s, the Survey of India had completed its "series of great triangles" from its base in Dehra Dun up to the northwestern town of Peshawar (Map 2.2).[50] The Survey's mapping of Kashmir began in 1854, paused during the rebellion, and recommenced in 1858. After recommencement, the Survey began to utilize the more precise trigonometric technique employing a theodolite that had become standard for other Survey of India maps further south.[51] The results were a series of detailed maps of the region in 1859 and 1861. Owing to altitude, its vastness, and the harshness of climate, Ladakh was not surveyed in the same way when mapping recommenced there in the 1860s. Instead it was mapped by "traverse" survey – sketched maps based on measured distances on the ground – akin to the method of the 1846–48 boundary commissions.

In 1865, William Johnson made a north-south traverse of the Aksai Chin. He followed the primary trade route through the region, but did not triangulate the distances to, and heights of, the mountains and hills scattered across the barren plateau. The resulting map was published in 1867 (Map 2.3). Johnson would later become the Dogra-appointed *wazīr-i-wazārat* ["district administrator"] of Ladakh. Johnson's survey, and the eventual "line" of mountains it produced, remained the basic cartographical representation of the region for the remainder of the

---

[50] NAI, Foreign, nos. 314–15, June 10, 1853, "Proposed Survey of Cashmere and the adjoining mountains."

[51] For a detailed description of this surveying process by the large boundary commissions and surveying parties of the late nineteenth century, see Hevia, *Imperial Security State*, 73–106.

Map 2.2 "Index Chart to the Great Trigonometrical Survey of India" (1870). Survey of India. PAHAR/Mountains of Central Asia Digital Dataset.

nineteenth century. It endures as one of the main sources for India's claims to the Aksai Chin today.[52] Critically, however, Johnson did not survey the mountains that formed the supposed outer perimeter of the Aksai Chin and a possible edge of the Indus watershed. Given the paucity of snowfall on the arid, largely glacier-less plateau, determining its water-partings was a nearly impossible task. Yet subsequent Survey of India maps began adding in a solid line of mountains, creating the illusion of an encircling mountain limit to the Aksai Chin. The 1876 "Index to Degree Sheets of the North West Himalaya Series," for instance, showed a neat

[52] Lamb, *Sino-Indian Border*, 8–9.

Map 2.3 "Map of the Country between Leh and Ilchi Showing the Routes Taken by Mr. Johnson Civil Assist. G. T. Survey in 1865" (1867). Royal Geographical Society. Wikipedia Commons.

line of mountains winding through sheets 36, 38, and 39 (Map 2.4). But when you go to those specific sheets, they are blank (Map 2.5). Modern satellite images, courtesy of Google Maps, make it clear that no such ring of mountains exists (Map 2.6)!

The increased interest in commercial ventures in Central Asia, coupled with growing concerns about the Russian Empire looming in from the north, pushed the Survey of India to produce more detailed maps of "trans-frontier" regions – representations of the limits of British territory, however vaguely defined that territory may have been. However, political uncertainties and the occasional unfriendly welcome in regions beyond British territories forced the Survey to produce these maps more covertly, often with the aid of trained Indians, known as pundits.

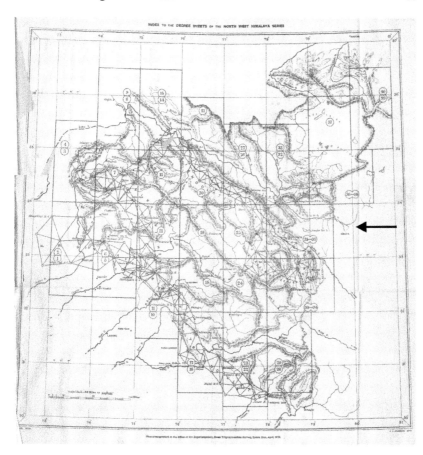

Map 2.4 "Index to Degree Sheets of the North West Himalaya Series" (1876). Survey of India. The arrow points to Pangong Lake, for reference to Map 2.6 below. PAHAR/Mountains of Central Asia Digital Dataset.

The pundits – often from the hills but sometimes from Bengal or other plains areas – were trained by the Survey of India to take part in covert intelligence gathering missions beyond the borders of India. Often disguised as pilgrims or traders, these agents were equipped with an array of hidden instruments to facilitate their work – practices made famous by Kipling's portrayal of Anglo-Russian Himalayan intrigue in *Kim* (1901). These highly praised "human instruments" – as Kapil Raj has styled them – formed a hybrid colonial scientific practice utilizing the expertise

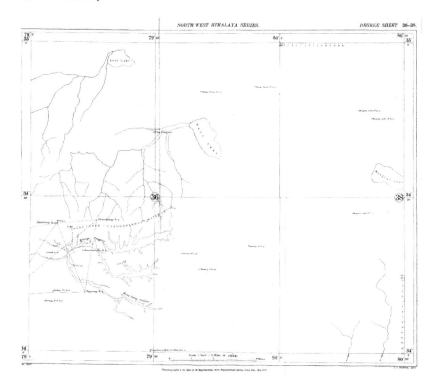

Map 2.5 "North West Himalaya Series degree sheet 36–38" (1877). Survey of India. Note the absence of the mountain range illustrated in the index to these degree sheets (Map 2.4); this, despite the fact that the degree sheet here is meant to accompany the index, published a year earlier. PAHAR/Mountains of Central Asia Digital Dataset.

of both colonizers and colonized.[53] The maps that the pundits and other Indian surveyors produced served to fill in the blank trans-frontier spaces on the Survey of India's maps. They also made it even clearer to central administrators that the government of India needed more precise demarcations of the frontier. Regarding the earlier 1846–48 boundary commissions in Ladakh, for instance, administrators complained that the resulting "information and the maps [were] so conflicting, that it [was] impossible to say what was the boundary."[54] Due to the conflicting maps,

[53] Raj, *Relocating Modern Science*.
[54] NAI, Foreign, Political A, nos. 240-41A, May 1870, "Boundary between Cashmere and Lingti."

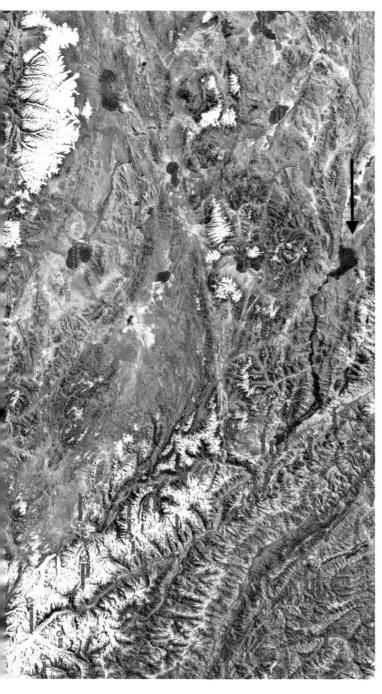

Map 2.6 A Google Maps image of the lower Aksai Chin. Arrow points to Pangong Lake for reference to Map 2.4. Note the absence of any linear north-south mountain ridge, despite its representation on the 1876 Survey of India index map and subsequent maps.

the government of India determined that a new boundary commission should ignore the 1846–48 boundary and that "the whole question should be re-investigated *de novo*." Therefore, in the 1870s, renewed attempts were made to determine Ladakh's boundaries, again applying the water-parting principle.[55] "To fix the boundary on the permanent water-shed," wrote the secretary to the government of the Punjab to the foreign secretary, is "to act on a clear and distinct principle."[56]

The government of India's Foreign Department indexes show a significant spike in boundary commissions by the early 1870s – a trend that would only accelerate until the turn of the century. This new wave of attempts at border demarcation came in part because earlier commissions, like those in the northwestern Himalaya, were increasingly seen as technically deficient "traverse" surveys that had produced inaccurate maps. The new efforts were also the result of an increasingly scientific approach to boundary settlement: one where teams of surveyors, naturalists, and boundary experts, like the aforementioned Thomas Holdich, would systematically "lay down" a borderline using standardized practices centered on identifying natural markers, or, when necessary, creating them. Experts like Holdich represented a new generation of frontier experts who employed the latest precision surveying instruments to generate an increasingly detailed accounting of imperial territory. Most of the major bilateral boundary commissions – the Anglo-Russian Afghan Boundary Commission, the Anglo-Russian Pamir Boundary Commission, and the Sino-British Burma Boundary Commission – succeeded in producing highly detailed demarcated borders, even if these borders were often ignored locally.[57] But the northwestern Himalaya proved a different case. The combination of the high altitude, the inhospitable climate, and the difficulty in determining a legible water-parting line in the Aksai Chin, produced a series of hypothetical border configurations. While those who attempted to survey parts of it fretted about the lack of geographical information available, imperial administrators were more concerned with eliminating "no-

---

[55] NAI, Foreign, Political A, nos. 10–12, May 1872, "Boundary between Spiti and Ladakh"; and NAI, Foreign, Political A, nos. 203–6, January 1873, "Settlement of the Spiti and Ladakh boundary."

[56] NAI, Foreign, Political A, May 1873, nos. 10–12.

[57] On bilateral boundary commissions, see, for example, B. D. Hopkins, "The Bounds of Identity: The Goldsmid Mission and the Delineation of the Perso–Afghan Border in the Nineteenth Century," *Journal of Global History* 2, no. 2 (2007): 233–54; Hevia, *Imperial Security State*; and Francesca Fuoli, "Incorporating North-Western Afghanistan into the British Empire: Experiments in Indirect Rule through the Making of an Imperial Frontier, 1884–87," *Afghanistan* 1, no. 1 (2018).

man's lands" like the Aksai Chin, which represented a threatening and incongruent "nonstate space."[58]

In 1879, Viceroy Lord Lytton articulated the first general frontier policy for northern India – a policy with roots going back beyond the first Himalayan boundary commissions. "The natural boundary of India," he wrote, "is formed by the convergence of the great mountain ranges of the Himalayas and of the Hindu Kush. ... [If] we resolve that no foreign interference can be permitted on this side of the mountains, or within the drainage system of the Indus, we shall have laid down a natural line of frontier which is distinct, intelligible, and likely to be respected."[59]

As the specter of Russian and Chinese advances in Central Asia provoked deepening anxieties in Calcutta, Shimla, and London, more resources were spent on surveying and demarcating the northern and eastern edges of Kashmir. These projects became covert, classified, and militarized. In 1876, Captain Henry Trotter made a trans-Himalayan survey and produced a map, fragments of which ended up in several Indian newspapers. The government reacted angrily to this publication, and subsequently deemed reports on trans-frontier survey operations "strictly confidential."[60] In 1884, the government of India ordered that notifications of boundary demarcations were not to appear in the *Gazette of India*.[61] Access to trans-frontier maps was formally restricted in 1885.[62] And regular intelligence gathering on the frontier became routine, organized through the recently formed Intelligence Branch that played a critical role in operations on the Afghan frontier.[63]

In 1888, Captain Henry Ramsay, the British Joint Commissioner at Ladakh, wrote to his superiors in the government of India's Foreign Department, urging them to consider defining the boundaries in northern and eastern Kashmir once again.[64] His predecessor, Ney Elias, who by then had become a frontier expert whose advice would be sought by the government of India on political frontiers from Afghanistan to Siam, responded dismissively. Elias wrote that he believed that "complete surveys [had] long ago been made by the regular survey of India, of all the

---

[58] Scott, *The Art of Not Being Governed*, 10–11.

[59] IOR/PS/Letters and Enclosures from India, Vol. 21, no. 49, February 28, 1879.

[60] Henry Trotter, *Account of the Survey Operations in Connection with the Mission to Yarkand and Kashghar in 1873–74 ...* (Calcutta: The Foreign Department Press, 1875).

[61] NAI, Foreign, A Political E, nos. 201–22, June 1884.

[62] NAI Foreign, Secret F, nos. 1–3, November 1885. "Trans-frontier information. Publication of frontier maps containing only sketchy Survey(s) permitted."

[63] For a history of the Intelligence Branch, see Hevia, *Imperial Security State*.

[64] NAI, Foreign, Secret Frontier, March 1889, nos. 115–16. "Frontier between Ladakh and Chinese-Turkestan."

country up to limits of the Indus system watershed."[65] But after much back and forth with the Foreign Department, officials concluded that the available maps (the Johnson map, and those that followed) did not inspire much confidence in the exact location of the Indus watershed, thus calling into question their conception of the northern frontier. While much of the subcontinent was mapped with the precision of trigonometric surveys, the difficult terrain of the Aksai Chin and the sketchy traverse surveys of Johnson and the pundits did not allow for a satisfactorily whole carto-graphic image upon which to demarcate a complete borderline.

The British resident in Kashmir wrote to the foreign secretary of India, Mortimer Durand, that he was of the "opinion that the adjustment of the whole northern and north-western frontier of Kashmir should not be further postponed." He continued,

The recent development of Imperial policy and the measures taken within the last three or four years to secure against attack or surprise routes leading from Central Asia or Afghanistan to India make it, I think, undesirable longer to defer the settlement of this boundary. ... I would advise that some officer ... should be sent early this year confidentially and quite quietly, ... accompanied with *two or three clever mappers to work out on the spot the best scientific frontier to include the most inaccessible portions.* ... Scientific accuracy need not be prescribed as so essential relatively as military features, and in this way I hope the Government of India would within the present year, be furnished with a valuable report, showing the best scientific boundary for the north and north-western frontier of Kashmir. Thus the work of a future delimitation commission would be rendered comparatively simple.[66]

A scientific frontier, as defined in 1907 by the former viceroy, George Curzon, was "a Frontier which unites natural and strategical strength."[67] The period term "scientific" reflected a process of merging precise geo-graphical information with military or political strategy, and revealed the development of geopolitics as an analytic frame derived from the premise that geography was a determining factor in the success or failure of states. Frontiers were "the razor's edge" upon which the "life or death" of nations rested; their strategic aspects could shift alongside the geopolitical fluctu-ations of imperial politics.[68] As maps came to include greater technical detail, they often retained symbolic references to early renderings of solid, parallel mountain ranges that made for the appearance of a concrete and legible border. But the certainty of solid lines on large-scale maps – and the geographical principles upon which they apparently rested – continued to belie deeper uncertainties on the ground.

[65] NAI.
[66] NAI, Foreign, Secret Frontier, March 1889, nos. 115–16. "Frontier between Ladakh and Chinese-Turkestan." My emphasis.
[67] Curzon, *Frontiers*, 26.   [68] Curzon, 7.

The water-parting principle, which in theory had previously offered such a clear means of removing any disputes, became increasingly difficult to apply on the ground. Curzon remarked in his 1907 Oxford lecture on frontiers: "In every mountain border, where the entire mountainous belt does not fall under the control of a single Power, the crest or water-divide is the best and fairest line of division; for it is not exposed to physical change, it is always capable of identification, and no instruments are required to fix it."[69] But this "fairest line" was itself not always clear. Curzon went on to note "the well-known geographical fact that in the greatest mountain systems of the world, for instance, the Himalayas and the Andes, the water-divide is not identical with the highest crest, but is beyond it and at a lower elevation."[70] By this time, Curzon's was hardly an original observation.

This inconvenient geological situation – which Strachey had described in his 1854 *Physical Geography of Western Tibet* – provoked heated debates in the highest echelons of the imperial government. The War Office's Director of Military Intelligence, John Ardagh – with an eye to the tactical advantages of keeping potential enemies off the high ground – advocated refraining from more precise demarcation in the Karakoram, in the hopes of coaxing China into the expansive lower terrain of Kashgaria and the Tarim Basin while retaining effective occupation of the glacial high ground.[71] Strategically speaking, Ardagh wanted the Chinese to occupy the vast and inhospitable western Tarim Basin in order to prevent Russia from surreptitiously taking over that no-man's land. But this departed from the water-parting principle insofar as it gave up what was then believed to be the northeastern reaches of the Indus watershed.

Throughout the last three decades of the nineteenth century, military and civilian strategists struggled to agree where the strategic or natural frontiers would lie. Military advisors appreciated keeping potential enemies off the high ground; however, doing so conflicted with the natural water-parting principle, which offered both sides – theoretically at least – access to the heights. Civilian administrators tended to favor the less stringent amalgamation of boundary pillars, bodies of water, and mountains ridges that reduced the range of territory to govern. By 1890, a vague strategy had coalesced: "The Government have now decided that, for the present at any rate, the limits of the Indus watershed should be considered as the boundary of the Kashmir territories to the north, and that the line of natural water-parting . . . should be regarded as

---

[69] Curzon, 19.   [70] Curzon, 19–20.
[71] NAI, Foreign, Secret F, November, nos. 110–14. "Kashmir-Frontier. Memorandum by Sir John Ardagh."

the limit of our political jurisdiction."[72] In other words, the political line that marked the northern edge of India would be coterminous with the limit of the Indus watershed. In choosing this model, military logic co-existed with the indeterminacy of the often undemarcated watershed limits. But given the dearth of trigonometric-based survey maps of the northern and eastern edges of Ladakh, the Survey of India was obliged to rely on the sketchier shapes of a handful of traverse surveys when representing the limit of the watershed. The result was the production of two types of map: maps that showed borders relying on a handful of precise points and a speculative line representing a suggested water-parting, and maps that showed no borders at all.

On March 14, 1899, this ambiguous arrangement was formalized in a memorandum sent to the Qing Government by Claude MacDonald, the British Minster at Peking. Echoing the East India Company's language to the 1846–48 boundary commissioners, MacDonald wrote to the Zongli Yamen[73] proposing "that for the sake of avoiding any dispute or uncertainty in the future, a clear understanding should be come to with the Chinese Government as to the frontier between the two States." Yet the memo also went on to assert that "it will not be necessary to mark out the frontier. . . . The natural frontier is the crest of a range of mighty mountains, a great part of which is quite inaccessible." It was sufficient from the British perspective to outline the prominent features of the Indus watershed in the memo, and to cite this line described on a map of the "Russo-Chinese frontier brought by the late Minister, Hung Chun, from St. Petersburg, and in possession of the Yamen."[74] The vague description in the letter, which generates to this day much debate between India and China, suggested a line that largely followed what the British understood to be the Indus watershed limit, though they still did not have a satisfactory map to represent the whole region. As the viceroy, Lord Elgin, had earlier written to the Secretary of State for India, "we regret that we have no map to show the whole line either accurately or on a large scale."[75]

When Fanny Bullock Workman and her husband, Dr. Hunter Workman, requested permission from the government of India in 1912 to survey the Siachen glacier in the Karakoram, north of Ladakh, their

---

[72] NAI, Foreign, Secret F, November, nos. 110–14. "Kashmir-Frontier. Memorandum by Sir John Ardagh."

[73] The Zongli Yamen was China's Foreign Affairs body, established in 1861 and replaced with a ministerial Foreign Office in 1901.

[74] NAI, Foreign, Secret F, August 1899, nos. 168–201. There is no known surviving version of this map.

[75] Lamb, *The Sino-Indian Border in Ladakh*, 7.

expedition was given approval contingent on the inclusion of a Survey of India surveyor. The Secretary to the Foreign Department, Henry McMahon – who, like his ministerial predecessor, Mortimer Durand, would have his own infamous boundary line – acknowledged that the Workman expedition would help to confirm or adjust an earlier survey. Based on the premise that "We understand the watershed of the Indus to be our boundary and have thought that the Karakoram was that watershed," McMahon then asserted that since the watershed determined the boundary, the government of India was *not bound to adhere to the Karakoram if it is proved not to be the watershed, but will claim the real watershed as our boundary.*[76]

Further south, the Swedish explorer Sven Hedin was tracing the origins of the Indus watershed in Western Tibet. His discovery in 1907 of the perpendicular "trans-Himalaya" range complicated Humboldt's purely parallel vision of the Himalayas. In doing so, he noted that the Indus and Brahmaputra watersheds were incongruent with the mountains that were assumed to form a natural, "scientific" boundary. "The Trans-Himalaya," Hedin wrote, "is not only a watershed of the first rank, but is also a geographical boundary of exceptional importance."[77] Hedin's discovery came under criticism from subsequent generations of geographers, who argued that the so-called trans-Himalaya was an ill-defined mountain area. If Hedin proved anything, it was that watersheds could cause as much trouble in boundary making as rivers, or any other natural or human-made object.

The decades following MacDonald's and Hedin's revised lines revealed patterns much like those evident in the decades that preceded them: periods of intense interest in boundary-making, followed by years of neglect; continued restriction and standardization of maps (including the standardization of map colors and symbols) that eventually produced an agreed-upon restricted zone after independence for all transborder maps; and continued debates, between central and regional, and military and civilian administrators, about what should be done to address frontier problems.

By the twentieth century the frontier had become an idea and a space suffused with security concerns and represented by restricted trans-frontier maps. But in the northwestern Himalaya – as with other parts of the Himalayan frontier – the natural objects considered capable of providing a strong and legible border instead produced continued

[76] NAI, Foreign, Frontier B, May 1912, nos. 125–26. "Contention that the real watershed of the Indus is the (1) Kashmir Boundary if it is proved that the (2) Karakoram range is not the water shed." My emphasis.
[77] Hedin, *Trans-Himalaya*, 1:273.

complications. The vastness of the land to be surveyed and mapped, the continued insistence on a legible water-parting line as the northern limit of India, and the increased restriction of "trans-frontier" information yielded political maps without borders.

2.4   Conclusion

A century after Governor-General Hardinge had requested "clear and well defined boundaries," the British still lacked a satisfactory border in the northwestern Himalaya. This was reflected, most graphically, by the production of maps that failed to include any borders in the region. It would become clear after independence in 1947 that "Survey of India maps issued in 1865, 1903, 1917, 1929, 1936, and 1938 [did] *not show any boundary at all* in the western (i.e. Ladakh) sector."[78] These borderless maps, supposedly precise, included the formal representation of territorial ignorance (e.g., Maps 2.7 and 2.8).

In the British imperial context, the practice of imbuing maps with authority involved transforming *terra incognita* into colonial territory: a process that oscillated between surveying the land and rendering it on paper. This cartographical thinking imbued maps with increasing authority. When, for instance, American arbiters were charged with resolving boundary disputes in Guyana, they went in search of maps and documents in Europe, presuming the scientific accuracy and the completeness of the work British surveyors had done on the ground in the tropics of South America. In appearing to present physicality, cartographic images attempt to settle the political and technological struggles they represent.

The cartographical construction of the northwestern Himalayan frontier was itself an epistemological development of the eighteenth and nineteenth centuries, drawing on the work of a number of geographers, most prominently "the scientific traveller *par excellence*,"[79] Alexander von Humboldt. For British surveyors and administrators of the mid-nineteenth century, the naturalness of the great Himalayan barrier – and its apparent linearity – could be reinforced through its water-partings, which increasingly acted as territorial demarcators and formed the basis of a major principle of international boundary making enshrined in international law by the twentieth century. The rise of cartographical thinking illustrates both the growing authority of colonial (and

---

[78] National Archives of the United Kingdom (NAUK). DO 196/190, 1962, "India's Himalayan Frontier." My emphasis.

[79] Kapil Raj, "La Construction de L'empire de La Géographie: L'odyssée Des Arpenteurs de Sa Très Gracieuse Majesté, La Reine Victoria, En Asie Centrale," *Annales. Histoire, Sciences Sociales* 52, no. 5 (1997): 1157.

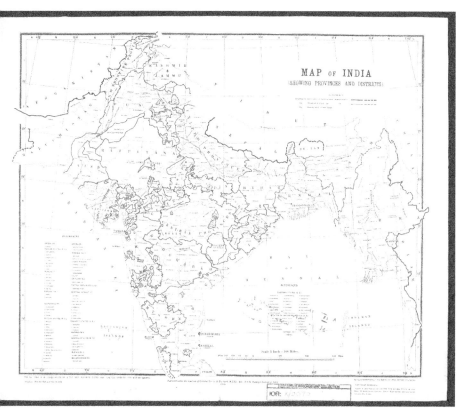

Map 2.7 "Map of India (Showing Provinces and Districts)" (1936). Survey of India. First edition published in 1915; this is the fourth edition. IOR/X/9070. Courtesy British Library.

eventually postcolonial) maps, and the evolving logics of border making. Surveying and map making came to represent a vision of a space organized and triangulated through a set of specific technologies of measurement and vision. But the clarity of that vision was often obstructed by complex mountainous landscapes, as was the case in Ladakh and the broader northwestern Himalaya.

The story of mapping the northwestern Himalaya demonstrates that it is important to disaggregate three apparently interwoven aspects of these colonial maps as historical sources: first, the representation of land and water rendered on the map from a variety of surveying practices and

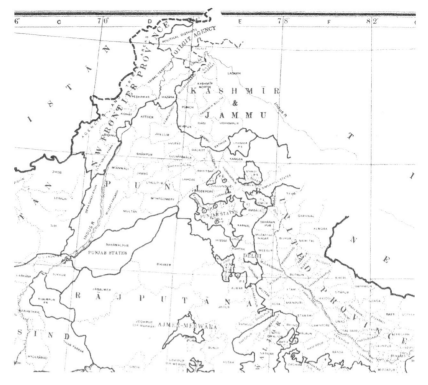

Map 2.8 Detail of Map 2.7.

speculations; second, the lines drawn over that representation to denote
political units and their limits (in other words: territory); and third, the
cartographic and geographic rationales used to render and determine the
first and the second aspects. While historians of the Himalayan borderland
do acknowledge inaccuracies on maps – particularly those produced before
1899 – as sources of disputes arising from this first aspect, they tend to
ignore the third aspect: the process and the rationale involved in making the
land, and its supposedly natural boundaries, conform to the map.

As explored in this chapter, certain practices and products worked to
facilitate this shift to a more border-centric world. Paying closer attention
to these practices – the rise of the science of surveying, and the coeval rise
of the geographical sciences – and products – maps, survey reports, the
regular publications of the Royal Geographical Society – can reveal the
deeply uneven texture of the process of border making. Such an analysis
can not only denaturalize maps, but also denaturalize frontiers and the

supposedly natural foundations upon which they were established. The history of the long-elusive border in Ladakh – a boundary supposedly derived from mountain systems and watersheds – offers a perfect test case for such a revision. The production of borderless maps of the northwestern Himalayan region reflected the simultaneous lack of sufficiently precise information and unwillingness to acknowledge that lack. It also reflected the unsuccessful application of a geographical concept – the water-parting principle – meant to provide a clear means of determining natural *and* political limits. The nature in natural was all too human.

3 Communication
Roads, Regulation, and the British Joint Commissioners

The British are the road-makers of Tibet.[1]
– Charles Bell, *Portrait of the Dalai Lama*, 1946

Following the 1846 Treaties of Lahore and Amritsar,[2] which gave the East India Company control over the newly formed princely state of Jammu and Kashmir, Governor-General Henry Hardinge penned a letter to the "Vizer [*sic*] of Lhassa-Gartok," the *gar.dpon* (governor) of Western Tibet.[3] It was to be delivered to the *gar.dpon* by the boundary commissioners Alexander Cunningham and P.A. Vans Agnew, who Hardinge had tasked with determining in the northwestern Himalaya "a clear and well defined boundary in a quarter likely to come little under observation."[4] In the letter, Hardinge articulated his hope for free trade between the new British dependency of Jammu and Kashmir and the Chinese dependency of Tibet.[5] He also stated that the East India Company had taken the liberty of modifying the 1842 Treaty of Chushul between the recently defeated Sikh Empire and the government of Tibet, signed after General Zorawar Singh's death at the hands of a Sino-Tibetan army. "Such persons," the modification went, "as may in future proceed from China to Ladakh or to the British Territory, its dependencies, or

---

[1] According to Charles Bell, this was a "Tibetan prophecy, which [he] had heard many years before." Charles Bell, *Portrait of the Dalai Lama* (London: Collins, 1946), 204.

[2] These treaties together marked the end of the First Anglo-Sikh War (Treaty of Lahore) and granted the Raja of Jammu rule of Kashmir, creating the state of Jammu and Kashmir (Treaty of Amritsar). The Treaty of Amritsar also gave paramountcy over the newly created state to the British East India Company.

[3] This title referred to the governor(s) of Western Tibet (Tib. *gar.dpon*, sometimes also spelled *sgar.dpon*) posted at Gartok, a trade mart along the bank of the upper Indus on the Leh-Lhasa route in far Western Tibet.

[4] "Governor General to Vizer [*sic*] of Lhassa-Gartok." NAI, Foreign, S.C., December 26, 1846, nos. 1331–43. "Instructions for laying down the boundary between the territory of Maharajah Golap Sing and the British Government."

[5] Tibet's status as a dependency of China became increasingly nominal over the latter half of the nineteenth century.

from Ladakh or the British territory and its dependencies to China *are not to be obstructed on the road.*"[6]

Hardinge repeatedly emphasized the importance of free travel and the need to identify accessible routes to markets beyond the limits of the Company's territory. Echoing Hardinge's instructions on the importance of locating and improving these conduits of commerce, Alexander Cunningham wrote from the "high road through Kulu to Ladak" that substantial modifications should be made to the course of that road to provide better access to the mountainous region of Ladakh and the trade that passed through it.[7] For Hardinge and for Cunningham, the development of mountain roads was the *sine qua non* of communication and commercial development on the imperial frontier. Though in reality the routes these officials referenced were often simple footpaths prone to frequent blockage and destruction – not the macadamized (or "metalled")[8] roads common in the plains of India by the mid-nineteenth century – these same modest tracks carried the aspirations and anxieties of the growing imperial state.

Roads are, at first glance, the opposite of borders, as they enhance movement and connect far-flung locales. But the imperial state in India, in the latter half of the nineteenth century, increasingly approached roads under the same logic and with the same end as borders: regulating the movement of people and goods, and establishing influence, if not always effective control, over neighboring regions. For all their ubiquity, roads rarely receive attention from historians as anything more than anonymous infrastructural technologies associated with trade, travel, and the expansion of the state – though recently several scholars have explored the histories of specific roads and the communities they impacted.[9] Yet as tools of political power and catalysts for commerce

[6] "Governor General to Vizer [*sic*] of Lhassa-Gartok." NAI, Foreign, S.C., December 26, 1846, nos. 1331–43. Instructions for laying down the boundary between the territory of Maharajah Golap Sing and the British Government." My emphasis.

[7] NAI, Foreign, S.C., August 28, 1847, nos. 162–64. "Instructions for [Captain Alexander Cunningham's] guidance on his approaching Mission to the Thibetan Frontier." Imbricating himself in the history of colonial exploration of, and expansion into, the region, Cunningham noted that "it is remarkable that we crossed the Bara-Lacha on the anniversary of the day on which Moorcroft had crossed it twenty-six years before us."

[8] The process of macadamization, named after the Scottish engineer John Loudon McAdam who first employed it around 1820, involves a layer of single-sized crushed stone placed in shallow lifts and compacted thoroughly before being topped by a layer of finer grained stone dust. Macadamization simplified earlier processes that required greater depths of stone and steeper cambers to roads.

[9] These include Joseph A. Amato, *On Foot: A History of Walking* (New York: New York University Press, 2004), which explores the long social history of walking in the Western world; Joe Moran, *On Roads: A Hidden History* (London: Profile Books, 2009), which

developed in particular locales at particular times, roads are also the point at which the changing aspirations of the state meet the environmental realities of particular lived spaces. As such, these reticular spaces are ideal objects of inquiry for examining the shifting frontier priorities of the imperial state. This chapter will focus on two roads of crucial importance to the British frontier in the northwestern Himalaya: the Hindustan–Tibet Road and the Indo-Yarkand Treaty Road.

Examining the historical development of these frontier roads also reveals notable examples of uneven infrastructural development, both within Britain and across its rapidly growing empire.[10] The imperial state in nineteenth-century India did not attempt the uniform approach to road building seen in Jo Guldi's examination of Britain's "invention" of the "infrastructure state."[11] Unlike the more systematic extension of roads across the periphery of Scotland in the eighteenth and early nineteenth centuries, British administrators in the Himalaya were willing to invest in so-called experiments like the Hindustan–Tibet Road, particularly when access to new markets in Central Asia offered the potential for commercial growth. This divergence between metropolitan policies and opportunistic imperial "experiments" inverts the arc of Guldi's *Roads to Power*. Whereas the historical road networks Guldi examined in Britain were born out of military intervention and eventually led to enhanced commerce and movement, the Himalayan roads examined in this chapter shifted in their purpose: from experiments in enhancing commerce and movement, to instruments of imperial security.[12] Thus we find examples of Himalayan trans-frontier roads left intentionally unimproved, to *prevent* "free access to

examines roads in the north of England; and Bruce D. Epperson, *Roads through the Everglades: The Building of the Ingraham Highway, the Tamiami Trail and Conners Highway, 1914–1931* (Jefferson, NC: McFarland, 2016), which explores the particular political, technological, and environmental factors at work in the construction of a road in southern Florida. (My thanks to Rob Butler for the Amato and Moran references.) There are also several notable histories of the trade routes collectively known as the Silk Road, though they tend to focus on economic and cultural exchange rather than on the development behind the routes themselves. See, for instance, James Millward, *Eurasian Crossroads: A History of Xinjiang* (New York: Columbia University Press, 2008); Valerie Hansen, *The Silk Road: A New History* (New York: Oxford University Press, 2012); and Susan Whitfield and Ursula Sims-Williams, *The Silk Road: Trade, Travel, War, and Faith* (London: British Library, 2004). For recent anthropological work most relevant to the region discussed in this chapter, see Jonathan Demenge, "The Political Ecology of Road Construction in Ladakh" (Sussex, University of Sussex, 2011).

[10] Road construction in the Punjab, for instance, was approached far more systematically than in the mountainous Himalaya.

[11] Jo Guldi, *Roads to Power: How Britain Invented the Infrastructure State* (Cambridge, MA: Harvard University Press, 2012).

[12] JKSA-J, 1924, 417/F-52. "Insertation of a rule in Kashmir Visitors' Rules regarding preventing the entry into Tibet of undesirable Indians"; and "Submission to His Highness the Maharaja Sahib Bahadur in Council, August 12, 1924."

every road into [India]."[13] In other words, by the early twentieth century roads had become a feature of the frontier complex: a key infrastructural instrument of imperial security and geopolitical thinking.[14]

This chapter focuses on the changing imperial encounter with, and expansion of, roads in the northwestern Himalaya. It begins with a brief examination of the first major British road-building endeavor in the region: the Hindustan–Tibet Road. The chapter then shifts to the colonial "man on the spot" in Ladakh: the British Joint Commissioner (BJC). From 1870 until the end of British rule in India, the BJC was tasked with overseeing "the Treaty Road" – a term used to describe the major route connecting Kashmir to Ladakh via the Zoji Pass and Ladakh to Yarkand via the Karakoram Pass.[15] This chapter explores this important frontier role in depth, using long-overlooked archival sources to show how the BJC regulated trade, gathered commercial intelligence, and controlled the flow of people across the mountainous region on a series of roads that he continually attempted to improve. Finally, the chapter examines the increased emphasis on the military role of roads by revisiting the Hindustan–Tibet Road and the Treaty Road at the turn of the twentieth century, in the context of both Younghusband's invasion of Tibet and the expanding imperial security state in India.

This chapter illustrates, quite simply, that roads create constant tension for the colonial state. These objects reflect the limits of the state's ability to gather information, the extent of its aspirations to commercial growth, and the increase of security concerns that so often accompanied the accumulation of colonial knowledge. The possibilities of commercial growth induced the colonial state to expend human and financial resources on developing trade. This increase in attention to what sources refer to as "communication" with the regions beyond the imperial frontier then required added political oversight, which in turn increased concerns

---

[13] Captain F. E. Younghusband, to the Secretary to the Foreign Department, August 1, 1890. NAI, Foreign, Keep-with ("K.W.") for Secret F, October 1890, nos. 14–31. "Notices in English and Persian to be posted at Suget, Kilian, Kugiar, Sanju, and Polu, prohibiting Travellers and explorers (European) from Central Asia from crossing the frontier of British India and States subordinate to it without a passport from the Government of India."

[14] For an overview of changes in the imperial policies of access via border roads, see Mahnaz Z. Ispahani, *Roads and Rivals: The Political Uses of Access in the Borderlands of Asia* (Ithaca, NY: Cornell University Press, 1989). For policies specific to the northeast of colonial India, see Lipokmar Dzuvichu, "Roads and the Raj: The Politics of Road Building in Colonial Naga Hills, 1860s–1910s," *Indian Economic and Social History Review* 50, no. 473 (2013): 473–94.

[15] The road was sometimes referred to as the "Leh-Yarkand Road" or the "Indo-Yarkand Road." While the BJC's jurisdiction was generally restricted to the segment from the Zoji Pass to the Karakoram Pass, the term "Treaty Road" was often used to refer the routes extending beyond those two points to Kashmir and Yarkand.

over what the imperial state did not know – which in turn encouraged the accumulation of trans-frontier commercial and political information. Thus, by the time of Younghusband's 1903–4 invasion of Tibet, frontier roads had taken on a Janus-faced role: keeping regions beyond India "open" and accessible, but working to restrict the ingress of unwanted trans-frontier groups. The interconnected histories of several prominent – if rather humble-looking – roads in the northwestern Himalaya illustrates these broader frontier trends.

3.1   Trade, Servitude, and the Hindustan–Tibet Road

The 1846 codification of Britain's relations with its newly formed dependency of Jammu and Kashmir made the northwestern Himalaya one of the most peaceful portions of a still vaguely defined imperial perimeter in India.[16] Sparsely populated and enclosed by some of the world's highest peaks, the region could be thoroughly explored, lightly administered, and easily defended. This stability convinced James Broun-Ramsay, the Earl of Dalhousie (governor-general of India from 1847 to 56 and a regular visitor to the northwestern Himalaya), to explore the potential expansion of trade routes through the mountains, in part to access the primary object of commercial interest: pashmina.[17]

Pashmina was initially referred to as "shawl wool" by the British. It would quickly become known as cashmere – reflecting the antiquated English spelling of the region in which it was manufactured. Properly speaking, pashmina is the material woven from *pashm*, the downy under-coat of the Tibetan *byang.ra*. Originating high up on the Tibetan Plateau in the goat herds of the seminomadic Changpa, the combed *pashm* was traded annually to Ladakhi or Kashmiri middlemen. The middlemen sold the wool to Kashmiri merchants who, in turn, sold it to merchants from the great shawl-weaving houses of the Kashmir Valley. European traders first encountered Kashmiri shawls in the eighteenth century: shawls marked by a characteristic woven design, often described as a teardrop with a bent tip, or as the forward bending crest of a rooster.[18]

---

[16] This was especially true when compared to the tumult that continued on the northwestern edges of the British Empire in India. (Note: Sections of this first part come from Gardner, "Ready Materials.")

[17] Dalhousie regularly visited Kalpa in Kinnaur, then known as Chini.

[18] Chitralekha Zutshi, "Designed for Eternity: Kashmiri Shawls, Empire, and Cultures of Production and Consumption in Mid-Victorian Britain," *Journal of British Studies* 48, no. 2 (2009): 420–40. The Bengali term *kalgā* (headdress) and Hindi term *kalgī* (crest, plume) are derived from a Turkic term for the forward-bending plumage of a rooster, frequently used to adorn a sultan's turban. I owe my thanks to Dipesh Chakrabarty for this etymological tidbit.

This design inspired the popular Western textile motif known today as "paisley" – named after the Scottish town that first began producing imitations of the Kashmiri pattern.

The long-established network of (mostly) Muslim traders known as the Lhasa Khaché[19] – stretching through Ladakh from Kashmir to Lhasa – further illustrated the powerful influence of the pashmina trade throughout the broader region. These trade routes were reinforced by the connections between the Buddhist centers of central Tibet and the Tibetan Buddhist centers of the western Himalaya. The reciprocal flow, between these centers, of pilgrims, monastic students, and traders ensured a well-worn network dotted with villages that could provide fresh supplies of food, as well as ponies, yaks, or donkeys for transportation.

Like the Sikhs and Dogras, the British wanted access to these trade routes, and to the potentially lucrative materials flowing along them. The first major British step toward gaining this access was the construction of the Hindustan–Tibet Road: extending from the plains of northern India up to Shimla, and then northeastward to Kinnaur, with two further planned branches leading north to Ladakh. This project, begun in the spring of 1850, utilized nearly one million laborers in its five-year initial construction phase.[20] In its first years, more than 60 percent of the labor used was unpaid, furnished by the individual hill states as part of an agreement to offer indentured service (known as *begār*) to their suzerain rulers.

The initial justifications for the road were threefold. First, over time, the completed road could open up a commercial route to Tibet: one that would give the British dependable access to Central Asian goods and markets. Early in 1850, the Earl of Dalhousie wrote that, "this road had been mentioned to me before as being of great importance with reference to the large trade which it is believed might be attracted to the plains of India from the countries beyond the Himalayan range."[21] In particular, the British would gain access to *pashm*, the raw material for pashmina: the exotic and luxurious fabric in high demand, by this time, among the Victorian British upper classes.

Second, the widening of the first stages of the road would quickly ease the difficulties of a growing number of British tourists from India visiting the hills, some to partake of the sanatoria multiplying there. This rationale

[19] See Chapter 1.
[20] United Kingdom, "Minutes and Correspondence in Reference to the Project of the Hindostan and Thibet Road, with Reports of Major Kennedy and Lieutenant Briggs Relating Thereto; and, an Account of the Expenditure Incurred in the Construction of the New Road between Kalha and Dugshai."
[21] United Kingdom, House of Commons 1857, 4.

was, perhaps, the main reason why so much work was done so quickly. By 1850, British officials were increasingly escaping to the milder climate of the hills.[22] Following the Rebellion of 1857, this trend intensified. Beyond growing fears of disease and "degeneration" in the plains, as Barbara and Thomas Metcalf have noted, the hills were also "meant to reproduce England."[23] These "hill stations" became not only sites of refuge and leisure, but also sites of governance – most notably in the case of Shimla, the summer capital of the British Raj.

The third reason the British gave for the road's construction was the abolition of the *begār* system of indentured servitude, which, in the tradition of ironic logics of rule in South Asia, they themselves had exploited. As John Bray has shown, forms of obligatory labor – most commonly referred to by the generic Urdu/Persian term *begār* – had long been present in the western Himalayan hill states, Ladakh, Kashmir, and Tibet. This *corvée* labor had been used in road construction in the region at least as far back as the sixteenth century.[24] For the British, however, the system of local semifeudal obligations between hill chiefs and their peasantry offered a cheap and convenient means of travel in regions where commercial transport was otherwise costly or not available. In particular, *begār* allowed for transport to and around the growing number of hill stations, which the British were building in the foothills of the Himalayas. "As embodied in their settlement agreements," Ramachandra Guha notes, "landholders were required to provide, for all government officials on tour and for white travellers (e.g., shikaris and mountaineers), several distinct sets of services."[25] These included laborers for carrying loads and building temporary rest huts, as well as provisions. According to the papers on the Hindustan–Tibet Road's construction, the use of these indentured laborers appears to have been most widespread on the initial segment of the road, running from the plains at Kalka up to Shimla (Figure 3.1). Dalhousie wrote in 1850 that his "first experience of the system, when my camp came to Simla in April 1849, satisfied me that it was a great and crying evil, and I have since that time both seen and heard much that has not only confirmed my conviction of the reality of the oppression, but has determined me to omit no effort to effect its removal."[26] For Dalhousie,

---

[22] See Pamela Kanwar, *Imperial Simla: The Political Culture of the Raj* (Delhi: Oxford University Press, 1990); and Dane Kennedy, *The Magic Mountains: Hill Stations and the British Raj* (Berkeley: University of California Press, 1996).

[23] Tom Metcalf and Barbara Metcalf, *A Concise History of Modern India* (Cambridge: Cambridge University Press, 2001), 111.

[24] Bray, "Corvée Transport Labour," 46.

[25] Ramachandra Guha, *The Unquiet Woods: Ecological Change and Peasant Resistance in the Himalaya* (Berkeley: University of California Press, 2000), 25.

[26] United Kingdom, House of Commons 1857, 3.

Figure 3.1 Samuel Bourne, "The view from the new road at Pangi – the Great Chini Peaks in the background" (1866). © Victoria and Albert Museum, London.

the "first step towards this end was the formation of a road from Simla to the plains at Kalka, capable of being easily and safely travelled by baggage animals."[27]

The expansion of access to Shimla and alleviation of *begār* may have been the most immediate reasons for expanding the existing rough road between the plains and the summer capital, but neither reason was deemed a major factor in the construction of much of the rest of the road, which extended beyond Shimla along the Sutlej and into the mountains toward the Tibetan Plateau. In the case of *begār*, colonial officials occasionally mentioned but largely ignored the problem, for the remainder of British rule. The practice continued in parts of the Northwestern Himalaya, such as Ladakh, beyond independence in 1947.[28]

---

[27] United Kingdom, 3.
[28] The reincarnate lama and preeminent political figure of postindependence Ladakh, Kushok Bakula Rinpoche, noted this problem in nearly identical letters to Sheikh Abdullah and Jawaharlal Nehru in 1951. See Ganesan, Deputy Secretary to Govt. of

The papers concerning the initial phase of construction of the Hindustan–Tibet Road detail the technological and physical struggles to master the rivers, mountains, and passes of this terrain. The British attempt to intervene physically in this mountainous landscape represented both an ambitious, laborious undertaking and a substantial financial investment. Regarding the determination of the exact route of the road, one superintendent, Lieutenant David Briggs, wrote:

> It ... appears beyond a doubt that the best line between Thibet and Hindostan, whether in a commercial, mathematical, or political point of view, is one from the uplands of Chang Tang through Bassahir and Simlah to the plains near Kalka. Here and here only has the awful barrier of the Himalayahs been pierced and its ramifications threaded by the waters of the Sutluj, so that passes of great elevation do not present themselves, and the mathematical correctness of the line is not impaired. This is the line that has been adopted for the Hindostan and Thibet Road. ... When completed, the keen reproach uttered by Moorcroft thirty-five years ago, will have lost its point and applicability.[29]

Recall William Moorcroft's insistence on the viability and profitability of Central Asian trade through the northwestern Himalaya. His views had been met with little interest by the directors of the East India Company decades earlier.[30] But under Dalhousie's expansionist policies, commercial opportunities in Central Asia seemed increasingly viable.

Despite the grandiosity of the road-building endeavor and the concurrent rhetoric of experimentality, the project itself was placed in the hands of military engineers, who spoke of it in the dry language of technological challenge. Major J.P. Kennedy, the first superintendent tasked with overseeing the road's construction, wrote regarding the planning process that "the obviously correct mathematical line for a road passing from the plains northward through the Hill States, offering at once a commercial communication with Central Asia through the Hill States, and an approach to our several sanitary stations, was indicated by the course of the rivers Jumna, with some of its tributaries, and the Sutlej."[31] Kennedy's statement reflected an assertion earlier expressed by Alexander Cunningham while on assignment in Ladakh as a boundary

India, Ministry of States. NAI, Ministry of State (Kashmir), Secret, 19(16)-K52. "Political Developments in Ladakh," April 30, 1952; and "Buddhists in Ladakh; Representations from head Lama of Ladakh; General position re: Ladakh."

[29] Here, Lieutenant Briggs, supervisor of much of the Hindustan–Tibet Road's construction, cites William Moorcroft's unheeded warning (c. 1820) that "whether [Tibetans and Central Asians] shall be clothed with the broadcloth of Russia or of England ... with hardware of every description from Petersburgh [i.e., St. Petersburg] or Birmingham, is entirely in the decision of the Government of British India." United Kingdom, House of Commons 1857, 73.

[30] See Chapter 1.   [31] United Kingdom, House of Commons 1857, 6–7.

commissioner, namely, that "mathematically" rerouting, expanding, or grading existing paths alongside the region's major rivers could reduce the friction of movement across this mountainous landscape, thereby "opening up" regions beyond the frontier to British commercial development.

Initially the Hindustan–Tibet Road project employed an average of 3,000 laborers daily. This number steadily increased. The irregular arrival of conscripted labor proved to be a continual problem for the overseers. One superintendent exasperatedly wrote in 1851: "When at last the numbers [of laborers] were down to so low an ebb that the native chiefs (threatened by the Superintendent of the Hill States) became alarmed, a large influx of wild hill-men was poured upon the road, a sufficiency of tools was wanting for so great an increase, and could not be procured at a moment's warning; the mass was utterly ignorant of the work required of them."[32]

The lack of consistent labor and the apparent failure of the local chiefs to provide food and shelter for their own finally forced the road's superintendents to pay more of their laborers a bare minimum wage. This increased cost resulted in a reduced expenditure on the construction of routes deemed less critical. The road from Shimla to Ladakh, via Kullu, was considered one such route.[33] Dalhousie described it as one of several branches "intended to open up the commerce of central Asia with Hindustan . . . of importance also, but its completion is of less immediate consequence."[34] Enhancing access to the increasing number of British sanatoria in the hills became the principal short-term consideration of the road builders.

The project faced numerous technological challenges over the next five years. Rocks impeding the road's course resulted in the experimental utilization of heavy quantities of gunpowder to demolish them. (Similar technologies designed for military use were employed in surveying.) While the latter portion of the Hindustan–Tibet Road's proposed route in Kinnaur was surrounded by relatively barren land, Briggs suggested that certain areas immediately surrounding the road could be planted with deodar, so that "in 20 years . . . the Government will be in possession of the finest timber in India."[35] This potentially innovative method of replenishing timber supplies – depleted as a result of high demand for temporary bridges, workers' lodgings, and cooking fuel – never came to fruition. However, other regions of the Himalaya became heavily utilized timber sources, particularly from the 1860s onward.

---

[32] United Kingdom, House of Commons 1857, 32.
[33] This is the route discussed by the boundary commissioner Alexander Cunningham at the start of this chapter.
[34] United Kingdom, House of Commons 1857, 12.   [35] United Kingdom, 44.

Throughout the documents relating to the road's construction there is scant mention of the working conditions of the people who built it. One temporary superintendent, however, revealingly wrote that "the road coolies unquestionably suffer, and are mulet [i.e., mules] in every possible way, though this would be denied, and stoutly, and which is my firm belief, makes the coolies detest every one and every thing connected with the road."[36] Injury and fatality statistics were not kept for the native workers, though occasional reports on "casualties of European troops" suggested that the numbers of Indian deaths were likely considerable – since there were thousands of native laborers for each European troop, and since the dangers of road building were many and varied. One casualty report for British troops read: "One man Private George Lewis severely wounded by the accidental blowing up of a rock and who died at Dughai on the twentieth December 1850. Another man Private William Smedley killed by falling from a precipice 7th April 1851."[37]

In addition to those conscripted through *corvée* labor and those who worked freely, thousands of prisoners were also used to build sections of the road. "Not the least remarkable circumstance connected with this work is, that it was constructed almost entirely by prisoners, and without a single accident. The night reliefs were alone composed of free labourers, and a few of the same class during the day, assisted the convicts in wheeling barrows, and in such work as their chains rendered irksome."[38] These remarks give a passing glance at the degree of coercion that accompanied this massive infrastructural undertaking.

By 1855, as construction slowly proceeded closer to "Chinese Tartary," Briggs optimistically looked beyond the commercial value of the road, suggesting that in the lower elevations there might one day be a colony of British retirees whose sons could supply the base of a growing and "acclimated" army.

It has been stated by some, that the annual repairs of this road will be enormous. . . . As traffic increases, it will probably be necessary to metal[39] certain portions of the line, but it is to be supposed that the increased traffic will afford increased income. But far above and beyond these considerations, is the opening out of the fertile vallies of these mountains to future European colonists. . . . All, and far more than the early colonists of America ever promised themselves, is to be found here, where under the blessings of a mild and paternal government, the

---

[36] United Kingdom, 60.
[37] NAI, Foreign, Political B, December 22, 1852, no. 278. "Casualties of European troops on the HTR."
[38] United Kingdom, 47.
[39] That is, to use broken stones to reinforce the surface of the road, possibly through macadamization.

colonist might increase his store, as *fully assured of safety to life and property, as if the scene were in the heart of Great Britain, instead of under the shadows of the mighty Himalayahs.* Instead of permitting the old worn-out European pensioner to idle away all that is left to him of life, under the scorching sun of Chunar, it might be worthy the attention of government to give him a cottage and a spot that he might call his own within some of these elevated vallies; where, with something to occupy his time, he might, under proper superintendence, lay the foundations of an European colony; the youth of which, educated to a military life ... might furnish our Indian army with recruits as strong, and better educated and accli-mated, than the mother country does produce.[40]

Briggs's optimism for potential "European colonists" highlights the perception of the region as a secure space in which British pensioners and children might flourish – a space far away from any perceived external threats or, indeed, from any border that required defending.

Though Briggs's plan was never formally implemented, his tone reflects an optimism and experimentality found as a common theme in early writings about the road. The governor-general himself echoed this attitude. Responding to an earlier report by Briggs, Dalhousie triumphantly wrote:

The whole thing was experimental. People scoffed at the idea of being able to form a level road through these enormous mountains at all. No estimate could be formed of the expense, for no data existed by which to calculate it. Any reference to the Military Board[41] would have been useless for this reason. I, therefore, took upon myself the responsibility of ordering its construction at once, directly under my own authority. I venture to think that the experiment has been eminently successful.[42]

The governor-general's tone here suggests that the project, or the tech-nical challenge of it, may have been its own end. The road's construction illustrated – to some at least – that one of the most challenging landscapes on earth could be "tamed."

By the time of the Rebellion of 1857, the road had reached just beyond Sarahan, approximately 100 miles beyond Shimla toward Western Tibet.

---

[40] United Kingdom, House of Commons 1857, 80–81. My emphasis.

[41] First established in 1785, the Military Boards were composed of various top military personnel within each of the three presidencies of India (Bengal, Bombay, and Madras). They grew to be quite powerful governing bodies; too powerful, from certain points of view. Dalhousie happily abolished the institution in 1855, noting that when he had first come to India the Military Boards were "omnipotent and omnipresent." Dalhousie wrote that the institution "managed everything and marred everything. It had under it the Commissariat, the Ordnance, the Powder Factory, the Gun Foundry, the Department of Public Works, the Studs and divers other things. One by one, I have got the departments withdrawn and now the Board itself, supposed to be immortal and invulnerable, is dead and buried. So may all Boards perish." H. A. Young, *The East India Company's Arsenals & Manufactories* (Oxford: Clarendon Press, 1937), 17.

[42] United Kingdom, House of Commons, 1857, 54.

Work resumed in 1861, but at a smaller scale and with a goal of making "a road suitable for pack mules only."[43] A fatal accident in 1864 of a British officer convinced the government to close the upper branch of the road through Sarahan and "that solid roadways be made to replace the wooden galleries which then traversed the cliff faces." Work recommenced several years later, stopped again in 1869, and started again in 1874–75. When it stopped yet again, in 1875, it was still "4.5 marches short of its objective" of the frontier around the Shipki-*la*.[44] As was the case of much of the road, the route up to this pass followed a preexisting "native path." The mountain ridges near the Shipki-*la* signaled, roughly, where the Chinese frontier was understood to begin.

The massive undertaking of the Hindustan–Tibet road's construction – particularly in the wider portions closer to the plains – required a vast amount of labor. Additionally, it generated a considerable paper trail: detailed accountings of the progress made, and the technological processes involved, in surveying, constructing, and recording the project. The failure of the road to produce any significant commercial results, however, led to British reluctance to continue developing routes to Central Asia and Tibet from the region south of Ladakh. By the mid-1870s, we find references to the road being occasionally used by a growing number of hunters, tourists, geologists, and botanists, but rarely by traders of any sort. One anonymous commentator in the *Pall Mall Gazette*, reviewing Major T. C. Montgomerie's "Routes in the Western Himalaya, Kashmir, &c," noted that "no attempt has been made to continue 'the great Hindustan and Tibet road' past Pangay[45] to the frontier of Chinese Tartary, and we understand the Indian Government has no intention of expending money on any such continuation at present." The reviewer went on to acknowledge that commercial and military rationales grew more contradictory as the road neared the frontier. "The Government has been blamed for not [continuing the road to the frontier] on the alleged ground that without the completion of this road to the Chinese border the part which has been made is useless for the purpose of developing traffic; but … it was really rather for military than commercial purposes that the road was constructed as far as Pangay."[46] The reviewer's insistence on the primacy of a military

---

[43] NAI, Foreign, Political A, April 1869, nos. 141–42; and NAI, Foreign, Secret E, September 1908, nos. 407–17, 503. "Report by Major S.H. Powell on the proposed extension of the Hindustan-Tibet to Shipki, with estimates of cost."

[44] The Tibetan and Ladakhi suffix "*la*" refers to a mountain pass. Hence, Ladakh (*la.dwags*) means "land of passes."

[45] See Figure 3.1 for a photograph of the road at "Pangi."

[46] *The Pall Mall Gazette*, July 15, 1874.

rationale behind the road's construction close to the frontier suggests that by the 1870s the road was already being understood primarily as an instrument of imperial security and only secondarily as a conduit for trade. But the questionable strategic value of the road's location casts doubts on whether such an undertaking would have ever been financed for purely military reasons, and without an anticipated revenue source.[47]

Furthermore, in all of the Parliamentary papers concerning the road's construction and in Dalhousie's own published writings there is no mention of stationing troops along its path beyond Shimla, or of the construction of any garrison beyond those temporary structures built to house EIC officers involved in the project. As his invasion of Burma revealed, Dalhousie was not a governor-general who shied away from military projects. Besides being known for his ruthless expansion of British possessions in South Asia (through conquest and his infamous Doctrine of Lapse), Dalhousie left behind him a tremendous series of public works (roads, telegraph lines, irrigation systems, and the beginnings of a railway system.) But again, he never articulated a connection between the Hindustan–Tibet Road and these broader infrastructural projects. Perhaps, then, the road was primarily a pet project of his – simply an "experiment," as he frequently described it, but one with the possible benefit of added revenue from trade in pashmina and an easy conduit for travelers seeking outdoor adventure. Or perhaps it was built, like many a monument, to symbolize territorial dominance and the challenge of the undertaking. One thing remains certain: whatever motivations spurred the initial construction of the Hindustan–Tibet Road, frontier security or control was not among them.

In any case, by the 1870s it was clear to the imperial government that, in the words of the Duke of Argyll (then Secretary of State for India), "the commercial value of the road in question has been much exaggerated, and that the outlay on it should, for the future, be confined within the narrowest possible limits."[48] The duke went on to suggest that, while he agreed further funding should be minimal due to financial constraints, he

---

[47] The road was originally directed at the trade marts of western Tibet, most notably Gartok, that were found along the route that paralleled the arc of the Himalayas from central Tibet to the Karakoram and the Silk Road entrepôts of the Tarim Basin. But apart from these small seasonal trading centers, there were few strategic "targets" that would require a military presence – and the corresponding construction of a military road. The road north from Ladakh to Yarkand was a far more direct route to Central Asia, while the routes through Sikkim and the Chumbi Valley were the most direct access routes to Lhasa and Shigatse.

[48] Duke of Argyll, Secretary of State for India to Government of India, February 24, 1870. NAI, Foreign, Political A, April 1870, no. 120. "No further expense to be incurred on the Hindoostan and Thibet Road for the present."

believed that the road's potential role as "an alternative route ... into Chinese Tartary, is a matter of considerable importance, and one which should not be lost sight of when a favourable opportunity occurs."

3.2   The Treaty Road and the British Joint Commissioners

In the years following the Rebellion of 1857, the British renewed their interest in the commercial potential of Central Asia. However, they did so by focusing on the region north of the line of the Hindustan–Tibet Road, running from the plains of the Punjab through Kashmir and Ladakh. In 1867, the government of India sent Dr. Henry Cayley[49] to Kashmir and Ladakh to gather information on trade with Yarkand, Kashgar, and the broader region known to the British as Eastern – or Chinese – Turkestan.[50] The British pressured the Maharaja of Jammu and Kashmir to acquiesce to the "experimental measure" of posting a British officer in Ladakh, though his officials there were already displeased by Cayley's presence.[51] After three years of travel throughout the region, Cayley wrote a report praising its commercial potential. Key to this potential was a series of narrow paths: variable in quality but all capable of substantial improvement that would lead to greater traffic and trade.[52]

On April 2, 1870, the Government of India and the Maharaja of Jammu and Kashmir signed a treaty meant to expand British access to Central Asian markets.[53] The treaty began by declaring that, "with the consent of the Maharaja, officers of the British Government will be appointed to survey the trade routes through the Maharaja's territories from the British frontier of Lahoul to the territories of

---

[49] Cayley, trained as a physician at London's King's College Hospital, had joined the Indian Medical Service in 1857 and served as a military surgeon during the Rebellion of 1857. For a detailed account of Cayley's diplomatic and medical mission to Ladakh, see John Bray, "Dr Henry Cayley in Ladakh: Medicine, Trade and Diplomacy on India's Northern Frontier," in *Tibetan and Himalayan Healing – An Anthology for Anthony Aris*, ed. Charles Ramble and Ulrike Roesler (Kathmandu: Vajra Books, 2015), 81–95.

[50] NAI, Foreign, Political A, July 1870, nos. 90–115. "Appointment of Dr. Cayley as first joint commissioner for the new route to Eastern Turkistan."

[51] W. S. Seton-Karr, Secy to Govt. of India, Foreign Dept., to T. H. Thornton, Secretary to Government of Punjab, November 9, 1868. NAI, Foreign, Political A, November 1868, no. 82. "Wish of the Maharaja that the appointment of a British officer to Ladakh should not be renewed next season."

[52] IOR/L/PS/20/226. "Reports on the trade routes through Ladakh to Yarkand, by Dr H Cayley, on special duty at Ladakh, and W H Reynolds, Assistant Surveyor; with opinion of Maj T G Montgomerie, Officiating Superintendent, Grand Trigonometrical Survey of India, on routes between Punjab and Turkistan, and connected papers, 1870–71."

[53] NAI, Foreign, Political A, July 1870, nos. 73–118. "Treaty with the Maharaja of Cashmere for improving communications between British India and Eastern Turkistan."

the Ruler of Yarkund."[54] It went on to state that whichever route was determined by the surveyors as "best suited for the development of trade with Eastern Turkestan, shall be declared by the Maharaja a free highway in perpetuity and at all times for all travellers and traders."[55] For "the supervision and maintenance of the road in its entire length through the Maharaja's territories," the treaty mandated the appointment of two commissioners tasked with enforcing regulations and settling "disputes between carriers, traders, travellers, or others using the road."[56] One of these two was the British Joint Commissioner (BJC). The other was typically the Maharaja's representative and chief administrator in Ladakh: the *wazīr-i-wazārat*.

The treaty defined the jurisdiction of the British Joint Commissioner, confining it – at least, on paper – to a certain amount of space surrounding the road itself:

The jurisdiction of the Commissioners shall be defined by a line on each side of the road at a maximum width of two Statute *koss*,[57] except where it may be deemed by the Commissioners necessary to include a wide extent for grazing grounds. Within this maximum width the Surveyors appointed under Article 1 shall demarcate and map the limits of jurisdiction which may be decided on by the Commissioners as most suitable, including grazing grounds; and the jurisdiction of the Commissioners shall not extend beyond the limits so demarcated.[58]

The routes to be identified by the British Joint Commissioner and *wazīr-i-wazārat* would come to be called the "Treaty Road." The British Joint Commissioner was in effect a district commissioner of a road stretching across the territory of a princely state under the indirect rule of the British. While his jurisdiction was technically restricted to the road and its immediate environs, in practice these officers often exceeded the treaty's mandate, exerting pressure on the *wazīr-i-wazārat* either directly in Ladakh's capital, Leh, or indirectly through the BJC's superior, the "Officer on Special Duty in Kashmir" (later titled the Resident in Kashmir).

The BJC – in keeping with practices Cayley had initiated – was tasked with keeping diaries and trade statistics, and forwarding them to his superiors in the Foreign Department by way of the Resident in Kashmir. Diaries were sent weekly, fortnightly, or monthly; they were regularly inspected and initialed by the secretary to the Foreign Department and the viceroy. These diaries and trade reports reveal the

[54] C. U. Aitchison, ed., *A Collection of Treaties, Engagements, and Sanads, Relating to India and Neighbouring Countries* (Calcutta: Office of the Superintendent of the Government Printing, India, 1892), 9:360–62.

[55] Aitchison, *A Collection of Treaties*, 360–62.   [56] Aitchison.

[57] One *kos* is roughly 2.25 miles.   [58] Aitchison, *A Collection of Treaties*, 360–62.

central position of the Treaty Road in the political and commercial life of an imperial administrator on the frontier, as well as insights into day-to-day events in Ladakh.[59] In the typology of space enumerated in Chapter 1, the commissioners viewed Ladakh primarily in the political and material modes.

While the activities of the BJC and the *wazīr-i-wazārat* stretched well beyond road repair, one of the most striking features of the voluminous diaries they kept is the preeminent position of information about the state of the roads.[60] Throughout the hundreds of surviving "Ladakh Diaries" held at the National Archives of India, it is clear that the condition of roads was an essential precondition for all other kinds of commercial and political information. Those mundane details – the amount of snow on the passes, the states of the paths themselves, the feed available at roadside serais, the structural integrity of bridges, and more – shaped all other information about communication, intelligence, and trade.

3.2.1   Commercial Intelligence: Dr. Henry Cayley and Robert Shaw

The British signatory to the 1870 commercial treaty between Britain and the Maharaja of Jammu and Kashmir was not Dr. Henry Cayley, but instead Thomas Douglas Forsyth. Forsyth, a career administrator and diplomat, had long argued for the expansion of trade between India and Yarkand, a Silk Road entrepôt around the western Tarim Basim. In the summer of 1870, he led an expedition to Yarkand accompanied by Robert Shaw, a tea planter with similar hopes and ambitions for Central Asian trade. Following Forsyth's signing of the treaty in 1870, Cayley was sent to Ladakh for a period limited to six months. When, in 1873, the government of India wished to appoint a permanent Resident at the Kashmir *Darbār*,[61] "the Maharaja suggested as a compromise that the British Joint Commissioner might be allowed to remain at Leh throughout the year," a solution that the British accepted until the appointment of the Officer on Special Duty in Kashmir in 1877.[62]

---

[59] On the relationship between diaries and frontier governance in the eastern Himalaya, see Bérénice Guyot-Réchard, "Tour Diaries and Itinerant Governance in the Eastern Himalayas, 1909–1962," *The Historical Journal* 60, no. 4 (2017): 1023–46.

[60] This is equally so for the few surviving records of the *wazīr-i-wazārat*. See JKSA-J, File 924, *rapot-i majmū'ī-yi wazārat-i ladākh bābat-i sāl-i [19]39 wa 1940* [General Report of the Ministry of Ladakh for the year 1883–84 CE].

[61] The term darbār referred to the court of a ruler of a princely state as well as his or her ministers and government – hereafter "darbar."

[62] Resident in Kashmir to Foreign Department, October 25, 1887. NAI, Foreign, Frontier A, April 1888, nos. 164–65. "Desire of the Kashmir Darbar to constitute the sale of 'Kut' root in Leh, a state monopoly."

Cayley's first task in Ladakh was to determine a precise and optimal location for the road he was to govern. Of this process, he wrote,

My journey will, of course, take time, . . . but it is most important that the future trade route beyond the Changchenmo [far-eastern Ladakh] should be definitely settled, and I can only do this satisfactorily by personally examining all the different routes. I shall be able afterwards, in consultation with Pundit Bukshi Ram [the *wazīr-i-wazārat*], to lay down the road through Ladakh Proper, and arrange for serais &c.[63]

After months surveying these regions, Cayley and Bukshi Ram gave instructions to crews tasked with improving the selected routes, largely comprising local inhabitants conscripted for short-term bouts of unpaid labor. Returning to Ladakh in 1873 after a year's interlude, Cayley revealed that the "road from the Indus to the Changchenmo by Fantsi is now excellent, and serais have already been built at several places which I pointed out last year." Besides overseeing the initial improvement to several branches of the Treaty Road, Cayley spent much of his time in Leh overseeing a small medical practice and training a native doctor.[64]

Cayley's regular memoranda to the Foreign Department joined similar reports submitted from locations along the Indian frontier with Tibet. This flow of information helped the imperial government weigh the relative merits of different trade routes to Tibet and Central Asia. As early as 1874, administrators in the Foreign Department were remarking that, for access to Tibet, "the route by Darjeeling [in the central Himalaya] will probably be found the easiest to develop, and therefore the most attractive to trade."[65] But this did not dissuade numerous officials from promoting Ladakh as an established and suitable access point for Tibetan and Central Asian markets. Cayley's reports on the riches of Central Asian towns like Yarkand and Kashgar painted an optimistic picture of commercial opportunities across the mountains.

Cayley's successor Robert Shaw, appointed in 1871, was equally enthused about the prospects of Central Asian trade along the Treaty Road. Beyond Shaw's own interests in private trade, some of this enthusiasm was no doubt the result of attention paid to the region by the very

---

[63] NAI, Foreign, Political A, August 1870, nos. 242–55. "Weekly narrative of events connected with the mission to Ladakh."

[64] NAI, Foreign, Political A, October 1873, nos. 167–78. "Ladakh Diary From 4 to 31 August and from 1 to 14 September 1873." This also illustrates John Bray's point about how medicine, diplomacy, and trade often worked together through the early British encounter with Ladakh. See John Bray, "Dr Henry Cayley in Ladakh."

[65] NAI, Foreign, Political A, 1874, nos. 289–91. "Trade route between Thibet and Central Asia." From Secretary of State for India to Government of India, India Office, London, July 2, 1874.

top of the imperial administration. "A special report on the road has been called for by His Excellency the Viceroy," Shaw noted, "and will be furnished, according to instructions, on my arrival at Leh."[66] The result of the initial "efforts of Government in opening out the road and encouraging the mule traffic is one of very great importance." Shaw had already made efforts back in Britain to sell the potential value of Central Asian trade. "When advocating the claims of the Turkistan market to the attention of English manufacturers and merchants," Shaw wrote in his Ladakh diary in July 1873, "I was met by the objection that the local carriage to be obtained in the remote hill districts through which the route passes would be insufficient for the transport of a trade of any importance." But the initial improvements made to the main routes solved this carriage problem "in the most satisfactory manner." However, Shaw's visit to the road in southeastern Ladakh (Rupshu) proved that not all locals – whether paid or coerced – could be relied upon to improve the roads or provide the necessary carriage. "Experience shows," he wrote, "that it is a futile waste of funds to send general directions to Tibetan headmen to improve the road."

The Ladakh Diaries, as the Foreign Department quickly came to label the commissioners' reports, provide a detailed glimpse into the daily life of the BJC and the traders and local officials he regularly encountered. While the form the diaries took varied over time, and the level of detail varied according to the enthusiasm of each officer, the entries invariably focused on the conditions of the roads, and on the variety of experiences linked to them. In the entries' day-to-day style we catch glimpses of the lives (and deaths) of those passing through the region. For example, one daily entry simply noted that "the dead body of a Hajjee [Muslim pilgrim] was lying near the camping-ground of Malikshah, on the old road. Another dead body is reported to be lying at Nischoo, on the original route via Lingzithang."[67]

Other entries reflected logistical difficulties that traders often brought to the BJC's attention. "[The] dak [mail] runners on the road have not been supplied with food at their respective stations, as promised when they were sent out, and are consequently in great distress." In response, the BJC sent "Rupees 5 for provisions for all the men along the road, with orders for all to return to Lahoul as the season is so far advanced."[68] The

---

[66] BJC on Special Duty, Ladakh to Sec of Punjab Govt., July 18, 1873. NAI, Foreign, Political A, September 1873, no. 27. "Ladakh Diary from 25 June to 3 August 1873."
[67] NAI, Foreign, Political A, February 1872, nos. 52–65. "Ladakh Diary from twentieth August to 25 Nov. 1871."
[68] NAI, Foreign, Political A, March 1872, nos. 402–4. "Ladakh Diary from 12 to 18 Nov 1871."

road was the center of the BJC's world; all information he provided to the government of India depended on its condition.

The Ladakh Diaries for the first half of the 1870s reveal a theme that would continue for the remainder of British rule in India. Roads were endlessly improvable. Yet when satisfactory improvements did not lead to dramatic surges in trade revenue (see the trade figures compiled in Figure 3.2), blame was cast on the continued poor conditions of the roads and the seasonal variability in their opening, or on the damages caused by unexpected floods or rock slides. In a certain sense, the condition of the Treaty Road became a Rorschach test for the British administrators. The BJCs could see endless possibilities and endless problems simultaneously, in the series of humble paths they were tasked with regulating and improving. However, by the late 1870s, events in Central Asia would push the government of India to approach these roads from a new perspective. Information, rather than goods, became the more valuable commodity traveling along them.

3.2.2   Political Intelligence: Ney Elias and Henry Ramsay

Though largely forgotten today, Ney Elias was one of the best-known British explorers of the late nineteenth century.[69] Both he and Henry Morton Stanley won the Royal Geographical Society's top gold medals in 1873: the Founder's Medal and the Patron's Medal, respectively.[70] Elias became the British Joint Commissioner in Ladakh in 1877. Unlike his predecessors, who were primarily tasked with developing commercial connections with Central Asia, Elias was instructed to keep a close watch on political events beyond the frontier – particularly in Kashgar and Yarkand.[71] Robert Shaw, who Elias replaced as BJC, was sent to Srinagar to become the top British official stationed there, in the newly created role of "Officer on Special Duty in Kashmir" (later renamed "Resident in Kashmir"). Elias would report directly to Shaw, who

---

[69] Gerald Morgan, *Ney Elias: Explorer and Envoy Extraordinary in High Asia* (London: George Allen & Unwin, 1971), 15. Morgan is, admittedly, a rather fawning and strangely psychoanalytical biographer, which might be accounted for by the author's own relation to Elias.

[70] In receiving the Society's top prize for a combination of daring travel and information gathering in Central Asia or Tibet, Elias joined a pantheon of colonial-era Himalayan explorers, that included Henry Strachey (1852), Thomas Thomson (1866), Robert Shaw (1872), Nain Singh (1877), Henry Trotter (1878), Thomas Holdich (1887), Francis Younghusband (1890), Hamilton Bower (1894), George Curzon (1895), Sven Hedin (1898), and many others.

[71] Morgan, *Ney Elias*, 109; and NAI, Foreign, Secret, 206–29, April 1878. "Ney Elias, British Joint Commissioner, Ladakh. Appointed to officiate as British Joint Commissioner and directed to collect information of events in Eastern Turkestan."

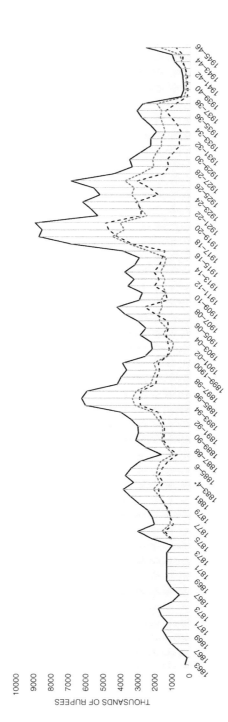

Figure 3.2 Total import and export figures via Ladakh (1863–1946). Compiled from annual trade statistics submitted by the British Joint Commissioners in Ladakh. NAI and IOR, British Library.

would report to the secretary to the Foreign Department. In each report to the secretary, Shaw would send along the most recent Ladakh Diaries, with his own summaries included. He would then direct the Foreign Department's attention to any particularly pressing matters.

The main reason Elias was appointed BJC in 1877 was to gather intelligence on the northwestern Himalayan frontier, especially concerning Russian encroachment on India. The need for intelligence had become pressing after the death, earlier in May 1877, of Ya'qub Beg. Beg was a critical figure, from the British point of view, for staving off Russian and Chinese incursions in the area.[72] In 1862 the population of Eastern Turkestan had revolted against the Qing imperial authorities who had controlled the region for over a century. Ya'qub Beg, a strongman from the Khanate of Khoqand (in present-day Tajikistan) emerged as ruler of the whole region. As a result of a slow trickle of information about the revolt, Eastern Turkestan became an object of concern for the British and Russian governments, both of which saw diplomatic and economic opportunities opened up by the Qing defeat. In his account of traveling through the region in 1868–69, Robert Shaw had noted that the Qing retreat brought massive upheaval to the region, with Kirghiz nomads looting Kashgar and committing various atrocities against the city's population. Beg was able to restore order with a string of executions in Kashgar.[73] In addition to lauding the great commercial potential of Eastern Turkestan, Shaw also noted the advantage of having Beg's territories interposed between the British, Russian, and Chinese empires. But this convenient buffer was eroded with the Qing reconquest of the Tarim Basin in 1876, and given the final blow with Beg's death in 1877. Seeing this block to Russian and Chinese expansion removed, the government of India began to pay closer attention to events on their otherwise quiet northwestern Himalayan frontier. To oversee this intelligence gathering, they sent Ney Elias to Ladakh as BJC, with the hope that he might also travel directly to Kashgar to report on the situation there. But excessive snows across the Karakoram Pass prevented Elias from going to Kashgar in 1878. Elias remained in Ladakh instead, and began to gather intelligence from traders, state officials, and pilgrims.

Roads were synonymous with a broad sense of communication. For Elias, the great value of the Treaty Road was less as a path for the expansion of commerce and more as a pipeline for the gathering of

---

[72] Alder, *British India's Northern Frontier*, 25, 123; and Hodong Kim, *Holy War in China: The Muslim Rebellion and State in Chinese Central Asia, 1864–1877* (Stanford, CA: Stanford University Press, 2004).

[73] Robert Shaw, *Visits to High Tartary, Yarkand, and Kashgar (Formerly Chinese Tartary) and Return Journey over the Karakoram Pass* (London: J. Murray, 1871), 50.

information. "The trade hardly came up to Shaw's enthusiastic prom-
ises," wrote Elias soon after commencing his duties in Leh.[74] During
Elias's eight years as the British Joint Commissioner, he oversaw the
gathering of intelligence that regularly informed the government's views
on Central Asia, particularly in terms of Russian advances and the Qing
reconquest of Eastern Turkestan (renamed Xinjiang, or "New Frontier,"
in 1884). But while his principal object of interest was the often vague
political goings-on beyond the frontier, Elias ended up gathering a good
deal of information on how people and information circulated across
Ladakh. At a basic level, his diaries describe the conditions of movement
across the major regional routes. They also contain statistics as to who,
and what passed along those roads.

Statistics like those in Table 3.1 reveal a shift in the kinds of information the British Joint Commissioner in Ladakh was meant to collect. For
Elias, it was not enough to simply register the value of the goods carried
along the Treaty Road. He was concerned with the people moving along
it, too – for besides goods, they brought information. From this regularly
collected intelligence, Elias provided the government of India with an
increasingly detailed image of the kinds of people who crossed the vague
northern frontier of India. He also gathered crucial historical information
on the region that would help make him a frontier expert after his time
as BJC.

If Ney Elias projected confidence in his ability to extract useful information about Ladakh and the regions beyond the northern frontier of
India, Captain Henry Ramsay, who succeeded Elias as BJC in 1886,
exuded anxiety regarding the limits of British control in the region. Like
Elias, Ramsay focused primarily on expanding communication along the
Treaty Road for the purpose of gathering political intelligence from
beyond the frontier. However, a number of issues surfaced during his
tenure as BJC that cast doubts on how well he knew the road, and the
people, he was tasked to supervise.

The first of these occurred in 1887, when Ramsay realized that
a particular root, used in incense and medicine, was being traded along
the Treaty Road in a particular way. "The case has arisen through the
interference by Kashmir authorities in British subject traders of Leh, in
order to prevent them from trading in the 'kut' root which has been made
a State monopoly in the rest of Kashmir and is subject to special local
rules."[75]

---

[74] Morgan, *Ney Elias*, 111.
[75] Resident in Kashmir, October 25, 1887. NAI, Foreign, Frontier A, April 1888, nos.
164–65. "Desire of the Kashmir Darbar to constitute the sale of 'Kut' root in Leh, a state
monopoly."

Table 3.1 *Ney Elias's compilation of the "number of men and cattle composing the inward caravans of 1882"*

Routes	Men							Horses[a]				Camels	Other laden animals			
	Merchants	Attendants	Laden coolies	Pilgrims to Mecca	Women	Children	Total of people	Laden	Ridden	For sale	Total		Bullocks	Donkeys	Sheep and goats	Total
India via Kulu	52	362	252	–	2	–	668	1,767	36	–	1,803	–	–	35	765	800
India via Rampur	3	15	–	–	–	–	18	5	3	–	8	–	–	43	–	43
India via Kashmir	42	153	–	63	11	5	274	1,059	119	–	1,178	–	–	–	–	–
Changthan (Tibet)	52	1,447	85	–	–	–	1,584	1,391	104	–	1,495	–	859	2,551	36,010	39,420
Turkestan	68	426	–	110	10	–	614	1,641	198	237	2,076	22	–	44	–	66
Local from Maharaja's territory	133	2,801	722	–	–	–	3,656	1,682	10	107	1,799	–	693	3,363	–	4,056
Total	350	5,204	1,059	173	23	5	6,814	7,545	470	344	8,359	22	1,552	6,036	36,775	44,385

Note: Elias notes in his remarks that "outward caravans are estimated as equal to inward caravans; none remain at Leh."
[a] It is likely that the category of "horses" includes ponies and mules.
Source: Ney Elias Papers. Royal Geographical Society.

The circulation of this root, which British officials initially confused with betel nut used in chewing *pān*, raised the question of whether the Treaty of 1870 prevented the Kashmir Darbar from "issuing rules within the limits of the jurisdiction of the Joint Commissioners."[76]

From 1870 to 1879, when the matter first came to their attention, the BJCs had considered the entire town of Leh to be within their purview. In 1888, Ramsay's superior in Kashmir also noted the difficulty in delimiting local and "through trade," which were "so closely allied that it would be difficult to know how far taxes on the latter affected the former." Yet they also acknowledged that "the treaty had its origin for the security of the through trade only." This uncertainty pointed to a larger jurisdictional issue.

The Foreign Department acknowledged that "the limits of the jurisdiction of the Joint Commissioner have never been clearly defined."[77] As the "free high road" had yet to be determined at the time of the 1870 treaty, the "jurisdiction was to be defined by a line on each side of the road at a maximum width of 2 statute *kos*, with exceptions where grazing grounds should prove necessary." However, the only clause in the Treaty that the government of India had subsequently insisted upon was that Leh was to be "'an obligatory point' on any trade route that might be chosen." After many memoranda went back and forth between the government of India, the Officer on Special Duty in Kashmir, and the BJC, it was decided to let the matter of the trade in "kut" drop. The decision not to press the Maharaja's government was allegedly made to avoid "excit[ing] feelings of irritation and suspicion in the minds of the Darbar, quite out of proportion to the value of the commercial advantages gained."

Both Elias and Ramsay were aware of tensions between certain exceptional features of their posting and the desire for uniformity in governance. Ramsay expressed repeated concerns about the existence of the long-established reciprocal tribute mission between Ladakh and Tibet, as well as other instances of customary relations with neighboring polities that cast doubt on the nature of British paramountcy over the region. If Ladakhis continued to send a triennial tribute mission to Lhasa (known as the Lopchak), then, Ramsay feared, the political meaning of any border would be eroded. In 1889, Ramsay insisted that the Lopchak and other missions should be abolished, citing his understanding of international law to defend his position.[78]

---

[76] Resident in Kashmir.   [77] Resident in Kashmir.

[78] Ramsay wrote that "it is incompatible with our dignity as a leading Power that the petty State of Lhassa should treat Ladak, which by right of conquest belongs to one of our Indian feudatory chiefs, as being politically subordinate to Lhassa." Ramsay went so far as to cite chapter and page (chapter 2, p. 52) of Henry Wheaton's *Elements of International Law* (1864 edition). Ramsay noted that in Wheaton's canonical text, "it is there laid

Several years earlier, Ney Elias had been more circumspect. "Were Ladak a portion of India, either in territory or population," Elias wrote in 1885, "it might be necessary to administer it in uniformity with the rest of the country; but it is entirely separate as regards the one [territory], and distinct and exceptional as regards the other [population]."[79] Elias was referring to the fact that Ladakh was part of the princely state of Jammu and Kashmir and, as such, subject to the internal rule of the Maharaja. Culturally, it was also quite distinct from that of the plains. "A country like Ladak," Elias continued, "is scarcely to be found among the administrations of India, and its people are, as yet, at all events, too rude and ignorant to appreciate the refinement of a lightly organized rule, while they are too few and too isolated to render it worth while to break down the self-governing institutions to which they are wedded, as a race, *for the sake of obtaining symmetry*."[80] The tension between "obtaining symmetry" and accepting anomalies surfaces in the persistence of debates over Ladakhi territory and sovereignty – including the aforesaid tribute missions between Ladakh and Tibet – that will be discussed in detail in Chapter 4.

While Elias's and Ramsay's tenures as BJC witnessed a greater focus on intelligence gathering, the condition of roads remained a primary concern. On the eve of his departure as BJC, Elias detailed the environmental obstacles to road upkeep:

In reforming the administration of Ladak, there is no subject of greater importance than improved means of communication. The external trade in every direction and the ordinary internal traffic of the province are carried on, at present, under most unfavourable conditions, on account of roads being periodically broken down by snow or rain, and bridges being carried away by freshets in the streams; while in some places traffic is entirely put a stop to, for weeks at a time, during the flood season, for want of a bridge or ferry to supply the place of the ford used in the dry season. To show the importance of keeping up the trade routes between India and Central Asia would be superfluous; it has been insisted on by every Political Agent who has been in Ladak since 1866, and has been acknowledged by Government in their treaty of 1870 with the Kashmir State, which provides, above all things, for promoting trade between India and Turkistan.[81]

down that treaties, whether real or personal, remain in force, 'so long as the nation exists as an independent State.' In the case in point, neither Ladak or Jamu now exist as independent States; therefore the Lhassa treaties between Leh and Lhassa would come within its scope." NAI, Foreign, Secret F, September 1889, nos. 211–17. "Lhassa authorities still recognize the Ex-Raja of Ladakh as in power and ignore the Kashmir Wazir."

[79] Ney Elias. NAI, Foreign, Secret F, March 1886, no. 5. "Ladaki Diaries for October, November, and December 1885 and for January 1886."

[80] Ibid. My emphasis.

[81] Ney Elias. NAI, Foreign, Secret F, March 1886, no. 5. "Ladaki Diaries for October, November, and December 1885 and for January 1886."

The challenges identified by Elias reflected the seasonal unpredictability of consistent "communication" via the Treaty Road.

3.2.3   The Case of Haberhaver

In July 1890, the Resident in Kashmir forwarded a letter from Captain Ramsay in Ladakh that raised concerns about the ability of the British to regulate travel across its frontier roads. It concerned "the movements of a *soi-disant* Austrian named Haverhaver [*sic*], at present at Panamik or Shahidulla" (settlements along the Treaty Road between Leh and Yarkand) who wished to come to Ladakh.[82] Lieutenant Hamilton Bower, who encountered Haberhaver in Kashgar while on an expedition to Eastern Turkestan, provided the Foreign Department with some sparse and rather strange biographical details about him. "Mr. Haberhaver gives out that he was born at Buda Pesth, but was brought up in the Caucasus. He speaks only German, Russian and Turki, and would have people believe he is very anti-Russian, as he abuses all things Russian. He has house property at Samarkand, where he lives with a Russian lady, the wife of some other man."[83]

While apparently being held up by Kirghiz nomads at Shahidulla, the Austrian penned a letter in German to Ramsay seeking permission to enter Ladakh, sending it along with a group of traders headed south. Translated by the head of the Moravian missionary at Leh, Reverend Friedrich Redslob, Haberhaver's letter claimed that he was on a mission to collect butterflies. "The British Museum for Natural History in London sent me to make collections," he wrote, "and for that purpose in regard of entomology, I am on an exploration trip from Europe through Turkistan. If you kindly will give me permission, I should like to collect butterflies and beetles in the Maharaja's territory. I am an Austrian subject, and am accompanied by a Muhammadan servant. Hoping you will favor me with an answer."[84] Captain Ramsay sent his response with two Kashmiri sepoys (soldiers) who took the Treaty Road to Panamik. The sepoys were to prevent the Austrian from proceeding any closer to Leh. Ramsay informed Haberhaver that as he had "no passport from the British Government, he could not be allowed to come on to Ladak, and that he should return at once to Chinese Turkistan."[85] When the two sepoys reached Panamik, they discovered Haberhaver had already been

[82] NAI, Foreign, Keep-with for Secret F, October 1890, nos. 14–31. "Notices in English and Persian to be posted at Suget, Kilian, Kugiar, Sanju, and Polu, prohibiting Travellers and explorers (European) from Central Asia from crossing the frontier of British India and States subordinate to it without a passport from the Government of India."
[83] NAI.   [84] NAI.   [85] NAI.

there two days. After reading Ramsay's letter, Haberhaver at first refused to turn back, "saying that no notice had been put up at Shahidulla forbidding Europeans to proceed in the Leh direction."

Bower gave further details about Haberhaver to the Foreign Department once he returned from a failed attempt to track down the murderer of the Scottish trader Andrew Dalgleish in Kashgar and Yarkand.[86] Bower noted, and the secretary of the Foreign Department agreed, that Haberhaver was "probably harmless, for it does not appear what the Russians are to gain from the explorations of a man of this class. Still, that our action may be consistent it is better he should go back."[87] By mid-August 1890 the Resident in Kashmir suggested that Haberhaver be escorted back to Chinese Turkestan by Captain Francis Younghusband, who was set to embark on an extensive survey of the region.[88] Younghusband weighed in on Haberhaver's case while in Leh, pointing out "the impolicy of allowing foreigners to become acquainted with the approaches to India."[89]

As a result of this episode, Ramsay asked the Foreign Department for "definite orders as to the treatment to be accorded to Europeans entering Ladak from the Turkistan direction."[90] For his part, he thought that "no person other than a pure Asiatic should be permitted to cross our frontier at Shahidulla, unless in possession of a British passport authorizing the visit." And he would apply the rule to Europeans as well as British subjects, "for, if this is not done, it would be easy for foreigners to come down, and pass themselves off as British subjects, from Malta, Canada, or any other distant part of our Empire." The Resident in Kashmir added to Ramsay's report the recommendation that notices be posted "on the passes prohibiting travellers from Central Asia from entering" India.[91] The Foreign Department approved, and Captain Ramsay was assigned to post such a notice on the road north of the Karakoram Pass, wherever the frontier of India was determined to be.[92]

[86] This episode will be discussed in Chapter 5. Andrew Dalgleish was murdered near the Karakoram Pass in April 1888, apparently by a Pathan trader named Daud Mohammed.

[87] NAI, Foreign, Keep-with for Secret F, October 1890, nos. 14–31. "Notices in English and Persian."

[88] Younghusband, the nephew of Robert Shaw, had been born in the hill station of Murree and joined the army at a young age. He became an intrepid explorer whose intelligence-gathering journal from Peking to Yarkand in 1886–87 made him well known across India and Britain. Patrick French, *Younghusband: The Last Great Imperial Adventurer* (London: HarperCollins, 1994).

[89] NAI, Foreign, Keep-with for Secret F, October 1890, nos. 14–31. "Notices in English and Persian."

[90] NAI.

[91] NAI, referencing NAI, Foreign, Secret F, February 1890, nos. 59–84; and NAI, Foreign, Secret F, July 1890, nos. 212–13.

[92] See Chapter 2 for the development of the "Water–Parting Principle" in boundary demarcation and the problem of the "moving" Indus watershed.

The matter was significant enough for the secretary to the Foreign Department to seek advice from Ney Elias. Elias suggested that notices be put up along the road at Suget (or Duget), near Shahidulla.[93] "Captain Younghusband might be directed to arrange with the Yarkand Amban," Elias wrote. "He might explain what we want to do (to stop Europeans unprovided with passes), give him a notice in English and Persian, and ask him to send it out to the Kirghiz with an order to post it in a conspicuous position."[94] Elias suggested a modification to Ramsay's recommendation and drafted a letter reflecting those changes to be carried to Younghusband in Leh. As the Foreign Department realized that there was no demarcated limit of British territory in the region, even though all had agreed that the limit of the "Indus Watershed System" should form that border, the government was quick to insist on some ambiguity as to the exact point at which British territory began. In order to avoid recognizing Shahidulla and Suget as Chinese territory, the secretary to the Foreign Department suggested that Younghusband's "request to the Chinese might be so worded as to avoid an admission of what is the frontier."

Viceroy Lansdowne agreed with the letter to the Chinese, though he fretted over the possible ambiguity of the notice: "A clumsily worded document might do mischief."[95] Nonetheless, Ney Elias drafted the notice, the viceroy and Foreign Department agreed to his wording, and the text was sent to Younghusband who then accompanied the unfortunate Haberhaver back to Yarkand. The posted notice ran as follows:

Inconvenience having arisen in consequence of attempts made by persons unprovided with the requisite authority to cross the frontiers of British India and the States subordinate to it, it is hereby notified, for the information of all travellers and explorers, that no British, European, or American subject is permitted to cross the land frontier of British India, or the States subordinate to it, without a passport from the Foreign Department of the Indian Government, and that all persons not furnished with such passports will be sent back from the first post at which they may arrive in British or British feudatory territory.[96]

Soon, similar rules were drafted for those moving in the opposite direction, from India to Central Asia. By the early twentieth century the

---

[93] Elias suggested that the Chinese might be in a better position to post the notice at Suget, since "Turdi Kol," the leader of the nomadic Kirghiz who had held Haberhaver for a month, could not be counted on to still be there at Shahidulla.

[94] NAI, Foreign, Keep-with for Secret F, October 1890, nos. 14–31. "Notices in English and Persian."

[95] NAI. Dated September 3, 1890. From Viceroy Lansdowne.

[96] NAI, Foreign, Keep-with for Secret F, October 1890, nos. 14–31. "Notices in English and Persian."

British exerted pressure on the government of Jammu and Kashmir to formally enact prohibitions against those traveling close to the frontier, whether Britons, Europeans, Americans, or British Indian subjects. The Kashmir Visitors' Rules, first published in 1906 and revised in subsequent decades, prohibited from entering Tibet and Central Asia all "undesirable Indians ... other than those who have already by usage traded or resided in Tibet elsewhere than at the marts and persons such as carriers, cartmen, labourers and regular petty traders." Ladakh's capital, Leh, became "the most suitable limit of travel for Indians in the direction of Chinese Turkistan and Tibet."[97]

These restrictions were further extended in the early 1930s, when it was determined that the Indus River in Ladakh would form the limit to restrict the "ingress of individuals from Chinese Turkestan into Kashmir by Leh route and egress from Kashmir to Chinese Turkestan." Only those "in possession of British passports, travellers' or pilgrims' passes or other travel documents duly granted ... by a recognised British authority shall travel North or South of the River Sindh in Ladakh."[98]

This growing desire to restrict entry and exit initially arose from late nineteenth- and early twentieth-century fears over the advance of the Russian Empire. Far from being the lighthearted "Great Game" portrayed in the pages of Kipling's *Kim*, the geopolitical struggle across India's mountainous periphery produced acute anxieties.[99] The consummate imperial adventurer Francis Younghusband supported Ramsay's refusal to let Haberhaver enter Ladakh on the grounds that Russia be denied any and all knowledge of the approaches to India. The episode with Haberhaver recalled an earlier attempt by a Russian explorer, named Gromchevsky, to travel south of Kashgar. Younghusband noted gravely:

Good-natured unthinking people may say that there is nothing to see, and that they can do no harm by coming through; and the foreigners themselves may say, as, according to Bower, Gromchevsky did when he was turned back, that "the Government of India take no interest in scientific enquiry." But we have to remember that Russia is advancing on India and striving to gain a knowledge of

---

[97] JKSA-J. "Tibet (entry into). Insertation of a rule in Kashmir Visitors' Rules regarding preventing the entry into Tibet of undesirable Indians." 1924, 417/F-52. "Submission to His Highness the Maharaja Sahib Bahadur in Council, dated Gulmarg the 12th August 1924."

[98] Maharaja Hari Singh, February 14, 1936. NAI, Foreign, 127-X (Secret), 1936. "Control of ingress into and egress from Ladakh (Kashmir) and Gilgit over the land frontier between India and Chinese Turkestan. Ladakh Frontier Crossing Regulation"; and JKSA-J, 1932, 534/V.B.32. "Limits of travel in the direction of Gilgit and Ladakh."

[99] For a critique of the "Great Game" narrative, see the introduction to Hevia, *Imperial Security State*.

every possible means of access to it, and that, if the case were reversed, and we were edging our way towards Turkistan, we should be very glad if our agents were allowed free access to every road into the country, and opportunities of calculating out exactly how many men could advance by each, or estimating the character and disposition of the people as possible allies.[100]

This "knowledge of every possible means of access" to India was central to the military strategies of keeping India secure. Foremost in the imperial arsenal of military intelligence, as James Hevia has recently shown, were military reports and route books, which instructed military leaders on the best routes for moving troops to particular frontier locales.[101] Accurate information was crucial to the utility of these manuals. When the Resident in Kashmir forwarded the Ladakh Diaries to the Foreign Department in July 1891, he noted that the mail from "Captain Younghusband [had] taken 20 days on the road which is reported to be much damaged by snow." He also noted that it "may interest I.B. [Intelligence Branch] to know that the info in the Route Books regarding distances and supplies between Simla and Leh is incorrect."[102] The precise location of these routes was key to the mobilization of forces across the frontier, a task implemented a decade later when Younghusband led the British invasion of Tibet.

3.3   The British Invasion of Tibet and the Regulation of Himalayan Roads

By the turn of the twentieth century, Himalayan road building had become unambiguously tied to a unified frontier policy that was asserted by the imperial government and articulated by a number of frontier experts, including Thomas Holdich, Alfred Lyall, and the arch-imperialist himself, the viceroy George Curzon. Roads had become key defensive and offensive instruments of the imperial state. They were the principal subject of manuals for military mobilization, which instructed officers on the optimal lines of movement for troops to and beyond the frontier. Over the last decades of the nineteenth century the central government of India's approach to its territorial periphery shifted from a policy of many individual frontiers to a unitary one. Referring to the development of roads and railways in that corner of India, the Secretary of State for India in 1884 insisted that the North-West Frontier and others

---

[100] Captain F. E. Younghusband, to the Foreign Secretary, August 1, 1890. NAI, Foreign, Keep-with for Secret F, October 1890, nos. 14–31. "Notices in English and Persian."

[101] Hevia, *Imperial Security State.*

[102] NAI, Foreign, Frontier B, November 1891, nos. 84–94. "Ladakh Diaries for the period from 1st Feb to 30th September."

"must be considered as a whole."[103] This changing territorial vision reconfigured the states lying beyond the formal limits of the empire into protectorates, "buffer states," and "spheres of influence" – categories detailed by numerous notable frontier experts, perhaps most famously by Curzon in the *Frontiers* (1907) lecture he delivered shortly after concluding his tenure as viceroy of India.[104]

Tibet was notably absent from this growing array. Its "closed" policy and its ambiguous status vis-à-vis the Qing Empire made it at once an object of fascination for British explorers and a growing concern as a neighboring state that refused to engage in diplomatic and commercial relations with British India – however long it had interacted with Ladakh and the plains of India via the Himalayan polities to its south and west. In 1903, two letters from the viceroy to Lhasa, once again hoping to open up talks, were returned unopened.[105] This perceived blow to British prestige magnified long simmering fears over Russian "intriguing" in Tibet via the Buryat monk Dorjieff. The government of India's awareness of this growing Russian influence "became intolerable to the Raj."[106] Younghusband's invasion of Tibet in 1903–4 was its response.

Walter Lawrence, the British officer overseeing the land settlement report in Kashmir, justified this move by pointing to the "unneighborly trespass of our good friends the Russians."[107] He bemoaned the apparent Russian provocation that forced Britain's hand and caused the sad end to the idyllic reclusiveness of Tibet, then justified the brutal onslaught with which Britain broke it open. "For eight long months, that quiet, pacific political officer, Colonel Younghusband, has been perched on the cold mountains vainly endeavoring to convince the fatuous monks of Lhasa that he was there on serious business." When his patience ran out the British mowed down the Tibetan soldiers, whose antiquated muskets proved no match for the British Maxim guns at Guru.[108] "Such lessons,"

---

[103] NAI, Foreign, Secret F, October 1885, nos. 118–28. "Construction of roads and railways for the purpose of improving the defences of the North-West Frontier of India." No. 120. "Extract from a Telegram from the Secretary of State," November 27, 1884.

[104] Curzon, *Frontiers*.

[105] Viceroy Lansdowne to His Majesty's Charge d'Affaires at St. Petersburg, November 17, 1903, in "Appendix 10: The Tibet Question," in Geoffrey Drage, *Russian Affairs* (London: John Murray, 1904), 719.

[106] Alex McKay, *Tibet and the British Raj: The Frontier Cadre, 1904–1947* (Richmond, UK: Curzon, 1997), 7. Dorjieff was a Buryat monk attendant to the thirteenth Dalai Lama who visited St. Petersburg at the Dalai Lama's request.

[107] Walter Lawrence, "The British Mission to Tibet," *The North American Review* 178, no. 571 (1904): 869–70.

[108] At the battle of Guru (March 31, 1904), the British killed nearly 700 disarmed and retreating Tibetans, wounding another 200. They suffered just twelve casualties themselves. The disproportionate military force used by the expedition and the subsequent

Lawrence asserted, "act as a tonic on the great continent of India, and as a prophylactic on our restless neighbors beyond the frontier."[109]

The invasion by the enterprising, if hardly "quiet and pacific," Younghusband had been commissioned by Viceroy George Curzon. In the months leading up to it, reports were gathered in Darjeeling and Sikkim from Tibetan traders who were "firmly under the impression that war will shortly be declared between the British Government and Tibet. They give as their reasons for this impression the repairing of the Sikkim road, the heavy transport of rations from Siliguri to Rungpo, and the presence of a large body of troops in Darjeeling."[110] Roughly 600 Kashmiri ponies and their drivers had in fact been sent to Sikkim to help Younghusband assemble his Tibet Frontier Commission.[111]

Though the route the expedition took was far away from Ladakh, the invasion revealed how the British viewed its frontier roads as a key tool of imperial security.[112] So did its aftermath. Quickly concluding a treaty with the Tibetan government in 1904, Younghusband signaled the necessity of improving the roads connecting India and Tibet. "We have just broken down the barriers of exclusion which the Tibetans have kept up against us for so many years," Younghusband wrote.[113] "It is eminently desirable that we should keep Tibet thoroughly accessible, and that the Tibetans should continue to realise that they are accessible, and that no such natural barrier, as that which the Nathu and Jelap roads cross, lies between us and them." With the "political object of keeping Tibet open and accessible and easily connected with India and with the commercial object of getting round obstacles which stand in the way of a promising trade," Younghusband urged the government of India to construct "a

looting of various monasteries belied Curzon's attempts "to fulfill the role and ultimate destiny of the British Empire as the arbiter of moral justice in the colonial situation." It divided the British metropolitan populace over the legitimacy of imperial interventions and made subsequent governments – in Britain and in India – more reluctant to engage in similar military aggressions. Michael Carrington, "Officers, Gentlemen and Thieves: The Looting of Monasteries during the 1903/4 Younghusband Mission to Tibet," *Modern Asian Studies* 37, no. 1 (2003): 86.

[109] Lawrence, "The British Mission to Tibet," 871.

[110] J. H. E. Garrett, Deputy Commissioner of Darjeeling, to the Chief Secretary to the Government of Bengal, May 12, 1903. NAI, Foreign, Secret E, November 1903, nos. 40–80. No. 43: "Weekly 'Darjeeling Confidential Frontier Reports.' Information regarding Tibetan traders named Jhampa Nagovang and Jhampala."

[111] NAI, Foreign, External, December 1903, 1–13, Part B. "Supply of Kashmir Ponies for the Tibet Frontier Commission."

[112] Carole McGranahan, "Empire Out of Bounds: Tibet in the Era of Decolonization," in *Imperial Formations*, ed. Ann Laura Stoler et al. (Santa Fe: School for Advanced Research Press, 2007), 177.

[113] NAI, Foreign, Secret E, March 1905, nos. 101–70. No. 141: "Instruction to Mr. Bell to enquire into the matter of disputed territory between Bhutan and India."

thoroughly good <u>line of communication</u>" through the central Himalayan Chumbi Valley to Tibet.[114] The Hindustan–Tibet Road was to be improved likewise. Once Younghusband returned to India, a flurry of books like Edmund Candler's *The Unveiling of Lhasa* (1905), Perceval Landon's *The Opening of Tibet* (1905), and Thomas Holdich's *Tibet, The Mysterious* (1906) soon followed to celebrate his conquest and its implications.[115]

3.3.1   The Hindustan–Tibet Road, Again

After Younghusband's invasion of Tibet in 1903–4, improvements to the Hindustan–Tibet Road were revisited with a view to both its commercial and military warrant.[116] In 1905, the Resident in Kashmir, E. G. Colvin, wrote optimistically to the secretary of the Foreign Department that "the effect of the Tibet Mission on Ladakh Trade [is] interesting. I am of the opinion that the considerable trade which already exists between Leh and Western Tibet would be very considerably increased if measures were taken to improve communications."[117] The government decided to focus first on the stretch south of Ladakh by allocating funds to improve the mule track up to the Shipki-*la*, neglected by the government ever since the Duke of Argyll nixed its expansion in the mid-1870s. The military rationales that were interspersed with commercial justifications reflected an accepted policy of roads as the principal instruments of frontier security. Indeed, progress reports submitted in 1906 and 1908 acknowledged that "the imports from Western Tibet along the Hindustan–Tibet road continue to decrease," though this was attributed, in part, "to the fact that while the uncompleted portion of that road [is] scarcely passable by laden sheep and goats, and its rivers are unbridged, other communications with Tibet are

[114] Ibid. Younghusband's emphasis.
[115] In an example of life mirroring fiction, Landon cites Kipling's *Kim* (London: Macmillan, 1901) numerous times in *The Opening of Tibet*, referencing the truthfulness of Kipling's representation of the country and its inhabitants. Perceval Landon, *The Opening of Tibet; an Account of Lhasa and the Country and People of Central Tibet and of the Progress of the Mission Sent There by the English Government in the Year 1903–4; Written, with the Help of All the Principal Persons of the Mission* (New York: Doubleday, Page, 1905). References to Kipling's *Kim* occur on numerous pages, including 103, 192, 228, and 250. It is also worth noting that Younghusband had read *Kim* prior to the mission, though I have yet to come across Younghusband referencing the book himself. See also Edmund Candler, *The Unveiling of Lhasa* (London: Arnold, 1905), and Thomas Hungerford Holdich, *Tibet, the Mysterious* (New York: F. A. Stokes, 1906).
[116] NAI, Foreign, Secret E, November 1903, "Tibet Negotiations"; and NAI, Foreign, Secret E, February 1905.
[117] NAI, Foreign, Frontier A, March 1905, nos. 3–9. "Report on the trade between India and Ladakh, and between India and Russian and Chinese Turkestan *via* Ladakh for the year 1903–1904."

being gradually improved."[118] Despite the development of these "other communications," the Hindustan–Tibet Road was still seen as providing dependable access to Tibet, worth the cost of upkeep for political, not just commercial, reasons. Not least, the route to the Shipki Pass could be accessed for most of the year, a substantial benefit in a region cut off from the rest of India for half the year when the passes were snowed in.

In September 1908, the road was expanded in its final fifty miles up to the Shipki Pass. "The new portion of the road is to be of the same standard as the furthest sections of the present mule road, the width being 8 feet (in the most difficult places 6 feet), and the ruling gradient one in seven, with occasional lengths of one in six. The Sutlej and one important tributary stream [is] to be crossed by light suspension bridges."[119] In November 1912, after several years of discussions across various departments of the government of India, the British trade agent, recently stationed in Western Tibet at Gartok, submitted an estimate for the further extension of the Hindustan–Tibet Road into Tibet, from the Shipki Pass to Gartok. "If it is desirable to keep permanent relations with Tibet, the first thing required to secure this object will be to improve our trade routes up to Tibetan borders and then to improve the Tibetan internal routes. The Government have taken the work of completing the Hindustan–Tibet road as far as Shipkee. This route will greatly improve not only our commercial interest but political as well."[120]

But the trade agent's request was postponed by his superiors in light of the diplomatic status of Tibet and the limits of its territory. On March 18, 1913, A. H. McMahon, the Secretary to the Foreign Department, wrote that "the Government of India do not consider it desirable at present to take up the question of the improvement of the route from Shipki to Gartok. Should our relations with Tibet shortly be placed on a more definite footing, the matter of the improvement of the route can be taken up then."[121] McMahon was about to embark on a protracted tripartite conference at Shimla that included Tibetan and Chinese representatives. The resulting "McMahon Line" was never fully demarcated on the ground but was instead hastily superimposed over a map of the borderlands; like the infamous "Durand Line," it would become a source of territorial disputes after independence.

[118] NAI, Foreign, Secret E, September 1908, nos. 407–17, p. 503. "Report by Major S.H. Powell on the proposed extension of the Hindustan-Tibet to Shipki, with estimates of cost." See also NAI, Foreign, Secret E, November 1908, nos. 118–58. "Progress on the Hindustan-Tibet Road."
[119] Ibid.
[120] NAI, Foreign, Secret E., May 1913, nos. 220–23. "Administration report of the Gartok Trade Agency for the year 1912," November 12, 1912.
[121] NAI, Foreign, External, April 1913, 46, Part B. "Question of the improvement of Hindustan-Tibet road from Shipki to Gartok."

Figure 3.3 Jawaharlal Nehru, Louis and Edwina Mountbatten, and an
unknown woman in a car on the Hindustan–Tibet Road in Shimla
(1948). The sign reads "Tibet 182 [miles]." Wikipedia Commons.

Writing in 1935, the career political officer Olaf Caroe acknowledged that the "Hindustan–Tibet road from Simla onwards to Shipki
in Tibet and eventually to Gartok has a certain international importance." It was one of only two roads into Western Tibet (the other
being through Garhwal and Kumaon) where the government maintained a trade agent. Caroe noted that the government's Tibet policy
was "to keep that country to the greatest possible extent within the
Indian orbit, both politically and commercially." Acknowledging that
the "key position" in Tibet was Lhasa, he insisted that, "the maintenance of commercial relations between Northern India and
Western Tibet has a definite importance from the point of view of
the Foreign Dept. and the external relations of the Govt. of India on
this part of the India frontier" (Figure 3.3). He noted that "if there
were no road to Gartok either via Simla or Almora our relations with

Tibet would certainly suffer. ... From this point of view the maintenance of the Hindustan–Tibet road should certainly be a liability of the Govt. of India and not of the Punjab State."[122]

3.3.2   The Treaty Road, Again

Following his invasion of Tibet, Younghusband was sent to Srinagar to become the Resident in Kashmir. He was to oversee the British Joint Commissioner in Ladakh and the British Consulate-General at Kashgar who had been stationed there beginning in 1890 to better oversee intelligence gathering.[123] The early twentieth-century Ladakh Diaries continued to reflect the preeminent importance of the conditions of the Treaty Road for political and commercial concerns. And improvements to the road continued. The number of grain godowns along the Treaty Road increased, though the Kashmir authorities often found it difficult to stock them.[124] Unseasonable snow, flooding, and diseases afflicting animals were of common concern.[125] In 1905, for instance, rinderpest broke out among yaks in the region. The BJC – then typically referred to as the Assistant to the Resident in Kashmir for Leh – requested a veterinarian to examine the yaks used for carriage of goods across the passes of the Treaty Road. "The death of the yaks," the BJC wrote, "is causing bad blocks on the Trade Road as the ponies have now to carry all the loads and their numbers are of course limited." This caused weeks-long delays in the transports of goods and the overworking of ponies, which were already in short supply, according to traders, owing to Russians buying ponies around Kashgar for use in Andijan.[126]

---

[122] NAI, Foreign, 1935, 375-P. "Question of maintenance of the Hindustan-Tibet Road (s)," July 9, 1935. Caroe would become the Chief Secretary of the North West Frontier Province in 1937, the Secretary to the External Affairs Department in 1939, and the Governor of the North West Frontier Province in 1946. After retiring along with the Raj, Caroe set about writing numerous books, including Olaf Caroe, *Soviet Empire: The Turks of Central Asia and Stalinism* (London: Macmillan, 1953), and Olaf Caroe, *The Pathans: 550 B.C.–A.D. 1957* (London: Macmillan, 1958).

[123] NAI, Foreign, Frontier, November 1906, nos. 56–66A, Part B. "Leh Diary(ies) for the period 12th June to 1st September 1906." The Qing Government did not officially recognize the British Consul in Kashgar until 1908.

[124] NAI, Foreign, Frontier, June 1904, nos. 110–11, p. 161. "Ladakh. Supplies. Difficulty experienced by the Kashmir Darbar in obtaining grain for stocking the godowns established on the road between the Zogi and Karakoram Passes for the requirements of Central Asian traders."

[125] NAI, Foreign, Frontier, November 1906, nos. 56–66A, Part B. "Leh Diary(ies) for the period 12th June to 1st September 1906."

[126] NAI, Foreign, Frontier, January 1906, nos. 98–107, Part B. "Leh Diary for period 4th June to the 14th October 1905."

By this time the BJC spent only the warmer months in Ladakh, returning to Srinagar before snow closed the passes in the early autumn. Younghusband directed the BJCs under his command to spend as much time as possible out on the Treaty Road. This trend continued until the last BJC left in 1946. The best part of their months in Ladakh each year was spent overseeing repairs to the track and bridges comprising the Treaty Road, as well as keeping tabs on the incoming and outgoing trade caravans. They also had to issue passes for the small number of Europeans and Americans who went to Ladakh in the summer months to travel or hunt. While this last group represented a type of traveler present in the region since the 1870s, they were now more closely regulated and charged more for the services they received. One soldier on leave from the army to hunt apparently complained about the cost of carriage across the Zoji-*la* (the pass between Kashmir and Ladakh). The BJC wrote regretfully that "one cannot help noting that it is very hard on the sporting subaltern who spends his leave in shooting to have to pay Rs. 100 or more in order to cross this pass."[127]

The British Joint Commissioners still wrote of commercial potential in the trade with Yarkand, though less frequently about the same with Tibet; by the twentieth century, the latter was carried on most successfully via Sikkim and the Chumbi Valley, the part of the central Himalaya closest to the major Tibetan centers of Lhasa and Shigatse. Still, an improved Central Asian trade harbored two notable sources of hope. First was the increased flow of *charas* (hashish) along the Treaty Road, including a particularly strong surge in the trade around 1895 (visible in Table 3.1 as the first major spike). This "extremely important article in the Central Asian Trade" was also "the largest medium of exchange in the Leh Bazar between the Yarkandi and Punjabi trader." Fluctuations in quality and quantity generated occasional seasons where the godowns of Leh were left filled with the drug. The BJC went so far as to appoint a Charas Officer whose sole purview was overseeing this commodity-currency. The second cause for hope came with the Russian Revolution of 1917.[128] Referring back to the graph in Table 3.1, one of the few notable spikes in revenue from the Indo-Yarkand trade occurred immediately after 1917. "Anarchy in Russia has paralysed Russian trade with Central Asia," wrote the Resident in Kashmir to the Secretary of the

---

[127] NAI, Foreign, Frontier, September 1909, nos. 42–45, Part B. "Leh Diaries from 30th June to 15th August 1909."

[128] For the significance of *charas*, see Captain S. B. Patterson, Assistant to the Resident in Kashmir for Leh. NAI, Foreign, Frontier A, March 1905, nos. 3–9: "Report on the trade between India and Ladakh, and between India and Russian and Chinese Turkestan *via* Ladakh for the year 1903–1904."

Foreign and Political Department in 1919. This "resulted in an enormous increase in the trade between British India and Central Asia," which "impos[ed] a heavy strain on the very limited transport facilities available on the Treaty road between Srinagar and Leh."[129]

But many of the improvements requested by the BJC were denied, the result of a major policy change that occurred after Younghusband's invasion of Tibet and his tenure as Resident in Kashmir. This policy was directly antagonistic to the development of trade along the Treaty Road. The Treaty Road itself had become an instrument of security. It was to be improved up to Leh, but the branch running from the Nubra Valley in northern Ladakh across the Karakoram Pass to Yarkand was not. In 1904, "the question as to the desirability of improving the Leh-Yarkand trade route was discussed" by the Foreign Department, and it decided that "*on military grounds, it was undesirable to improve it to any greater extent than had been done in the past.*"[130] The strategic rationale for leaving the road in a bad state was less apparent with the Hindustan–Tibet Road farther south. The continued threat of Russia to the north led military strategists to regard the Leh-Yarkand route as a potential invasion route.[131] Weighing in on another round of recommendations for road improvement by the BJC in 1910, Viceroy Minto agreed not to improve it. Though he recognized the advantages of road improvement "from a commercial point of view," "our policy as to the northern communications into India has hitherto been very clear, and for political reasons I am quite opposed to reversing it."[132] The nonimprovement policy was maintained following the end of the First World War when "war conditions" continued to severely restrict budgeting for infrastructure, though it was acknowledged that certain facilities were required for military concerns.

It is understood that as much pony transport as can be made available is required for military purposes. In the circumstances as military exigencies must preponderate at present it will be difficult if not undesirable to do anything towards

[129] Lieut-Col. A D'A.G. Bannerman, Resident in Kashmir, to Sir Hamilton Grant, Foreign Sec. Foreign and Political Dept., August 2, 1918. NAI, Foreign, Frontier, February 1919, nos. 69–71, Part B.

[130] NAI, Foreign, Secret F, June 1910, nos. 6–8, Part A. "Proposal to improve the Leh-Yarkand trade route." My emphasis.

[131] NAI, Foreign, Frontier A, June 1906, nos. 102–3. "Objection to the extensive improvement of the Leh-Yarkand route on strategical grounds. Approval to some slight improvements on the section between Murgo and Kazil Augar to save the loss of life in animals at present occasioned by bad gradients."

[132] NAI, Foreign, Frontier A, June 1906, nos. 102–3. "Objection to the extensive improvement of the Leh-Yarkand route on strategical grounds. Approval to some slight improvements on the section between Murgo and Kazil Augar to save the loss of life in animals at present occasioned by bad gradients."

improving the present transport facilities existing on the treaty road between Srinagar and Leh, more especially as some of the export trade mentioned in the Resident's letter must find its way through Central Asia into enemy hands. In this connection it should be noted that both dyes and leather would appear to be among the articles of which the export to all destinations is prohibited.[133]

Frontier roads had become, first and foremost, infrastructural instruments of imperial security.

3.4   Conclusion

By the turn of the century, imperial policy shifted from a focus on several frontiers to a policy connecting frontier locales to each other. The histories of the Hindustan–Tibet Road and the Treaty Road through Ladakh reveal this shift. Initially, each project was encouraged largely by the perceived potential of commercial markets beyond British India. With the growing awareness of political changes in Central Asia and the encroachment of the Russian Empire, these roads gradually became subsumed under larger rubrics of security, even if local administrators still frequently promoted the roads' commercial potential. Thus the Hindustan–Tibet Road became a secondary avenue to Tibet following Younghusband's invasion in 1903–4, while the Indo-Yarkand Treaty Road became an access point to Central Asia and thus a potential invasion route to defend – albeit less likely than the one military strategists hypothesized running through Afghanistan.[134] The two roads examined here evolved through particular histories that increasingly emphasized their role as regulatory mechanisms of the frontier, and, as such, of the empire. Roads that were meant to decrease the friction of moving through mountainous terrain and promote connections with regions beyond India were transformed into tools for restricting potentially dangerous "transfrontier" people.

Finally, it is worth noting that roads themselves are not static objects. They are, as Joe Moran has observed, palimpsests – objects "laid on top of earlier versions like overwritten texts."[135] The two roads examined in this chapter were further widened in the mid-twentieth century for motorized vehicles. Private cars and trucks were allowed along the Hindustan–Tibet Road only in 1946, a boon to apple farmers in Kinnaur, Kullu, and Shimla, who could more easily sell their produce

[133] NAI, Foreign, Frontier, February 1919, nos. 69–71, Part B.
[134] See, for instance, Chief of Staff's Division Army Headquarters, India, *A Study of the Existing Strategical Conditions on the North-West Frontier* (Simla: Government Central Branch Press, 1909).
[135] Moran, *On Roads: A Hidden History*, 1.

Figure 3.4 A typical sign from HIMANK, a division of the Borders
Road Organization (BRO) in Ladakh. Wikipedia Commons.

in the plains.[136] While the first motorized vehicle to reach Ladakh was
an Indian Army plane in 1948,[137] it was followed by tanks and trucks
entering Ladakh from Kashmir along the Treaty Road, and by troops
arriving from the south along the road from Kullu. In 1960, the administration of these and other mountain roads along the Indian border was
handed over to the Indian Army's Border Roads Organization (BRO).
India's ongoing territorial disputes with China and Pakistan have
ensured a highly visible military presence across these border regions.
The continued improvement of these roads is now unambiguously
spoken of in terms of security, and the roadsides in Ladakh and other
border regions are littered with patriotic messages and amusing slogans
and innuendoes that suggest both the danger of the mountain roads
("Darling I like you, but not so fast") and the technical challenge and
significance of road building (Figure 3.4). In this last sense, at least, we
hear echoes of Dalhousie's triumphal "experiment": "People scoffed at
the idea of being able to form a level road through these enormous
mountains at all."[138] But as for the dreams of Dalhousie's predecessor,
Hardinge's "free" and "unobstructed" road to Central Asia and Tibet
has become anything but.

---

[136] Himachal Pradesh State Archive-Shimla (hereafter HPSA-S). "Motor Lorry Transport
Scheme on H. T. Road."
[137] See Figure 7.1.   [138] United Kingdom, House of Commons 1857, 54.

4 Reading the Border
Gazetteers, Tribute Missions, and the Problem with Goats

When Syed [Ahmed Khan] went around with the *Gazette* [*of India*], he brought in lakhs;

When the sheikh went around showing the Qur'an, he received not a single paisa.[1]

– Akbar Allahabadi

The true territorial unit of Indian history is, indeed, much smaller than the British District.[2]

– William Wilson Hunter

By the 1870s the Government of India began issuing instructions to administrators for compiling district entries for *The Imperial Gazetteer of India*.[3] The entries were to begin with a "short paragraph giving the name of the District, its latitude and longitude, boundaries, area in square miles, and the estimated population." "Care should be taken," the directions continued, "that the latitudes and longitudes and area are procured from the Surveyor-General's Department, and that the area represents the true size of the District, allowing for any recent transfers of parganas,[4] or changes in the boundary." The district gazetteers that soon accompanied the *Imperial Gazetteer* delivered an even more detailed formal order of

---

[1] *Syed ūṭhe jō gazeṭ le ke to lākhoṇ lāe; shaikẖ Qurān dikhāte phire paisā na milā.* Akbar Ilāhābādī, *Kulliyyāt-i Akbar Illāhābādī*, ed. Aḥmad Maḥfūẓ, vol. 1, 2 vols. (Naʾi Dihlī: Qaumī kaunsil barā'e furoẖ-i Urdū zabān, 2002). The *Gazette of India* was (and continues to be) an annual Government of India publication that lists new laws, official appointments, and government reports, in addition to financial figures (revenue and costs). One *lākh* equals 100,000 rupees. A paisa is one-hundredth of a rupee. My translation.

[2] William Wilson Hunter, Preface to the 1881 edition of the William Wilson Hunter, *The Imperial Gazetteer of India* (London: Trüber, 1881), 1:xviiii.

[3] NAI, Department of Agriculture, Revenue and Commerce, Statistics, General B. 1872. William Wilson Hunter, *Heads of Information Required for the Imperial Gazetteer of India, with Rules for the Spelling of Indian Proper Names* (Simla: Government Central Press, 1871).

[4] The *paraganā* was an administrative unit employed by the Mughals and other South Asian dynasties. The British formally abolished them (and the revenue system associated with them) with their permanent settlements but retained them as geographical terms that often overlapped with their own districts.

information in their initial "descriptive" section. Boundaries, latitude and longitude, and area were followed by subsections on the district's "natural divisions and hill system," "river system, and lakes," geology and botany, "characteristic or noteworthy wild animals," and meteorology.[5] There followed accounts of the district's history, population, public health, religions, tribes and castes, and languages. The gazetteer then continued with sections devoted to economic and administrative subjects.

By the end of the nineteenth century the gazetteer was a ubiquitous and indispensable tool for colonial officials "on the spot" and for administrators in the central government. Over the course of formal British rule in India, more than 1,400 editions of district, provincial, and imperial gazetteers were published.[6] These authoritative guides were used frequently by all levels of government, consistently arranged, and regularly revised. Their form illustrated a basic epistemological premise behind the colonial state's assumption of who, and what, it governed. These manuals asserted the central importance of a clearly demarcated border in defining their human and territorial subjects. Establishing this narrow, linear limit to imperial territory, in turn, reflected a global transformation in how geography shaped political thinking.

Writers of travelogues and histories across the world had long begun their works with what had become a convention for the genre: a brief physical description of the particular place concerned. The nineteenth century, however, witnessed a major expansion in the volume and authority of geographical information included in both public and private writings on historical, ethnographic, and political subjects. In particular, the growth and inclusion of this information in official reference manuals illustrates both Foucault's insights concerning the rise of governmentality – that is, the organized practices by which the state governs its subjects – and the development of the state's principal objects of concern and analysis: population and territory. Historians of empire have applied this general observation to an array of information-gathering practices under the capacious rubric of "colonial knowledge." Scholars of colonial South Asia, in particular, have noted how this colonial knowledge was largely driven by the development of the statistical sciences in the nineteenth and

---

[5] J. M. Douie to All Revenue Officers in the Punjab, 1890. HPSA-S. "Circular issuing instructions for the preparation of Final Settlement Reports, and the revision and maintenance of District Gazetteers"; and HPSA-S Appendix B, No. 63, S. No. 1077, Deputy Commissioner, Kangra, Head 40, file N. 40(1) "Rules for the preparation of district gazetteers," dated May 8, 1903.

[6] Robert C. Emmett, "The Gazetteers of India: Their Origins and Development during the Nineteenth Century" (MA thesis, University of Chicago, 1976).

early twentieth centuries.[7] This transformation in governance was fed by
technocratic practices ranging from ethnographic and linguistic studies to
the development of census-related statistics and military intelligence –
distinct forms of officially generated "objective" knowledge that Bernard
S. Cohn referred to collectively as "surveys."[8] These regularized the
bureaucratic documentation of territory and population. Those reference
manuals focusing on population, such as the census and ethnographic
surveys, defined their colonial subjects through an increasingly complex
social taxonomy. Those focusing on territory, such as district-level gazetteers and military route books, defined their subjects by first precisely
delimiting their dimensions.

Within those manuals focused on territory, geography asserted
a fundamental role in the ordering of information, a role resonating
with another insight of Foucault's. In *The Order of Things* (*Les mots et les
choses*, 1966) and *The Archaeology of Knowledge* (*L'Archéologie du Savoir*,
1969), Foucault demonstrated how systems of knowledge shift over time
in accordance with their internal *epistemes* – that is, with "the totality of
relations that can be discovered, for a given period, between the sciences
when one analyses them at the level of discursive regularities."[9] We can
simply observe here that "discursive regularities" and a consistent "order
of things" emerged in nineteenth-century imperial manuals of governance, most notably within detailed district-level gazetteers. This order
placed geographical information before the social, historical, economic,

---

[7] The category of colonial knowledge originates from the work of Foucault and Said. For the
most notable historical work on colonial knowledge in the past two decades see Bernard
S. Cohn, *Colonialism and Its Forms of Knowledge: The British in India* (Princeton, NJ:
Princeton University Press, 1996); Bayly, *Empire and Information: Intelligence Gathering
and Social Communication in India, 1780–1870*; Nicholas B. Dirks, *Castes of Mind:
Colonialism and the Making of Modern India* (Princeton, NJ: Princeton University Press,
2011); Hopkins, *Modern Afghanistan*; and Hevia, *Imperial Security State*. For a succinct
survey of the pre-2008 canon of "colonial knowledge" literature, see Tony Ballantyne,
"Colonial Knowledge," in *The British Empire: Themes and Perspectives*, ed. Sarah Stockwell
(Malden, MA: Blackwell, 2008), 177–97.

[8] Cohn uses the term in several essays, but most notably in Bernard S. Cohn, "The Census,
Social Structure and Objectification in South Asia," in *An Anthropologist among the
Historians and Other Essays* (Delhi: Oxford University Press, 1987), 224–54.

[9] Or, earlier on in Foucault's rather rambling definition, "the total set of relations that unite,
at a given period, the discursive practices that give rise to epistemological figures, sciences,
and possibly formalized systems." Foucault, *The Archaeology of Knowledge*, 191. I use
Foucault's term here in a very general sense, given that the "discursive regularities" and
"orders of things" at hand here are distinct from the subjects Foucault actually examines in
his work on epistemes. (In *The Order of Things*, e.g., Foucault examines the disciplines of
biology, economics, and linguistics.) In a similar vein, we might also think of Thomas
Kuhn's paradigms – sets of concepts and practices that define a scientific discipline at any
particular period of time. Thomas S. Kuhn, *The Structure of Scientific Revolutions*, 2nd ed.
(Chicago: University of Chicago Press, 1970).

and political. Such consistency in relating increasingly distinct subjects of inquiry suggested a new and particular mode of seeing space and people: formally separating the two and rendering them static. By placing geography before people and their history, these manuals increasingly defined the people of a district in relation to the geographical features used to bound them. This episteme harbored a clear geographical determinism, particularly the later "scientific" variant associated with geographers like the prolific Ellsworth Huntington, whose contributions to *Explorations in Turkestan* (1905) articulated a deterministic view of "Climate and History."[10] Not incidentally, this deterministic geography reflected the rise of geopolitics, as will be shown in Chapter 6.

This chapter focuses on two different colonial approaches to "reading" the northwestern Himalaya, particularly the borderlines that British administrators in India presumed ran – or insisted should run – through it. I use the term "reading" because, unlike the pluralistic ways one might "see," reading requires a fixed set of symbols, a cohesive grammar, and a cultural context that delimits possible outcomes of understanding. As James C. Scott has shown, because its "vision" is imperfect, the state may attempt to render its territory and population legible through various "distance-demolishing technologies." Its vision thus enhanced, the state then makes sense of what it "sees" by ordering its objects in certain ways, providing a kind of grammar for accessing this information. Moving from seeing to reading requires the development of "discursive regularities" that bespeak a particular epistemic language. British officials and explorers attempted to craft this language by formalizing an order of geographical information, producing and bequeathing to subsequent generations of colonial (and eventually postcolonial)[11] administrators texts to reference and revise. In making a legible border primary in this process, the state increasingly employed geographical science to produce borderlands.

---

[10] Raphael Pumpelly, ed., *Explorations in Turkestan, with an Account of the Basin of Eastern Persia and Sistan. Expedition of 1903, under the Direction of Raphael Pumpelly* (Washington, DC: Carnegie Institution of Washington, 1905). Huntington later developed this geographical determinism in his *Climate and Civilization* (New York: Harper, 1915), in which he made extensive use of the writings of British frontier experts like the surveyor Thomas Holdich and the Viceroy of India and *Frontiers* author George Curzon (e.g., p. 303). Huntington further elaborated his environmental determinism in numerous works, including his *The Pulse of Asia, a Journey in Central Asia Illustrating the Geographic Basis of History* (Boston: Houghton, Mifflin, 1919); *The Character of Races as Influenced by Physical Environment, Natural Selection and Historical Development* (New York: C. Scribner's Sons, 1924); and (with Sumner Cushing) *Principles of Human Geography* (New York: John Wiley, 1934).

[11] District gazetteers are still produced in India today.

As Chapter 2 illustrated, the development of standardized surveying techniques, apparently natural boundary objects, and more numerous maps with greater ascribed authority reflected an emerging geographical episteme. Gazetteers were one of several genres of reference works that assembled and synthesized a "complete" set of individual pieces of information. Lorraine Daston and Peter Galison have likewise referred to atlases – compilations of all available maps of a given subject – as "systematic compilations of working objects."[12] For both the gazetteer and the atlas, the various information-gathering practices these "working objects" represented helped to craft an increasingly unified image of imperial India and its constituent administrative parts. But the informational (and cartographical) unification of India belied deeper uncertainties about its frontiers. Those uncertainties produced a second kind of reading in which administrators struggled to understand transregional political relations and the movements of people, animals, and water across the region.

This chapter divides into two parts. First, it traces the genealogy of the gazetteer to reveal the growing prominence of detailed descriptions of borders in particular and geographical information in general. This geographical episteme was manifest in increasingly standardized and widely circulated reference manuals: gazetteers, settlement reports, route books, and military reports. These amounted to a top-down model of organizing information about imperial territories and populations, from the level of the directly administered district or indirectly administered princely state, to the empire as a whole.[13]

The second half of this chapter examines case studies that challenged such top-down – or perhaps "border-in" – readings of imperial space-as-territory in different ways. Though seemingly insignificant, these cases drew an extraordinary level of response from the imperial state, often involving voluminous engagement from the highest imperial officials. One set of cases centered on the limits of Ladakhi sovereignty as it related to territory. These involved debates over the Maharaja of Jammu and Kashmir's *jāgīr*[14] in Tibet on the one hand and concerns over the triennial

---

[12] Lorraine Daston and Peter Galison, *Objectivity* (New York: Zone Books, 2007), 22.

[13] The authoring department, it should be noted, varied depending on whether the subject was part of (directly administered) British India (gazetteers published directly by the provincial government) or whether it was an indirectly administered dependency covered by the Foreign Department (gazetteers published by the Intelligence Branch).

[14] A *jāgīr* was "a rent-free estate obtained as a grant in perpetuity" (Platts Dictionary of Urdu DSAL). Those who held them were often referred to as *jāgīrdārs*, though in the archives of the princely state of Jammu and Kashmir, the most common term for such land grants at the sub-state level was the Persian term *muāfīdār*. This *jāgīr* in particular was the result of an earlier Ladakhi enclave, *Men.ser*, discussed below.

Ladakhi "tribute" mission to Lhasa and the annual reciprocal mission from Lhasa (the Lopchak [*lo.phyag*] and Chaba [*La.dwags gzhung. tshong*], respectively) on the other.[15] A second set of local challenges to a top-down model of imperial territory involved taxation and borders. These cases include an abduction of Ladakhi trader Lha.rgyal by Tibetan authorities, and debates between Tibetan, Kashmiri, and British officials over where pastoralists were to pay taxes when fixed boundaries on the ground were rarely known and respected by transhumant peoples. Each case casts doubt on the ability of the imperial state to represent and impose a border and, therefore, casts doubt on the very category of territory.

4.1   Top-Down Information

4.1.1   Defining the Object of Inquiry

Rulers have long sought to collect information on the people and places they govern by compiling historical, ethnographic, and geographical information into reference manuals. In China, early prototypes of what later came to be known as gazetteers (called generally *difang zhi*) have been dated to the Han dynasty (202 BCE–220 CE), while the first known version of a form of gazetteer that would later proliferate was compiled in the Jin dynasty (265–420 CE).[16] The fourth-century *Chronicles of Huayang* contained biographies of notable figures, chronicles of notable events, and some geographical information on the region around Mount Hua. More than a millennium later in South Asia, the Mughal Emperor Akbar's vizier, Abu'l Fazl Allami, compiled similar information in his sixteenth-century *Ai'n-i-Akbari* ("the Regulations of Akbar").[17] In the third volume of that work, Abu'l Fazl briefly describes the borders of Hindustan after giving a detailed account of the administrative and military structures of the Mughal Empire. He asserted that Hindustan was surrounded by oceans – with the mountainous "intermediate" region between it and China also likened to an ocean. In contrast to his earlier detailing of regional and subregional administrative divisions (*ṣūba* and

---

[15] These debates return throughout the latter half of the nineteenth century and the early twentieth century and extend beyond Ladakh to include "tribute" missions in Sikkim and Bhutan. There are numerous recommendations, particularly from several British Joint Commissioners (Elias, Ramsay) to discontinue them. See, for instance, NAI, Foreign, Secret F, September 1889, nos. 211–17.

[16] Thanks to Jesse Watson for this information.

[17] http://persian.packhum.org/persian/main?url=pf%3Ffile%3D00702053%26ct%3D0.

sarkār, respectively), however, Abu'l Fazl only briefly describes Hindustan's territorial extent.[18]

In Britain, several self-described gazetteers were published in the eighteenth century, containing alphabetized descriptions of villages, towns, cities, and other locales. In the Enlightenment spirit that yielded monumental compilations like Diderot and d'Alembert's *Encyclopédie* (1751–72) and Johnson's *A Dictionary of the English Language* (1755), Richard Brooke's *General Gazetteer* (1762) sought to improve on Britons' supposed ignorance of world geography – indeed, of their own.[19] In his preface Brooke complained that "the description of our own country has been greatly neglected, as if it was hardly worth our notice, though it ought to be the first and principal object of enquiry to every Briton." In a telling analogy, Brooke continued: "This is not unlike the sending young [*sic*] gentlemen abroad to visit foreign parts, before they have obtained any adequate knowledge of the laws, constitution, trade, product, and geography of the realm in which they drew their first breath."[20] By comparing the "grand tour" of the youthful elite to an education in a variety of subjects, Brooke asserted the fundamental importance of geographical knowledge for a whole variety of practical and scholarly reasons. He enumerates these at length, and it is worth recounting them in detail.

As for the usefulness of geography in general, nothing need be said, it being a study now greatly in vogue; and there are none but the very dregs of the people that have not some occasion or other to be acquainted therewith. It is absolutely

---

[18] For more on the Mughal conception of borders, see Jos Gommans, "The Silent Frontier of South Asia, c. AD 1100–1800," *Journal of World History* 9, no. 1 (1998): 1–23; and "Western Expansion, Indian Reaction: Mughal Empire and British Raj," in J. C. Heesterman, *The Inner Conflict of Tradition: Essays in Indian Ritual, Kingship, and Society* (Chicago: University of Chicago Press, 1985). Both authors suggest that internal imperial frontiers were more significant than exterior borders. For a history of the frontiers of the princely states, see Eric Lewis Beverley, *Hyderabad, British India, and the World: Muslim Networks and Minor Sovereignty, c. 1850–1950* (Cambridge: Cambridge University Press, 2015).

[19] The full title ran Richard Brooke, *The General Gazetteer, or, Compendious Geographical Dictionary Containing a Description of All the Empires Kingdoms, States, Republics, Provinces, Cities, Chief Towns, Forts, Fortresses, Castles, Citadels, Seas, Harbours, Bays, Rivers, Lakes, Mountains, Capes, and Promontories in the Known World; Together with the Government, Policy, Customs, Manners, and Religion of the Inhabitants; the Extent, Bounds, and Natural Productions of Each Country; and the Trade, Manufactures, and Curiosities of the Cities and Towns; Their Longitude, Latitude, Bearing and Distances in English Miles from Remarkable Places; as Also, the Sieges They Have Undergone, and the Battles That Have Been Fought near Them, down to This Present Year: Including, an Authentic Account of the Counties, Cities and Market-Towns in England and Wales; as Also the Villages with Fairs, the Days on Which They Are Kept According to the New Stile; as Well as the Cattle, Goods and Merchandises That Are Sold Thereat* (London: J. Newbery, 1762).

[20] Brooke, iii.

necessary to men of letters, because no history can be well understood without it: as also to politicians, it being impossible to understand the true interest of different states and countries, without the knowledge of this science. Officers, both by sea and land, have great need of it, because it lets them into the nature and circumstances of places and towns, and enables them to take their measures accordingly. Merchants and traders ought to study it beyond all doubt, because it assists them in taking prudent measures in order to establish a beneficial commerce. In short, all those who have either interest or curiosity to know any thing of the transactions of the world, or are desirous of forming some judgment of the different events, which happen in the times of war or peace, ought not to be ignorant of geography.[21]

Whether for the scholar, the military man, or the merchant, then, geography was to be a foundational body of knowledge. Aside from its evident utility, by the eighteenth century geography had also become immensely popular through the medium of travel literature; Richard Grove has recently deemed it "the single most widely read and sought-after category of English literature."[22] By the end of the eighteenth century other gazetteers, like Clement Cruttwell's *A Gazetteer of France* (1793), appeared with roughly the same order of information as Brooke's: first, a brief sketch of borders, area, mountains, and rivers; then descriptions of the inhabitants, their history, culture, trade, and political organization.[23]

Particularly in Western Europe, the eighteenth century witnessed a rapid rise in the use of technological and statistical practices designed to generate more detailed information by which the state could better understand and control its population and territory.[24] Though not exclusively state-sponsored, these initiatives often sought out statistical, cartographical, and technological means to address problems associated with public health, revenue generation, and agriculture. In the case of eighteenth-century Ireland, as Patrick Carroll has shown, a colonial periphery became a site of experimentation in "engineering land into the state," a process Carroll calls *technoterritorialization*.[25] At the core of such

---

[21] Brooke, iii–iv.

[22] Richard H. Grove, *Green Imperialism: Colonial Expansion, Tropical Island Edens, and the Origins of Environmentalism, 1600–1860* (Cambridge: Cambridge University Press, 1995), 54. To back up this claim, Grove cites Peter James Marshall and G. Williams, *The Great Map of Mankind: British Perceptions of the World in the Age of Enlightenment* (London: Dent, 1982), 54–59.

[23] Clement Cruttwell, *A Gazetteer of France: Containing Every City, Town, and Village in That Extensive Country … / Illustrated with a Map Divided into Departments* (London: Printed for G. G. J. and J. Robinson, 1793).

[24] Hevia, *Imperial Security State*, 107.

[25] Carroll writes, "I use the term *technoterritoriality* to emphasize the theoretical point that the issue of territory, in the context of the modern state, is only partly captured by reference to coercive or sovereign dominion within a landmass (which can include territorial waters, islands, and colonies). Modern territoriality involves engineering land *into the state* in a way

practices was a belief in the benefit of organized information for state administration. Thus John Sinclair's *Statistical Account of Scotland* (1790s–1800s) – modeled in certain ways on eighteenth-century Prussian land surveys – used parish questionnaires to gather information on geography, population, agricultural and other productions, and the welfare of its people.[26]

In 1815, Walter Hamilton published *The East India Gazetteer*.[27] The "plan [it] usually followed," he noted, "is that of Brooke's, Crutwell's, and other Gazetteers,"[28] while its "geographical basis" came from Arrowsmith's 1804 "six sheet map of Hindostan" (Map 4.1), which exhibited "the most correct delineation of this part of Asia hitherto presented to the public."[29] That is, besides the general order of information already established by Brooke's and Crutwell's gazetteers, Hamilton shaped his work according to the most current maps available. In attempting to "class the whole" of Hindustan, Hamilton acknowledged earlier works of geography, including Abu'l Fazl Allami's *Ai'n-i-Akbari*, which he acknowledged was precise in its definition of local boundaries albeit "wrong in many instances" on the boundaries of the whole country.[30] Hamilton's is a good example of the degree to which cartographical thinking increasingly shaped the organization of written descriptive information.

In the century between the Battle of Plassey (1757) and the Rebellion of 1857, military successes transformed the British East India Company from a coastal, factory-based trading company into an imperial power. Its first task, therefore, was to survey and define the spaces it sought to control and govern, which also entailed exploring and defining neighboring regions to better determine the limits of British territory. This task was

that extends, through particularizing scientific practices, the depth and reach of state power." Carroll, *Science, Culture and Modern State Formation*, 161. In other cases, as John Brewer has persuasively shown, information gathering exercises were tied to an effective centralized "fiscal-military state" capable of generating income and managing debt through centralized institutions. John Brewer, *The Sinews of Power: War, Money and the English State, 1688–1783* (Cambridge, MA: Harvard University Press, 1988).

[26] See Fredrik Albritton Jonsson, *Enlightenment's Frontier: The Scottish Highlands and the Origins of Environmentalism* (New Haven, CT: Yale University Press, 2013), 54–57.

[27] Walter Hamilton, *The East India Gazetteer; Containing Particular Descriptions of the Empires, Kingdoms, Principalities, Provinces, Cities, Towns, Districts, Fortresses, Harbours, Rivers, Lakes, &c. of Hindostan, and the Adjacent Countries, India beyond the Ganges, and the Eastern Archipelago; Together with Sketches of the Manners, Customs, Institutions, Agriculture, Commerce, Manufactures, Revenues, Population, Castes, Religion, History, &c. of Their Various Inhabitants* (London: J. Murray, 1815).

[28] Hamilton, x–xi.   [29] Hamilton, viii.

[30] Hamilton, xii–xiii. Here Hamilton is referring to Abu'l Fazl's relatively precise detailing of the rivers and streams that were frequently used in Mughal India as demarcators of the regional (*sūba*) and sub-regional (*sarkār*) administrative divisions, though not, as noted in the earlier passage on the metaphorical northern "ocean," with the northern Himalayan limits.

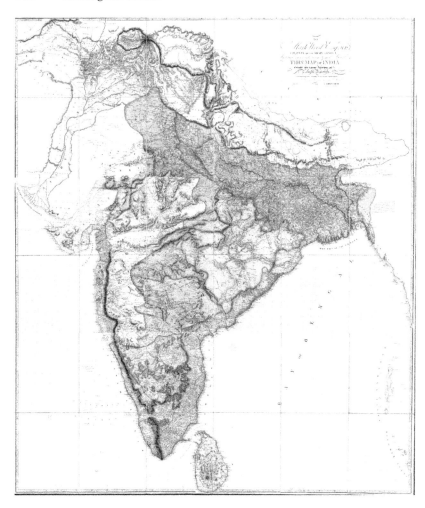

Map 4.1 "Six sheet map of Hindostan" (1804). Aaron Arrowsmith. PAHAR/Mountains of Central Asia Digital Dataset. Note the linearity with which the Himalayas and other mountain ranges are represented.

accomplished in a number of early nineteenth-century works by scholar-administrators that sought to bring together all the useful information that could be gained from a study of a particular neighboring region. Foremost among these were Francis Buchanan's *A Journey from Madras Through the Countries of Mysore, Canara, and Malabar* (1807) and *An Account of the Kingdom of Nepal* (1819), Mountstuart Elphinstone's

Account of the Kingdom of Caubul (1815), John Malcolm's *History of Persia* (1815), and James Tod's *Annals and Antiquities of Rajast'han* (1829–32). These works followed the convention of beginning histories with a brief geographical description – a natural move given that the subject itself was a geographical expression. Elphinstone gathered his information gathered during a diplomatic mission to the Afghan court of Shah Shujah Durrani in 1808–9.[31] Malcolm, who succeeded Elphinstone as Governor of Bombay and had undertaken a similarly ambitious diplomatic mission to Persia in 1801, drew upon troves of Persian documents collected while in India to complete his work. Translations of these documents in turn formed a major portion of Hamilton's sources for *The East India Gazetteer*.[32] Likewise, Tod's work drew on a vast array of materials collected while in various military and administrative postings. In all these works geography was prioritized as first-order information. Like Brooke before him, Tod made this assumption explicit, writing in his *Annals and Antiquities of Rajast'han*: "The basis of this work is the geography of the country, the historical and statistical portion being *consequent and subordinate thereto*."[33]

While Tod's and Malcolm's works devote a few sparse pages to a general setting of the scene, Elphinstone dedicated the whole first book of his first volume (some eighty-four pages) to a systematic detailing of geography. He relegated his travel narrative to his introduction, thus segregating the experiential narrative from the systematic and static – or statistical – accounting of his subject.[34] Unsurprisingly, Elphinstone began with borders. In addition to enclosing a calculable area, borderlines ostensibly also reflected the notion of discrete and unambiguous sovereignty. In his *Account of the Kingdom of Caubul*, Elphinstone used the *khutba* – the weekly sermon in which a ruler's name is inserted into prayers – and the inscription of coins with rulers' names as the two best

---

[31] Bayly, *Empire and Information*, 128. Bayly notes the dates as 1808–10.

[32] Hamilton, *The East India Gazetteer*, xi: "a very considerable portion of the most valuable information contained in this publication will be found to be entirely new, being extracted from various unpublished manuscripts, collected by Sir John Malcolm, while he filled important official and diplomatic situations in Hindostan and Persia, and communicated by him in the most handsome and liberal manner."

[33] James Tod, *Annals and Antiquities of Rajast'han* (London: George Routledge, 1914), 1:2. My emphasis.

[34] Examples of official and private *Tours* and *Journeys* are too numerous to merit enumeration. For one such example of an official tour, see Clements R. Markham, ed., *Narratives of the Mission of George Bogle to Tibet, and of the Journey of Thomas Manning to Lhasa, edited, with notes, and introduction and lives of Mr Bogle and Mr Manning* (1876). For private examples, see Thomas Pennant's *A Tour in Scotland and Voyage to the Hebrides* (1772); Samuel Johnson, *Journey to the Western Islands of Scotland* (1775); James Boswell, *Journal of a Tour to the Hebrides with Samuel Johnson LL.D.* (1786); or Arthur Young's *Tour of Ireland* (1780).

"tests" for determining how far Afghan sovereignty extended.[35] This assumed that the allegiance of any given community could be "fixed" like a point on map, ignoring the reality that coins, even more than allegiances, could move. His tests also suggested a looser notion of sovereignty, one that perhaps reflected the overlapping and fluctuating political configurations in South Asia at that time.

Alongside his religious and numismatic tests, Elphinstone posited "natural divisions" to bound the range of Shah Shujah's rule, suggesting that more mappable objects were better indicators of the physical limits of sovereignty. While this comported, in a very general sense, with older practices like Abu'l Fazl's description of the actual and metaphorical "oceans" surrounding Hindustan, Elphinstone adduced a greater degree of systematic detail to assert and describe the "natural" boundaries separating "Hindoostaun and [the Kingdom of] Caubul."[36] These were fixed markers following in the separating lines of watersheds, foreshadowing the later nineteenth-century concept of the "water-parting principle," a topic discussed in the second chapter of this book.

At the conclusion of his first chapter, which detailed mountains, rivers, and deserts, Elphinstone revealed that he had fact defined something new, a unified territory enclosed by ostensibly natural boundary lines: "*The Afghauns have no general name for their country*; but that of Afghaunistaun, which was probably first employed in Persia, is frequently used in books, and is not unknown to the inhabitants of the country to which it applies. I shall, therefore, use it in future to express the country of which I have just described the limits."[37] Adopting the old Persian descriptor "Afghaunistaun," Elphinstone gave it new precise and geographically determined borders. These limits were reinforced – at least for the mountainous northern and eastern regions – on the map made by Elphinstone's official surveyor, Lieutenant John Macartney.

As Alexander Cunningham did later for Ladakh, Elphinstone thus constructed borderlines around his object of study. His statement quoted above clearly confirms a key assertion of Ben Hopkins's *Making of Modern Afghanistan*: that the geographic expression called "Afghanistan" was largely a product of the early nineteenth-century British official mind.[38] Hopkins further noted that colonial visions of territory in that era imposed "Westphalian state forms" over alternative

---

[35] Mountstuart Elphinstone, *An Account of the Kingdom of Caubul, and Its Dependencies in Persia, Tartary, and India; Comprising a View of the Afghaun Nation, and a History of the Dooraunee Monarchy* (London: Longman, Hurst, Rees, Orme, and Brown, 1815), 1:112.
[36] Elphinstone, 1:116.   [37] Elphinstone, 1:125. My emphasis.
[38] Hopkins, *Modern Afghanistan*, 11.

indigenous concepts of space.[39] Nor was Elphinstone's preoccupation with borders restricted to Afghanistan; it was becoming customary across the growing British Empire.[40]

Like Afghanistan before Elphinstone's *Account*, Ladakh was *terra incognita* to the East India Company. Hamilton's 1815 *East India Gazetteer* said that its "limits are wholly undefined, and the interior has been but imperfectly explored. ... We are so little acquainted with the interior of this province, that it has never been accurately ascertained what religion the natives profess; but from their geographical position, and other circumstances, it is probable they follow the doctrines of Buddha."[41]

The first colonial official to write extensively on Ladakh was William Moorcroft, who spent two years there (September 1820–22).[42] During that time, Moorcroft and his traveling companion, George Trebeck, kept voluminous journals that would later be edited and published by the English orientalist Horace Hayman Wilson. Along with Alexander Cunningham's 1854 book, *Ladák, Physical, Statistical, and Historical*, Moorcroft and Trebeck's *Travels*, would form the bedrock of subsequent colonial understandings of the region. Cunningham wrote admiringly that Moorcroft's "account of the country is marked by great shrewdness of observation, and by the most scrupulous accuracy. A more truthful chronicler than Moorcroft never lived."[43]

When Wilson later compiled the journals of Moorcroft and Trebeck in the 1840s, he placed Moorcroft's description of the boundaries and physical extent of Ladakh in the first descriptive section of the region. Wilson's table of contents is telling: "Description of Ladakh – Limits – Extent – Surface – Rivers – [details on specific rivers] – [varieties of

---

[39] Hopkins, "The Bounds of Identity."

[40] Hopkins, *Modern Afghanistan*, 12. For more on this connection to Mountstuart Elphinstone and the "Elphinstonian episteme," see Kyle Gardner, "Elphinstone, Geography, and the Specter of Afghanistan in the Himalaya," in *Mountstuart Elphinstone in South Asia: Pioneer of British Colonial Rule* (London: Hurst, 2019).

[41] Hamilton, *The East India Gazetteer*, 482. In 1815 it was still assumed, as maps of the time indicate, that Ladakh was on the Ganges, not the Indus. The second *East India Gazetteer* entry for "Lahdack" references a town that is most likely Leh. "A town in the province of Lahdack, placed in the maps in Lat 35*N. Long. 78* 10' E. but as the geography of the province is as yet very uncertain, it is probable that when better explored a new position will be assigned to this place. Merchants travelling from Hindostan to Yarchand in Chinese Tartary rendezvous at this place, from whence they proceed in a body, travelling the greatest part of the way along the banks of the Indus, which they assert comes within two days journey of Lahdack. If true, this fact would materially alter the geography of this part of Asia, but the natives are generally so loose and inaccurate in their observations, that it cannot be depended on." Hamilton, *The East India Gazetteer*, 482–83. Those natives, not surprisingly, were right.

[42] Cunningham, *Ladák*, 7.   [43] Cunningham, 7.

plants] – Animals – Minerals."[44] Though Moorcroft's observations on Ladakh's "Limits" – which he variously referred to as "borders," "boundaries," and "frontiers" – referenced specific locations on routes that he traversed or learned about from informants, he nevertheless introduced his detailed studies of the region with a description of a polity broadly bounded by natural and political borders:[45]

Ladakh is bounded on the north-east by the mountains which divide it from the Chinese province of Khoten, and on the east and south-east by Rodokh and Chan-than, dependencies of Lassa: on the south by the British province of Bisahar, and by the hill states of Kulu and Chamba. The latter also extends along the south-west till it is met by Kashmir. ... The north is bounded by the Karakoram mountains and Yarkand. / The precise extent of Ladakh can scarcely be stated without an actual survey; but our different excursions, and the information we collected, enabled us to form an estimate, which is, probably, not far wide of the truth. From north to south, or from the foot of the Karakoram mountains to the fort of Trankar in Piti [Spiti], the distance is rather more than two hundred miles; and from east to west, or from the La Ganskiel pass to that of Zoje La, it cannot be less than two hundred and fifty. The outline, however, is irregular, being contracted on the north-west and south-west, and the whole area may not much exceed thirty thousand square miles.[46]

Moorcroft's treatments thus proceeded on the straightforward assumption that Ladakh was to be enclosed in borderlines and determined to be a territory of square miles bounded by similar territories ("Rodokh and Chan'than," etc.).

In the preface he wrote for Moorcroft's compiled journals, Horace Hayman Wilson employed a telling geographical image about this whole new genre of information: "The embassy of Mr. Elphinstone to Kabul, in 1808 ... was the means of introducing us to much new knowledge of countries beyond the Indian Caucasus; and more recently, the travels of Lieut. Burnes ... have completed *the line of information* from Kabul to Bokhara, and connected it with that obtained by Fraser and Connolly in Khorasan." The greater purpose of such lines was clear to the 1846 boundary commission led by Alexander Cunningham and Patrick Alexander Vans Agnew (see Chapter 2). They were to set the boundary between the newly formed Jammu and Kashmir state and the East India

---

[44] William Moorcroft and George Trebeck, *Travels in the Himalayan Provinces of Hindustan and the Panjab; in Ladakh and Kashmir; in Peshawar, Kabul, Kunduz, and Bokhara; from 1819 to 1825*, ed. Horace Hayman Wilson (London: John Murray, 1841), 1:x.

[45] Moorcroft and Trebeck, *Travels*, 1:x. For example, in volume 1, Moorcroft notes, "Along the eastern frontier of Ladakh, in an almost semicircular line, is the province of Chan-than" (p. 360). On page 390, he refers to the "border of Chinese Turkistan" without giving any precise location. And on page 440, he notes that "the boundary of Ladakh was pointed out to us as extending from the angle of a hill about five miles to the east, to the low pass of La Ganskiel, on the road to Gardokh, about fourteen miles distant to the southward."

[46] Moorcroft and Trebeck, 1:258–59.

Company's directly held western Himalayan territories in Kullu, Lahoul, and Tehri-Garhwal. Cunningham noted that this was because "the British Government determined to remove the most common cause of all disputes in the East – an unsettled boundary."[47]

Like Elphinstone's *Account of the Kingdom of Caubul*, the organizational structure of Cunningham's *Ladák* suggested a basic premise: information about place should precede information about people, their society, culture, history, and language(s).

The two texts followed a consistent ordering of geographical information, beginning with boundary lines before detailing the mountain systems, water systems, and climate within those lines. But it is fair to ask how one could write about "the Kingdom of Caubul" or "Ladak" without first describing what is meant by these places. In fact it was far from obvious that, when Elphinstone or Cunningham appeared on the scene, these were fully bounded or fixed territories on the order of post-Westphalian (more accurately, post-Congress of Vienna) European states. While Elphinstone sought to define the extent of the territory of the Kingdom of Caubul, Cunningham and the other boundary commissioners were given a mandate to "lay down" the boundaries of Ladakh, thus explicitly acknowledging that preexisting markers of territorial limits were insufficient for the territorializing purposes of the growing imperial state.

When it came time for Cunningham to publish his findings, he drew heavily on Moorcroft. His introduction fixed Ladakh in time and space – asserting that the oldest mention of the region could be found in the writings of Ptolemy and briefly outlining the major mountain ranges bounding the region.[48] His first substantive section, on geography, largely followed Moorcroft's general description regarding the "boundaries and extent" of Ladakh:

On the north it is divided by the Kárákoram mountains from the Chinese district of Kotan. To the east and south-east are the Chinese districts of Rudok and Chumurti; and to the south are the districts of Lahul and Spiti, now attached to British India, bur formerly belonging to Ladák. To the west lie Kashmir and Balti, the former separated by the western Himalaya, and the latter by an imaginary line drawn from the mouth of the Dras river to the sources of the Nubra river. / Its greatest extent is from north-west to south-east, from the head of the Dras river, in longitude 75* 30' to Chibra, on the Indus, in longitude 79* 10', a distance of 240 miles. Its greatest breadth is 290 miles, from the Kárákoram Pass, in north latitude 35* 25'. Its mean length is 200 miles, and its mean breadth 150 miles. Its whole extent is therefore only 30,000 square miles.[49]

---

[47] Cunningham, *Ladák*, 13.   [48] Cunningham, 3.   [49] Cunningham, 17–18.

Cunningham's inclusion of lines of longitude and latitude and his frequent detailing of measured distances ("feet" is the most commonly used word in his book apart from "stop words"[50]) suggests an added degree of precision that Moorcroft had marked as lacking in the absence of precise surveys. Yet Cunningham's similar figure for Ladakh's square mileage indicates either his continued reliance on Moorcroft's boundaries or similar means of calculation.[51] Cunningham then went on to delineate the "natural divisions of the country" along the mountains and drainage basins of the Indus, reflecting his mandate to make the "water-partings" (the edges of abutting watersheds) the eastern and northern boundaries of the region. As shown in Table 4.1, only after Cunningham detailed the major constituent geographical features did he proceed to discuss the people who inhabited the region, their material production, history, and language. Texts like Elphinstone's and Cunningham's were the privately published forebears of the official genre of gazetteer.

4.1.2   Gazetteers: Ordering Information

In later decades the place of geography in the growing volume of official colonial publications became graphically – and consistently – illustrated by official gazetteers published by the British Government of India. Historians have long accepted that colonial knowledge was central to the history of British rule in India. This knowledge became more systematic after the reconstruction of British rule in 1858. As the British Raj became more security-conscious, it increasingly employed statistical and ethnographic information to attempt to better control the large swathes of people and territory of India. This strategy of organized information was most apparent in the official gazetteers that emerged in the second half of the nineteenth century.

While the term "gazetteer" generally signified a "geographical index or dictionary" in the eighteenth century, it took on a much more expansive meaning for the British in the second half of the nineteenth century, particularly when the government of India began to focus on the production of detailed district-level volumes. The bibliographer Henry

---

[50] In Cunningham's *Ladák*, "feet" occurs roughly 704 times, while "Ladak" occurs only 579 (coincidentally, the same number of times that "Ladakh" appears in the first volume of Moorcroft and Trebeck's *Travels*). The next most frequently used words are "river" and "mile" at 392 and 336 times, respectively. To calculate this I uploaded an OCR version of Cunningham's text to the data-scraping site http://voyant-tools.org. "Stop words" are the most common words – typically definite and indefinite articles, prepositions, etc. – that can be removed by computing programs to search more effectively for keywords.

[51] I.e., through either the use of on-the-ground measurements or the use of a map.

Table 4.1 *Comparison of contents of Elphinstone's and Cunningham's texts*

Account of the Kingdom of Caubul (1815)	Ladák, physical, statistical, historical (1854)
Introduction	Introduction
Book 1: Geographical Description of Afghaunistaun	Geography [incl. "General Description" and "Boundaries and Extent"]
1: Situation and Boundaries of Afghaunistaun	Mountains
2: Mountains of Afghaunistaun	Rivers
3: Rivers of Afghaunistaun	Lakes and Springs
4: Natural and Political Divisions of Afghaunistaun	Roads, Passes, Bridges
5: Of the Climate of Afghaunistaun – Rain	Climate
6: Animals, Vegetables, and Minerals of Afghaunistaun	Productions
Book 2: General Account of the Inhabitants of Afghaunistan	Commerce
1: Introduction, Origin, and Early History of the Afghauns	Government
2: Divisions and Government of the Afghaun Nation	People
3: Marriages, Condition of Women, Funerals, etc.	History
4: Education, Language, and Literature of the Afghauns	Religion
5: Religion, Sects, Moolahs, Superstitions, etc.	Language
6: Hospitality, Predatory Habits, etc.	Comparison of the Various Alpine Dialects, from the Indus to the Ghagra
7: Manners, Customs, and Character of the Afghauns	Magnetical Observations
8: Of the Inhabitants of Towns	Meteorological Observations
9: Of the Great	
10: Trade of Caubul	
11: Husbandry of Caubul	
12: Taujiks, Hindkees, and Other Inhabitants of Afghaunistaun	

Scholberg defined this particular British colonial form of the genre as follows: "A district gazetteer is a comprehensive description of a district or state of British India ... including historical, archeological, political, economic, sociological, commercial and statistical data."[52] Missing

---

[52] Henry Scholberg, *The District Gazetteers of British India: A Bibliography* (Zug, Switzerland: Inter Documentation Company, 1970), iv.

from Scholberg's definition is the geographical element found in eighteenth-century examples and the works of Elphinstone, Cunningham, et al. – an omission all the more surprising given that each district gazetteer begins with a detailed section devoted to geography.[53] But Scholberg did acknowledge the variety of precursors to the official gazetteers, singling out Cunningham's *Ladák* in particular:

> One of the finest examples of a book which was not intended to be a district gazetteer when it was written, but which falls beautifully into the genre of district gazetteers is Brevet Major Alexander Cunningham's *Ladák, Physical, Statistical, and Historical; with Notices of Surrounding Countries*. This is a 485-page work published in 1854 that, as its title implies, describes the district of Ladakh in the manner which was to be typical of district gazetteers of a later time.[54]

Though a dozen or more works like Cunningham's *Ladák* were published privately from 1800 through the 1850s, the government of India began to realize after the Rebellion of 1857 that it should invest in the systematic production of such guides for both its directly and indirectly administered territories, as well as for some of the neighboring regions such as Central Asia and Afghanistan. In 1869, the viceroy of India Lord Mayo commissioned William Wilson Hunter "to visit the various provincial governments with a view to submit a comprehensive scheme for utilizing the information already collected; for prescribing the principles to be thenceforth adopted; and the consolidation into one work [of] the whole of the materials."[55] These were to be systematic manuals for administrators and secondarily for scholars. The early district gazetteers, many of which Hunter himself compiled, were to feed information to the *Imperial Gazetteer*. Hunter modeled his project on two notable predecessors: "When I started, I had two national enterprises in my mind: the *Aí'n-i-Akbari*, or statistical survey of India, conducted three hundred years ago by the Finance Minister of Akbar, the greatest of Mughal Emperors; and the military survey of Egypt, executed by France in the first quarter of the present century.[56] The former is a masterpiece of administrative detail, the latter a brilliant effort of organized research."[57] Hunter's invocation of these two works suggested both the grand scale his twelve-year undertaking was to pursue and the level of detail he sought to include.

---

[53] OED Online, s.v. "Gazetteer, n."   [54] Scholberg, *District Gazetteers*, 53.
[55] Scholberg, 5–6.
[56] *Description de L'Egypte, Ou Recueil Des Observations et Des Recherches Qui Ont Été Faites En Egypte Pendant l'Expédition de l'Armée Française*, 36 vols. (Paris, 1821).
[57] William Wilson Hunter, preface to *The Imperial Gazetteer of India*, 1:xxix–xxx.

As Maureen L. P. Patterson has noted, until 1869 "district accounts were haphazardly produced and were not uniform in format or coverage."[58] But from the late 1870s onward, the district gazetteers and the *Imperial Gazetteer* alike followed a consistent order of presentation, as did compliers and editors of the genre like Edwin T. Atkinson and the prolific Denzil Ibbetson for ease of access and reference.[59] *Imperial Gazetteers* were issued to all major administrative posts along with a copy of the latest relevant district or similar local gazetteer. For instance, the list of books held by the British Joint Commissioners stationed at Leh in Ladakh always included, from its initial publication in 1890 on, a copy of the *Gazetteer of Kashmír and Ladák*. This self-consciously scholarly gazetteer listed its sources in its introduction, following the model typical of the provincial and district gazetteers which all drew on a growing volume of ethnographic sources to provide support for the information they presented. In the case of the *Gazetteer of Kashmír and Ladák*, Cunningham's *Ladák* and Moorcroft's *Travels* unsurprisingly headed the long list of accounts used to compile the information presented.[60] Following independence, the Republic of India continued to update and publish many of these manuals – the gazetteers of Jammu and Kashmir being no exception.

Other official documents were meant to provide supplemental kinds of information to the gazetteers. A circular sent to all revenue officers in the Punjab from the senior secretary to the financial commissioner of the government of the Punjab noted, for instance, that "the Final Settlement Report should not ordinarily contain historical or descriptive material, which properly belongs to the Gazetteer. It should be what its name implies, a report of the settlement operations just completed."[61] Nevertheless, as this circular went on to note, the Settlement Officer should have already submitted an "Assessment or Revenue Rate Report" which was to begin with "an account of the Physical Geography of the

---

[58] Maureen L. P. Patterson, *South Asian Civilizations: A Bibliographic Synthesis* (Chicago: University of Chicago Press, 1981), xvii.

[59] E.g., Edwin T. Atkinson, *The Himalayan Districts of the North-Western Provinces of India* (Allahabad: North-western Provinces' Govt. Press, 1882); Denzil Ibbetson, *Gazetteer of the Gújrát District, 1883–84, Compiled and Published under the Authority of the Punjab Government* (Lahore: Arya Press, 1884).

[60] Intelligence Branch, *Gazetteer of Kashmír and Ladák, Together with Routes in the Territories of the Maharaja of Jamú and Kashmír. Compiled (for Political and Military Reference) under the Direction of the Quarter Master General in India in the Intelligence Branch* (Calcutta: Superintendent of Government Printing, India, 1890). It is worth noting that Elphinstone's *Account of the Kingdom of Caubul* was absent in these lists.

[61] J. M. Douie to All Revenue Officers in the Punjab, 1890. HPSA-S Circular issuing instructions for "the preparation of Final Settlement Reports, and the revision and maintenance of District Gazetteers; and Appendix B in HPSA-S, B. No. 63, S. No. 1077, Deputy Commissioner, Kangra, Head 40, file N. 40(1) "Rules for the preparation of district gazetteers," dated May 8, 1903. My emphasis.

tract." Thus, geographical information was seen as prerequisite for other organized forms of colonial knowledge. These forms – whether gazetteer or settlement report – were often produced by the same officials. As the aforementioned circular reminded him, it was also the duty of the Settlement Officer "to draft a new edition of the *Gazetteer* of the district. In doing so, *he must in every respect conform to the plan of the Gazetteer already published, and the order in which the subjects are there arranged should under no circumstances be departed from, as uniformity in this respect is a valuable addition to the usefulness of the* Gazetteers."[62]

Like other forms of official information, such as military statistics or settlement reports, the gazetteer was packaged in a particular standardized form with an anticipated order of information (Table 4.2).[63] Knowing exactly where certain kinds of facts were to be found was a key aspect of its utility. An administrator could pick up a copy of any gazetteer and know where to find information on a district's roads, trade, or spoken languages. But beyond functionality, the consistent ordering also reflected how different kinds of facts were meant to relate to one another. The "order of things" in the gazetteers suggested that geographical information epistemically preceded social, historical, economic, and political subjects. The first subject of the gazetteer was to establish precise and complete borders around its subject and articulate the "natural divisions" that supported those boundaries.

4.1.3   Settlement Reports, Route Books, Military Reports

It is worth noting that gazetteers were by no means the only manuals of governance on this model. Other official manuals, including settlement reports, route books, and military reports, were frequently produced and widely circulated to serve specific purposes, from revenue collection or moving military troops.

Settlement reports varied across time and space in South Asia in terms of the land-tenure model adopted (zamindari, ryotwari, or mahalwari). Indeed, the earliest settlements (i.e., the Permanent Settlement of Bengal, 1793) were not compiled into specific reports, but rather formed parts of larger legislation (i.e., the Cornwallis Code of 1793). Yet these established the basic practices that would later yield the standardized kinds of settlement reports common by the second half of the nineteenth century. Whether written early or late their purposes were the same: to establish an accounting of agricultural land revenues to better determine taxes to be extracted

[62] Douie.   [63] Hevia, *Imperial Security State*, 4.

Table 4.2 *Initial contents and section descriptions of provincial and district gazetteers*

Chapter 1: Descriptive[a]	
A. Physical Aspects	(a) Name in vernacular, with derivation if known; area.
	(b) Boundaries and general configuration, including natural divisions and hill system; scenery generally.
	(c) River system, and lakes.
	(d) Brief sketch of Geology and Botany (Arrangements are being made for the writing of special articles on these subject [*sic*] by experts.)
	(e) Characteristic or noteworthy wild animals, etc.
B. Meteorology	(a) General account of climate in different parts; mean temperature where recorded.
	(b) General account of rainfall, with averages for chief natural divisions, noticing its relative variability in different parts of the district and its fluctuations in past years.
	(c) Notable cyclones, earthquakes, and floods.
C. History	A general knowledge of Indian history should be assumed on the part of the readers of the District articles, and the latter need only mention the various historic States of which the District has formed part, the date of its coming under British rule, and any especially noteworthy events which have occurred within it. Interesting archeological remains should also be noted.
D. Population	Distribution of population by natural or administrative divisions; number of towns and villages according to 1901 Census; population at last four censuses with explanations of striking variations; residential characteristics of towns and villages, *i.e.* the grouping of houses in the town and village areas; movement of population and migration; occupations.

[a] These descriptions come from an appendix titled "Sketch of Contents of the Different Sections of the Provincial Gazetteer with Notes, Where Necessary, Regarding the Special Treatment of Subjects in District Gazetteers." However, the sections themselves directly align with an earlier appendix, "Table of Contents of District Gazetteers." I have not been able to find a similar description given for *District Gazetteers*, so I have utilized the *Provincial Gazetteer* descriptions with the assumption that since it exactly follows the contents of the *District Gazetteers*, the descriptions for those contents will be similar.

and to establish clear lines of ownership for determining property rights. As with gazetteers, this process again required ascertaining a precise description of the region under examination. Table 4.3 illustrates the order of information given for the Ladakh Settlement by the authorities of Jammu and Kashmir at the behest of the British government.

Table 4.3 *Contents of preliminary report of Ladakh Settlement (1908)*

Chapter 1: Descriptive
  Tract under Settlement
  Boundaries
  Natural Divisions
  Physical Features
  Area
  Climate
  Rain and Snow-fall
  Inhabitants
  Population
Chapter II: Short Revenue and Political History
Chapter III: Present Settlement
Chapter IV: General Conditions
Chapter V: Tenures and Tenancy Rules
Chapter VI: Matters Relating to Assessment
Chapter VII: Miscellaneous
Chapter VII: Miscellaneous

Source: Jammu and Kashmir State Archive, Leh Branch (hereafter JKSA-L). Chaudhri Mohamad, *Preliminary Report of Ladakh Settlement* (Jammu: Ranbir Prakesh Press, 1908).

Similarly, in the context of military intelligence, military reports and route books offered convenient, portable information to those concerned with security on and beyond the imperial frontier. As James Hevia has observed, "within the imperial security apparatus, the military report was the essential form of summary for storing the military statistics of other states or well-developed territories."[64] The difference between the gazetteer and the military report, Hevia notes, concerns the range of information and its application. Gazetteers sought to present "virtually everything that was factually known about the particular locale," while the military report organized "detailed information that might be of importance for planning, mobilizing, and executing a campaign." Hevia illustrates this with a typical example of the genre, the 1906 Military Report on Afghanistan.

The volume begins with the main geographical features of Afghanistan and moves on to communications, fortresses and defenses, climate, resources, history (in this case, primarily British military adventures in Afghanistan), ethnology, administration, and the current military and political situation. By the 1890s, the

---

[64] Hevia, 107–8. Hevia goes on to note that "adjacent to the military report were two other genres – the handbook, which was usually a detailed collection of factual information on a foreign army, and the Who's Who, which provided biographical information on foreign personages."

structural order of the military report that can be seen in this one on Afghanistan, with only slight variations such as references to harbors and naval capabilities, was firmly in place. Each book was of a uniform size, shape, paper quality and type-face, and the small format made them easily portable.[65]

The route book, in turn, instructed military leaders on the best means of moving troops to a particular location. Across the genres, however – route book, military report, settlement report, or the gazetteer – the primary position of geographical information emphasized the epistemic axiom that place often preceded people in the eyes of the imperial state. This epistemic assertion was emphatic for strategic territories like Ladakh, viewed by the imperial government principally in terms of its position as a frontier. Like the gazetteer, the reference manuals for governance and security reflected both the concrete utility of having facts at hand and the more abstract epistemic assumptions of the state. Administrators could read these manuals for facts (the term "manual" itself signals the use of the book in hand), but their contents also reflected the imperial state's attempt to "read" places and peoples and to situate them – trigonome-trically, in case of geographical information – within a broader informa-tional order. This ordering was a crucial prerequisite for viewing the world *geopolitically* (as a series of interconnected territories dependent on geographical features) and *geostrategically* (utilizing those geographical features to the advantage of the state).[66]

4.2   Reading from the Ground Up: Sovereignty, Territory, and Tribute

Viewing a district, province, princely state, or empire as a static territory with fixed borderlines, often attached to "natural" features and a historically cohesive population, made sense to the British imperial state, even if the empire's disposition toward expansion meant that those borders frequently changed.[67] The model of organizing imperial space by territory is a political concept that has received thoughtful treatment by several prominent scholars of European history and political theory. Stuart Elden's recent exploration of the emergence of this idea within Western political thought provides a working definition to test in the imperial context. For Elden, as was noted in the introduction,

[65] Hevia, 108.
[66] Another definition of "geostrategy" would be Brzezinski's: "the strategic management of geopolitical interests." Zbigniew Brzezinski, *The Grand Chessboard: American Primacy and Its Geostrategic Imperatives* (New York: Basic Books, 1997), xiv.
[67] This was noted by imperial administrators, such as Alfred Lyall in "Frontiers and Protectorates" and George Curzon in *Frontiers*.

territory is, broadly speaking, a historically produced "bounded space under the control of a group of people, usually a state."[68] Borders are thus the necessary prerequisite of territory and of the process of generating and defining territory: territorialization.

At the local level the establishment of clearly defined linear borders allowed for the key extractive activity of the state (imperial, or otherwise): taxation. As Owen Lattimore noted, walls – as physical manifestations of borders – work not just to keep "barbarians" out but to help keep taxpayers in.[69] At a wider level, precise borderlines also clearly symbolized the state's sovereignty, jurisdiction, and physical position relative to neighboring states. This clarity, it is worth noting, was not always in the interest of imperial administrators. As noted by numerous frontiers experts, there were multiple frontiers at which the empire ended.[70] The arrangement of frontiers and concomitant "buffer states" and "spheres of influence" sometimes led to ambiguous policy positions. Nonetheless, by the end of the nineteenth century the imperial British state insisted on increasingly precise language, location, and techniques to "delimit and demarcate" its territorial boundaries.[71] The concepts of frontiers and boundaries became increasingly distinct. Whatever political aspirations might have existed for the spaces beyond the administrative boundary, it was crucial to have the empire's formal limits known, marked, and in accordance with a set of standardized practices.[72] Where this boundary was still uncertain, the central government repeatedly encouraged its local administrators to clarify those limits for the purposes of maps, gazetteers, and military reports, so as to better exercise judicial authority over its subjects and minimize the potential for conflicts with neighboring states.

By emphasizing borders as the first condition for legibility, the imperial state often came into conflict with populations that regularly transgressed them. In addition to nomadic groups, traders, and pilgrims, long-

---

[68] Elden, *The Birth of Territory*, 322.

[69] A point James C. Scott also makes in the concluding chapter of *Against the Grain: A Deep History of the Earliest States* (New Haven, CT: Yale University Press, 2017).

[70] See, for instance, Henry Bathurst Hanna, *India's Scientific Frontier: Where Is It? What Is It?* (Westminster: Archibald Constable, 1895); Thomas H. Holdich, *The Indian Borderland, 1880–1900* (London: Methuen, 1901); and Holdich, *Political Frontiers and Boundary Making*.

[71] Henry McMahon gave these two terms distinct technical meanings. "'Delimitation' I have taken to comprise the determination of a boundary line by treaty or otherwise, and its definition in written, verbal terms; 'demarcation' to comprise the actual laying down of a boundary line on the ground, and its definition by boundary pillars or other similar physical means." A. Henry McMahon, "International Boundaries," *Journal of the Royal Society of Arts* 84, no. 4330 (1935): 4.

[72] Lyall, "Frontiers and Protectorates."

established political relationships throughout the Himalaya often challenged Westphalian notions of ostensibly sovereign and "perfectly equal" states. Precolonial customary relations between political actors like the *rgyal.po* of Ladakh and the Ganden Phodrang (dGa'.ldan Pho.brang) of Central Tibet were either dismissed by the British imperial state or seen as threats that could undermine the jurisdictional power of the border. Long-running historical patterns of pastoralism and season-dependent trade challenged state-imposed borders as well. As outstanding studies of the dynamics between plains and hill societies have shown, peoples who regularly move pose a deep threat to the state's legibility practices like census taking, taxation, and the regulation of a fixed population – practices which were all reflected in manuals of governance like district gazetteers.[73] A legible population required a legible territory and, therefore, a legible border.

Even though the political structures of Ladakh depended in part on the extraction of labor and revenue from a static peasant base, its economy was closely tied to the influx of goods from short- and medium-distance trade. Participating in segments of long-distance trans-Himalayan trade between Kashmir and the plains of India on one side and Tibet, Kashgar, and Yarkand on the other generated crucial revenue as well. As illustrated in Chapter 1, the rulers of precolonial Ladakh had generally been comfortable with the movement of traders, pilgrims, and seminomadic pastoralists. Indeed, these mobile peoples carried the economic lifeblood of the region. Their traded goods were typically taxed at the border points established through treaties like the one signed between the rulers of Ladakh and central Tibet at Tingmosgang in 1684.[74] The revenue generated from this settlement came in addition to the annual tithes paid to local monasteries as determined by local assessments on the holdings of agriculturalist families. Individuals and families were responsible for paying these costs, often in kind or with their own labor. Traders, nomads, and agriculturalists each paid different forms of tax. Consistency here mattered little to the *rgyal.*

---

[73] Neeladri Bhattacharya, "Predicaments of Mobility: Peddlers and Itinerants in Nineteenth Century Northwestern India," in *Society and Circulation: Mobile People and Itinerant Cultures in South Asia, 1750–1950*, ed. Claude Markovits, Jacques Pouchepadass, and Sanjay Subrahmanyam (Delhi: Permanent Black, 2003); David Gilmartin, "Scientific Empire and Imperial Science: Colonialism and Irrigation Technology in the Indus Basin," *The Journal of Asian Studies* 53, no. 4 (1994): 1127–49; David Gilmartin, *Blood and Water: The Indus River Basin in Modern History* (Berkeley: University of California Press, 2015); and Scott, *The Art of Not Being Governed*. In Scott's description of Zomia, what distinguishes the region is its relative statelessness, its relative equality, and the inability to effectively impose taxation (pp. 19–20).
[74] See Chapter 1.

po and his ministers who gathered much of their own revenue by direct or indirect participation in trade (the *rgyal.po* himself was known as the "Chief Trader of Ladakh"[75]).

Transcending Ladakh's minimally defined territorial limits were the religious and political relationships it maintained through a series of customary "tribute" missions; these also functioned to promote long-distance trade in high-value items like tea, gold, *charas* (hashish), and *pashm*. But the presumed political relationships represented by these tribute missions provoked anxieties among British frontier officials, as evidenced by Captain Henry Ramsay's attempts to abolish the *Lopchak* (the triennial Ladakhi tribute mission to Lhasa). The risk, for the British, was that a relationship which made sovereignty more ambiguous would erode, or erase, the political meaning of the border. What coherence or meaning could the borders inscribed on their maps and described in their gazetteers have, if they failed to sufficiently enclose a legible political entity? Further complicating the political ambiguity around the tribute missions were examples of noncontiguous or poorly defined territory that cast doubt on the very shape of Ladakh. Like other regions with undefined borders, or in cases of princely states with territorial enclaves elsewhere, information about Ladakh became less authoritative when the territory itself faded into indeterminate space.

The following sections explore case studies offering an alternative to the top-down reading of the landscape presented in the gazetteers and official publications. They include disputes over Ladakhi territory within Tibet, questions of tribute crossing British-imposed borders, grazing rights for seminomadic populations, taxation, and land change caused by natural disasters. They all reveal precolonial spatial configurations still rooted in the Himalayan locale, below the level of state-imposed territorial legibility. They illustrate how moving peoples and changing landscapes produced challenges for a state modeled on a static and enclosed vision of territory.

4.2.1   The Lopchak (lo.phyag) and Chaba (La.dwags gzhung.tshong)

In 1889, the former British Joint Commissioner in Ladakh, Ney Elias, responded to a request from Henry Mortimer Durand, the secretary of the Foreign Department, to provide context to concerns over apparent tribute missions between Ladakh and Tibet. No longer the chief British administrator in Ladakh, Elias had become an expert consulted on a wide

---

[75] Bray, "Lopchak."

array of frontier issues, ranging from Afghanistan to Siam.[76] "Briefly stated," Elias began his assessment,

[The British Joint Commissioner in Ladakh] Captain Ramsay comes to the conclusion (1) that the [deposed] Raja of Ladakh pays tribute to the Lhassa authorities; (2) that the Wazir of Ladakh [the Dogra-appointed *wazīr-i-wazārat*] sends tribute to the Chinese Ambans at Lhassa; (3) that Lhassa refuses to recognise that Ladakh belongs now to Kashmir, but affects to consider the Ladakh Rajas to be in power as heretofore; and (4) that Lhassa treats the Raja with some civility and treats the Kashmir Wazir with insolence. Captain Ramsay says the periodical missions can be stopped, and recommends that they should be stopped; he also recommends that the Raja should be removed from Ladakh together with his whole family, that the Wazir should not be allowed to correspond with the Lhassa authorities or with the Chinese authorities in Turkistan, and that Government should "arrange with the Darbar for a British administration of Ladakh."[77]

The tribute to which Henry Ramsay referred was the triennial Lopchak from Ladakh to Lhasa and the reciprocal annual *gzhung.tshong*, also known to Ladakhis as the Chaba (lit. "tea man") because of the main Tibetan commodity traded on the mission.[78]

While irregular gift exchanges preceded the 1684 Treaty of Tingmosgang, the treaty formally established these missions between the *rgyal.po* of Ladakh and the central Tibetan government. According to the *La.dwags rGyal.rabs*, the treaty signaled the formal establishment of regular commercial relations between the ruling regimes of both Ladakh and Tibet.[79] On the Lopchak, the Ladakhi emissaries brought the treasurer of the Central Tibetan government gold, saffron, calico, and soft cotton cloth,[80] along with smaller gifts for the heads of the major monasteries. In return, the Chaba mission brought Sichuanese tea and other goods from Lhasa. As John Bray has observed, the basic form of the mission changed little between 1684 and 1950, when the last Lopchak is recorded.[81] The reciprocal missions benefited from *'u.lag* (*corvée* labor, or *begār*) for their transport along the Leh–Lhasa route, while the note in the *La.dwags rGyal.rabs* to the effect that the mission also included 200 animals

---

[76] See Chapter 3 for Elias's time as British Joint Commissioner and Chapter 6 for his later boundary commission work. For his biography more generally, see Morgan, *Ney Elias*.

[77] NAI, Foreign, Secret F, September 1889, nos. 211–17. "Lhassa authorities still recognize the Ex-Raja of Ladakh as in power and ignore the Kashmir Wazir."

[78] Bray, "Lopchak."

[79] Bray. The two regimes were the rNam.rgyal dynasty of Ladakh and the Ganden Phodrang of Central Tibet.

[80] *La.dwags rGyal.rabs*, Vol. 2, 42. "Soft cotton cloth" is Francke's translation of *bab.sta*.

[81] Central Intelligence Agency, Information Report, "Ladakh (Kashmir)-Tibet Trade/ Proposed Organization of 1950 Lobchag Mission," November 7, 1952.

besides riding horses and servants suggested that the commercial goals of the mission went well beyond the formal gift giving.[82]

The *La.dwags rGyal.rabs* also recorded a similar reciprocal gift exchange with Kashmir in which the *rgyal.po* of Ladakh presented the ruler of Kashmir with eighteen piebald horses, eighteen pods of musk, and eighteen white yak tails.[83] In exchange, the *rgyal.po* received a *jāgīr* (rent-free estate) at Naushahr in the Kashmir Valley. It is likely that this gift exchange ended with the Dogra invasion of Ladakh in 1834. In 1842 the Raja of Jammu, Gulab Singh, shored up his conquest of Ladakh by concluding a treaty signed by his representative, representatives of the Emperor of China, and the "Lama Guru of Lhasa" (the Dalai Lama).[84] The Lopchak was reaffirmed and continued under the watch of the newly appointed chief Dogra official in Ladakh, the *wazīr-i-wazārat*.[85]

Moorcroft and Cunningham both remarked on the Lopchak during their time in Ladakh. But it was only with the British Joint Commissioners Ney Elias and Henry Ramsay in the 1870s and 1880s that the implications of a tribute mission began to arouse anxieties at the top of the imperial bureaucracy. When Durand wrote to Elias for advice, he was doing so in the context of other concerns across the Himalayan frontier, particularly British India's relationship with Sikkim. There, in 1886, a small Tibetan militia had arrived in the vicinity of the Jelap Pass in response to reports of British road building. British troops responded with force in 1888, pushing the Tibetan soldiers across the Jelap Pass, the same route that Francis Younghusband's forces would take fifteen years later to invade Tibet.

Consulting with authorities like Elias across the Indo-Tibetan frontierlands, the Foreign Department began to perceive a broader pattern in trans-frontier political relationships. "These papers," Durand wrote regarding the British Joint Commissioner's memorandum on the

---

[82] Bray, "Lopchak."

[83] Bray. Bray notes that "two of the sets of gifts – the musk and the yak tails – correspond to the presents offered by Deldan Namgyal to Aurangzeb two decades earlier."

[84] JKSA-J. "Treaty between Ladakh and Tibet: 1920, 276/RP-4."

[85] The treaty reaffirmed that "the Darbar and Lhassa people ... will carry on the trade in Shawl, Pasham and Tea as before, by way of Ladak; and if any one of the Sri Raja's enemies comes to our territories and says anything against the Raja, we will not listen to him, and will not allow him to remain in our country; and whatever traders come from Ladak shall experience no difficulty from our side. We will not act otherwise but in the same manner as it has been prescribed in this meeting regarding the fixing of the Ladak frontier and the keeping open of the road for the traffic in Shawl, Pasham and Tea. We will observe our pledge to God, Gaitri and Pasi." Captain H. Ramsay to Colonel Parry Nisbet, June 23, 1889. NAI, Foreign, Secret F, September 1889, nos. 211–17. "Lhassa authorities still recognize the Ex-Raja of Ladakh as in power and ignore the Kashmir Wazir."

Lopchak, "come opportunely and show that Chinese and Tibetan pretensions in regard to Sikkim are not an isolated case, but part of a - system."[86] Durand shared Ramsay's concerns with the political officer in Sikkim, A. W. Paul, who expressed fears of Tibetan inroads into the British protectorate of Sikkim. In response to Durand's request, Paul wrote that the Lopchak mission

appears common to several other States: as Captain Ramsay points out the word is Lo-phyag (pronounced Lo-cha or in Ladakhi Lob-cha). Jueschke translate it "Embassy sent every year to the King to renew the oath of allegiance": Csoma de Körös translates it "Respects or homage paid every year by envoys to a superior lord." The Bhutanese call their agent or vakil according to Lauva Ugyen Gyatsho Lo-lchak-pa (Lo-cha-pa) which is evidently the same word misspelt, as I can find no such word in the dictionary as "Lchak."[87]

In reading the Ladakhi instance of tribute with Lhasa as part of a systemic series of relationships, Durand and other senior imperial officials began to see patterns in trans-frontier behavior. Not for the last time, the sense of political insecurity along the frontier inspired recommendations of taking direct control of the imperial periphery instead of relying on dependent states to do so.[88] Failing that step, however, Durand suggested greater oversight by the BJC. In August 1889, he forwarded the collected opinions of his frontier experts to the viceroy. On the matter of the Lopchak, he wrote: "I do not see how it is possible for any one to argue that the letters and presents in this case are purely complimentary and mean nothing. See particularly the answers of the Ambans. I have no doubt that the sending of them should be stopped, but I think we had better take no action until the Sikkim matter is settled."[89]

On August 16, 1889, the viceroy wrote to the Secretary of State for India: "There can, in our opinion, be no doubt that the Chinese and Tibetan pretensions in regard to Sikkim are part of a system, and that unless they are steadily resisted, we shall have much difficulty hereafter in dealing with the Himalayan States."[90] But there were also signs that the Government of Tibet in Lhasa was beginning to recognize a British frontier in Ladakh. In a letter from the *munshi* (clerk) of the Ladakh

---

[86] Durand to Viceroy. NAI, Foreign, Secret F, September 1889, nos. 211–17. "Lhassa authorities still recognize the Ex-Raja of Ladakh as in power and ignore the Kashmir Wazir."

[87] A. W. Paul, Esq. to Sir Mortimer Durand, August 14. 1889. NAI, Foreign, Secret F, September 1889, nos. 211–17. "Lhassa authorities still recognize the Ex-Raja of Ladakh as in power and ignore the Kashmir Wazir." The translation errors here are bountiful.

[88] Captain H. Ramsay to Colonel Parry Nisbet, June 23, 1889. NAI, Foreign, Secret F, September 1889, nos. 211–17. "Lhassa authorities still recognize the Ex-Raja of Ladakh as in power and ignore the Kashmir Wazir."

[89] Ramsay.   [90] Ramsay.

Agency Office to Ramsay in December 1889, the unnamed *munshi* noted that he had heard from two prominent Ladakhi traders, Hajis Haider Shah and Nasir Shah, that the leader of the *Chaba* had sent a report to Lhasa regarding the state of affairs in Ladakh. The Kashmir state, "at the suggestion of the British Government, [had], through the Wazir of Ladakh, placed a guard of sepoys on the frontier, and [the leader of the Chaba sent] them the report in order that they may be aware of it."[91] Nevertheless, this possible recognition of a frontier did little to assuage the British regarding the basic problem of the tribute missions.

Writing from Ladakh, Henry Ramsay continued to express his concern to his superiors, invoking his understanding of international law to bolster his case for alarm. "It is incompatible with our dignity as a leading Power that the petty State of Lhassa should treat Ladak, which by right of conquest belongs to one of our Indian feudatory chiefs, as being politically subordinate to Lhassa. For the international law on this point, please see Wheaton, Chapter 2, page 52."[92] Ramsay was so concerned by the continued political implications of the tribute missions that he submitted his May 1890 monthly diary directly to the Foreign Department in Shimla, breaking protocol by bypassing his superior officer in Srinagar.[93] Ramsay's fear was triggered by a report he had gathered from traders passing through Leh that the Leh-Yarkand road had been closed as a result of Tibetan concerns over Russian explorers traveling toward the "Leh–Lhasa frontier." His continued alarms, as well as his decision to abolish a passport system to make it easier for peasants unable to pay a newly raised tax, even triggered a formal letter from the Maharaja of Jammu and Kashmir to the Resident in Kashmir, complaining about Ramsay's "interference in the internal administration of Ladak."[94]

Against Ramsay's protests, Durand and the viceroy chose to let the matter drop. It resurfaced in 1899, when the new British Joint Commissioner, Captain R. L. Kennion, came to realize that the Jammu and Kashmir state government had started advancing money to the Lopchak mission as an official investment in the Leh–Lhasa trade. The prospect of a guaranteed 67 percent return on its investment appealed to

[91] Munshi of Ladakh Agency Office to the British Joint-Commissioner, Ladakh, November 25, 1889. NAI, Foreign, Frontier: Sec E, December, 182.

[92] Munshi.

[93] NAI, Foreign, Frontier Part B, July 1890, nos. 153–58. "Proposal of the British Joint Commissioner, Ladak, to put a stop to the trade between Ladak and Lhassa."

[94] Late Raja Amar Singh Ji Bahadur to Col. W. F., Resident in Kashmir, December 1890. JKSA-J, Persian Records, "Copy of a letter no. 1508, dated Dec. 1890 from Late Raja Amar Singh Ji Bahadur to Col. W. F., Resident in Kashmir, complaining against the interference in the internal adm of Ladakh Capt. Ramsay, BJC Leh and his conduct in flouting the orders of the state council."

the Kashmir Darbar, which had little concern that the mission might appear to be a form of tribute paid to Tibet, or China. But like his predecessors, Kennion concluded that "The triennial Lapchak [was] ... a pernicious anomaly which should be abolished as soon as possible." He also noted the existence of numerous other commercial missions. "The Triennial Lapchak is not the only commercial mission of the kind between Ladakh and Tibet, though the important one. In addition there are ten annual missions between either Leh and Lhassa or Leh and Gartok, ... all of which are entitled to a fixed amount of free carriage." But Kennion also saw reasons to keep these missions running, given the reluctance of the Tibetan government to allow the British into their country.[95] In 1900, it was decided that Kennion should travel to Western Tibet with a letter from Viceroy Curzon in an attempt to communicate with the government of Tibet. But he was rebuffed by the *gar. dpons* at Gartok, and returned to Leh. His rejection was added to the growing list of "intolerable treatment" by Tibet that would push the British to invade in 1903–4.[96]

From the perspective of the government of Jammu and Kashmir, given the guaranteed return on its investment, the missions did not seem to threaten their political standing vis-à-vis Tibet.[97] In February 1906 the Maharaja's officials released an order responding to renewed British threats to end the mission. "It is not desirable," the letter read, "to discontinue the sending of the Lapchak mission to Lhassa nor is it advisable that the concessions hitherto allowed to the Choba Mission, within State territories should be discontinued."[98] However, the Kashmir

---

[95] This was, after all, still four years before Younghusband's invasion in December 1903. Kennion went on to write, "So long however as the Lhassa Government maintains with success the ancient close border system, I am of opinion that it would be premature to abolish these, the almost only means of intercourse between Ladakh and Lhassa; but the sooner a way can be found to break through the cast iron hedge the Lhassa theocracy has set round the country, the better for any one and especially for the people of Tibet itself." Like many "men on the spot" before him, Kennion appreciated the possibility of commercial growth, though this often oscillated with the security concerns of increased transfrontier traffic. NAI, Foreign Department. "Lapchak Mission. Information regarding the Kashmir Frontier." Frontier B, November 1899. 141–46. Diary for 15th August to 15th September 1899.

[96] Bray, "Lopchak," 21; Kennion's official report is in OIOC/L/P&S/7/135, No 11. R. L. Kennion, *Sport and Life in the Further Himalaya* (Edinburgh: William Blackwood, 1910), 241–61.

[97] NAI, Foreign, Frontier B, November 1899, nos. 141–46. "Lapchak Mission. Information regarding the Kashmir Frontier." Diary for 15th August to 15th September 1899.

[98] Maharaja of Jammu and Kashmir, February 6, 1906. NAI, Foreign, Frontier, June 1906, no. 100, Part B., in File No. 376-X (Sec) 1932. "Supply to the Director-General of Commercial Intelligence of information regarding the leader of the Lapchak Mission and the trade in tourquoises between Ladakh and Lhassa."

government's statement noted a growing problem, the exploitation of the zamindars (landed peasants) in their obligation to provide *corvée* labor.[99] "This will be secured by directing that so much transport as is necessary to be supplied for the purposes of these two Missions ... should be obtained as heretofore but that payment for such transport at the rates recommended by the Wazir-i-Wazarat should be made by the Darbar."[100]

On the Tibetan side, similar appeals by peasants aggrieved by the obligation to offer unpaid labor in assisting the missions reached the thirteenth Dalai Lama in Lhasa. From 1930 until the last Lopchak in 1950, the Tibetan government "discontinued the practice of providing free transport, not only to the 'Lapchak' Mission, but also to their own officials travelling on duty."[101] The Political Officer in Sikkim wrote in 1933 that "His Holiness the Dalai Lama appears to have been so impressed with the hardships caused to the peasants by requisitions for free transport that he himself now uses his own private transport when travelling. Formerly free transport was always levied."

Like the Lopchak, Chaba, and other trade and tribute missions, the exchange of letters between the Nono of Spiti and the (deposed) *rgyal.po* of Ladakh also raised concerns among British administrators. Spiti was transferred to East India Company control in 1846.[102] In 1889, when he was raising alarms about the Lopchak, Captain Ramsay also brought this annual exchange of letters to the attention of his superiors in the Foreign Department. Ramsay's superior, the Resident in Kashmir, wrote to the Kashmir Darbar about this "Custom, considered objectionable, whereby an annual interchange of letters and presents passes between the Ruler of Spitti and the Wazir of Ladakh."[103] After addressing his superiors, he received the order that the Punjab government was requested to "order the Nono of Spiti to put a stop to the custom, and I am asked to thank the Durbar for the courtesy shown in the matter, at the same time however, to request that the Wazir of Ladakh may be required to renounce all

---

[99] These zamindars are not to be confused with the large-scale landowners found in much of North India.

[100] NAI, Foreign, Frontier, June 1906, no. 100, Part B., in File No. 376-X (Sec) 1932.

[101] F. Williamson Political officer in Sikkim to deputy Sec. Foreign and Political Dept., January 23, 1933. NAI, Foreign, File No. 376-X (Sec) 1932. For the last Lopchak, see: Central Intelligence Agency, Information Report, "Ladakh (Kashmir)-Tibet Trade/ Proposed Organization of 1950 Lobchag Mission."

[102] NAI, Foreign, Frontier A, September 1889, nos. 28–32. "Annual interchange of letters and presents between the Nono of Spiti and the Wazir and the Raja of Ladakh."

[103] Resident in Kashmir, to the President of Council and Prime Minister to His Highness the Maharaja of Jammu and Kashmir, September 3, 1889. JKSA-J, General Records, letter No. 1106. "Discontinuance of the practice of interchange of letters and presents between the Ruler of Spitti and the Wazir of Ladakh."

intercourse of this kind with Spiti and to forbid the Raja of Ladakh to receive such letters and presents in future."[104]

These concerns over the political meaning of the Lopchak and Chaba were never to be found in the pages of the *Gazetteer of Kashmír and Ladák*, which reduced the mission to a commercial event. On the "*The Lap Chuk*" the *Gazetteer* simply noted: "Under the treaty of 1842, a commercial caravan goes every third year from Ladák to Lhása, under the charge of an agent, who is a Kashmír official, and is known by the name of the 'Lap Chuk.' He takes and brings back presents and letters to and from the Ladák and Tibetán authorities."[105] A later accounting in the alphabetical portion of the *Gazetteer* detailed the route taken by the mission, but the *Gazetteer* never mentioned the repeated and voluminous concerns that the Lopchak and other customary missions raised regarding a British dependency's relations with a neighboring political entity.

4.2.2   Other Questions of Tribute: The Problem of "Tribute Goats"

"Tribute," it is worth noting, can be a controversial term among historians. In modern Chinese historiography, for instance, it has been the subject of heated debates centered on questions of self-perception by the Qing state. In the "tribute system" described by historian John Fairbank, China's foreign relations were conducted through an "asymmetric" and sino-centric model whereby the benevolent Qing emperor received gifts from the inferior states beyond China. This asymmetry is often encapsulated by the reluctance of the Qianlong Emperor's court to treat with the British embassy of George Macartney's in 1793. James Hevia's *Cherishing Men from Afar* (1995) challenged this model by revealing the ways in which Qing relations with their tributary states and foreign powers was more reflective of "imperial formations" and the performance of rulership than of any kind of internally originated policy of isolation, intransigence, or outright dismissal of all "barbarians." The Manchu rulers of the Qing dynasty were, after all, foreign conquerors overseeing a multiethnic empire. Their position at the "center" had to be constructed through careful strategies of governance and performance. These strategies included "spatial techniques" such as imperial tours of inspection, the erection of multilingual stelae, and the promotion of mapping territory.[106] Given British observations of the Macartney embassy to the court of the Qianlong Emperor, a perception of tributary relations could

---

[104] Resident in Kashmir.
[105] Intelligence Branch, *Gazetteer of Kashmír and Ladák*, 120.
[106] Peter C. Perdue, *China Marches West: The Qing Conquest of Central Eurasia* (Cambridge, MA: Harvard University Press, 2005), 409–61.

be read as an affront to the "perfect equality" between Westphalian sovereign states. British perceptions of a Chinese worldview shaped their own reciprocal view of China, replete with long-lasting tropes of "arrogance," "intransigence," and the need to "save face."[107]

In a similar vein of argument to those historians who rejected Fairbank's "tribute system," John Bray has argued that the success of the Lopchak (running as it did every 3 years for more than 250 years) was largely due to its capacity to absorb multiple interpretations on the part of its participants, while still adhering to a prescribed "guest ritual" and bi-directional gift giving, two key features noted by Hevia in his examination of tribute in the Qing context. But as in Fairbank's model, the success of the Lopchak also rested on its ability to facilitate significant economic exchange irrespective of any strong institutional relation between Lhasa and Leh. The fact that the Lopchak was frequently carried out by members of Ladakh's principal Muslim trading community, the Arghons, suggests the commercial value of the mission as much as the easy intermingling of the region's Buddhist and Muslim communities.

While certain British administrators sought to minimize the Lopchak and Chaba *as* tribute missions with political meaning, they insisted upon upholding the clauses of treaties involving symbolic or nominal tribute offered *to them*. The case in point is Article 10 of the 1846 Treaty of Amritsar which stated that "Maharaja Golab Sing acknowledges the supremacy of the British Government, and will in token of such supremacy present annually to the British Government one horse, twelve perfect shawl goats of approved breed (six male and six female), and three pairs of Cashmere shawls."[108] These tokens also symbolized the object of greatest interest in the Ladakh trade, the precious *pashm* "shawl wool" used in the production of Kashmir's famed pashmina textiles. The annual receipt of the requisite "tribute shawls" was dutifully recorded by the Foreign Department, which passed along the shawls to Britain's monarch.[109] Occasionally there was official quibbling about the diminished quality of the shawls, but there was no debate about whether these symbols of allegiance were to be demanded. On the other hand, the issue of the "twelve perfect shawl goats of approved breed" proved more difficult.

---

[107] Hevia, *Cherishing Men from Afar.*

[108] C. U. Aitchison, *A Collection of Treaties, Engagements, and Sunnuds Relating to India and Neighbouring Countries* (Calcutta: Bengal Printing Company, 1863), 2:377.

[109] See, for instance, NAI, Foreign, Part A, September 1860. "Receipt of tribute shawls from Cashmere"; NAI, Foreign, Political A, March 1870, nos. 100–103. "Despatch for the Cashmere Tribute Shawls for presentation to Her Majesty"; and NAI, Foreign, Internal, March 1908, nos. 93–97. "Kashmir" Tribute Shawl(s) for the year 1907," which included the remark that the "quality of the shawls received this year is inferior to the quality of the shawls received last year."

The archives of the Foreign, Revenue, and Agricultural Departments all record numerous attempts across the 1870s to transplant these goats to other parts of India and the empire in the hopes of cultivating pashmina elsewhere and reducing Jammu and Kashmir's monopoly on it. But climate proved to be a critical factor. Taken away from their high-altitude environment, the goats quickly died. Initially, officials tried sending them to neighboring Himalayan regions, but as one official noted, "the goats do not thrive in Chamba, Kulu or Hazara, in fact in any part of the Northern Punjab."[110] Subsequent attempts to send them to Kumaon also failed. Officials began to think of still further destinations for the handful of goats they annually received from the Kashmir Darbar. These unfortunate goats came from the herds of the transhumant Changpa, who moved them from their summer pastures on the Changthang plateau in eastern Ladakh to the *wazīr-i-wazārat* in Leh, who in turn sent them to the government of Kashmir in Srinagar.

When the Himalayan trial failed, the secretary of the Revenue Department suggested that the goats might be "deported" to either Tasmania or New Zealand. He calculated the costs of passage by boat and suggested that February would be the ideal time of year for the passage. But some officials rightly worried that this solution would not solve the annual problem. Revenue officials also wondered why they "should go out of [their] way to enable New Zealand and Tasmania to compete against Kashmir."[111] After the viceroy weighed in, the deportation experiment was "negatived." How, then, to avoid breaking the terms of the treaty? The first suggestion was to annually decline them. This the viceroy rejected: "I do not think that we should give up this established tribute or decline to accept the goats. It does not the least signify from a political point of view what is done with them."[112]

The second suggestion came in 1883. The government of India decided that it would seek to modify the treaty to allow for *pashm* wool to be given in lieu of the goats. Ney Elias provided the crucial information for determining the correct exchange rate: the average yield per goat was eight to nine ounces of *pashm* (underbelly wool only). Over a goat's average lifespan this amounted to roughly three to three and one-third pounds. The viceroy accepted the figures and the Maharaja's government

---

[110] NAI, Foreign, Political A, March 1882, nos. 79–81. "Question of the locality where the Kashmir Tribute Shawl Goats would thrive."

[111] NAI.

[112] Revenue and Agricultural Department to Foreign Department, May 23, 1882. NAI, Foreign, Political A, June 1882, nos. 136–39. "Breeding arrangements of the Kashmir shawl goats left to Punjab Government."

soon agreed to modify the treaty.[113] Various indices scattered throughout the National Archives of India show that the receipt of the tribute shawls continued until at least 1935. There is even a record of an instance when Rs. 106 was recovered from an insurance company after the tribute shawls were "lost or damaged" aboard the *SS Canara* in 1911.[114] But after 1883, there was at least some relief for the small batch of goats that had annually been brought down from the Tibetan Plateau to satisfy the British insistence on tribute. This symbolic transaction reflected a pressing and continual need for the British to assert sovereignty over its territory.

4.2.3   Men.ser

One of its more unusual features of the 1684 Treaty of Tingmosgang was a provision that granted rights to the Ladakhi *rgyal.po* for a settlement near the holy mountain and lake of Mount Kailash and Lake Manasarovar in Western Tibet, territory that, following the Tibet–Ladakh–Mughal War (1679–84), was controlled by administrators from the Central Tibetan government. This village, called Men.ser,[115] was transferred after the formal annexation of Ladakh in 1842 to the Dogra Raja of Jammu, who shortly thereafter became the first Maharaja of Jammu and Kashmir. By then the village was spoken of in terms a *jāgīr*, or deeded land.

The use of the term *jāgīr* by the governments of Jammu and Kashmir and British India is itself significant. Typically, a *jāgīr* was a land grant of an area extending beyond a single village and included a requirement of military service.[116] Most often a *jāgīr* was granted by a monarch to a feudatory prince. If this is the meaning intended by the term, it acknowledges that in this case the Tibetan government was making the Maharaja one such prince. While these sorts of arrangements were not unknown across South Asia, this modest settlement complicated any notion of unambiguous sovereignty separating Kashmir and Tibet, and, by extension, between the British Empire and the Qing Empire.

[113] NAI, Foreign, A Political E, July 1883, nos. 229–30. "Correspondence with Kashmir regarding Treaty of 1846, Article X (pashm)."
[114] NAI, Foreign, Internal, June 1911, no. 24, Part B. "Recovery from the Insurance Company of R106-12–0 on account of contribution to general average paid on the insured consignment shipped per SS. Canara containing Tribute shawls." The ship would be wrecked off Mauritius in 1914, See www.plimsoll.org/images/39031_tcm4-3 35153.pdf.
[115] Also written in an alternative manuscript of the *La.dwags rGyal.rabs* as sMon.tsher and recorded in English records variously as Mensar, Min sar, Misar, and Misar Tarjum.
[116] Though in parts of North India, this type of arrangement was sometimes referred to as *umli* or *mukasa* when encompassing a single village or town.

Moorcroft visited Men.ser while exploring Western Tibet. He noted that the settlement consisted of "but one house made of bricks baked in the sun, and five tents of goat herds."[117] In 1882, the Officer on Special Duty in Kashmir, the direct superior to the British Joint Commissioner in Ladakh, wrote on the subject to the then under-secretary to the Foreign Department, Henry Mortimer Durand: "Some time ago I asked [Ney] Elias to try whether he could ascertain anything about the Maharaja's *jagir* in Chinese territory."[118] Elias responded with a long memorandum outlining the history of the subject.

"The whole of the country drained by the Indus beyond the present boundary of Ladak," Elias began, invoking the now standard use of the watershed as a boundary object, "and extending south-eastward . . . to the watershed of the Tan-pu or Brahmaputra – belonged originally to the Ladak Rajas."[119] There followed a peculiar account of how the region came to belong to Ladakh, likely mistaking it for a Bhutanese territorial enclave nearby (Dar.chen, near Mount Kailash).[120] Instead of Ladakh's territorial loss of western Tibetan territory following the Tibet–Ladakh–Mughal War, Elias insisted that "Mipan Angpo," the head of the Drukpa Kagyu sect (who Elias wrongly assumed to be the "Raja" of Ladakh), give the provinces of Gartok and Rudok to the Dalai Lama as an act of piety after recovering from serious illness. He retained "for himself only some grazing grounds about two marches north-west of the Mansarowar Lake on the road to Gartok. These grazing grounds are known as Min-Sar and the spot is marked on the latest edition of the Surveyor-General's map of Turkestan as "Misar Tarjum." The distance from Leh by the direct, or winter, route which follows the valley of the Indus, is about 17

---

[117] William Moorcroft, "A Journey to Lake Manasarovara in Undes, a Province of Little Tibet," *Asiatic Researches; or, Transactions of the Society, Instituted in Bengal* 12 (1816): 380–536.

[118] F. Henvey, Officer on Special Duty in Kashmir, to H. M. Durand, Under-Secretary to Government of India, Foreign Department. September 25, 1880. NAI, Foreign, Secret, August 1882, no. 320.

[119] NAI, Foreign, Secret, August 1882, no. 320. "Memorandum by Mr. Elias on relations of Maharaja of Kashmir with Thibet (Chinese)."

[120] According to John Bray, "both sets of enclaves share a common origin in that they date back to the period when the Kings of Ladakh controlled the whole of Western Tibet (mNga'.ris skor.gsum). The link with Bhutan arises because of the Ladakhi royal family's association with the Drukpa Kagyupa sect. This association dates back to at least the end of the sixteenth century: in 1577 King Jamyang Namgyal (Jams.dbyang rNam.rgyal, r. c.1595–1616) of Ladakh, who stood in a priest/patron relationship with the Drukpa leader Padma Karpo (1527–1592), sponsored the building of a tantra school on his territory." John Bray, "Ladakhi and Bhutanese Enclaves in Tibet," page 2. Updated version of an article first published in *Recent Research on Ladakh 7*, ed. Thierry Dodin and Heinz Räther, Ulmer Kulturanthropologische Schriften 8 (Ulm: Abteilung Anthropologie, Universität Ulm, 1997), 89–104.

marches."[121] Elias painted a bleak image of this location's population. The inhabitants were poor, nomadic Champas, he wrote. "There is only one house and the number of tents is estimated at about 40." The annual revenue the Maharaja's government drew from it was fixed by treaty at six yaks, sixty sheep, forty goats, and fifty rupees and was typically collected by the Lopchak officials returning from Lhasa.

Elias's superior, the Officer on Special Duty in Kashmir, detailed the village's peculiar taxation. When the Lopchak mission passed through the village, it collected the *sa.khral*, or rent (lit. "land tax"), which was owed to Kashmir, but which was then given to the authorities at Lhasa as part of the Lopchak tribute mission. "Whatever the Kashmiris may think of the sah-tal [*sa.khral*] and presents, I have no doubt the Chinese regard them as tribute." Yet Elias also acknowledged a degree of ambiguity in the customary relations exhibited in the Lopchak. "The distinction between presents of ceremony or friendship on the one hand, and tribute as a sign of dependence or vassalage on the other, is frequently very loosely drawn by Asiatics, and the names of their taxes, duties, &c., do not always designate accurately the purpose for which they are levied."[122] For the British, the complexities of historical relationships that often included palimpsestic overlapping sovereignties were reduced to a racial trait and definitional problem. Government concerns over Men.ser continued until 1947, when the Indian government inherited the problem.[123]

As with Men.ser, other occasional problems arose that provoked uncertainty over sovereignty and territory. The first layer was the practical difficulty of accessing the region to extract its revenue, however paltry. This inaccessibility forced administrators to grapple with the question of what, precisely, it meant to actually control the area. The *Gazetteer of Kashmír and Ladák* quickly pointed out that it is held by the Maharaja, but acknowledged the difficulty of access, owing to its location within Tibetan territory. "Under the treaty of 1842, which ended the expedition led by Guláb Singh's Zorawár Singh, against Ladák and Tibet, the district of Min-Sar was made over by the Tibetán authorities to Guláb Singh and his heirs as a *jagír*." The *Gazetteer* noted that "its pecuniary value is insignificant. The small revenue is collected annually by a Kashmír official deputed by the Maharája's *wazir* at Léh. Mr. Elias states that

---

[121] NAI, Foreign, Secret, August 1882, no. 320. "Memorandum by Mr. Elias on relations of Maharaja of Kashmir with Thibet (Chinese)."

[122] NAI, Foreign, Secret, August 1882, no. 320. Letter from Ney Elias in Leh, September 20, 1880.

[123] See, for instance, NAI, Foreign, Secret E, November 1900, nos. 55–57, p. 81. "Suggestions connected with the exercise of control over the Minsar *jagir* in Tibet owned by the Maharaja of Kashmir"; and John Bray, "Ladakhi and Bhutanese Enclaves in Tibet," in Dodin and Räther, *Recent Research on Ladakh 7*, 89–104.

Mr. Johnson, when wazir, tried to visit the *jagír*, but was prevented by the Chinese officials in Gartok." Yet British administrators frequently mentioned this "insignificant" *jāgīr*, suggesting that its value was symbolic, not fiscal. The tone of the *Gazetteer* registers only the faintest sense of political tension when it concludes that "some political significance attaches to the *jagír*, because there is reason to doubt whether the Maharája does not pay tribute on account of it to the Chinese."[124] Like the Lopchak, these small instances that challenged British notions of sovereign and territorial congruency – provoking anxieties at the highest levels of government – produced a second reading of Ladakh: one that failed in small but significant ways to conform to the rationalized form found in imperial manuals of governance.

4.2.4   Jurisdictional Problems: Lha.rgyal and Dog.po Kar.po

Besides complications deriving from historical customary relations and noncontiguous territory, a second major point of British concern involved the basic understanding of borderlines and the problems posed to them by moving people.

On August 3, 1918, the Resident in Kashmir wrote to the Foreign secretary in the Foreign and Political Department.

It would seem that one, Hlagyel [Lha.rgyal], a native of Pangong, Ladakh, went to Rudok in Tibet some years ago and there by honest means, as is alleged, accumulated a fortune consisting of 30 yaks, 2 ponies and a large flock of sheep and goats. With these he and his wives whom he had married at Lhassa, returned to Pangong and lived there peaceably until last year when he took his flocks to graze in a nala[125] named Dokpo Karpo in the Changchemo basin. While there, a party of Tibetans from Rudok came and forcibly carried him off across the Tibetan border together with his wives and flocks. / *There is no doubt that Dokpo Karpo, where the abduction took place, is well within the border of the Kashmir State, as shown on the survey maps.* It is equally certain that the man Hlagyel is a Kashmir subject. As to whether, in the course of his sojourn in Tibet, he also acquired Tibetan nationality there is no information forthcoming. / Whatever the status of Hlagyel in Tibet, however, there can be no justification for his forcible removal from State territory and it is to this that the Kashmir Darbar takes exception.[126]

---

[124] *Gazetteer of Kashmir and Ladák*, 120.

[125] A nala is typically a watercourse, channel, or canal, sometimes dried up.

[126] NAI, Foreign, External, April 1920, nos. 213–27, Part B. "Agreement alleged to have been entered into with the representatives of the Ruok Jongpen by a British official in Ladakh governing the status of Ladakhis in Tibet." See also IOR/R/2/1066/87A, File No. 310 of 1919. "Abduction of one Hlagyal of Ladakh by Tibetans. Ladakh-Tibet Frontier question." My emphasis.

The apparent abduction of Lha.rgyal generated a surprising degree of alarm within the Kashmir state government and the government of India. It reflected the fundamental problem that across the northern and eastern reaches of Ladakh the border, on the ground at least, did not exist. It might be recorded on maps and described in the *Gazetteer of Kashmír and Ladák*, but for the traders and nomadic Changpa who regularly circulated through the region, there was no definite, linear marking of territory to determine where Ladakh ended and Tibet began. This was especially true of the regions where the Changpa typically took their animals to graze, north of the well-trodden Leh–Lhasa route.

The Tibetans alleged that Lha.rgyal lived with wife who was a subject of Ding.med in Rudok, which fell under Tibetan jurisdiction. He had failed to pay taxes while residing with his flocks there in the winter. This suggests that Tibetans considered him a *mak.pa*, that is a man who moves in with his wife, while she retains control over her family property rights – typically in an ancestral village. This practice is common across Ladakh where, due to limited property, polyandry and matrilineal property control is common. The villagers in Ding.med apparently petitioned the *gar. dpon*s at Rudok to be "made a regular tax payer there."[127]

Meanwhile the British Joint Commissioner contacted his superior, the Resident in Kashmir, who consulted his survey maps and brought them to the Kashmir Darbar to discuss the location of the abduction, near a dried stream (Hindi/Urdu: *nālā*) known as Dog.po Kar.po ("white narrows"). The Resident asserted that the Government Survey maps showed this to be "well within the Kashmir State." Yet the maps consulted would not have contained any demarcated border in eastern Ladakh: a confusion, the Resident explained, that resulted from earlier failed attempts to determine a boundary with Tibetan officials in Western Tibet. The *gar. dpon*s at Gartok mentioned a place referred to simply as "O-ith," but the *gar.dpon*s "frankly admitted that none of them had ever been there and knew nothing about the boundary line personally; the report submitted to the Lhassa government to the effect that Dak-po-kar-po Nullah was within the Rudock District was purely founded on the statement made by the Goba (headman) as well as the people of U-Jang Parganah where the said Nullah is situated."[128]

It soon turned out that each group questioned had a different understanding about where Tibetan control ended and Ladakhi control began. The people living around Pangong Lake (like the headman, or *mgo.ba*,

---

[127] NAI.
[128] British Trade Agent, Gartok, to the Superintendent, Hill States, Shimla, August 1, 1921. NAI, Foreign, External Branch, January 1922, nos. 4–19. "Matters in dispute between the Kashmir Darbar and the Tibetan Government."

just quoted) stated that there was a stream to the east of the lake that marked Tibetan (or at least Rudok's) control. Others suggested the cluster of mountains to the south east of the plains near Pangong Lake. Others had still more conflicting accounts of the *sa.mtsham*, owing to a similar conflict fifteen years earlier involving grazing rights near the nulla.[129] "Under these circumstances," the Resident concluded, "it has become very difficult for me to proceed with this case and to ascertain the real boundary near Dak-po Kar-po Nullah without finding out a pucca [true] boundary." The Resident did not consider that asking people long accustomed to practicing transhumance to locate a borderline might have been a futile undertaking.

In August 1921, the British trade agent stationed at Gartok[130] acknowledged in a report to his superior that he had heard of other abduction cases similar to that of Lha.rgyal. For instance, "one Ganbo, a native of Ladakh territory," had written a letter as follows:[131]

Sir, we beg to state that we are the Raiyet [*ra'īyat*] of Ruksho Goba [headman] of Ladakh territory.[132] Some 12 years ago we came to Tibet and settled at Dungbo (Daba District). The cause of our coming to Tibet was that one year on account of heavy snowfall there was a heavy toll of mortality amongst sheep and goats entrusted to us by the said Goba and the replacement of which (to complete number) became out of our power, so owing to his fear we left Ladakh for Dungbo where Daba Jangpon did not tax us for three years. The fourth year he levied tax on us making us his regular Raiyet with a promise that we may return to our country, if we please, after paying this tax for three years. Now nine years have gone [and] we are not allowed to go home. We have been requesting to the Daba Jangpon for his permission from the last three years but of no avail. I therefore request you to kindly cause my release from Daba Jangpon's possession to return to Ladakh with my wife Showang and two daughters Palmo and Sanam Dahna. signed Gunbo [Gon.bo] of Dungbo.[133]

---

[129] British Trade Agent.

[130] This was the posting that the British demanded following Younghusband's mission to "open" Tibet in 1903–4. "It was intended in 1913 that the appointment of British Trade Agent at Gartok should be whole-time but owing to the failure in erecting a house for him, due to the obstructiveness of the Garpons (between 1905 and 1923), he was permitted to make his winter quarters at Poo and later Simla." NAI, File No. 89-X (Secret) 1927. "Disabilities suffered by Indian traders in Western Tibet."

[131] NAI, Foreign, External Branch, January 1922, nos. 4–19. "Matters in dispute between the Kashmir Darbar and the Tibetan Government."

[132] That is, he held a small-hold tenancy (which he referred to by the Hindi/Urdu/Persian term *ra'īyat*) under the headman (mgo.ba) of the region of the Changthang (byang. thang) plateau northwest of Tso (lake) Moriri known variously as Rup.sho or Rup.shu, a high-altitude expansive region in which the Changpa often brought their herds during the summer months.

[133] NAI, Foreign, External Branch, January 1922, nos. 4–19. "Matters in dispute between the Kashmir Darbar and the Tibetan Government."

Over subsequent years, at least fifty-nine cases surfaced of Tibetans evading local taxes by fleeing to Ladakh.[134] In 1927, E. B. Wakefield, the officer then in charge of the British Trade Agency at Gartok, wrote of his frustrated attempt to find the border between Western Tibet and Ladakh. Part of the problem rested with faulty information provided by gazetteers and maps. "And now came the great disappointment: the trade route marked on the map between Deboche and Demchok, simply didn't exist!"[135] Wakefield was critical of the previous *gar.dpon* of Rudok, who was a "blood-thirsty tyrant" owing to the absence of regular pay from Lhasa and his penchant for physically abusing travelers. Fortunately, he had recently been recalled to Lhasa to face murder charges and the new *gar.dpon* "leaves Indian traders severely alone – he has even reduced the taxes on them from 10 per cent to 2 per cent: for he respects and is frightened of the British." This, it turned out, was because the *gar.dpon* "was educated at Rugby!!! being sent there in 1914 ... with three other Tibetan boys of good family at the expense of his Government as an experiment."[136] The decision by the central Government of Tibet to station this aristocrat chosen for an "elite" and "modern" education at Rugby at a remote posting in Western Tibet suggests some wariness toward Britain on the part of the Tibetan government following the Younghusband mission.

Based on Wakefield and the BJC's correspondence, the Resident in Kashmir surmised that "without the boundary being settled, settlement of other questions will remain difficult."[137] His superiors in the Political Department proposed another boundary commission. "I think, with the Resident, that a settlement of the boundary might help matters," though they were hesitant to go to the trouble of a commission if all that was at stake were "grazing grounds."[138] The Assistant Surveyor-General added to the skepticism in stating that "a case can be made out for *any* frontier here. ... There is no settled boundary. The Chang-pas (Nomads) graze when and where they will. The area is vast and the Chang-pas very few. The rainfall is scanty and the Chang-pas must move to suitable grazing grounds. Political boundaries mean exactly nothing to them; if they were demarcated, they would still mean nothing."[139]

[134] NAI, External Affairs Department, File No. 27-X 1937 (Secret).
[135] NAI, Foreign, File No. 89-X (Secret) 1927. "Disabilities suffered by Indian traders in Western Tibet."
[136] For more on this education experiment, see Kyle Gardner, "The Education Complex: Imperial Anxieties and the Case of Five Tibetans in England, 1913–1914" (MA thesis, University of Chicago, 2011).
[137] NAI, External Affairs Department, File No. 27-X 1937 (Secret), 19.   [138] NAI, 28.
[139] NAI. "Note by Major K. Mason, Assistant Surveyor General Dated the 13th January 1928," 22–23.

In response, the Resident in Kashmir wrote:

I am inclined to think that until such time as a definite boundary is fixed it will be impossible to decide to which Government the inhabitants of the disputed area are subject. ... The two questions of trade facilities and the return of subjects seem to me to be so intimately bound up with the boundary question that until this is fixed we shall be faced from time to time with disputes between the two Governments, of which equitable settlements will be well-nigh impossible. I therefore suggest that Government take into their serious consideration the problem of getting the boundary settled once and for all.[140]

Although debates continued into the 1930s about Dog.po Kar.po, the unsettled boundary, and the question of extradition treaties between Tibet and British India, no arrangement proved satisfactory to all parties concerned. Lha.rgyal and Gonbo were both eventually returned to Ladakh, Kashmir balked at the omission of an "independent" boundary commissioner to demarcate the borderline, and the Changpa continued to graze their animals across the wide and arid expanse of the western Byang.thang plateau. Only in 1962 was an effective border imposed across this region at the conclusion of the Sino-Indian War: it was revealingly named the Line of Actual Control (LAC).

4.3   Conclusion

This chapter opened with quotations from two very different figures in late nineteenth-century India. Both reflect the power of official, organized information. The Urdu poet Akbar Allahabadi's satirical couplet on the value of the annual *Gazette of India* in extracting money from people reveals the authoritative function of official publications. The *Gazettes* were not only used by district commissioners or central administrators, but gave local elites various resources, not least a place in which to inscribe their social prominence. These manuals gained immense power over time. Lists of notable families within the *Gazette of India* granted those families prestige, while its statistical details were often produced as evidence in litigation over property boundaries, the legal status of various social groups, or the historical status of certain local families.[141] Information from the annually published *Gazettes* often found its way into the gazetteers, particularly the detailed district versions that included sections on the area's local boundaries, apparent

---

[140] NAI, 66 (in pencil). Letter from the Resident in Kashmir, December 8, 1927.
[141] Thanks to C. M. Naim for bringing this practice to my attention.

ethnic and religious composition, and the history and political role of prominent families. Thus, the gazetteers, along with the *Gazette of India* and other widely circulated official publications, profoundly shaped the territorial, social, and political understandings of colonial officials and local elites alike. Settlement reports and district gazetteers granted historical legitimacy and, at times, legal validity.

The second quotation came from the "father" of the *Imperial Gazetteer*, William Wilson Hunter. He acknowledged in his preface to the 1881 edition that the "true territorial unit of Indian history" was "indeed, much smaller than the British District."[142] "He who would study the history of Oudh [Awadh]," he continued, "must search for it in the *paraná* or parish; in other parts of India, the *zamíndári* or estate is the historical unit." This notion of a "true territorial unit" to history is intriguing. It suggested, perhaps, that a historical subject required a fixed spatial referent. But if an archetypal Indian *pargana* or *zamindari* were the "true" unit Hunter had in mind, his statement also contained an irony since it conceded a degree of artificiality in the British District.[143] The district did not correlate directly to a historically sensible unit of space but represented a rationalized space utilizing the careful manipulation of mountains and water systems to make boundary objects and boundary-making principles.

The model of territory presented in British imperial manuals of governance represented a fixed object delimited by borderlines. The precise work of surveyors, boundary commissioners, and settlement officers imposed lines onto the landscape and, more importantly, onto the maps and treaties in which sovereignty was increasingly vested. This model of territory demanded a particularly static vision of a population confined within it. This idea was not confined to British India but was emerging across imperial territories and North America as part of the broader territorialization of the globe in the modern period.[144] By the

---

[142] William Wilson Hunter, preface to the 1881 edition of the *Imperial Gazetteer*, xviii.

[143] Like his contemporary Henry Maine, Hunter was probably envisioning an atavistic, primitive village.

[144] In fact, some of the earliest nineteenth-century gazetteers that provided detailed information about the location of borders were produced at the state level in the United States. For instance, the prolific American gazetteer writer John Hayward began his 1849 *Gazetteer of New Hampshire* by introducing a revised structure for the volumes. "We have adopted a new arrangement in our work which, it is thought, will be found more convenient for reference than any in our former publications of the kind. After a brief geographical description, biographical sketches, etc., are given the *Boundaries* of the towns under a distinct head; the *First Settlers* and *First Ministers* come next, and are seen at a glance; then are given the *Manufactures* in the towns when practicable; and then some of the most important *Productions of the Soil*. The *Distances* come last, though not the least important item to the traveller." John Hayward, *A gazetteer of New Hampshire*,

late nineteenth century, the genre reflected an emerging global form of knowledge that began with a legible border and systematic outline of a geographically sensible territory. This territory was presented as natural and rational, but also disciplined and sanitized – free from the complications that would challenge the meaning of the border.

And yet for colonial administrators like the British Joint Commissioners in Ladakh, a range of preexisting relations and movements complicated the autonomy of the gazetteer's subject. Long-established customary arrangements between Ladakh and Tibet and other regions blurred the neat notion of sovereignty presumed to be recognized by the establishment of borders. Furthermore, the position of the enclave of Men.ser vis-à-vis the princely state of Jammu and Kashmir, British India, Tibet, and China reflected the imperial powers' much wider problem in dealing with non-contiguous territory in an age when complete and legible borders were becoming de rigueur. Likewise, incidents like the abductions of Lha.rgyal and Gon.bo showed that borderlines drawn on paper were often irrelevant to the lived experience of moving populations. People started and stopped at unpredictable moments across the seasons, and lands near rivers and streams were reconstructed or reassessed depending on the changes made to them by floodwaters. Such local challenges demonstrated that the static, top-down model of the region of Ladakh conveyed by official information did not reflect practical political and environmental realities on the ground. It was one thing to read the landscape for information to be added to gazetteers and other manuals of governance; it was quite another to read historically inscribed customary relations and seasonal movements of people and their livestock, as well as preexisting, overlapping sovereignties that had not been adjudicated.

The most striking feature of the examples of Lha.rgyal's abduction, the tribute goats, and the Lopchak lay in the degree of concern that these rather insignificant problems elicited from the imperial state. Each of these cases produced hundreds of pages of official documentation, involved – at times – multiple Viceroys and Secretaries of State for

containing descriptions of all the counties, towns, and districts in the state; also of its principal mountains, rivers, waterfalls, harbors, islands, and fashionable resorts. To which are added, statistical accounts of its agriculture, commerce and manufactures (Boston: J. P. Jewett, 1849), 3. Previously, in an 1846 version of his *A gazetteer of Massachusetts* ... (Boston: J. Hayward, 1846), he had insisted on a purely alphabetical structure, noting that "in many particulars the plan of this work is new: the descriptions of the counties and towns comprise their location, natural characteristics, general appearance, &c.; but those items of information common to all, such as population, valuation, schools, dates of incorporation, &c. &c., are arranged alphabetically, in tabular form, thereby presenting many of the most important items, without crowding the whole together indiscriminately, and, as stated on page 320, in a 'mode best adapted for reference and comparison.'"

India, and provoked repeated discussions about the need for direct control of Ladakh as a frontier region – or indeed for bringing the whole of India's periphery under direct administration.[145] The prospect of a dependent state of the British Empire paying tribute to a foreign power, or the inability of the state to determine which individuals belonged to it owing to a failure to know or enforce mapped borderlines, was deeply troubling to imperial administrators. It turns out that a motley assortment of nomads, traders, and goats proved to be quite significant symbols of the limits of imperial state legibility.

---

[145] Various administrators made this recommendation on at least seven separate occasions. See Chapter 5, note 27.

Invasion Anxieties and Frontier Heroes

March 26, 1888. "Here I am on the border of habitation and to-morrow morning will put off for the howling desolate waste."[1] Thus began Andrew Dalgleish's last letter to his friend Dr. Suraj Bal, written just before the young Scottish trader and British informant set off across the "no-man's land" of the Aksai Chin. Bal was the grandly titled *wazīr-i-wazārat*, the district administrator of Ladakh. Dalgleish had spent a decade and a half traversing the routes from India to Kashgar and Yarkand, working first for the short-lived Central Asian Trading Company and then as an independent trader and informant feeding the British imperial government commercial and political intelligence on Russian and Chinese activities in Central Asia.[2] He had lived in Yarkand for several years, married a Yarkandi woman,[3] learned Uyghur, and earned a good sum of money through his trade in high-value items like pashmina and silver – items that had been

---

[1] NAI, Foreign, Frontier A, July 1888, no. 81. "Transcript copy of a letter, dated the 26th March 1888, from Mr. A Dalgleish, to Dr. Suraj Bal, Camp Shijok [Shyok] village." Dalgleish's letter continued, "The Nubra Tartars with their eighteen ponies are here with me. The six drivers with Tashi Sonam as their chief, are well chosen, and the ponies as good as can be expected at this time of the year. But they have come instead of being well stored for the journey, as one who thinks of going only to church, *i.e.*, with their coat only on their back. So I have had to outfit them and also their ponies and am now pleased to state that the little caravan is neat, and as perfect as can be made, in this part of the world. They wish to take the goods all the way to Yarkand and from there return to Leh with another caravan of goods; so that I will have no changing at Shahedullah and they will make some money out of the transaction. I will be kind to them and endeavor to get them goods from Yarkand to Leh and whatever they also may require. / And now farewell, my dear friend, with many thanks (not the thanks of that two-legged thing, a shopkeeper), but the thanks of a true heart for all your kind assistance, and believe me will kindest regards, &c. / P.S. – The sepoy who deserted has not turned up here; but there is a tall robust Panjabi with the Yarkand caravan. I have had a look at him, and I don't think he is else what he calls himself, *i.e.*, a fakir, *en route* to Turkistan to try his fortune there."

[2] For the history of the Central Asian Trading Company, see Bir Good Gill, "The Venture of the Central Asian Trading Company in Eastern Turkistan, 1874–5," *Asian Affairs* 31, no. 2 (2000): 181–88. NAI, Foreign, Secret F, February 1883, nos. 184–95. "Employment of Dalgleish (Mr. A) for one year as a news-agent during his trading journey to Yarkand. Rupees 4,000 placed at his disposal."

[3] The Russian Consul at Kashgar found a lock of her hair among Dalgleish's possessions. These ended up, along with Dalgleish's gun and some articles of clothing, "in the

crossing the Karakoram for centuries. Because of his diminutive stature he was sometimes referred to affectionately by officials of the princely state of Jammu and Kashmir as "Chhota Sahib" (Little Sir).[4]

On April 8, 1888, Dalgleish was killed on the northern side of the Karakoram Pass. His apparent murderer was Daud Mohammed Khan, a trader from Afghanistan. According to testimony given to British and Kashmiri officials by several Ladakhis in the caravan, others involved included Usman, a Yarkandi trader based in Andijan; Gulban, a Pathan trader; two elderly Andijanis and one Kashgari, all returning from the *Haj*; and Bakhsh, a Punjabi *fakīr*.[5] Daud Mohammed and Dalgleish had known each other for years and were friends according to Dalgleish's Kashmiri servant, Muhammad Jan. Daud Mohammed had recently fallen into debt with moneylenders in Amritsar and then again in Leh, and Dalgleish had lent him money. They had met two weeks earlier in northern Ladakh and, together with a caravan of eighteen people drawn from a wide variety of locations, had reached the Karakoram Pass on April 8, slowly shoveling their way across the pass through deepening snow and setting up camp on the north slope. Although the detailed testimony of Dalgleish's servant and three Ladakhi *kiraiyakash* (pony drivers)[6] does not reveal the reasons behind the attack, they agree that Daud Mohammed invited Dalgleish into his tent for tea, their daily habit for a fortnight while on the road. Some thirty minutes later Daud Mohammed shot Dalgleish at least once. Dalgleish managed to escape the tent but not the sword that Daud Mohammed carried.

---

possession of a Chinaman." V. N. Petrovsky to Her Majesty's Consul at St. Petersburgh, 24th September / 6th October [calendar variations] 1888. NAI, Foreign, Frontier A, January 1889, no. 84. The difference in date is due to the variation between the Western Gregorian calendar and the Russian Julian calendar; the latter was used up to early 1918.

[4] NAI, Foreign, Political A, March 1878, nos. 261–68. "Ladakh diaries from 17th November to 31st December."

[5] Captain H. Ramsay, British Joint Commissioner, Ladakh, to Trevor Chichele Plowden, Resident in Kashmir, May 17, 1888. NAI, Foreign, Frontier A, July 1888, no. 93; and "Mr. Dalgleish's Murderer," *The Times of India*, June 28, 1890.

[6] *Kiraiyakash* were typically "Arghons," descendants of Kashmiri merchants settled across Ladakh who rented their guide services and labor, along with their horses, yaks, or mules, for segments of the long-haul trade routes. Yaks were typically used only for the passes where footing could be treacherous, while ponies, horses, mules, and donkeys were utilized for longer segments of the journey; accordingly, yaks suffered much higher rates of mortality. Unexpected snowfall, crevasses, and the lack of pasturage could often kill whole caravan-loads of animals (and, much more rarely, the humans guiding them). *Kiraiyakash* is also etymologically a Persian portmanteau of "kiraya" or rent, and "kash" which comes from the infinitive "kashidan" (i.e., to pull), meaning someone who charges a fee to "pull" or transport people. I am grateful to Naveena Naqvi for pointing out the Persian etymology.

After ordering one of his muleteers to strangle Dalgleish's dog next to its master's head (the dog had remained in Dalgleish's tent apparently due to frostbitten paws), Daud Mohammed impressed a number of the victim's hired Ladakhi pony drivers to accompany him one stage northward toward Yarkand. There he had the *kiraiyakash* "shorn of their pigtails" and cut off Muhammad Jan's beard, telling him that he "should not in future serve the English, and this is your mark." Then, in a moment of apparent grandeur, Daud Mohammed proclaimed himself "lord of the wilderness [*jangal*]." The Ladakhi *kiraiyakash* and Muhammad Jan were allowed to return to collect their employer's body. After eighteen days on the Leh-Yarkand road, they returned it to Leh for autopsy and burial.

The postmortem examination conducted by Dr. Karl Marx, a Moravian missionary living in Ladakh, largely confirmed the testimony of the pony drivers: Dalgleish had been struck by two bullets and fourteen to sixteen sword strokes. His Kashmiri servant and three Ladakhi *kiraiyakash* gave detailed and fairly consistent testimony to the local British and Kashmiri officials. The Joint Commissioner, the British counterpart to the Dogra-appointed *wazīr-i-wazārat*, then contacted his superior, the British Resident at Srinagar, who in turn wrote to the Foreign Department in Shimla. News of the murder and descriptions of the murderer and his travel companions were quickly telegraphed to Afghanistan, China, Persia, and Russia, along with a "dead or alive" reward for Daud Mohammed, of 5,000 rupees.[7]

The motive for the murder was never conclusively determined. The British Resident in Kashmir gave a range of possible answers to his superior in Shimla, Henry Mortimer Durand.

The simplest explanation that Dad Muhammad [*sic*] being himself in difficulties killed Mr. Dalgleish for the sake of his property is probably the true one. Against this supposition is the omission to search the deceased's person which would have placed Dad Muhammad in possession of Rs. 5,200, together with a gold ring; and also his conduct in letting the Bhots [Ladakhis] take back their ponies which compelled him to leave Mr. Dalgleish's property at Wahab Jilga until he could return with transport for it. Another explanation is revenge for some slight or quarrel, but there is no evidence to support this theory; on the contrary, Mr. Dalgleish appears to have been on excellent terms with Dad Muhammed. Or, again, there may have been a political motive for the crime, for it was pretty well known that Mr. Dalgleish was an emissary of the Government of India and combined the collection of political intelligence with his mercantile operations.[8]

---

[7] The figure was determined by the Finance Department to be comparable to that offered for the capture of Twet Nga Lu, a Burmese resistance leader in the third and final Anglo-Burmese War (1885).

[8] NAI, Foreign Department, Frontier A, July 1888, no. 92: Resident in Kashmir to H. M. Durand, Sec., Foreign Dept.

One might add to this a few even more speculative motives: Could Daud Mohammed's actions have been anticolonial, perhaps for recent British aggressions in Afghanistan? Was it motivated by religious difference, a case of so-called fanaticism?[9] Or, still less plausible, could Daud Mohammed's attack have been caused by the effects of extreme altitude and cold temperatures? There simply is not enough documentation to venture to solve this century-old murder case, but its dramatic nature tempts speculation.

Daud Mohammed was eventually caught by Russians in Samarkand in 1890, but apparently hanged himself in prison before he could be sent back to British India.[10] This disappointed the British Joint Commissioner in Ladakh who had hoped to execute Daud Mohammed and his alleged accomplices "during the trade season, when all the Central Asian world" would be in Leh.[11] Henry Mortimer Durand, the secretary to the Foreign Department, had further hoped that the hanging could be done "on some conspicuous spot on the line of road" to act as a clear deterrent to those who would dare attack a British citizen.[12] The renowned British soldier, explorer, and evangelist of empire, Francis Younghusband, gravely commented that Dalgleish was one of the "true missionaries of all that is best in our civilization."[13] When Younghusband crossed the Karakoram Pass

---

[9] The British applied the term "fanatic" to individuals who supposedly held "extreme" views, usually against the imperial state, derived from religious belief. On this North-West Frontier, where it was used most frequently, it typically referred to Muslim Pathans, but elsewhere in the imperial archive are numerous references to Hindu "fanatics." For the development of this trope, see Zak Leonard, "Muslim Fanaticism as Ambiguous Trope: A Study in Polemical Mutation," in *Mountstuart Elphinstone in South Asia: Pioneer of British Colonial Rule* (London: Hurst, 2019).

[10] The author John Buchan would later write about the fate of Daud Mohammed Khan: "Suddenly there came news from Samarkand that the Pathan [i.e., Daud Mohammed] had been caught there and was now in a Russian prison. Two of the emissaries who had gone in that direction had arrived in Samarkand and had found Dad Mahomed sitting on a box in the bazaar. One of them stopped and engaged him in conversation, while the other went off to the Governor, who happened to be the famous General Kuropatkin. Kuropatkin, on opening Bower's letter, at once sent a party of Cossacks to the bazaar and had Dad Mahomed arrested. / It was arranged to send him to India, and preparations were made for an armed escort to bring him back over the Russian border; but news arrived that the criminal had cheated justice, for he had hung himself in his cell. *Nevertheless, the power of British law was vindicated, and the story of the unrelenting pursuit throughout Central Asia had an immense moral effect in all that mountain country.*" John Buchan, *A Book of Escapes and Hurried Journeys* (Boston: Houghton Mifflin, 1923). My emphasis.

[11] Ramsay to Plowden, June 10, 1888. NAI, Foreign, Frontier A, July 1888, Keep-with 1, p. 5. "Murder of Mr. Andrew Dalgleish, a British trader, beyond the Karakoram range, while *en route* from India to Chinese Turkistan."

[12] Ramsay to Plowden. Durand to Plowden.

[13] Francis E. Younghusband, *The Heart of a Continent: A Narrative of Travels in Manchuria, across the Gobi Desert, through the Himalayas, the Pamirs, and Chitral, 1884–1894*, 3rd ed. (New York: Scribner, 1896).

a year after Dalgleish's murder, he observed that there, "on the dividing-line between India and Central Asia, in the very core of these lofty mountain ranges ... had fallen the one solitary Englishman who had tried to make his home in Central Asia ... treacherously murdered in a fit of fanaticism or temper by one who was a stranger like himself" (Map 5.1). But the exact nature and extent of that "dividing-line between India and Central Asia" was still far from apparent to the imperial state.

Besides maintaining British prestige, the search for Dalgleish's killer provoked deeper anxieties about the British imperial state and its territory. Who had jurisdiction over the murder scene, on the "howling desolate waste" of the Switzerland-sized plateau today generally referred to as the Aksai Chin?[14] Neither China, Britain, Russia, nor any of their

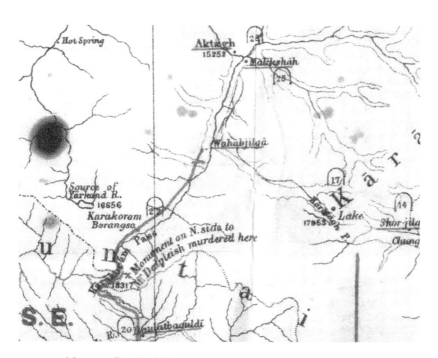

Map 5.1 Detail of "Territories of the Maharaja of Jammoo and Kashmir" (1903). Note that "Monument on N. side to Mr. Dalgleish murdered here" is visible above the point marking the Karakoram Pass. PAHAR/Mountains of Central Asia Digital Dataset.

[14] Technically speaking, the region now generally referred to as the Aksai Chin includes two other distinct plateaux that historically have been referred to as the Lingshi Tang and the Chang Chenmo (Tibetan: "great northern").

protectorates effectively controlled the region north of the Karakoram Pass.[15] Although central to the worgld's highest major network of cultural and commercial exchange, it was effectively a "no-man's land."[16] The episode of Andrew Dalgleish's murder near the Karakoram Pass and the effects it had on the government of India spoke to two central challenges facing colonial officials regarding the imperial frontier in the northwestern Himalaya. They centered on definition and control: where should the northern border of India be, and how could it be controlled? By drawing the imperial government's attention to this nonstate space stretching across the north of India, Dalgleish's murder hastened efforts to establish a territorial border through the broad Himalaya and its neighboring mountain regions.

This chapter reexamines border making, roads, and geographical epistemes in the context of growing security concerns – particularly in terms of those people and groups who regularly crossed the frontier. The 1880s marked a turning point in imperial security and frontier policy. The jurisdictional uncertainties surrounding Andrew Dalgleish's murder in 1888 and the threat of unwanted incursions reflected two key challenges to rendering population and territory legible: foreign penetration and nonstate space. Amid the escalating tensions between Britain and Russia, the Aksai Chin could no longer function as an acceptable vague buffer frontier. Instead, the British government of India increasingly required demarcation of a borderline through this "no-man's land." Surveying, border demarcation, and the regulation of roads all fell under an overarching rubric of imperial security. Geography thus became explicitly linked to the needs of the state. The wide circulation of frontier experts like Ney Elias, Mortimer Durand, Henry McMahon, and Thomas Holdich demonstrated this fusion. Altogether, these developments reflected a new, geopolitical way of seeing space – a mode of seeing that was distinct from, and frequently in conflict with, indigenous modes.

5.1   Beyond the Frontier

In 1883, a series of memoranda began circulating through the Government of India's Foreign Department. So-called trans-frontier

---

[15] The British at the time claimed the Karakoram Pass as their northernmost boundary based on the water-parting principle, by which the limits of the Indus watershed defined their northern boundary. Several years later they would change their minds and suggest the northern base of the Karakoram Pass, only to return to the water-parting line at the pass in 1896, where it has more or less remained.

[16] NAI, Foreign, Frontier A, July 1888, no. 94.

men were crossing into India from Afghanistan. They were entering the Punjab and making their way to the princely state of Hyderabad in southern India, generating anxiety among colonial officials.[17] Unlike the Powindah merchants and other nomadic groups[18] who regularly made that crossing to trade horses and goods, these men were moving south in search of work, or, as one British administrator suspected, "for a row."[19] The nizam's government in Hyderabad asked the Foreign Department to restrict their movements, fearing instability from a glut of unemployed migrants. But British attempts to post observers at rail-heads and along major roads predictably failed to produce any results – in part because the British were not even sure how to distinguish the unwanted trans-frontier men from other trans-frontier groups that regularly traversed the Indo-Afghan borderland.[20] They were not buying train tickets and they were not crossing at the few towns with border check-points. The frontier, after all, was quite permeable – and often still not precisely defined by any complete borderline.

---

[17] For the long history of colonial anxiety in regard to Afghans, particularly those headed to Hyderabad, see Hopkins, *Modern Afghanistan*; Seema Alavi, "'Fugitive Mullahs and Outlawed Fanatics': Indian Muslims in Nineteenth Century Trans-Asiatic Imperial Rivalries," *Modern Asian Studies* 45, no. 6 (2011): 1337–82; Chandra Mallampalli, *A Muslim Conspiracy in British India? Politics and Paranoia in the Early Nineteenth Century Deccan* (Cambridge: Cambridge University Press, 2017).

[18] Generally called *Kōchī* in Afghanistan. For a study of the complex movements of these "trans-frontier" groups on the North-West Frontier, see Neeladri Bhattacharya, "Predicaments of Mobility: Peddlers and Itinerants in Nineteenth Century Northwestern India," in *Society and Circulation: Mobile People and Itinerant Cultures in South Asia, 1750–1950*, ed. Claude Markovits, Jacques Pouchepadass, and Sanjay Subrahmanyam (Delhi: Permanent Black, 2003), 163–214, 168.

[19] NAI, Foreign, A Political I, June 1884, nos. 131–32. "Restrictions on the movements of trans-frontier men towards the Decan." The undersecretary to the Foreign Department, W. Lee-Warner, wrote in May 1884, "Eliminating traders, two classes of [trans-frontier men], pour into the Nizam's territory. Pathans, Rohillas, and others, who are on the look out for service or for a row, and whose trouble to ourselves would commence by taking part in plundering or dacoity expeditions in the Native States. The second class has been frequently troublesome to Bombay District Officers, and the Home Department has plenty of information about them. They call themselves usually Mekranis, or Khurasanis, and they come down from Biluchistan and southern Afghanistan. They are a sort of turbulent gypsy tribe. . . . They move in gangs of some scores, invade British territory, and when met by strong measures, separate and dribble away into the Nizam's territories again. . . . These I expect are the men about whom Baroda was anxious. . . . The Punjab Government at present watches the railway stations."

[20] Colonel A. H. Bamfield, Inspector-General of Police, Punjab, to Secretary, Government of Punjab, June 27, 1883. NAI, Foreign, A Political I, September 1883, nos. 183–85. "The District Superintendents of Police at Jhelum, Amritsar, Jullundur, and Umballa were accordingly directed to place men who could distinguish Central Asian pilgrims from Afghan vagrants at the railway stations, so that such persons might be brought in a conciliatory manner to the District Superintendents of Police and granted the necessary passport."

"To the centre of any empire," Manan Ahmed recently wrote, "the frontier is a site of anxiety, of potential harm, of barbarians who could be marching towards the gate."[21] In the case of the northern frontier of India in the latter nineteenth century, the "gates" were mountain passes and the "barbarians" came in two forms: Russians moving southward from Central Asia, and the "trans-frontier men" who inhabited and regularly moved across the regions the British insisted should be considered frontiers and buffer states. The first section of this chapter addresses the major imperial responses to these apparent threats in terms of border-making practices. First I examine British concerns over trans-frontier penetration in the 1880s and 1890s and the strategies employed to establish boundary lines and eliminate "no-man's lands." I then trace how the late nineteenth-century Russian threat easily shifted into a Soviet threat in the 1920s, 1930s, and 1940s, generating concerns that would be passed on to the postindependence government of India.

5.1.1   Invasion and Anxiety on the Periphery

Despite Thomas Holdich's assertion that the Himalayan range was "the finest natural combination of boundary and barrier that exists in the world," it was crossed with great regularity in multiple directions by many different groups.[22] From Baloch and Afghan traders in the west, to merchants and monks crisscrossing the Indo-Tibetan frontier, to pilgrims on the Haj and traders from Central Asia, the mountainous edges of the subcontinent were home to people with a habit of moving. These regions were also home to many of the so-called martial races: Dogras, Pathans, Kumaunis, Garhwalis, and Gurkhas.[23] Forming the top strata of the post-1857 colonial military-racial classificatory schema, these groups struck the British as ideal army recruits in part because of the vigorous mountain climates whence they came.[24]

Movement across the mountainous periphery of India both generated and exacerbated ongoing concerns within the British Government of India, just as its own commercial and political designs on the lands beyond India simmered with anxieties over unknown incursions into their empire. By the 1870s, with the growing threat of Russian encroachment, British officials redoubled their efforts to define India's borders as

---

[21] Ahmed, "Adam's Mirror."
[22] Holdich, Political Frontiers and Boundary Making, 280.
[23] See Heather Streets-Salter, Martial Races: The Military, Race and Masculinity in British Imperial Culture, 1857–1914 (Manchester, UK: Manchester University Press, 2004); and Hevia, Imperial Security State, 178–80, 204–8.
[24] This is in contrast to the alleged degenerative effects of the plains.

precisely as possible. They realized that trans-frontier peoples, like nomads more generally, were difficult to control, and that their continued movement reflected a general vulnerability to invasion from beyond. Such hypothetical invasions were beginning to be imagined and planned for by military strategists in the Intelligence Branch of the Indian Army, one of the world's earliest intelligence gathering organizations.[25]

Invasion fears were intensified by the fact that much of India's periphery was not directly ruled by the British Government of India but was composed of princely states with varying degrees of internal autonomy. As the Resident at Hyderabad wrote regarding those unemployed Afghans causing concern in the 1880s, "it is almost entirely owing to the presence of Native States within British India that trans-frontier men come across in inconvenient numbers, and that it is only within those Native States that the ordinary police and the ordinary laws of the land are unable to cope with them."[26] Repeated proposals to create a thin strip of territory surrounding all of India and directly controlled by the central government never materialized, but certain frontier areas – like Gilgit to the north of Kashmir – were temporarily administered by the central government when local rulers were deemed to be inefficient or untrustworthy. Plans to do the same with Ladakh, or the whole of Jammu and Kashmir, were proposed by several frontier administrators and experts on at least seven separate occasions between 1880 and 1947.[27]

---

[25] London War Office Intelligence Branch was founded in 1873 (Hevia, *Imperial Security State*, 54), while the India Army Intelligence Branch, which emulated that of the War Office, was founded under the Quartermaster General in India in 1878.

[26] NAI, Foreign, A Political I, June 1884, nos. 131–32. "Restrictions on the movements of trans-frontier men towards the Decan."

[27] (1) NAI, Foreign, Secret F, February 1888 nos. 198–206. "Proposed appointment of a secret commission to consider a future military frontier line to be held for the protection of India"; (2) NAI, Foreign, Secret F, September 1889, nos. 211–17. "Lhassa authorities still recognize the Ex-Raja of Ladakh as in power and ignore the Kashmir Wazir"; (3) NAI, Foreign, Secret E., May 1918, nos. 146–47. "Effect on the Indo-Tibet Frontier of the grant of Self-Government in India. Question of the creation of a non-self-governing belt of India to act as a buffer between self-governing India and Tibet, Nepal, Sikkim, Bhutan and Kashmir"; (4) NAI, Foreign and Political, No. 364-X. of 1924–27 (Secret). "Soviet propaganda, and measures to counteract Soviet activities in the North. Measures suggested for adoption in the Gilgit Agency and dealt with separately. . . . Taking over the independent territories lying between the Gilgit Agency and the North West Frontier Province and Chitral"; (5) NAI, External Affairs Department (predecessor to Ministry of External Affairs), 1940, No. 798-X. "Ladakh Affairs"; (6) NAI, External Affairs Department, No. 329 C.A. (Sec.) of 1944. "Payment to the Kashmir Government of a sum of Rs. 8,000/- on account of expenditure incurred on the entry of Kazaks into India. Question of lease of Ladakh Province from the Kashmir Government"; and (7) NAI, External Affairs Department, No. 258-C.A. (Secret), 1947. "Question of surrender by Jammu and Kashmir State to the Centre, the effective control and administration of its external frontier and taking over of the Ladakh Tehsil."

As illustrated in Chapter 3, frontier roads became both causes of and solutions to imperial security concerns. Conduits like the Treaty Road through Ladakh that had been improved in attempts to develop trade with Central Asia became, by the turn of the century, means of regulating and restricting movement – whether of "undesirable" Central Asians or Europeans like the bizarre Austro-Hungarian Haberhaver who was supposedly there in search of butterflies. In addition to improving oversight of the roads themselves, broader restrictions were put in place by the early twentieth century to address the problem of trans-frontier men. In 1901, for instance, selling them "arms, ammunition, and warlike stores" was prohibited.[28] And beginning in 1914 these "tribesmen" had to carry passports.[29] But the greatest power these groups posed undoubtedly lay in their ability to generate fear in the government of India and in the imperial British public more broadly.

Accounts of their putative "outrages" had brought trans-frontier groups to the attention of the British and Indian metropolitan publics before the Rebellion of 1857. These rare accounts became more frequent – and visible – by the turn of the century. An April 1920 editorial in the *Madras Mail*, republished in the Sunday *Times*, introduced one such event on "that most interesting part of India – the Frontier."[30] The author, a Member of Parliament, described the frontier as follows: "This is a long range of mountains which shuts off India from Tibet, Afghanistan and Persia, penetrated by gorges and passes that are inhabited by tribes of the greatest scoundrels now living on the face of the earth." In language typical of such pieces, the author described in his "Call to Action" an incident in which a British officer's wife was abducted near Peshawar by a party of Afridi tribesmen who apparently tore her out of bed, forced her to march into the hills at dagger point, and subjected her to such treatment that was "not necessary to enlarge" upon. For this "blow to our prestige" the author demanded an accounting of the incident from the Secretary of State for India and recommended more roads be built to ensure faster retaliation against such groups and greater control over such regions. Three years later in Kohat, the kidnapping of Molly Ellis, which was preceded by the murder of her mother, generated

---

[28] NAI, Foreign, Secret F, February 1901, nos. 122–34, 127. "Proposed amendment of the rule in order to prohibit licensed dealers from selling Arms, Ammunition, and Warlike Stores to Trans-border men." See also T. R. Moreman, "The Arms Trade and the North-West Frontier Pathan Tribes, 1890–1914," *The Journal of Imperial and Commonwealth History* 22, no. 2 (2008): 187–216.

[29] NAI, Foreign, General, Secret, June 1914, no. 3.

[30] NAI, Foreign, Frontier, August 1920, no. 48, Part b. The article in question was entitled, "The North-West Frontier: A Call to Action," by Sir William Joynson Hicks, Bt., M.P. published in the *Sunday Times* from the *Madras Mail*, April 6, 1920.

a similar degree of public alarm and resulted in British destruction of several villages after ransom had been paid and Molly returned.[31]

5.1.2   The "Boys with Digestions" and the Pundits

While the majority of frontier experts were associated with the work of boundary commissions that will be discussed in the next chapter, some gained renown through explorations beyond the frontier. These were the "boys with digestions," as Kipling styled them: hypermasculine paragons of the imperial British homosocial world.[32] Theirs was not simply a masculinity of physical strength and the occasional use of violence; as recent scholarship has established, it was also "a masculinist story" of solitary discipline and exploratory fantasy (Figure 5.1).[33] The dominant trope, purveyed in much popular fiction and nonfiction, had the young colonial officer "penetrating" the virgin lands beyond the frontier, or taming the lawless hills, evoking sexual metaphors without much taxing of the imagination.[34] For these men the two great theaters of empire in India were the North-West and Indo-Tibetan frontiers.[35] The former offered frequent opportunity for conquest and reconquest while the latter stubbornly refused to be "opened" until Younghusband's mission in 1903–4. Embodied by the otherworldly figure of "the Lama" in Kipling's novel, *Kim* (1901), Tibet was a "forbidden," "mysterious," and "unknown" land. The continual failure of the government of India to "open up" Tibet throughout the nineteenth century was often viewed by commentators as reflecting a "timid, wavering policy."[36]

---

[31] Victoria Schofield, *Afghan Frontier: Feuding and Fighting in Central Asia* (New York: Tauris Parke, 2003), 130–35. For a recent study on kidnapping on the North-West Frontier, see Kate Imy, "Kidnapping and a 'Confirmed Sodomite': An Intimate Enemy on the Northwest Frontier of India, 1915–1925," *Twentieth Century British History* 28, no. 1 (2017): 29–56.

[32] Rudyard Kipling, *Plain Tales from the Hills* (1888; repr., Oxford: Oxford University Press, 2001), 162.

[33] See Robert H. Macdonald, *The Language of Empire: Myths and Metaphors of Popular Imperialism, 1880–1918* (Manchester, UK: Manchester University Press, 1994); and Anne McClintock, *Imperial Leather: Race, Gender and Sexuality in the Colonial Contest* (New York: Routledge, 1995).

[34] For an example of this genre, see the Tales from the Outposts series.

[35] The North-West Frontier, as Lewis Wurgaft and others have detailed, was the preeminent locus of these fantasies. As James Hevia has noted with regard to the main characters of Kipling's "The Man Who Would Be King," "Kipling's stories are significant precisely because they formed Asia around such fantasies. Tales like this one fixed the continent as a space for unconventional men, where romantic adventure . . . lay just . . . over the next range of mountains." Hevia, *Imperial Security State*, 9.

[36] NAI, Foreign, Secret External, May 1887, no. 82. "Despatch to Secretary of State containing a complete account of the circumstances connected with the proposed British Mission to Tibet" and Extract from the "Englishman," dated January 31, 1887: "Public opinion strongly stirred by delay of Tibet Mission."

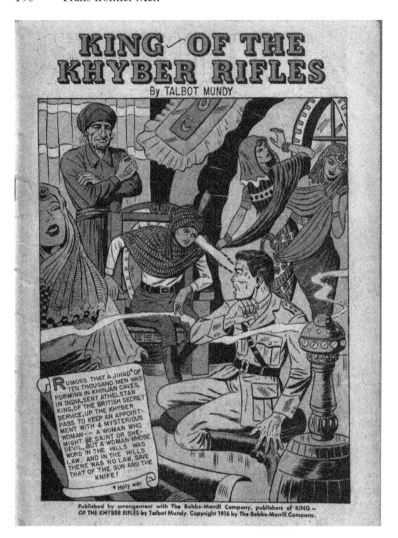

Figure 5.1 Talbot Mundy, *King of the Khyber Rifles* (1916). This example of masculinist frontier fantasy reads, "Rumors that a Jihad★ (★Holy war) of ten thousand men was forming in Khinjan Caves, in India, sent Athelstan King, of the British Secret Service, up the Khyber Pass to keep an appointment with a woman – a woman who might be saint or she-devil, but a woman whose word in the hills was law. And in the hills there was no law, save that of the gun and the knife." Collection of the author.

Francis Younghusband was the consummate frontier man, having achieved fame through his daring traverses in the Karakoram and his travels across China and Central Asia. These travels formed the basis of his first popular memoir, *The Heart of a Continent* (1896).[37] It recounted his journey from eastern China across the Gobi Desert to the northwestern Himalaya. Reflecting the emerging geopolitical view of Asia as both a "problem" and an object to be studied,[38] Younghusband's journey into the "heart" of Asia also implied the accumulation of expertise necessary to be a respected frontier man. Expertise was generated on the ground in Asia, not in London. True, men like Younghusband would later return to London and participate in the Royal Geographical Society, which circulated exploration reports, maps, and policy recommendations in the pages of its *Journal*. But ground zero for frontier expertise lay in the mountainous "heart" of Asia.

The Tibet Frontier Commission would also be known, tellingly, as the invasion of Tibet, and Younghusband would eventually be rewarded for his role therein with the position of Resident in Kashmir.[39] Durand believed that any aspiring political officer needed time on the frontier to "enable his superiors to judge of the stuff of which he was made and would assist them in forming an estimate of his capacity for general or special employment."[40] Men with "knowledge and brains" like Elias and Younghusband, Durand opined, should not be left to work in "humdrum routine."[41] They were suited for work on the frontier – especially, Durand added, if they were young and unmarried.[42]

Besides unwanted "trans-frontier men" and imperial adventurers, a third group of trans-frontier men figured on this scene. These were the pundits, a hybrid of native and colonial. Often from the hills but sometimes from Bengal and other parts of the plains, they were trained by the Survey of India to take part in covert intelligence gathering missions beyond the borders of India. Complicating the trope of "effeminate natives," these highly praised spies and surveyors were lauded for their bravery and sometimes rewarded with medals and titles by the imperial state. As prized "human instruments," the pundits generated critical trans-frontier information for the Survey of India and the imperial state.[43]

---

[37] Younghusband, *The Heart of a Continent*.   [38] See Hevia, *Imperial Security State*.
[39] NAI, Foreign, External, December 1903, nos. 1–13, Part B.
[40] Captain Prideaux to Mortimer Durand, April 25, 1892. NAI, Foreign, General, July 1892, 18–40.
[41] NAI, Foreign, Secret E, May 1887, no. 119. "Note by Elias, Mr. Ney, C.I.E on Tibet and his views as to the best means of obtaining access to that country."
[42] NAI.
[43] Kapil Raj, *Relocating Modern Science*. See also Robert Johnson, *Spying for Empire: The Great Game in Central and South Asia, 1757–1947* (St. Paul, MN: Greenhill Books, 2006).

One of the two most famous pundits was Sarat Chandra Das, the inspiration for Kipling's Hurree Chander Mukherjee, Kim's faithful servant.[44] He was also the author of one of the canonical Tibetan-English dictionaries and an extensive traveler in Tibet in the days before Younghusband's expedition forced it open.[45] On one such exploratory trip, Colman Macaulay, then the Finance Secretary of Bengal, wrote a poem commemorating each of the expedition's members. He evoked the dual language of effeminacy and masculinity by styling Das "A Hardy Son of Soft Bengal."[46]

The hagiographic quality ascribed to some of these surveyors is perfectly encapsulated in a story that Sir Henry McMahon told before the Royal Society of Arts about a surveying party in Seistan. "It befell one of our survey parties under the charge of an old and very experienced Indian surveyor, who, *overcome by his zeal to fill up a blank in our map*, ventured too far into that dread tract, the Dasht-i-Margo (Desert of Death) – a desert ... into which no one had ever been known to enter." The party ran out of water and when they finally stumbled across a pool, it was salty, thus "hasten[ing] their end." Only one member of the team remained, "an Indian survey subordinate, named Saidu." "But even at this awful moment," McMahon continued,

[Saidu] made duty his first care. He cut off from the surveyor's plane table the precious map for which so much had been risked, and knowing he could not long retain consciousness, he wrapped it round his waist in his waist-cloth and started off in the faint hope of surviving. For two days and nights, he said, he struggled on in a state of semi-consciousness, and woke up one night to find himself half lying in a pool of water. There a wandering Afghan found him and carried him on his back to the nearest habitation. Thus was a blank in the map filled up and its survey preserved. It cost us seven valuable lives.[47]

Despite the poet Rabindranath Tagore's assertion that "no one can give up his life for a map," McMahon's story suggests that in the patronizing colonial world of dutiful native surveyors and high-stakes mapping, there were those who would willingly die for the cause of imperial territorial legibility.[48]

[44] The other was Pundit Nain Singh Rawat.

[45] Derek Waller, *The Pundits: British Exploration of Tibet and Central Asia* (Lexington: University of Kentucky Press, 1990).

[46] Sarat Chandra Das, *Indian Pandits in the Land of Snow* (Calcutta: Baptist Mission Press, 1893). The full stanza reads, "And Sarat Chandra, hardy son / Of soft Bengal, whose wonderous store / Of Buddhist and Tibetan lore/ A place in fame's bright page has won / Friend of the Tashu Lama [i.e., Panchen Lama]'s line / Whose eyes have seen, the gleaming shrine / Of holy Lhassa, came to show / The wonders of the land of snow."

[47] A. H. McMahon, "International Boundaries," *Journal of the Royal Society of Arts* 84, no. 4330 (1935): 11–12. Proceedings of the Royal Society of Arts, inaugural address by the incoming Chairman of the Council, Wednesday, November 6, 1935.

[48] Tagore, quoted in Sumathi Ramaswamy, "Visualising India's Geo-Body: Globes, Maps, Bodyscapes," *Contributions to Indian Sociology* 36, nos. 1–2 (2002): 151.

5.2   The Macartney–MacDonald Line and the Problem of No-Man's Lands

Shifting our focus back to Ladakh and the northwestern Himalaya, the major "outrage" that stirred British opinion had been Andrew Dalgleish's murder in 1888, later immortalized by John Buchan in a short story in his *A Book of Escapes and Hurried Journeys* (1922). "The story of the unrelenting pursuit [of Dalgleish's killer] throughout Central Asia," Buchan wrote, "had an immense moral effect in all that mountain country. The tale of it was repeated at camp-fires and bazaars everywhere between Persia and China, till the Great War, with its far wilder romances, came to dim its memory."[49] Whatever its impression upon the British public, Dalgleish's murder reminded imperial administrators of another, more practical problem. The northern boundary of India had, in theory, already been established as the limit of the Indus watershed, but the government of India had yet to effectively demarcate that line or to gather precise details about its location. Here the northwestern Himalaya was increasingly the exception rather than the rule. The Afghan and Pamir boundary commissions, which included the prominent experts Thomas Holdich and Robert Wahab, were demarcated with great detail by the mid-1890s. Simultaneously, the British were undertaking a detailed demarcation of the Sino-Burmese boundary. The difference in the case of the northwestern Himalayan boundaries stemmed in part from the sheer harshness of the environment, which prohibited large survey parties from spending much time in the arid, high-desert region. But perceptions of territories beyond India as a "no-man's land" were also at work. The government of India continued debating whether or not to "induce the Chinese to occupy" the regions north and east of the Karakoram Pass in order to block potential Russian advances. This strategy was complicated by Kashmiri claims to Shahidulla, a small settlement north of the Karakoram along the Treaty Road.[50]

In 1865, Shahidulla was briefly occupied by troops from Jammu and Kashmir but was quickly abandoned and subsequently taken over by troops of Yaqub Beg. According to Ney Elias, when the Chinese retook Kashgaria they sent troops south to Shahidulla and taxed the Kirghiz nomads in the Karakash valley north of the settlement. In 1885, Pandit Radha Kishen, the *wazīr-i-wazārat* of Ladakh, heard of the discovery of

---

[49] Buchan, *A Book of Escapes*, 291.
[50] W. J. Cuningham, Foreign Secretary to Colonel R. Parry Nisbet, Resident in Kashmir, August 21, 1890. NAI, Foreign, Secret Frontier, October 1890, nos. 141–70, page 97. Keep-With No. 2: "Report from Younghusband (Captain) regarding the state of affairs in Shahidulla and the northern frontier of Kashmir."

a lapis lazuli mine in the Karakash valley and desired to send Kashmiri troops to retake it. Elias worried that this might "incense the Chinese and give rise to an awkward frontier question."[51] The government of India denied Radha Kishen's request and agreed with Elias that though a borderline had yet to be demarcated, Shahidulla clearly lay beyond the Indus watershed. This acknowledgment also revealed that the Chinese did not know where their own frontier was in the region.

In December 1888, the British Joint Commissioner in Ladakh, Captain Henry Ramsay, forwarded a secret memorandum to his superior, the Resident in Kashmir, Colonel Parry Nisbet.[52] The note precipitated a change in thinking about the northern frontier of India. Nisbet forwarded Ramsay's memo to Mortimer Durand, the secretary to the Foreign Department, adding that the "recent development of Imperial policy and the measures taken within the last three or four years to secure against attack or surprise routes leading from Central Asia or Afghanistan to India make it, I think, undesirable longer to defer the settlement of this boundary."[53] The ensuing discussion brought in a range of frontier experts. Ney Elias was again consulted. The viceroy, Lord Dufferin, was involved, as was Durand's assistant and eventual successor, W. J. Cuningham. For his part Ramsay voiced his anxieties about continuing relations between Ladakh and Tibet, particularly the triennial Lopchak tribute mission and the reciprocal Chaba discussed in the previous chapter. Ramsay reminded all that the northern frontier of Ladakh had never been defined and that "while some authorities placed it at Shahidulla, others placed it at the crest of the Karakoram Pass, which is as much as 79 miles south of Shahidulla."[54]

By the time Ramsay weighed in it had been three years since Ney Elias's note on the northern frontier, and during that time Russian advances in Turkestan had generated increased anxiety in India. In addition, Anglo-Russian tensions in Afghanistan had risen after the Panjdeh Incident in 1885, when a Russian incursion into Afghan territory threatened to

---

[51] NAI, Foreign, Secret F, November 1885, nos. 12–14. "Application of the Indus System to the boundary between Ladak and Chinese Turkistan."

[52] NAI, Foreign, Secret F, March 1889, nos. 115–16. "Frontier between Ladakh and Chinese-Turkestan."

[53] NAI. The "development of Imperial policy" and "measures" referred to an increased awareness of Russian advances in Central Asia and Eastern Turkestan and the growing need to address the possibility of an Afghan invasion. From the time of Henry Rawlinson's *England and Russia in the East* (1875), there had been a growing group of "forward policy" advocates. Rawlinson served as president of the Royal Geographical Society.

[54] NAI, Foreign, Secret F, March 1889, nos. 115–16. "Frontier between Ladakh and Chinese-Turkestan."

provoke a diplomatic crisis and war.[55] The need for unambiguous demarcations of the northern boundary of India became increasingly apparent, as
the "Forward Policy" advocated by Rawlinson, Sandeman, and others was
beginning to generate more friction across the frontier, not less. This policy
argued that Britain ought to be aggressive in claiming the farthest extent of
controllable territory and in seeking to establish favorable political conditions beyond its claimed border, usually in the form of "buffer states" or
"spheres of influence." Thus the British Government of India came to see
China, like Afghanistan, as a necessary bulwark against Russian advances.

   While arranging the return of Andrew Dalgleish's papers to Calcutta,
Henry Ramsay came across a memo "on the Chinese position in Yarkand,
in which Mr. Dalgleish wrote that the Chinese were very unwilling to
extend their territory southwestwards."[56] It was only after "frequent and
urgent recommendations made by [Dalgleish] to the Chinese authorities
at Yarkand, that they had sent troops to occupy the fort at Sirikol," north
of Shahidulla. Furthermore, Ramsay noted, the Chinese government's
"conduct in regard to Mr. Dalgleish's murder shows that the Yarkand
authorities do not regard the Karakoram Pass as their frontier." This
suggested that the Chinese did not consider the space immediately
north of the Karakoram Pass to be their territory, though, as Ramsay
wrote, the "truth of the matter probably is that the Chinese do not know
where their frontier is." Considering the history of unilateral boundary
commissions in the northwestern Himalaya up to that point, Ramsay's
conclusion held a good deal of unintended irony. "Indeed," he concluded, "how should [the Chinese know where the frontier is] for it
requires two parties to demarcate a frontier."

   Echoing Elias, Ramsay argued that for clear "geographical and ethnological reasons" the water-parting that included the Karakoram Pass was
the ideal borderline.[57] A proper demarcation was all the more necessary,
he added, for if the government of India continued to "permit affairs to
remain in their present condition, we must accept the fact that there is
a broad belt of 'no man's land' between Indian and Chinese territory."[58]

---

[55] Hevia, *Imperial Security State*, 96.
[56] NAI, Foreign, Secret F, March 1889, nos. 115–16. "Frontier between Ladakh and
   Chinese-Turkestan."
[57] Expanding later on this point, Ramsay wrote, "The watershed of the Indus system is our
   natural frontier at any rate as far east as the Karakash river (beyond this point the
   geographical argument would remain in favour of this boundary, but the ethnological
   argument would be against it, as people, if any, found east of the Karakash would be
   Tibetans and not Kirghiz or Central Asian Muhammadans)."
[58] Ramsay further argued that if the frontier had been formally demarcated, "the Chinese
   could not, without loss of dignity to which they would not submit, allow the Russians to
   enter upon that country, and at the same time the Russians would be aware of this and
   would be less likely to take such a step. In the same way if the Chinese agreed to give over

Although the matter continued to be "frequently under discussion," Viceroy Dufferin worried that demarcating a boundary with China around the Karakoram Pass would raise concerns over the Afghan-Chinese frontier as well.[59] The viceroy noted that the map of the neighboring Pamir region produced by Francis Younghusband on an earlier covert mission was too vague to bring to the Chinese.[60] Still, discussions of how to get the Chinese to occupy the no-man's land between the two empires continued. Reaffirming the limit of the Indus watershed system as at least part of the northern boundary of Ladakh, the British imperial government soon moved to push the Chinese to "effectively assert their claims to Shahidulla and the tract between the Kuen Lun and Karakoram Ranges," while prohibiting Kashmir from going beyond the Karakoram Pass.[61] Yet the Secretary of State for India added the caution that, "while we welcomed the interest which [the Chinese government displayed] in these remote places, we could not allow the ownership of them to be disposed of without reference to us and otherwise than by common consent."

The first major segment of the northern Indian frontier to be codified by treaty came with the agreement to demarcate the 1,500-mile boundary between India and Afghanistan in 1893; this would be known as the Durand Line after its chief architect and the British signatory. In an effort to extend this imperial perimeter still farther, the British Government decided in 1898 that it was no longer "impolitic to bring before the Chinese Government the question of the settlement of their boundaries with Kashmir, Hunza and Afghanistan."[62] William Cuningham, now head of the Foreign Department, wrote the Resident in Kashmir: "I recently had occasion to consult Younghusband on the question of the settlement with China of the boundaries of Hunza, Kashmir and Afghanistan." With the exception of two valley posts deemed strategic, this border would follow the water-parting of the main range. After consulting with Henry McMahon, who had accompanied Durand on

the 'no man's land' to us, the mere fact of its having been declared to be British territory would suffice to prevent Russian encroachment."

[59] W. J. Cuningham, Foreign Secretary to Colonel R. Parry Nisbet, Resident in Kashmir, August 21, 1890. NAI, Foreign, Secret Frontier, October 1890, nos. 141–70, page 97. Keep-With No. 2: "Report from Younghusband (Captain) regarding the state of affairs in Shahidulla and the northern frontier of Kashmir."

[60] Cuningham. Telegram from Her Majesty's Secretary of State, to Foreign Secretary, September 29, 1890.

[61] Secretary of State for India, to Deputy Secretary, Foreign Department, India. June 15, 1894. NAI, Foreign, Secret F, August 1894, nos. 26–33. "Chinese Boundary. Question of fixing the Chinese Boundary."

[62] NAI, Foreign, Secret Frontier, November 1898, nos. 110–14. "Kashmir-Frontier."

his 1892 mission to Kabul and was later posted to Gilgit as the political officer in 1897–98, this line was accepted.[63]

Cuningham also consulted Robert A. Wahab, who, like Thomas Holdich, had been a member of numerous surveys, including the Afghan Boundary Commission of 1884–86.[64] Cuningham sent Wahab the latest map of Eastern Turkestan, one compiled by Henry Trotter in the 1870s and marked up by Francis Younghusband with a hypothetical borderline in red and blue dotted lines,[65] and asked Wahab to produce a printed map based on Younghusband's revisions. But, he added, "it would be better *not* to indicate on it the true crests of the main ranges … for the map might be wanted for use in negotiations, and would be better for not indicating alternatives."[66] The map was forwarded to the viceroy, who sent it to the Secretary of State for India. After consulting with John Ardagh, the Director of Military Intelligence in the War Office, it was determined that the water-parting of the Karakoram should be established in writing between the Chinese and Indian governments as the boundary between the two empires. In April 1898 the Secretary of State told the viceroy that "no strategical advantage would be gained by going beyond the natural frontier and across mountains where no hostile advance is ever likely to be attempted."[67] What was needed, as Viceroy Elgin put it, was "an agreement with China describing the line in question by its better known topographical features, each power reciprocally engaging to respect the boundary thus defined."[68]

To that end the Foreign Office reached out to George Macartney, the consul-general at Kashgar who had been placed under the command of the Resident in Kashmir. Having been born and raised in Nanking, the

[63] William J. Cuningham, Foreign Secretary, to A. C. Talbot, Resident in Kashmir, August 1, 1898. NAI, Foreign, Secret Frontier, November 1898, nos. 110–14.
[64] William J. Cuningham, Foreign Secretary, to A. C. Talbot, Resident in Kashmir, August 1, 1898. NAI, Foreign, Secret Frontier, November 1898, nos. 110–14.
[65] India International Center (hereafter IIC), Himalayan Club Collection. Captain Henry Trotter, R.E. (Deputy-Superintendent, Great Trigonometrical Survey of India) *Account of the Survey Operations in connection with the Mission to Yarkand and Kashghar in 1873–74.* Extracted from the volume of reports submitted to the Government of India by Sir Douglas Forsyth, C.B., K.C.S.I., in charge of the mission (Calcutta: Printed at the Foreign Department Press, 1875).
[66] William Cuningham, Foreign Secretary, to Lieutenant-Colonel R. A. Wahab, September 4, 1898. NAI, Foreign, Secret F, November 1898, nos. 110–14.
[67] Secretary of State, London, to Viceroy, Simla, July 13, 1898. NAI, Foreign, Secret Frontier, November 1898, nos. 110–14. "Kashmir-Frontier. Memorandum by Sir John Ardagh, KCB, advocating the extension of British influence to regions beyond the northern frontier of India contiguous to Chinese Dominions for the purpose of frustrating a Russian advance on India via the Kilik Mintaka, Shimshal, Khunjerab, Mustagh, and Karakoram Passes."
[68] Secretary of State.

child of a Scottish father and Chinese mother, Macartney served as a Chinese interpreter on Younghusband's 1890 expedition. After Younghusband left in 1891, Macartney stayed on in Kashgar as the sole British representative in Central Asia. This remained an informal role until 1910, when Russia and China recognized him as British consul-general.[69] In the early 1890s, with very little instruction from the government of India, Macartney began gathering information on the region around Kashgar and Yarkand, including a map provided by Hung Ta-Chen, a senior Chinese official in Kashgar in 1893.[70] That gave the Foreign Office its first glimpse of what the Chinese understood to be its territorial limits in Xinjiang.

The Foreign Office then contacted Claude MacDonald, the British minister to the Chinese government, telling him to give the Chinese a description of a proposed "line of frontier" which was "so clearly denoted by geographical features that no difficulty [was] anticipated in its observance by the two Governments without the necessity for any demarcation on the spot."[71] To avoid incongruous Chinese claims to territory within the watershed – specifically a "shadowy" claim to sovereignty over Hunza" (north of Gilgit) – the British were prepared to push the rulers of Hunza to waive their claims to the Taghdumbash valley and Raskam if the Chinese waived their claim to Hunza.[72] The Foreign Office concluded its letter to MacDonald by stating that the "line now proposed, which is shown on the enclosed map, would form a good and well defined boundary, and I have to request you to approach the Tsungli Yamen on the subject, with a view to obtaining a settlement of the question in the direction indicated by the Government of India."[73]

The resulting letter of March 14, 1899, to the Chinese government proposed the border configuration later known as the Macartney–MacDonald Line.[74]

---

[69] C. P. Skrine and P. Nightingale, *Macartney at Kashgar* (1973); Katherine Prior, "Macartney, Sir George (1867–1945)," in *Oxford Dictionary of National Biography* (Oxford: Oxford University Press, 2004).

[70] Woodman, *Himalayan Frontiers*, 74–78.

[71] Foreign Office to Sir Claude MacDonald, December 14, 1898. NAI, Foreign, Secret Frontier, May 1899, no. 164, p. 193. "Indo-Chinese. Minister in China asked to address Tsungli Yamen regarding the line decided upon as the Boundary(ies) between Kashmir and its Dependencies and Chinese territory."

[72] Foreign Secretary to Resident in Kashmir, July 28, 1899. NAI, Foreign, Secret Frontier, August 1899, no. 198, p. 515. "Despatch addressed by Sir Claude MacDonald to the Tsungli Yamen regarding the Boundary(ies) between Chinese Turkistan, Afghanistan, Hunza, and Kashmir, and undertaking on behalf of the Indian Government to relinquish Hunza's claims to the Taghdumbash and Raskam if China will relinquish her claim to Hunza."

[73] Foreign Secretary to Resident in Kashmir.

[74] Viceroy to Secretary of State for India, July 27, 1899. NAI, Foreign, Secret E, September 1905, nos. 12–18, 15. "Definition of the boundary between Hunza and

Commencing on the Little Pamir, from the peak at which the Anglo-Russian Boundary Commission of 1895 ended their work, it runs south-east. . . . From the Karakoram Pass the crests of the range run nearly east for about half a degree (100 *li*), and then turn south to a little below the 35th parallel of north latitude. Rounding then what in our maps is shown as the source of the Karakash, the line of hills to be followed runs north-east to a point east of Kizil Jilga, and from there in a south-easterly direction follows the Lak Tsung Range until that meets the spur running south from the K'un-lun range, which has hitherto been shown on our maps as the eastern boundary of Ladakh. This is a little east of 80 [degrees] east longitude. / Your Highness and your Excellencies will see by examining this line that a large tract of country to the north of the great dividing range shown in Hung Chun's map as outside the Chinese boundary will be recognised as Chinese territory. / I beg your Highness and your Excellencies to consider the matter, and to favour me with an early reply.[75]

But there was no reply from the Chinese. Moreover, while the Macartney–MacDonald Line satisfied British imperial concerns to eliminate the no-man's north of Ladakh, it failed to address the continuing problem of trans-frontier men and the greater threat from the north.

5.3   Soviet Penetration

By the early twentieth century, threats of local border transgressions were easily extrapolated to the realm of geostrategic concern. This was due in part to anti-imperial nationalist movements as well as the growth of perceived transnational threats like Bolshevism and Pan-Islamism. In 1925, with the menace of imperial Russia replaced by that of Communist Russia, the Secretary of State for India received a telegram from India which he "regarded with some anxiety."[76] It seemed that "the Soviet Government while by no means abandoning its earlier line of 'attack' on India from Afghanistan and the north-west [was] taking advantage of the opportunity afforded by the condition of affairs in China to obtain and consolidate a position from which to launch also an

Chinese Turkestan as claimed by Sir C. Macdonald in 1899 and that which it is now recommended the Chinese Government should be invited to accept as part of the general settlement of all outstanding difficulties in Chinese Turkestan. Proposed modification of the latter so as to include the northern slope of the Kilik Pass for strategical reasons, rejected."

[75] Sir Claude M. MacDonald to the Tsung-li Yamên, March 14, 1899. Appendix 7 in Woodman, *Himalayan Frontiers*, 366–67.

[76] L. D. Wakely, Sec., Political Dept. India Office, London, October 8, 1925. NAI, Foreign F. No. 364-X. of 1924–27 (Secret). "Soviet propaganda, and measures to counteract Soviet activities in the North. Measures suggested for adoption in the Gilgit Agency and dealt with separately. Increase in the subsidies of Mirs and Governors of the Gilgit Agency. . . . Sanction of an increase in the Secret Service grant of the British Joint Commissioner in Leh."

attack from the north."[77] Besides, a "natural development of the policy that the Soviet Government appears to following in Hsin-Kiang and other parts of Central Asia" included extending its influence to Tibet. "To sum up," the secretary of state concluded, "it appears that if the policy which the Soviet Government is reported to be following in Central Asia and in China is allowed to be carried through unhindered, there is no sector of India's land frontier that will not eventually be threatened, in greater or lesser degree, with the danger of the infiltration of Bolshevik influences."

The deputy to the Secretary of the Foreign and Political Department responded that their office had obtained "secret and very reliable information that the Soviet Government, in certain eventualities, will endeavour to get into touch with our frontier tribes from the Pamirs with the object of stirring up trouble."[78] Establishing posts along the Yarkand-Leh Treaty Road would be one good means of addressing these concerns, he thought, though the consul-general at Kashgar, the Resident in Kashmir, and the General Staff Branch should first be consulted on the matter.

The Army's General Staff in the person of R. R. Maconachie replied that it was "doubtful whether the idea of a *detective cordon* along the Frontiers from Chitral to Burma [was] at all practical." But the Resident in Kashmir and his subordinate, the British Joint Commissioner, were more positive toward measures to be taken to combat "the Russian menace." Sir John Wood, the Resident in Kashmir, wrote that he fully supported the recommendations that his subordinates in Ladakh, Gilgit, and Kashgar had made, for the Soviets doubtless wanted "to turn Sinkiang into a Soviet Republic. ... It is the logical thing for the Russians to do as it will link up Soviet Turkestan with the new Soviet Republic of outer Mongolia."[79]

The Political Agent in Gilgit enumerated a list of specific steps to be taken. These included increasing the subsidies to the local mirs and governors, more training for the Gilgit Corps of Scouts, "taking over the Independent Territory lying between Gilgit Agency, the North West Frontier Province and Chitral," granting the Political Agent "special powers to deal with foreigners and undesirable British Indian Subjects," establishing aircraft landing grounds and telephone communications, increasing the Secret Service and Darbar present grants, and, of course, improving the roads up Gilgit while restricting roads beyond it to the border.

---

[77] Wakely.
[78] NAI, Foreign F. No. 364-X. of 1924–27 (Secret). "Soviet propaganda, and measures to counteract Soviet activities in the North."
[79] NAI.

Major Hinde, the BJC for Ladakh, had a more complex recommendation yet. He granted that Soviet movements between Yarkand and the
Karakoram would certainly be monitored by the consul-general in
Kashgar. Regarding those south of the Karakoram Pass, he told his
superior in Kashmir, "A glance at the map will show that for all practical
purposes there is only one pass which is feasible for travellers and that is
the one just North of Dipsang Plains. . . . South of the Dipsang, the Treaty
High Road makes a turn to the East over the Sasser Pass" and offers
another route along the Shyok river that could allow travelers to bypass
Leh and rejoin the Treaty Road at the Indus River five miles south of Leh
at Spituk.[80] "It is thus possible," Hinde concluded, "for travellers from
Chinese Turkestan to avoid Leh by using the Shyok route whether they
rejoin the Treary [sic] Road or not but *fortunately* this route is not open all
the year."[81] Tellingly, the seasonal inaccessibility of this route was now
a strength in the estimation of the British Joint Commissioner.

Regarding Soviet agents, Major Hinde noted that they "would hardly
attempt a journey from Yarkand to India on routes where most of the
travellers are known unless they have accomplices to shield them and
these accomplices would necessarily be traders or Hajis, probably the
latter." "Therefore," he concluded, "we may expect to find agents travelling with a party of Hajis."

But coordinating the issue of Haji passports with the consul-general at
Kashgar had already proved untenable, said Hinde. Instead, he proposed
(and the Resident in Kashmir concurred) that the "best and cheapest
method of keeping a watch on the ingress of undesirables from Chinese
Turkestan via Ladakh" was to have his assistant, the Special Charas
Officer at Leh, build a network of informants in the villages through
which a trans-frontier traveler was likely to pass. He proposed that his
Secret Service grant, which was set at a mere Rs. 50, should be increased
to Rs. 550. This would allow him to give a small monthly allowance to six
headmen in villages along the main routes into Ladakh for the six months
of the year that the passes were typically open.[82] These informants would
report the "arrival and departure of any teavellers [sic] who in any way
excite suspicion" to the Special Charas Officer in Leh, or to the "road
daroghas"[83] at Kargil and Dras, or the trade moharrirs (clerks) at
Panamik (which was open from June until November) and Tankse
(open all the year round). The Special Charas Officer would then send

---

[80] British Joint Commissioner, Ladakh, to the First Assistant to the Resident in Kashmir,
   February 26, 1926. NAI, Foreign, F. No. 364-X. of 1924–27 (Secret).
[81] My emphasis.
[82] These villages were Panamik, Spitak, Durgub, Upshi, Pashkyum, and Dras.
[83] *dārōghah*: headman of an office, official in charge.

a weekly report and telegraph important information. These recommendations were approved in May 1927.

Last to weigh in on the issue of Soviet ingress to India was Mr. V. Short of the Intelligence Bureau.[84] Referring to the Soviets, he wrote in March 1926,

> From their present organization in Central Asia, with their advance base at Tashkent, they have three main lines of penetration. / (1) The Central Line through Afghan Turkistan. / (2) The Eastern Line through Chinese Turkistan. / (3) The Western Line through Persian Turkistan. / The Central Line is the old established route, and ... is still very busy. There are, however, indications that the Eastern Line is now becoming more popular. The Russians have lately established Consulates in Chinese Turkistan, and are engaged in extending their trade agencies in that area; these will provide them with means of penetrating, via the Pamirs, into Gilgit and Chitral. ... I now come to the last link in the chain and one which, although it does not concern us directly, may possibly give rise to some anxiety. I refer to Kashmir State. The very position of this large state shows its importance, but the subject is very difficult.

Short's enumeration of routes – or "lines of penetration" – reflected a form of strategic thinking that developed out of a revolution in military organization and planning in the late nineteenth century, as seen in official documents like the Strategic Situation reports.[85] Not only had imperial policy shifted from addressing specific frontiers independently of each other but an integrated frontier policy also allowed for a calculus of potential invasion routes and the probability of each being used. This information – supplied in route books and other manuals of governance and military control discussed in Chapter 4 – was combined with intelligence gathered within India and beyond. Underscoring the threat of "Bolshevik propaganda," Mr. Short noted that "relations have been found to exist between the Red International, the All-India Trade Union Congress, and the Labour Swaraj Party."

5.4   Conclusion

A decade later, in 1935, the government of India brainstormed once again about ways to "sterilize the working of Soviet spies and agents penetrating Gilgit, Chitral and Ladakh." It is unclear as to how much of the "work" attributed to these "spies" was simply the circulation of Russian goods along trade routes, but reports from Secret Service agents posted in Leh, Gilgit, and Chitral make reference to several individuals who spoke of

---

[84] That is, the civilian intelligence service housed in the Home Department, which was distinct from the Indian Army's Intelligence Branch.

[85] See Hevia, *Imperial Security State*.

Bolshevism, including a doctor in Chitral whose father was allegedly Russian.[86] Unfortunately the Foreign Department files detailing "Anti-Soviet measures" in the 1930s are marked "destroyed" in the National Archives of India.[87] But severe measures were under discussion; the authors of the memo spent time debating the varying merits of the terms "liquidate," "sterilize," and "neutralize."[88] Alas, "the Germans have brought sterilization too much in the limelight from its meaning to be limited to our requirements," wrote the deputy Foreign Secretary in reference to eugenics and the rise of National Socialism in Germany. "I suggest neutralization."[89]

Following independence in 1947, the government of India continued to register reports of possible Soviet inroads. And following the victory of the Chinese Communist Party over the Kuomintang, threats of Communist Chinese inroads in northern India were added to the list of frontier concerns. These we will discuss in the final chapter.

---

[86] NAI, Foreign and Political, Secret. D.O. No. D.4126-X/35. August 1935. "Dear Lang," wrote Deputy Secretary Olaf Caroe in the Foreign Department, "We have had a good deal of information lately regarding the penetration of Russian agents into Chitral, Gilgit, and Ladakh, and as the problem in its bearing on Chitral and Gilgit is really a common one, I am desired to address both the administrations concerned, and ask them to pass the word to the Chitral and Gilgit Agencies for endeavors to be made to neutralize the efforts of such agents. O.K. Caroe to A.J. Hopkinson, Esq., Chief Secretary to Government N. W.F.P. and Lt. Col. L. E. Lang, Resident in Kashmir." See also NAI, Frontiers, no. 471-F of 1927 (Secret). "Bolshevik penetration on the Northern Frontier of India. Information regarding Ghol if father a Russian, who is employed as a doctor in Chitral."

[87] NAI, Frontiers, no. 354-X of 1924–27. (Secret). "Anti-Soviet measures."

[88] These authors were the Deputy Foreign Secretary, Olaf Caroe, and L. E. Lang, the Resident in Kashmir.

[89] NAI, External Affairs, 342-X (Secret) of 1935. "Penetration of Soviet Agents into Chitral, Gilgit and Ladakh and measures taken to neutralize their efforts."

6 The Birth of Geopolitics

Frontier Experts, Boundary Commissions, and Trans-frontier Information

> Frontiers are indeed the razor's edge on which hang suspended the modern issues of war or peace, of life or death to nations.
>
> – George Curzon, *Frontiers*, 1907

When Andrew Dalgleish was murdered near the Karakoram Pass in 1888, the government of India struggled to ascertain whether or not the scene of the crime was within their territorial jurisdiction.[1] Part of the problem stemmed from intensified concerns about where the border should be situated – a problem illustrated by the repeated attempts to survey the region and establish a border that conformed to still-evolving border-making principles. The trans-frontier groups that regularly moved along the Treaty Road from Ladakh to Yarkand resembled those moving across frontier regions: traders, pilgrims, and nomads. Increasingly concerned about them, the imperial state sent out boundary commissions that were much larger and more systematic than those of earlier decades. Members of these commissions, in turn, became part of the growing "military techno-elite" that emerged in the second half of the nineteenth century.[2]

The development of a coordinated strategic approach to managing and securing the frontiers of India thus reflected increased security concerns and improvements in intelligence gathering. It depended especially on a particular set of trans-frontier men. Their expertise was built upon years of technical surveying, participation in large-scale boundary commissions, and contributions to debates in the Royal Geographical Society and its publications.

---

[1] The Foreign Department eventually decided that he was murdered "beyond British jurisdiction," though there was still uncertainty for several years afterward as to whether the Karakoram Pass should be the frontier, or whether said frontier should be placed seventy-nine miles farther north at Shahidulla. See NAI, Foreign, Frontier A, July 1888, nos. 76–130. "Question of the powers of Administrator-General, Bengal to administer the estate of Dalgleish (Mr.), who was murdered beyond British jurisdiction, but whose property was brought to Leh."

[2] Hevia, *Imperial Security State*, 43.

Boundary commissions had begun decades earlier with the small, solitary endeavors of "knowledge entrepreneurs" like Alexander Cunningham, Henry Strachey, and Thomas Thomson.[3] By the 1880s the commissions had evolved into extensive, highly technical undertakings that might involve hundreds of people demarcating and mapping a line across diverse terrains, following a set of consistent border-making principles. The team typically included botanists and geologists, soldiers and draftsmen, porters and cooks, and lots and lots of animals. The key role belonged to the surveyors who triangulated and mapped the location of the border and its surroundings. The detailed records they produced formed the basis of the imperial state's understanding of its territorial limits.

The 1880s also witnessed the development of bureaucratic procedures for securing and circulating trans-frontier information, including restricted trans-frontier maps. For these new "frontier experts," imperial security concerns, geographical science, and the sense of masculine adventure we saw in the previous chapter went hand in hand.[4] As they traversed the empire, and circulated their writings and debates in the Royal Geographical Society's *Geographical Journal*, a new way of looking at frontiers and borders emerged. This chapter analyzes this new mode of seeing as a hybrid form of geography and imperial politics: geopolitics.

Coined in 1899 by Rudolf Kjellén, a conservative Swedish professor of political science, the term "geopolitics" signaled a new approach to international politics that emphasized the roles of territory, natural resources, and geographical information in forming and sustaining states.[5] This "science" conceived of the state as "a geographical organism or as a phenomenon in space," not the abstract and legalistic political entity it had long been held to be.[6] Instead, geography dictated "laws" of politics. Kjellén's term reflected interconnected trends in geography and imperial state formation decades in the making: the "laws" in question had been articulated in publications that were established venues for a wide range of geographical information. The premier English outlet was *The Geographical Journal* of the Royal Geographical Society. The

---

[3] The term is from Martin J. Bayly, *Taming the Imperial Imagination: Colonial Knowledge, International Relations, and the Anglo-Afghan Encounter, 1808–1878* (Cambridge: Cambridge University Press, 2016), 72.

[4] I use the category of frontier experts in a more general sense than Alex McKay's term of "Frontier Cadre," which he applied to the group of men who pushed for Tibetan policy (McKay, *Tibet and the British Raj: The Frontier Cadre, 1904–1947*), because many of the figures I treat had a transimperial agenda. They were less concerned with policy on any one particular frontier than in approaching frontiers and borders more generally and systematically.

[5] Agnew, *Geopolitics*.

[6] Brian W. Blouet, *Geopolitics and Globalization in the Twentieth Century* (London: Reaktion, 2001), 187n2.

Journal provided a forum for recent discoveries, geological theories, evolving surveying technologies, new maps, and newly discovered routes across imperial frontiers. When Francis Younghusband took leave from India to return to Britain in 1892, for instance, he wrote to Mortimer Durand, then the foreign secretary of India, that with "the sanction of the India Office" he had given a lecture before the Geographical Society, which was subsequently published in the *Journal*'s immediate predecessor, the *Proceedings of the Royal Geographical Society*.[7]

By the turn of the twentieth century the *Journal* had come to be dominated by British imperial frontier experts who debated the geographical basis of political questions and problems associated with, among other subjects, surveying and border making. When Thomas Holdich, the preeminent British boundary expert, was president of the Royal Geographical Society (1916–18), his vice-presidents included the former viceroy George Curzon and Francis Younghusband (both of whom would also serve as presidents). Henry McMahon, a veteran of numerous boundary commissions, a former foreign secretary of India, and the architect of the McMahon Line at the Shimla Conference, was one of the twenty-one Members of Council under Holdich. Together, these experts oversaw the fusion of geographical science and politics. A *Journal* review of Holdich's *Political Frontiers and Boundary Making* in 1917 noted that the author deemed "the first and greatest object of an international frontier to [be to] ensure peace and good-will between contiguous people by *putting a definite edge to the national political horizon*, so as to limit unauthorized expansion and trespass."[8] In short, geography had become politics by scientific means.

As noted in Chapter 4, the growth of territory as a central and precise object of interest to the state heightened the importance of determining rationalized borders while maintaining the looser senses of political influence implicit in the category of frontier. As the *sine qua non* of territory, borders became subjects of crucial importance to this new political "science." Thus, we understand why George Curzon stated grandly in 1907 that frontiers were "the razor's edge on which hang suspended the

---

[7] NAI, Foreign, General, July 1892, nos. 18–40, KW no. 2. Francis Younghusband to Sir Mortimer Durand, dated Eastern Villas Road, South Sea, March 2, 1892. The resulting published paper was Francis E. Younghusband, "Journeys in the Pamirs and Adjacent Countries," *Proceedings of the Royal Geographical Society and Monthly Record of Geography* 14, no. 4 (1892): 205–34. The *Proceedings of the Royal Geographical Society and Monthly Record of Geography* was renamed *The Geographical Journal* in January 1893.

[8] Review of Thomas Holdich's *Political Frontiers and Boundary Making* (1916). "Frontiers in Theory and Practice," *The Geographical Journal* 49, no. 1 (1917): 58. Emphasis given by the anonymous author of the review.

modern issues of war or peace, of life or death to nations."[9] Curzon's strange metaphor raises questions about the exact role of frontiers in the "life" of a nation, not to mention the function and size of razors. We will return to these questions at the conclusion of the book; for now, we can focus on one of its implications. Frontiers needed to be strong, legible, and controllable. Information about them was increasingly contained within restricted maps and reference manuals for governance and military operations. The triangulated position of demarcated boundaries – the "definite edge to the national political horizon" – enabled the state to better see itself geopolitically *and* geostrategically.[10] Legible borders enabled the imperial state to see itself as one of the globe's interconnected territories: territories dictated by the apparent laws of geography. The task of imperial strategists was to utilize those geographical features to the advantage of the state.

6.1   Thomas Holdich and the Expansion of Boundary Commissions

Between Cunningham's two Ladakh Boundary Commissions in the late 1840s and the new initiatives of the 1880s, surveying and boundary demarcation were dramatically transformed.[11] The scale of the new commissions' work revealed their geographical range, technological precision, and variety of professional expertise. No one man was more closely associated with the new type of enterprise than Thomas Hungerford Holdich (1843–1929). Holdich began his career in India as an assistant surveyor on the Bhutan Expedition (1865–66). His performance guaranteed him a permanent appointment in the Survey Department, which sent him to Abyssinia (1867–68) and on numerous surveys along the North-West Frontier. As a survey officer with the southern Afghanistan Field Force (Figure 6.1) during the Second Anglo-Afghan War (1878–80), he became "fascinated by the prospect of filling out the very incomplete maps of the region," and he "surveyed and gathered intelligence both during military operations and when engaged to lay out roads and railways through the border passes of Baluchistan and Afghanistan."[12] Subsequently, he served as a surveyor and cartographer on the Afghan

---

[9] Curzon, *Frontiers*, 7.   [10] "Frontiers in Theory and Practice."
[11] For an analysis of the Afghan Boundary Commission, see James Hevia, *Imperial Security State*, 92–106; and Fuoli, "Incorporating North-Western Afghanistan into the British Empire: Experiments in Indirect Rule through the Making of an Imperial Frontier, 1884–87."
[12] Elizabeth Baigent, "Holdich, Sir Thomas Hungerford (1843–1929)," in *Oxford Dictionary of National Biography* (Oxford: Oxford University Press, 2004).

Figure 6.1 Bourne & Shepherd, "A survey group in the Kurram" (1879). Photograph taken during the Second Afghan War. Thomas H. Holdich is seated center right, amid a team of surveyors. National Army Museum, London. NAM. 1955-04-42-18.

Boundary Commission (1884–85) and the Pamir Boundary Commission (1885), which created the famous Russian buffer and salient known as the Wakhan Corridor. In 1887, Holdich earned the Royal Geographical Society's top prize, the Founder's Medal, for his surveys in Afghanistan.[13]

By the time Holdich left India "he was the supreme authority on all matters connected with frontier delimitation and demarcation."[14] He would adjudicate the boundary dispute between Argentina and Chile in 1902 and publish nearly a dozen books on the subject of boundaries, frontiers, and border making. Throughout his career Holdich also published extensively in the *Geographical Journal* and became an active member of the Royal Geographical Society, serving on its governing council and finally as its president from 1916–18.

As a respected frontier expert Holdich, like Ney Elias, was regularly consulted by such senior administrators as Mortimer Durand, Henry

---

[13] Kenneth Mason and H. L. Crosthwait, "Colonel Sir Thomas Hungerford Holdich, K. C. M. G., K. C. I. E., C. B.," *The Geographical Journal* 75, no. 3 (1930): 212.
[14] Mason and Crosthwait, 209.

McMahon, and George Curzon. After retiring in 1898, Holdich broadened his reach across the globe, writing extensively on frontier and border-making problems in the Americas and Africa, as well as in Asia and Europe.[15] Unlike Elias, who was typically called in to advise on political matters on the frontier, Holdich was more often asked about technical aspects of demarcation and the geographical principles upon which they rested.[16] In 1902, for instance, he arbitrated a long-standing boundary dispute in Patagonia between Argentina and Chile. The standing 1881 treaty had failed to address the location of the border in sufficient detail to account for several watershed basins as well as extensive unsurveyed forests. Holdich spent several months in South America reviewing the available surveys and touring the area before he "established a boundary which is so far based on natural features, that it cannot be mistaken nor removed." He explained with some flourish that this new border "follow[ed] lines of lofty mountains, which interpose themselves in silent majesty between the ephemeral disputes and discords of human political strife. ... It is on the whole a strategic boundary."[17]

Over time, Holdich fashioned a classification system with a hierarchy of natural and artificial boundaries. His voluminous report on the Perso-Baluch Boundary Commission from 1896 defined "the best method of demarcation in uncivilized districts" along the lines of several "general principles." "The best and most recognizable natural boundary is"

a well-defined watershed; the higher and more inaccessible the better, but whether high or low, it is one which every trans-border savage recognizes *instructively* and which he feels to be *immoveable*. ... When artificial methods are a necessity, the only alternative is to erect pillars at all important points and to fix their position accurately by a survey process.[18] ... Unnecessary pillars should never by erected unless their safety can be secured, as the destruction of them may, and does, lead to the erroneous idea that the boundary itself has been impaired or destroyed. But apart from the temptation afforded to any casual trans-frontier outlaw to insult the British Government by the destruction of carefully erected boundary marks, there are natural causes which tend to destroy such artificial erections quite as surely as human vindictiveness or love of mischief.[19]

---

[15] For instance, his *Boundaries in Europe and the Near East* (London: Macmillan, 1918); "How Are We to Get Maps of Africa?," *The Geographical Journal* 18, no. 6 (1901): 590–601; and *The Countries of the King's Award* (London: Hurst and Blackett, 1904).

[16] Although he often focused on technical aspects in his official reports and published works, Holdich also enumerated the political and social benefits of effective borders.

[17] Holdich, *The Countries of the King's Award*, 411.

[18] I.e., by trigonometrically fixing those points to a universal grid of latitude and longitude.

[19] Colonel Thomas Holdich, Commissioner, Perso-Baluch Frontier, to Foreign Secretary, Government of India. NAI, Foreign, Secret External, October 1896, no. 41. My emphasis.

Holdich's "general principles" of demarcation not only aimed to stop a "trans-border savage" but also tied the utility of natural boundaries to their simultaneous existence on the land and on the survey map. Even in the case of a well-placed artificial marker, the map would ensure its durability. "Should the boundary marks themselves vanish," he concluded, "there should always remain a record of their position on the map, and a repetition of the same survey process will show precisely where the original site may have been."[20]

The "immoveable" watershed and mountain range, acting in tandem with the restricted trans-frontier map, provided the surest means of precisely identifying and defending imperial territory. The strength of a natural, scientifically determined border also complemented the work of men like Younghusband, ensuring that states beyond the border would be "chastened" in their independence and remain open to British influence.[21] An impermeable border was also an object that "every nomadic robber in the frontier [understood and was] perforce obliged to respect it as being quite beyond the limits of his powers of interference."[22]

At the core of this territorializing process was the expanded and systematized work of the boundary commission. The indices of the Foreign Department in the National Archives of India reveal a burst of large-scale boundary commissions in the 1880s. Holdich himself referenced this revolution in the preface to his *The Indian Borderland, 1880–1900* (1901), apropos of the surveys on the North-West Frontier where he spent most of his time in India. "During the last twenty-five years," he began, "a great change has been effected in the measure of our information about the regions of farther India on the north-west. Twenty-five years ago all that we knew of frontier geography was narrowed to a few lines running westward from India and terminating in the cities of the Afghan and Baluch highlands."[23]

The process of demarcation began to follow standardized procedures, with a small number of experts being consulted on the finer points of the process. Ney Elias and Thomas Holdich, for instance, were called in to advise the Afghan Boundary Commission in 1885–88. Elias would later also be consulted on the Anglo-Siamese Commission (1889–90) as well as

[20] Ibid.
[21] Thomas Holdich, *The Indian Borderland, 1880–1900* (London: Methuen, 1901), 49. Holdich is discussing a distinction between "British Baluchistan" and "'independent' Baluchistan," which includes "close political control where British interests are involved." Similar descriptions can be found in the discussions of Tibet's status vis-à-vis India.
[22] Colonel Thomas Holdich, Commissioner, Perso-Baluch Frontier, to Foreign Secretary, Government of India. NAI, Foreign, Secret External, October 1896, nos. 15–53.
[23] Holdich, *The Indian Borderland*, vii.

about boundary disputes between Badakhshan province and the North-West Frontier, Burma and Yunnan (1887), Rajputana (1888), Tibet and Sikkim (1889), Burma and Siam (1889), and Khorassan and Seistan (1892, 1896).[24]

Holdich took boundary demarcation to a far more scientific level than his predecessors, elaborating the systematic methods and rationales for utilizing "natural" and "artificial" boundaries.[25] By the 1890s, these geographically based considerations were being fused with "strategical" concerns, adding weight to the concept of the "Scientific Frontier." As illustrated in Chapter 2, that frontier, in the words of George Curzon, united "natural and strategical strength."[26] The strategic aspect included the kinds of military considerations that came from the Army General Staff and Intelligence Branch as codified in standardized manuals like route books. "From a military point of view," Holdich wrote,

the ideal to be aimed at in determining a frontier in mountainous country is that the line chosen should follow some prominent geographical feature, preferably the main watershed of the mountain system, and also that, to facilitate effective occupation if necessary, the communications up to the frontier should be such as to afford reasonable access to the line selected. A lateral communication running parallel to and a short distance in rear of the frontier is also a considerable asset.[27]

Thus, roads and other communication infrastructure like railways and telegraphs should work in tandem with an ideal natural border, which followed the apparently unambiguous water-parting principle, to form a "scientific frontier."

By the end of the nineteenth century, military experts like the Director of Military Intelligence in the War Office were regularly weighing in on boundary commissions, often suggesting minor deviations from the water-parting principle of natural boundaries to secure particular advantageous points along the demarcated line. John Ardagh, who served first as Director of Military Intelligence and then in the leadership of the Royal Geographical Society, regularly addressed boundary issues along the north of India. Military considerations not only went hand in hand with geographical concerns; they fused as a scientific ideal to be achieved through the application of a prescribed set of principles and implemented through a standard set of practices. Such expert consultation reflected

---

[24] NAI, Foreign, Secret F, June 1887 nos. 57–61. "Decorations of CMG proposed for Elias (Mr. Ney) for his services in Turkistan and Badakhshan."

[25] For an extensive account of these categories, see Thomas Holdich, *Political Frontiers and Boundary Making* (London: Macmillan, 1916).

[26] See Curzon, *Frontiers*, 19; and Hanna, *India's Scientific Frontier*.

[27] NAI, Foreign, Secret E., September 1915, nos. 76–101. "India. Definition of Indo-Tibetan Boundaries."

a growing ability to synthesize input from a range of imperial experts into the evolving calculus of border making across the remote northern limits of India.

6.2   Trans-frontier Information

Recall from the previous chapter the story Henry McMahon recounted of the surveying party that ran out of water in the desert of Seistan. The sole surviving member, the "Indian survey subordinate," named Saidu, "made duty his first care" by saving "the precious map for which so much had been risked."[28] As McMahon's recollection graphically detailed, the map was a critical tool for mastering the territory at the empire's edges. The zeal for filling blank spaces on maps – whether by native surveyors like Saidu or British experts like Holdich – reflected the intimate connections between imperial state formation, geography, and personal adventure. Determining boundaries was a major preoccupation of the Government of India's Foreign Department, and the accumulated man-years that the boundary commissions devoted to the task attested to the active, and complex, nature of the process. Just as the language of Partition often drew on surgical metaphors, so the language of border making frequently spoke of making the territorial "geo-body" whole through shaping, demarcating, mapping, and, ultimately, defending.[29] And just as surgical metaphors supposed an ameliorative precision that was never the case during Partition, so the shape of the body defined by maps was often "whole" only on paper. Entire segments failed to meet the technical demands established by the Survey and Foreign Departments. Yet this incompleteness does not detract from the power of the territory as a body metaphor – be it a feminine, anthropomorphic Mother India or Britannia, or an unnamed "no-man's land" awaiting an explorer and surveyor. As Sumathi Ramaswamy, J. R. Hale, and Thongchai Winichakul have each shown in different ways, a political map can render the nation-space, or geo-body, uniquely visible.[30] In that sense the new policy of restricting access to maps that emerged in the late nineteenth century demonstrated one of the more tangible shifts in the rhetoric of the border, selectively revealing or hiding its precise location as a means of controlling it.

---

[28] A. H. McMahon, "International Boundaries," *Journal of the Royal Society of Arts* 84, no. 4330 (1935): 11–12.
[29] Regarding Partition metaphors, see Chatterji, "The Fashioning of a Frontier," and Winichakul, *Siam Mapped*.
[30] Ramaswamy, "Visualising India's Geo-Body: Globes, Maps, Bodyscapes," 152.

As the specter of Russian advances in Central Asia provoked deepening anxieties in Calcutta, Delhi, Shimla, and London, trans-frontier surveys became covert, classified, and militarized. By the late 1870s reports on "trans-frontier" survey operations were stamped "strictly confidential." In 1884, the government of India ordered that notifications of boundary demarcations were not to appear in the *Gazette of India*.[31] That same year the Foreign Department reserved to itself the right of distributing all "Trans-Frontier Reports."[32] By the turn of the century the Foreign Department was producing secret monthly Trans-Frontier Journals, restricted to the viceroy and top secretaries of departments.[33] A Secret Service emerged alongside the Intelligence Branch and Army General Staff to better gather the information contained within these reports.

6.2.1   Trans-frontier Maps

Like trans-frontier information more broadly, maps underwent a dramatic change in the degree to which their geographical and political contents were restricted. By 1884, the Foreign Department required that all "Trans-Frontier Maps" first be vetted by their office before being published.[34] All of these maps became classed as "restricted" in 1885.[35] By 1888 the status of all "1 inch = 4 miles" trans-frontier maps was upgraded to "confidential."[36] When, in 1885, the Surveyor-General asked it for clarification on what precisely was meant by "trans-frontier," the Foreign Department's reply suggested some internal confusion that was not immediately resolved:

In another letter the office of the Surveyor-General has asked whether *frontier* maps, as distinct from *trans-frontier* maps, should be issued without reference to this office. The principle to adhere to would seem to be that no trans-frontier maps, *i.e.*, maps which contain topographical information about countries beyond the British border, such as Afghanistan, Nipal, Tibet, etc., etc., should be issued without our authority; but that maps of provinces, etc., in India containing only strips of the trans-frontier are at the disposal of the public?[37]

---

[31] NAI, Foreign, A Political E, June 1884, nos. 201–22.
[32] NAI, Foreign, A Pol E, August 1884, nos. 149–57.
[33] These reports typically highlighted commercial and political intelligence from regions such as the Trans-Caspia, Russian Turkestan, Afghanistan, Chinese Turkestan, Chitral, North-West Frontier, and Baluchistan. See, for instance, NAI, Foreign, Secret F, May 1908, nos. 271–73, 291.
[34] NAI, Foreign, Secret F, September 1884, nos. 554–56.
[35] NAI, Foreign, Secret F, November 1885, nos. 1–3.
[36] NAI, Foreign, Frontier B, April 1888, nos. 120–21.
[37] NAI Foreign, Secret F, November 1885, nos. 1–3.

Soon, the production of maps became more closely regulated and extensive debates followed over how best to standardize colors and symbols.[38]

In 1893 the Foreign Department reported to the Secretary of State for India that a "yellow wash" should be used for all non-British territory across the subcontinent.[39] The secretary of state, in response, suggested a more detailed set of colors: an orange wash would signify territories, such as Afghanistan, that were "within the sphere of British influence, but not under British protection or control." There ensued, one clerk wrote in summary, a discussion that "continued for six years, as to how to colour correctly the various territories comprised in the map of India." Initially, Chitral, Afghanistan "and any countries which are only within the British sphere of influence" were to be colored orange. But then one Foreign Department official asked what would be done with the tribal lands between British India and Afghanistan that fell beyond the Durand Line established by the Kabul Agreement of 1893? They were meant to be washed in yellow, to signify their status as non-British territory, but the Amir of Afghanistan, it was feared, would expect them to be colored the same as his territories. With the work of the Afghan Boundary Commission still ongoing, any ambiguous territorial designations might cause trouble with the Amir. "The varying extent of our interests in, and connection with, frontier tribal country would clearly be often most difficult to define; conditions are liable to frequent change; and, if the different washes were used more freely than above suggested, it would not be easy . . . to devise perfectly appropriate reference notes to show the distinction drawn between [orange and yellow]" one official noted.[40] "In any case," another replied, "I venture to think that, until we have *demarcated* the Amir's frontier, we should on no account send him a copy of the map of India with frontiers marked on it. He would not understand or believe any explanation we could offer him." The exasperated Secretary to the Foreign Department, W. J. Cuningham, had the final say. "I agree except that where the Durand line follows a range of mountains, like the Hindu Kush, the line may be sharp. To give the Amir a map with the Mohamand [*sic*] country tinted in indefinite graduated shades of orange and yellow is likely to raise trouble. . . . Defend me from more than one of these map cases at a time!"

[38] NAI, Foreign, Frontier, October 1893, nos. 344–45. "Revision of the map of India. Proposed distribution of colour washes and system of marking boundaries submitted for the approval of the Secretary of State."
[39] NAI, Foreign, Secret F, February 1908, nos. 40–51, 19. "History and definition of boundaries between Kashmir and Eastern Turkistan." And NAI, Foreign, Secret Frontier, June 1907, nos. 323–25.
[40] NAI, Foreign, Secret Frontier, June 1901, nos. 59–67, 75.

In 1899 Viceroy George Curzon settled the long-running color debate by ordering that no maps or external boundaries were to be colored or shown unless the borderlines had already been demarcated by a boundary commission.[41] This resulted in a range of partially borderless maps. Nonetheless, a standard set of colors did finally emerge after nearly two decades of internal debate: Native States were to be colored yellow and "British India and country under British control" was to be pink. "Border tribes under British control" would be orange, though this was soon changed to burnt sienna. ("No authority can be traced for the change, but the difficulty of mixing up a uniform shade of orange suggests an obvious reason."[42]) Foreign possessions in India were colored green while Afghanistan was to be pale blue.[43] In 1907 the Secretary of State for India weighed in on the map-coloring question and approved the existing colors, specifying as well the colors to be used for gazetteer maps and whether these regulations need extend to all general maps of India.

Maps were classified in three categories: "Public," "For Official Use Only," and "Secret."[44] Only a small number of officials were allowed access to the latter two categories.[45] The Surveyor-General also issued regulations for "the procedure for the submission to the Foreign Department or frontier officials concerned of frontier maps in the proof state for the insertion or verification of boundaries."[46]

---

[41] NAI; NAI, Foreign, External, September 1900, no. 37, part b; NAI, Foreign, Secret Frontier, June 1907, nos. 323–25. "Direction for map colors and secret maps"; NAI, Foreign, Secret Frontier, October 1893, nos. 344–45; NAI, Foreign, Secret Frontier, June 1901, nos. 59–67; and NAI, Foreign, Secret Frontier, October 1901, nos. 1–2.

[42] NAI.   [43] NAI, Foreign, Secret Frontier, February 1908, nos. 40–51, 19.

[44] These classifications read, respectively, "Maps in 'Class A. – Public' may be obtained on indent or by purchase from the Officer in charge, Map Record and Issue Office, Survey of India"; "Maps in 'Class B. – For Official use only' will only be issued to Officers in the service of the British Government. Applications for such maps on the prescribed form obtainable from the Officer in charge. Map Record and Issue Office, Survey of India"; and "Maps in 'Class C. – Secret' will only be issued to selected individuals. Applications for use of 'Class C. – Secret' maps will be addressed to, and disposed of, by the Chief of the General Staff, Army Headquarters. In order to ensure the safe custody and limited issue of such maps, the Chief of the General Staff is authorised to issue such additional instructions as may from time to time be necessary. . . . No alterations or additions to the list of "Class C. – Secret" maps may be made without the sanction of the Government of India in the Army Department." See NAI, Foreign, Secret Frontier, February 1919, 1. "Revised rules regarding the classification, issue and custody of maps."

[45] Officials authorized to "countersign indents for any map which is 'For Official use only'" included: "Secretaries to the Government of India, the Chief of the General Staff, General Officers Commanding Armies, Divisions, and Brigades, the Commandant, Staff College, Quetta, the Surveyor-General (for use of the Survey Department), and the Director, Geological Survey of India (for use of the Geological Survey Department)."

[46] NAI, Foreign, Frontier, December 1905, nos. 41–42, 33.

By 1906 a set of "rules regarding the definition of boundaries on all maps of India and of adjacent countries" was approved by the government of India.[47] In the future, "every map containing a frontier or trans-frontier boundary will be submitted to the Foreign Department for orders before publication." Second, "no portion of the external boundary of India shall be engraved or printed on any map unless it has been actually surveyed after demarcation." Third, "no boundary beyond the frontiers of India shall be engraved or printed on any of the general or standard maps published by the Survey of India unless it has been actually surveyed after demarcation." Fourth, "when the survey of any area in which such boundaries occur precedes demarcation, such boundaries will be shewn whenever possible on the plane table sections and be copied in blue on the original fair sheets." Finally,

two copies of every Frontier or trans-frontier map containing a boundary which has been shewn on the plane table section but not on the engraved or zinc plate (under rules 2 and 3) will be supplied to the Foreign Department shewing the boundaries as given on the plane table section, for those orders as to the numbers of copies which will be required by that department. These will be coloured by hand or specially printed but such coloured copies will be issued to no one without the express orders of the Foreign Department, and no boundary symbol will be used.

Of particular concern were the symbols to be used for distinguishing between surveyed and unsurveyed borders, and between the demarcated and undemarcated. "No portion of the external boundary of India and no boundary beyond the frontier should be shown *on the printed standard maps,* which has not been authoritatively demarcated and been surveyed by the Survey Staff, any boundary which has not been so demarcated being left blank. On the standard maps, therefore, which are issued to the public, there would be no symbol for undemarcated external or trans-frontier boundaries."[48]

For all these bureaucratic determinations, however, the supposed "frontier line of India" was still not consistently defined (Map 6.1).[49] The segments in the west that Holdich so extensively surveyed were clear, with two exceptions ("between Persia and the Chagal Agency of Baluchistan and between Afghanistan and the Dir-Chitral Agency of the North West Frontier Province"). For the disputed Perso-Baluch

[47] NAI, Foreign, Frontier A, September 1906, no. 108.
[48] NAI, Foreign, Frontier A, September 1906, no. 110. J. Wilson, Secretary of Revenue and Agriculture to Surveyor-General of India, August 14, 1906.
[49] NAI, Foreign, F. No. 422-F. 1922–23. "Frontiers of India. Question by a member of the Inchcape Committee reg. the frontier line of India. Preparation of information showing acquisition of territories on various Boundaries since 1878."

Map 6.1 Detail of "India Showing Provinces, States & Districts" (1947). Survey of India. Second Edition (First Edition 1938). Scale 1 inch to 70 miles. IOR/X/9079/2.

segment, it was determined that though it had been demarcated, it must still be shown on "official maps as indefinite because reexamination has shown that the demarcation was based on inaccurate data." The Foreign Department noted approvingly that the Durand Agreement of 1893 had laid down a clear line that "chiefly follow[ed] watersheds." Similarly, "the eastern boundary between India and Indo-China and Siam is definite and has been demarcated through most of its length." The northern boundary of Kashmir, however, was another matter.

This would-be borderline was still considered to be "absolutely indefinite."[50] "It is not shown at all on uncoloured official maps of India," wrote an official in the Foreign Department, "and on coloured maps it is supposed to be shown by a yellow wash which 'fades away imperceptibly' to the north." While acknowledging the attempts of the 1890s to induce China to claim everything up to the Karakoram Pass, this line, the official wrote, "cannot be regarded as either definite or authoritative. Part of the way it follows the watershed of the Karakoram Range, but the north-eastern section is almost entirely arbitrary."[51]

Yet the Foreign Department asserted that, with Ladakh's indefinite northern and eastern limits and one other exception, the northern boundary of India – including "the Punjab, the United Provinces, Bihar and Orissa and Sikkim" – was "definite and for the most part . . . demarcated." The other exception lay "north of Assam," where "the limits of British influence are indefinite."[52] It had been delimited by a treaty and a map, but had not yet been surveyed and demarcated on the ground. This part of the Himalayan border would become known as the McMahon Line, and emerged out of talks between Chinese, Tibetan, and British leaders in 1913.

6.3   Shimla and the McMahon Line

Between October 1913 and July 1914, plenipotentiaries of the newly formed Republic of China, the British Government of India, and the Government of Tibet gathered at Shimla to define the territorial limits and political status of Tibet. Tibet's ambiguous status vis-à-vis India and China and its undemarcated borders produced, said Viceroy Hardinge, a situation "of constant anxiety."[53] Even before the Younghusband expedition violently opened Tibet to the British, frontier policy had divided imperial politics. For Curzon and others subscribing to his "forward" policies in South Asia, Tibet represented a logical extension of a general strategy projecting loose political control over the Himalayan states (Bhutan, Nepal, Sikkim); at the same time it was a sensitive matter given Chinese claims to suzerainty over the mountainous region. By 1910, following an incursion by Zhao Erfeng, the British Government of India was worried that "China had come to the gates of India."[54] Following the Chinese Revolution of 1911, the British decided that the solution to the "Tibetan Question" – defining Tibet in relation to China

[50] NAI.   [51] NAI.   [52] NAI.
[53] "Viceroy on Indian Affairs: British Foreign Policy," *Times*, September 18, 1913.
[54] Premen Addy, *Tibet on the Imperial Chessboard: The Making of British Policy Towards Lhasa, 1899–1925* (Calcutta: Academic, 1984), 212.

and British India – should be a condition of their recognition of the new Chinese government. Specifically, the British made their diplomatic recognition of the new Chinese republic contingent upon China's recognition of Tibetan autonomy. On October 7, 1913, Yuan Shikai granted as much; the British recognized the Republic of China the same day.[55]

The Dalai Lama tactfully thanked the "Great British Government" for its kindness in deciding to hold a conference "between the British, Chinese and Tibetans regarding Chinese-Tibetan affairs."[56] Charles Bell noted the terms by which the Dalai Lama wished to define Tibet. He wanted "Tibet to manage her own internal affairs; To manage her own external affairs, consulting on important matters with the British; To have no Chinese High Commissioner, no other Chinese officials [Ambans], and no Chinese soldiers in Tibet; Tibet to include all the country eastward as far as Tachienlu."[57] The Dalai Lama, Bell continued, had a capacious picture of Tibet, including most of the land between central Tibet and Mongolia. Not surprisingly, the Chinese government wanted the opposite: a reassertion of its political control over Lhasa and the inclusion of Tibet within the boundaries of the Republic of China.

The British goals of the conference were twofold. First, they desired to secure the maintenance of peace and order on the Indo-Tibetan border,[58] and second, they wanted to ensure that the controlling influence at Lhasa was not overtly hostile to India or the frontier states.[59] On December 19, 1913, after two months of talks, British representative Henry McMahon decided that both the Tibetan and Chinese representatives should prepare cases to support their specific claims to territory and sovereignty. In a move suggesting that his stance as an equal arbiter was anything but, McMahon decided he would act as judge in determining which case was more compelling. The conference resumed on January 12, 1914 when Lonchen Shatra Paljor Dorje (the prime minister of Tibet) and "Ivan" Chen (Chen Yifan, the Special Commissioner for Foreign Affairs in Shanghai) presented their evidence.

---

[55] Jonathan D. Spence, *The Search for Modern China*, 2nd ed. (New York: W. W. Norton, 1999), 283; and Jerome Ch'en, *Yuan Shih-k'ai* (Stanford, CA: Stanford University Press, 1972), 142.

[56] IOR/L/P&S/10/400, Gould's translation of a letter from Dalai Lama to Basil Gould, July 10, 1913.

[57] Bell, *Portrait of the Dalai Lama*, 204. "Tachienlu" is Dajianlu, i.e., Kangding.

[58] Alastair Lamb, *The McMahon Line: A Study in the Relations between India, China and Tibet, 1904 to 1914, Volume II: Hardinge, McMahon and the Simla Conference*, vol. 2 (London: Routledge and Kegan Paul, 1966).

[59] Tsepon W. D. Shakabpa, *Tibet: A Political History* (New Haven, CT: Yale University Press, 1967), 252–53; and extract from Viscount Morley's speech in the House of Lords, October 17, 1913 (Hansards Debates).

The Tibetan case was substantial: more than ninety original Tibetan documents including "inscriptions of boundary pillars, census reports, tax and revenue records, extracts from written histories, registers of legal cases, lists of official appointments, monastic records, bonds of allegiance between territories and the Tibetan Government, and correspondence between the Chinese and Tibetan governments regarding certain territories."[60] The Chinese, on the other hand, presented but a single general statement for their claim, which rested on "effective occupation" and "Qing Dynasty relations with Tibet reclaimed by the new Chinese Republic."[61] As Carole McGranahan observes, "the status quo was interpreted differently by each: autonomous to the British, suzerain to the Chinese, and independent to the Tibetans."[62]

McMahon then presented the British position: a nonnegotiable "compromise" that included the radical division of Tibet into two zones: "Inner Tibet" and "Outer Tibet," a bifurcation that had no historical precedent, but was based loosely on the traditional regional divisions of central Tibet (*dbus.gtsang*), Kham (*khams*), and Amdo (*a.mdo*). As Political Officer in Sikkim and friend to the thirteenth Dalai Lama, Charles Bell noted that in "Outer Tibet the Dalai Lama retained practically complete control."[63]

After six months of discussions, a draft of the treaty was initialed by all three representatives and sent to their respective governments for final approval. Great Britain and Tibet approved the draft on July 3, 1914, but China did not.[64] As Bell wrote:

Two days after the Chinese, Tibetan and British plenipotentiaries had initialed the Convention, the Chinese Government telegraphed repudiating it. Tibet and Britain, however, recognised it as binding on themselves. China having repudiated the Convention, was of course entitled to none of the advantages, for instance, the opening to Chinese of Inner Tibet, which the Convention would have conferred upon her. ... In due course the British and Tibetan Plenipotentiaries signed the agreement in respect of the frontier, and that in respect of the trade regulations, thus making both a part of the Simla Convention.[65]

Just one month after the conclusion of the conference, Great Britain entered the First World War. Tibet had found – it believed – an ally in

---

[60] Carole McGranahan, "Empire and the Status of Tibet: British, Chinese, and Tibetan Negotiations, 1913–1934," in *The History of Tibet: Vol. III. The Modern Period: 1895–1959, the Encounter with Modernity*, ed. Alex McKay (London: RoutledgeCurzon, 2003), 270–71.

[61] McGranahan, 271.   [62] McGranahan, 280.

[63] Bell, *Portrait of the Dalai Lama*, 204–6.

[64] McGranahan, "Empire and the Status of Tibet," 269.

[65] Bell, *Portrait of the Dalai Lama*, 204–6.

Great Britain and the Dalai Lama offered to send a thousand Tibetan soldiers to fight alongside the British.[66] The empire would prove a fickle friend, however. The "Simla Agreement" of 1914 and early British documents relating to Tibet's political, diplomatic, and trade status, would long be used in the fight over historical recognition of an independent Tibetan state.[67] Ironically, the McMahon Line, by which the British projected its vision of a buffer region with China, became the basis on which the People's Republic of China created its Tibetan Autonomous Region model.[68]

Progress at the Shimla Conference was slowed down by the question of the boundary between Tibet and China, but by the broader and more ambiguous definition of Tibet's relationship to China as well. As a "perfectly equal" arbiter between the two other parties, Britain had the final say in drafting the treaty.[69] Britain's ambiguous position at the Shimla Conference, reflected its simultaneous insistence on establishing a border to differentiate Tibet from British India and China, its desire to appease the security interests of India by means of establishing an effective buffer state, and the historical claims of the Qing Empire to the territory of Tibet.[70] The resulting 550-mile McMahon Line dividing northeastern India from Tibet asserted a cartographic objectivity while ignoring the extent of surveying still to be done on the ground.

Thanks to the combined survey work of multiple boundary commissions in the eastern Himalaya and Burma, McMahon's line rested on an emerging vision of the Himalayan watershed. Surveys completed in 1911 and 1912 in the North-East Frontier "so added to [the government of India's] geographical knowledge" that it became possible for the first time

---

[66] K. Dhondup, *The Water-Bird and Other Years: A History of the Thirteenth Dalai Lama and After* (New Delhi: Rangwang, 1986), 54. The offer was not accepted.

[67] Until 2008 the British Government's position remained constant regarding China's suzerainty – but limited sovereignty – over Tibet. Britain was the sole state to maintain this view. Its position changed on October 29, 2008, when it recognized Chinese sovereignty over Tibet by issuing a statement on its website. India's current claim to a part of its northeast territories, for example, is largely based on the same agreements – notes exchanged during the Shimla Conference of 1914, which set the boundary between India and Tibet.

[68] McGranahan, "Empire and the Status of Tibet," 288.

[69] The language of the Simla Agreement of 1914 is filled with the terminology of diplomatic equality. For a discussion of "perfect equality" in British diplomacy, see James L. Hevia, *English Lessons: The Pedagogy of Imperialism in Nineteenth-Century China* (Durham, NC: Duke University Press, 2003).

[70] These ambiguities included dividing Tibet into two regions (Outer and Inner) while "recognizing that Tibet is under the suzerainty of China," at the same time "recognizing the special interest of Great Britain in virtue of the geographical position of Tibet," which prohibited China and Tibet from "enter[ing] into any negotiations or agreements regarding Tibet with one another." See Articles 2, 3, and 5 of the Simla Agreements of 1914, in Goldstein, *History of Modern Tibet*, 833.

to "make a general definition of the frontier line."[71] The surveyors began at the northernmost demarcated point of the Burma-Yunnan boundary and worked westward. With only two minor exceptions in Sikkim, the main watershed of the Himalayas formed the border between India and Tibet. This was in keeping with McMahon's demand that the line follow the limit of the watershed. As noted by Charles Bell, McMahon's "heart was set on having the boundary lines along high water-partings" instead of the border points already established.[72] Bell also observed that although at present the Indo-Tibetan frontier, "some 1,600 miles from Kashmir to beyond the north-eastern corner of Assam," was the "least troublesome" of India's frontiers, that situation could change with the granting of self-government.[73] Responding to a Foreign Department query about the impact of giving that status to the people of India, Bell noted that to avoid "constant friction" and "serious trouble" along the frontier, the government of India should implement and directly govern "a strip of land dividing [the border] from the self-governing communities of India." While never implemented, Bell's plan spoke to continued anxieties about the indirectly ruled territories along the frontier. Such a critical element of the imperial state should not be left in the hands of local powers. The growing importance of the frontier as "the razor's edge" determining "life or death to nations" revealed just how intimately tied politics and geography had become.[74]

6.4   The Birth of Geopolitics

Growing concerns over movements of trans-frontier groups, access to trans-frontier information, and the determination of lines that would define the imperial perimeter reflected a broader change in how geography and the state functioned together. By the turn of the twentieth century the imperial state came to see space in a particular new mode. Territory and the state were now co-terminus entities, and the border the *sine qua non* of the state's existence. This process of "re-visioning," as John Agnew and Stuart Elden have noted, dated back to Renaissance European notions of the world as "a structured whole."[75] But geography only emerged as a self-conscious science in the late nineteenth century.

---

[71] NAI, Foreign, Secret E., September 1915, nos. 76–101. "India. Definition of Indo-Tibetan Boundaries."
[72] Charles Bell to the Political Officer in Sikkim, October 5, 1919. NAI, Foreign, Secret E., February 1920, keep-with no. 112.
[73] Charles Bell, P. O. Sikkim, to A. H. Grant, November 13, 1917. NAI, Foreign, Secret E., May 1918, nos. 146–47.
[74] Curzon, *Frontiers*, 7.   [75] Agnew, *Geopolitics*, 11–12.

With his usual dramatic flourish, Thomas Holdich summed up this transformation: "Time was (and not so very long ago either) when the whole wide area of scientific knowledge embraced in the broad field of geography was narrowed to a ridiculous little educational streamlet which babbled of place-names and country products."[76] But by the time Holdich became a leading member of the RGS, those days were over. Geography was not only a science; it had become a *political* science. In the development of this geopolitics, the frontier experts of imperial India and the Royal Geographical Society played a leading role.

6.4.1   *The Royal Geographical Society and* The Geographical Journal

The Royal Geographical Society was founded in 1830 as the Geographical Society of London, "an institution to promote the 'advancement of geographical science.'"[77] Within its *Proceedings* – renamed *The Geographical Journal* in 1893 – explorers, scientists, and imperial administrators detailed and debated the territorialization of the globe. By the turn of the twentieth century its leaders were drawn largely from the ranks of imperial administrators, military commanders, and – more specifically – the frontier experts discussed above. In addition to granting these individuals seats in the invitation-only leadership of the society, the RGS also recognized their outstanding contributions to geography through its prestigious annual Gold Medal, subdivided between two prizes: the Founder's Medal and the Patron's Medal. These awards were increasingly given to explorers and surveyors of the Himalaya and Central Asia, including Alexander Burnes (1835), Henry Strachey (1852), T. G. Montgomerie (1865), Thomas Thomson (1866), Robert Shaw (1872), Ney Elias (1873), (pundit) Nain Singh[78] (1877), Henry Trotter (1878), Thomas Holdich (1887), Francis Younghusband (1890), Hamilton Bower (1894), George Curzon (1895), Sven Hedin (1898), Douglas Freshfield (1903[79]), H. H. Godwin-Austen (1910), Filippo Filippi (1915), Kenneth Mason

---

[76] Thomas H. Holdich, "Some Aspects of Political Geography," *The Geographical Journal* 34, no. 6 (1909): 593.

[77] The Geographical Society of London changed its name to the Royal Geographical Society in 1859: www.rgs.org/aboutus/history.htm. The Society's website tellingly glosses over its relationship with empire and colonial exploitation: "The history of the Society was closely allied for many of its earlier years with 'colonial' exploration in Africa, the Indian subcontinent, the polar regions, and central Asia especially."

[78] The famous pundit explorer Nain Singh Rawat (see p. 255n44) is one of the very few non-Europeans to receive the award, and the only one to do so in the nineteenth century.

[79] Awarded for work in the Caucasus, though he also worked extensively on the Indo-Tibetan frontier.

(1927), Tom Longstaff (1928), F. Kingdon-Ward (1930), Owen Lattimore (1942), and Halford Mackinder (1945).

As this string of dates suggests, Himalayan and Central Asian exploration intensified in the last quarter of the nineteenth century, at the same time that the membership of the RGS started enlisting greater numbers of imperial administrators. This was also the era of "high imperialism" or "new imperialism," when the dominant powers of the world sought to lay claim to all of the territory of the globe and eliminate nonstate spaces like the no-man's land of the Askai Chin. This heightened territorialization, following the Berlin Conference in 1885 and entailing the European Scramble for Africa, entailed as well a very practical convergence of colonial administration and the gathering of geographical information. "It is to the Imperial interest in African geography that I wish to draw particular attention," wrote Thomas Holdich in 1891 in describing the "application of Indian systems of geographical survey to Africa." Holdich asserted that "any really satisfactory and comprehensive scheme of survey must depend, in the first instance, on State support."[80] It also depended, as he later noted, upon the era's revolution in border-making technologies and their application to imperial frontiers.[81]

The pages of *The Geographical Journal* reflected this revolution, nowhere more so than in its numerous publications regarding Younghusband's invasion of Tibet in 1903–4. Here geography, empire, and territorial expansion came into an intimate relationship. In "Notes from Tibet," the mountaineer Douglas Freshfield introduced his compilation of observations sent to him by members of the Tibet Mission by first acknowledging the patronage of the then viceroy of India, George Curzon (who would later become the RGS's president in 1911). "Lord Curzon has recently forwarded to the Royal Geographical Society a set of thirteen photographs taken by Mr. Hayden, the geologist attached to the Tibetan Mission." Freshfield's notes were complemented by direct correspondence among Curzon, Sarat Chandra Das, Captain W. F. O'Connor, and Younghusband himself. Studies of geology ran alongside (nonclassified) maps, discussions of the "Military Aspect[s] of the Frontier," and, above all, "Roads to Tibet."[82]

---

[80] Thomas H. Holdich, "African Boundaries, and the Application of Indian Systems of Geographical Survey to Africa," *Proceedings of the Royal Geographical Society and Monthly Record of Geography* 13, no. 10 (1891): 597–98.

[81] Holdich, *The Indian Borderland, 1880–1900*, vii.

[82] Douglas W. Freshfield, "The Roads to Tibet," *The Geographical Journal* 23, no. 1 (1904): 79–91; Douglas W. Freshfield, "Tibet. I. Notes from Tibet," *The Geographical Journal* 23, no. 3 (1904): 361–66; L. A. Waddell, "Map of Lhasa and Its Environs," *The Geographical Journal* 23, no. 3 (1904): 366; F. J. Needham and H. J. Elwes, "The

This combination of travel narrative with geographical observations, description of routes, political information, botany, and cartography reflected the cumulative process through which geographical information was organized to gradually render frontier space more legible to the imperial state and to the scientific community that increasingly fell within that state. As was customary with the annual RGS Presidential Address, transcripts of conversations among prominent members of the society followed key articles. In these discussions, experts compared their experiences from the field as well as the finer points of methods used. Above all, these discussions served to generate implicit policy positions based on the topic under discussion. This was the beginning of geopolitics at work.

6.4.2   Geopolitics: Geography Becomes Security

The same year that Younghusband's invasion made big news across the RGS and the British public, Halford Mackinder presented to the Society his influential paper, "The Geographical Pivot of History." It was subsequently published in *The Geographical Journal*.[83] Mackinder articulated a relationship between geography and world (or "universal") history through what would become known as his "Heartland Theory." Like many a geographer, he began his discussion with a map.

In 400 years the outline of the map of the world has been completed with approximate accuracy. ... In Europe, North America, South America, Africa, and Australia there is scarcely a region left for the pegging out of a claim of ownership, unless as the result of a war between civilized or half-civilized powers. Even in Asia we are probably witnessing the last moves of the game first played by the horsemen of Yermak the Cossack and the shipmen of Vasco da Gama.[84]

Now it was time to make use of this geographical omniscience. "It appears to me, therefore," Mackinder observed,

that in the present decade we are for the first time in a position to attempt, with some degree of completeness, a correlation between the larger geographical and the larger historical generalizations. For the first time we can perceive something of the real proportion of features and events on the stage of the whole world, and

---

Roads to Tibet," *The Geographical Journal* 23, no. 3 (1904): 397–400; A. W. Paul, "The Roads to Tibet," *The Geographical Journal* 23, no. 4 (1904): 528–29. Emphasizing the dialogic nature of the *Journal*, the same issue included two brief responses to Douglas W. Freshfield's January article on "Roads to Tibet," noting earlier routes that had been explored in the 1880s.

[83] Mackinder, "The Geographical Pivot of History." The speech was delivered on January 25, 1904. Mackinder had been appointed Oxford's first professor of geography several years earlier.

[84] Mackinder, 421.

may seek a formula which shall express certain aspects, at any rate, of geographical causation in universal history. If we are fortunate, that formula should have a practical value as setting into perspective some of the competing forces in current international politics.[85]

Mackinder thus endeavored to describe "those physical features of the world" which he believed to be "most coercive of human action ... to exhibit human history as part of the life of the world organism. ... Man and not nature initiates," he stated, "but nature in large measure controls." Although this was not absolute geographical determinism, Mackinder thought that the life or death of states in history was controlled "in large measure" by geography.

Mackinder then launched into an elaboration of the key role played throughout human history by the Eurasian steppe. This area, "inaccessible to ships, but in antiquity ... open to the horse-riding nomads [and more recently train networks]," was "the pivot region of the world's politics." And this "heartland" was controlled by the Russian Empire. "There have been and are here," Mackinder concluded, "the conditions of a mobility of military and economic power of a far-reaching and yet limited character. Russia replaces the Mongol Empire. Her pressure on Finland, on Scandinavia, on Poland, on Turkey, on Persia, on India, and on China, replaces the centrifugal raids of the steppemen. In the world at large she occupies the central strategical position held by Germany in Europe."[86] World history, he asserted, was driven by the struggle between the heartland of Eurasia and the marginal regions and islands outside of it.

In the discussion that followed Mackinder's paper, the first to respond was Spencer Wilkinson, first Chichele Professor of Military History at Oxford. Like his American contemporary, Alfred Thayer Mahan, Wilkinson combined the study of history and geography to articulate theories about military strategy on land and at sea. On the question of applying Mackinder's theory to policy, Wilkinson noted that he wished more ministers of the current government "would give more time to studying their policy from the point of view that you cannot move any one piece without considering all the squares on the board."[87] The chess metaphor would remain a staple for geopolitical analysis throughout the twentieth century.[88] Wilkinson also worried that by focusing on the expansion of Russia within the Eurasian landmass, too little importance

[85] Mackinder, 422.   [86] Mackinder, 434–36.
[87] Spencer Wilkinson, Thomas Holdich, Mr. Amery, Mr. Hogarth and H. Mackinder, "The Geographical Pivot of History: Discussion," *The Geographical Journal* 23, no. 4 (1904): 4381.
[88] Brzezinski, *The Grand Chessboard*.

was given to the hegemonic status of Britain as a result of its sea power. Despite this objection, as well as several points concerning the legacies of ancient Rome and Greece and an unanswered observation by Thomas Holdich on the "impossible barrier" of Tibet, no one disputed the importance Mackinder granted to geography as a determinant of human history.

Mackinder promoted this view through an edited series on *Regions of the World*.[89] His theories were often invoked throughout the series, but they did not go uncontested. Mackinder's notion of global geographical "pivots," for instance, built off of the notion of the "Problem [or 'Question'] of Asia" articulated by strategists such as the American naval theorist Alfred Thayer Mahan.[90] Like Mackinder's "heartland," Mahan's "problem" revolved around the dominant position of Russia on the Eurasian landmass and the need for a multitude of other powers to contain it – not just the British Empire, but the United States and Japan as well. Unlike Mackinder, Mahan saw global dominance through the lens of sea power: the establishment of commercial networks during peacetime and the establishment of strategic military networks (including chokepoints, refueling stations, and canals) during wartime. For both Mackinder and Mahan, a deep understanding of geography (maritime or inland) was a necessary prerequisite to achieving political dominance and solving the problem of Asia, or any place else.

Borders and frontiers, often being at the edge of so-called pivots, were increasingly discussed in terms of their respective strengths and weaknesses. Ever since the late nineteenth century, the "scientific frontier" had been a cost-effective means of achieving political dominance and removing friction between states.[91] Thomas Holdich's detailed and prolific writings took the concept even further by enumerating the natural and strategic features that produced "strong" or "weak" borders. Holdich developed these ideas in the pages of *The Geographical Journal*, often in conversation with other frontier experts including his old friends Robert Wahab and Francis Younghusband.[92] While applauding Britain's arrival into the academic study of geography with Oxford's appointment of Mackinder and the establishment of a geography department, Holdich

---

[89] Thomas Holdich wrote the volume on *India* (London: Frowde, 1904)

[90] Mahan, *The Problem of Asia*.

[91] George N. Curzon, "The 'Scientific Frontier' an Accomplished Fact," *Nineteenth Century* 23, no. 136 (1888): 900–917. Cost efficiency is particularly emphasized in Hanna, *India's Scientific Frontier. Where Is It? What Is It?*

[92] Holdich refers to his "old friend" Robert Wahab in Thomas Holdich, Colonel Wahab, Colonel Maunsell, Mr. Bury, J. L. Myres, H. J. L. Beadnell, and D. G. Hogarth, "Problems in Exploration: Discussion," *The Geographical Journal* 32, no. 6 (1908): 563–70.

was quick to remind readers of the *Journal* that "practical geography" was of still greater importance.[93] "A knowledge of geography," Holdich wrote, "most intimately affects matters naval and military."[94] This theory and practice of geography was indistinguishable from political concerns regarding imperial security. Summing up the confluence of security, geography, and statecraft around the "problem of Asia," James Hevia writes:

> The theory and practice of security constituted Asia as a problem, one that demanded and justified interventions of many kinds. If Asians could not solve the problem of Asia – and by definition they could not, because they were unable to recognize either the causes or the solutions to the problem – then white men with the appropriate technologies of knowledge would do so. As British politicians, colonial administrators and military officers organized a security regime based on command of information about territory and military statistics, they also convinced themselves that their interventions were for the good of the indigenous populations.[95]

Thus had the study of geography become seamlessly integrated into the apparatus of the state. It also formed one of the first explicit bridges between science, state, and the academy.

When the Swedish political scientist Rudolf Kjellén coined the term "geopolitics" in 1899, he was building upon the work of his German teacher, Friedrich Ratzel, who was in turn influenced by Mahan's most famous work, *The Influence of Sea Power Upon History, 1660–1783*.[96] Ratzel and Kjellén's conservative *Geopolitik* did more than invoke a deterministic relationship between natural and human histories however. As Kjellén put it in *Der staat als Lebensform* [State as a Form of Life] (1916), the state was an organic entity that required a necessary *Lebensraum* ["living space"] for its *Volk*. The ideal autarkic *Reich* would govern a territory that was sufficiently capacious for its racially homogenous *Volk*, while cognizant of the strategic considerations of geography for bounding that *Raum*. Karl Haushofer built on this "applied science" of geopolitics in the pages of his *Zeitschrift für Geopolitik* [Journal for Geopolitics], founded in the mid-1920s. But after German *Geopolitik* was picked up in turn by Adolf Hitler and incorporated into the propaganda of the Third Reich, academics were quick to distance themselves from the German branch.

---

[93] Thomas H. Holdich, "The Use of Practical Geography Illustrated by Recent Frontier Operations," *The Geographical Journal* 13, no. 5 (1899): 465–77.
[94] Holdich. See also Peter Lumsden, Lieut.-Colonel Leverson, and H. J. Mackinder, "The Use of Practical Geography Illustrated by Recent Frontier Operations: Discussion," *The Geographical Journal* 13, no. 5 (1899): 477–80.
[95] Hevia, *Imperial Security State*, 251.
[96] Mahan, *The Influence of Sea Power upon History*.

Geopolitics hardly disappeared after 1945, however. As John Agnew has argued, "American containment and domino-effect doctrines of the Cold War ... had echoes of the older geopolitical models, such as Mackinder's 'Heartland' model, even though they lacked the formal grounding in the Big Picture that these models offered."[97] Zbigniew Brzezinski's *The Grand Chessboard* (1997) in many ways directly rehashes Mackinder and Mahan's models of Eurasian grand strategy in the context of post–Cold War American hegemony. Brzezinski does not explicitly invoke Mahan and cites Mackinder only once. Nevertheless, his insistence on the importance of "geopolitical pivots" (such as Turkey, Iran, and Ukraine) and the primary importance he assigns to Eurasia in shaping global power dynamics clearly echo the first generation of geopolitical theorists.

Following the Second World War, other, more critical, geopolitical approaches surfaced in the academy. Yves Lacoste's provocatively titled *La géographie, ça sert, d'abord, à faire la guerre* [Geography is, above all, used to make war], acknowledged that geospatial information had become intimately entwined in the military concerns of global powers.[98] According to Klaus Dodds, Lacoste was "one of the first to really consider how geopolitics was a form of political and strategic knowledge." And on the centenary of Mackinder's "The Geographical Pivot of History," historian Paul Kennedy observed that the legacy of the "heartland theory" survived in Washington, DC. "Right now [2004] with hundreds of thousands of US troops in the Eurasian rimlands and with an administration constantly explaining why it has to stay the course, it looks as if Washington is taking seriously Mackinder's injunction to ensure control of the geographical pivot of history."[99] Both Henry Kissinger and Zbigniew Brzezinski insisted that Mackinder's theory continued to affect post–Cold War international relations. More recently still, conservative scholars like Robert D. Kaplan have breathed new life into geopolitics by arguing for its continued relevance; indeed, one of his book titles asserts *The Revenge of Geography*.[100] Geography might have been considered the "imperial science" of the nineteenth century, but it became political science in the twentieth. At the center of this grand transformation in viewing political space was the idea of a strong and scientific borderline.

---

[97] Agnew, *Geopolitics*, 27.

[98] Yves Lacoste, *La géographie, ça sert, d'abord, à faire la guerre* (Paris: F. Maspero, 1982).

[99] Klaus Dodds and James Sidaway, "Halford Mackinder and the 'Geographical Pivot of History': A Centennial Retrospective," *The Geographical Journal* 170, no. 4 (2004): 292.

[100] Robert D. Kaplan, *The Revenge of Geography: What the Map Tells Us about Coming Conflicts and the Battle against Fate* (New York: Random House, 2012).

6.5   Conclusion: India's Inheritance

In conclusion, let us return to the more modest geographical and historical scales of Southern Asia and the end of British rule. Unlike the North-
West Frontier with the Durand Line and the North-East Frontier with the
McMahon Line, the northwestern Himalaya never inherited a single
"line" after independence. As with the McMahon and Durand Lines,
the general principle of following the water-parting of the Indus watershed had long been accepted as the ideal borderline in mountainous
terrain. But the arid Aksai Chin offered no clear mountain range upon
which to impose such a line. As post-1947 surveys would later reveal,
much of the Aksai Chin would actually drain its waters into the Tarim
Basin – a self-contained, endorheic watershed – instead of the Indus. But
by the time of the transfer of power to an independent India in 1947,
Ladakh still had a number of hypothetical borderlines. It had the Johnson
Line of 1865, the product of a traverse survey by William H. Johnson,
who likely sketched in (or had the Survey of India sketch in) a presumed
crescent of mountains that were not actually surveyed (and, in fact, never
existed). Then there was the Macartney–MacDonald Line suggested to
the Qing government in MacDonald's now-infamous memorandum,
based in part of an earlier Chinese map given to George Macartney in
Kashgar. And then there were the maps with no lines at all. This last
group of official documents – products of the standardization and restriction of imperial maps – officially acknowledged territorial illegibility. The
requirements for boundary demarcation in the mountainous northern
periphery of India had exceeded the amount of information available.
This illegibility, and the official practices that accompanied it, was
bequeathed to India at independence.

The northwestern Himalaya's continued borderlessness represented
a profound irony to the emerging geopolitical sensibilities of the frontier
experts who spent so much time concerned with a region containing
neither an immediate military threat nor a large commercial payoff. The
region had been one of the key imperial laboratories for border making
and the development of the geographical sciences. It was central to the
concerns of frontier experts and geographers across the globe. But by
1947, this once central crossroads of Asia had become a palimpsest of
frontier configurations – configurations that reflected a consensus on the
geopolitical significance of this mountainous and inhospitable space, but
with no detailed survey to support the hypothetical borderline.

When the Radcliffe Commission took six weeks to draw the lines that
would partition India, they dispensed with any of the rationalized border-
making principles that experts such as Holdich had taken such pains to

develop.[101] Instead, the commissioners used district census records to determine, by religious majority, which districts would belong to the future India and which to Pakistan. Louis Mountbatten, the last viceroy of India, even went so far as to state that it was in neither his nor Britain's interest to leave India and Pakistan with defensible borders.[102] Postindependence friction along the newly demarcated borderlines was of no concern to the imperial administrators eager to leave a country they could no longer control.

In Ladakh, the transfer of power registered little immediate attention. In 1946, the last British Joint Commissioner left Leh at the end of another lackluster trading season (see Table 3.1) and did not return the following summer. The Resident in Kashmir did not bother assigning someone to the posting when the transfer of power became apparent in early 1947. Under the dual layers of Dogra and British rule, Ladakh's political existence became tied to the princely state of Jammu and Kashmir. The exceptional and "asymmetrical" features of the region that Ney Elias and many other frontier experts had earlier noted complicated an already complex problem. The Dogras were a Hindu dynasty ruling over the Muslim-majority Kashmir Valley.[103] This princely state, in turn, had come to rule over Buddhist-majority Ladakh. The uncertainty as to which state Jammu and Kashmir would accede was mirrored within the state itself by concerns in Ladakh. Would it join India or Pakistan? By the early 1950s, a third option also materialized: Tibet.

The next chapter takes up the years between independence in 1947 and the Sino-Indian War of 1962. The geopolitical significance of the region, coupled with the post-1947 disputed status of Jammu and Kashmir, put Ladakh in a paradoxical position. It was simultaneously central to geopolitical tensions of enormous magnitude while rendered increasingly isolated as part of a still ambiguously defined territory. By becoming appended to the imperial-turned-national frontier, Ladakhis

---

[101] The Partition of India has generated a vast body of work. Recent notable histories include Joya Chatterji, *Bengal Divided: Hindu Communalism and Partition, 1932–1947* (Cambridge: Cambridge University Press, 1994); Yasmin Khan, *The Great Partition: The Making of India and Pakistan* (New Delhi: Penguin, 2007); and Vazira Fazila-Yacoobali Zamindar, *The Long Partition and the Making of Modern South Asia: Refugees, Boundaries, Histories* (New York: Columbia University Press, 2007).

[102] Chatterji, "The Fashioning of a Frontier," 193.

[103] See Mridu Rai, *Hindu Ruler, Muslim Subject: Islam, Rights, and the History of Kashmir* (Princeton, NJ: Princeton University Press, 2004); and Chitralekha Zutshi, *Languages of Belonging: Islam, Regional Identity, and the Making of Kashmir* (New York: Oxford University Press, 2004).

slowly became more aware of their isolated, peripheral position. More significantly, as postcolonial nationalism infused the young state's conception of itself, that nationalism became attached to the territory bequeathed to it. But the exact shape of that geo-body was still far from clear.

7 Lines of Control
From Empire to Nation-State

> In the high Himalayas, Gurkhas and Rajputs fled in disarray from the Chinese army; and in the upper reaches of my mind, another army was also destroyed.[1]
>
> – Salman Rushdie, *Midnight's Children*, 1981

A century after Governor-General Hardinge had first requested "clear and well defined boundaries," the British still lacked a satisfactory border in the northwestern Himalaya. Following independence from Britain in 1947, this uncertainty was reflected both on maps and in intragovernmental communications. These included the circulation of questionnaires asking local officials for information about the border's exact location.[2] Maps that showed "transboundary" areas continued to be subjected to "secret" classifications and restricted circulation.[3] Maps of maps, as in Map 7.1, which employed a "red line" to distinguish between domestic and transborder maps, were used to determine the reproduction and circulation of border-area maps.[4] Maps produced in the years immediately following independence continued to omit "undemarcated" borders. The indeterminacy of official maps had long been a standard practice of the British government of India. For instance, a 1962 Commonwealth Relations Office memo on the "India-China Border Question" remarked that "Survey of India maps issued in 1865, 1903, 1917, 1929, 1936, and 1938 *do not show any boundary at all* in the western

---

[1] In Rushdie's masterpiece, the Conference of Midnight's Children (those born at or close to midnight of August 15, 1947, when India gained independence) was disbanded at the end of the Sino-Indian War in 1962, breaking the psychic connection between the novel's chief protagonist, Saleem Sinai, and his fellow Midnight's Children. Salman Rushdie, *Midnight's Children* (New York: Alfred A. Knopf, 1981), 290.

[2] NAI, Ministry of States, 1-K/51, "Defence of North-North East Border of Jammu and Kashmir [and] certain aspects of the administration of Ladakh."

[3] NAI, Ministry of States, 14(11)-K/51, "Report regarding import of arms and ammunition into Ladakh"; and "Restriction on the sale, publication and distribution of maps. Supply of restricted maps to Part 'B' States." 34-AE/51.

[4] This practice continues today, much to the annoyance of scholars seeking access to historical maps of border areas.

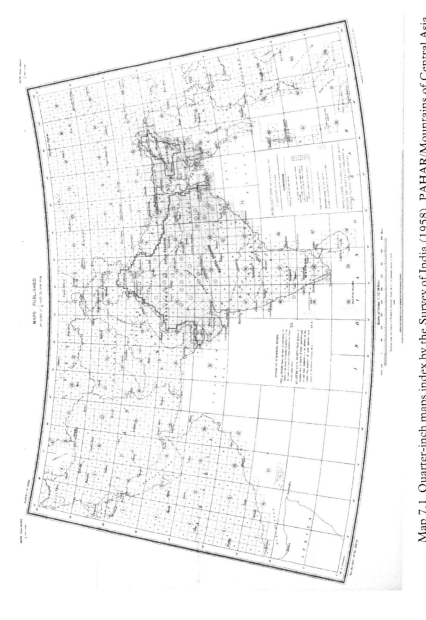

Map 7.1 Quarter-inch maps index by the Survey of India (1958). PAHAR/Mountains of Central Asia Digital Dataset.

(i.e. Ladakh) sector."[5] These borderless maps, and those that employed colors and washes to illustrate the same omission, reflected the unwillingness to formally represent territorial ignorance on supposedly precise maps.

The Sino-Indian War of 1962 imposed the first effective borderline on the region, the "Line of Actual Control." It failed to follow the line put forth in the 1899 MacDonald memorandum, the 1865 Johnson Line, or, indeed, the watershed of the Indus River. Maps produced in India still fail to show this de facto border, instead insisting on a version most closely resembling the 1865 Johnson Line, which reflected a hasty traverse survey across a vast region. Legislation was unsuccessfully introduced in 2016 to criminalize maps failing to represent India's claimed border, and a year earlier the Indian government banned Al-Jazeera from the air for five days for showing maps that excluded India's claimed territories occupied by Pakistan and China, a move the government labeled a "cartographic aggression."[6]

With the struggle for independence a new layer of power was added to the complex of practices and ideas surrounding the frontier: nationalism. Geography had already been transformed into a political science, producing a new way of seeing territory. With the coming of independence in 1947 it now fueled the creation of the "geo-body" of the nation – for Indians, a body that Partition had violently amputated at birth and that needed defending at all costs.[7] Internally, the young government was preoccupied with organizing the 554 princely states that acceded to India into fourteen administrative units.[8] Yet calls for statehood along linguistic, national, or religious lines have continued to occupy Indian politics from 1947 to the present. Despite what contemporary maps and politicians assert, the shape and anatomy of India is still changing.

While 1947 signaled a clear watershed in Indian history, 1962 constituted another major milestone in the territorializing the geo-body of the independent Indian state. Post-Partition wars over Kashmir, East Pakistan (later Bangladesh), and segments of the Sino-Indian borderlands generated violent border disputes and a host of ongoing uncertainties over territory.[9] Like Partition, the Sino-Indian War also marked

---

[5] NAUK. DO 196/190, 1962, "India's Himalayan Frontier." My emphasis.

[6] Pandey, "India Bans Al Jazeera for 5 Days over 'Incorrect' Kashmir Map."

[7] Winichakul, *Siam Mapped.*

[8] An entire ministry (the Ministry of States) was established to oversee this process. See V. P. Menon, *Integration of the Indian States* (New Delhi: Orient BlackSwan, 2014).

[9] Besides border disputes, this has included annexations and the production of territorial enclaves, counterenclaves, and even a counter-counterenclave. For the history of the India–Bangladesh enclaves, see van Schendel, "Stateless in South Asia."

a deep collective trauma for the new Indian state and a sudden halt to optimistic narratives of postindependence politics. This rupture is elegantly represented in Rushdie's fictional *Midnight's Children* (1981) by the simultaneous defeat of the Indian Army across the Himalaya and the destruction of the "Conference" of psychically connected children: all those born at the moment of India's independence (midnight, August 15, 1947).

This concluding chapter reviews major transitions and continuities in the broader northwestern Himalaya from the 1940s up to the outbreak of the Sino-Indian War in 1962. It begins by refocusing on Ladakh and the rise of communalism in its postindependence politics, a result of Partition and the uncertain status of the erstwhile princely state of Jammu and Kashmir. It then zooms out to show how Ladakh became the center of a geopolitical rivalry between India and China. With its geopolitical concerns vis-à-vis Pakistan and China, the government of India continued to see Ladakh as the British saw it: as a frontier region crucial to the defense of India and the balance of power in Asia. Nationalism magnified this need for a defensive perimeter. The territory of India was now synonymous with the idea of an independent nation of India – an idea that leaders like India's first prime minister, Jawaharlal Nehru, struggled hard to cement through rhetoric of "unity in diversity." The chapter concludes with a brief summary of how this inherited frontier complex has been applied in the postcolonial context.

7.1   Bakula Rinpoche, Sheikh Abdullah, and Jawaharlal Nehru: The Dual Specters of Communism and Communalism

Though it did not suffer the horrific violence and mass population displacements of Partition, Ladakh deeply felt the political fractures that accompanied independence. In particular, independence quickly catalyzed communal divisions between Ladakh's Buddhist and Muslim populations.[10] We can reconstruct these tensions – as well as a deeper, existential uncertainty regarding the region's future – from once-secret Ministry of State documents on Ladakh at the National Archives of India

---

[10] These tensions continue today. In September 2017, a petition from "the Buddhists of Ladakh" made its way to Prime Minister Modi in an unsuccessful effort to stop a consensual marriage between a Ladakhi Buddhist woman and a Ladakhi Muslim man. The petitioning Ladakh Buddhist Association used this as an instance of "love jihad," a recently coined term used predominantly by the Hindu right to describe the (often unfounded) pursuit of non-Muslim women by Muslim men who feign love in order to convert women to Islam. M. Saleem Pandit, "Ladakh Tense over Muslim-Buddhist 'Love Jihad' Marriage," *Times of India*, September 12, 2017.

in Delhi. Likewise, the correspondence between the emergent leader of Ladakh, Bakula Rinpoche, the head of the government in Jammu and Kashmir, Sheikh Abdullah, and Jawaharlal Nehru and officials in India's Ministry of State laid out multiple possible future political configurations for Ladakh.[11] Just as the central government of India feared the influence of the newly created Republic of Pakistan on the Muslim population of India, particularly in Kashmir, it also feared the influence of newly Communist China on the Buddhist population of Ladakh. In many ways, this continued and expanded upon British fears of "Bolshevik penetration" across the north of India from the 1920s to the 1940s.[12] The Indian state of Jammu and Kashmir, a fractured version of the princely state that preceded Partition, wrestled with its suspended and divided status vis-à-vis India and Pakistan.[13] In the stalemate that followed the first Indo-Pakistani War (1947–48; also referred to as the First Kashmir War), internal divisions grew across the state's political spectrum and within Sheikh Abdullah's newly dominant political party, the National Conference. The limited resources of the young Republic of India compounded these tensions, despite the consensus among those in the national government that Ladakh held an important, strategic position.[14] Above all, the correspondence among these regional and national leaders shows numerous instances of growing communal tensions. At every point Ladakhis were facing a basic political question: politically speaking, where did they belong? Though communal tensions would subside and flare up again in subsequent decades (especially during the late 1980s and early 1990s), they were never so existentially crucial as in the first days of independence.

In February 1948, militants from Pakistan attacked the Skardu branch of the Wazārat of Ladakh. The *wazīr-i-wazārat* and "a number of other high State officials" were killed, and the state treasury was raided.[15] That summer incursions into the remote Ladakhi region of Zangskar and up

---

[11] The Ministry of State was tasked with integrating the princely states.

[12] See Chapter 5. For continued fears of Soviet penetration of India via Ladakh in the 1940s, see NAI, Ministry of External Affairs, 798-X, 1940. "Ladakh Affairs."

[13] This is a massive and complex history that has been ably told by, inter alia, Chitralekha Zutshi, *Languages of Belonging: Islam, Regional Identity, and the Making of Kashmir* (New Delhi: Permanent Black, 2003); and Mridu Rai, *Hindu Ruler, Muslim Subject: Islam, Rights, and the History of Kashmir* (New Delhi: Permanent Black, 2004).

[14] There are numerous newspaper and official sources to support this view. See, for example, "Strategic Position of Ladakh," *Times of India*, June 26, 1949, p. 7; and "Ladakh – Kashmir's Strategic Frontier Province: Regent Visits Land of Lamas," *Times of India*, October 5, 1952, p. 10.

[15] NAI, Ministry of States, 12(79)-P, 1948. "Ladakh treasury attack. Question in the Constituent Assembly of India (Legislative) by Dr. Bakhsji Tek Chand in respect of State officials who were attacked and the State treasury which was looted in Ladakh."

Figure 7.1 Ladakhis and Indian Army soldiers posing next to an Indian Army DC-3 at the hastily constructed airfield near Leh (1948). Photograph courtesy of Nawang Tsering Shakspo. Reproduced with his permission.

the Indus valley toward Leh were eventually routed by a combination of local militia, a battalion of Gurkhas marching up from Kullu, and soldiers flown into a hastily constructed airfield near Leh. The plane was the first motorized vehicle to reach Ladakh (Figure 7.1) and gave rise to the (likely apocryphal) story that locals greeted the plane with bales of hay, assuming that it was an auspicious "wind horse" (rlung.rta) and hungry after its flight.

Ladakh's indigenous leaders quickly protested the neglect and mistreatment of their region by state officials. The leading voice was the nineteenth Bakula Rinpoche, a reincarnate lama from the Matho branch of one of the royal families of Ladakh. The nineteenth Bakula had recently returned from Tibet, where he had attained the degree of Geshe Lharampa (the highest possible in the Gelukpa sect of Tibetan Buddhism). This degree had been bestowed in the presence of the young fourteenth Dalai Lama in 1940, during the Tibetan leader's enthronement ceremonies in Lhasa. Bakula traveled to New Delhi in 1949 to meet with Jawaharlal Nehru and discuss a number of political issues in Ladakh – including a particularly rapacious state administrator and systemic neglect on everything from education to roads. As Nehru expressed his interest in visiting Ladakh, the rinpoche later sent him a letter of invitation to come visit the "deserted State."[16] Nehru,

---

[16] NAI, External Affairs Department, "Exchange of message between Prince Pendup, Ladakh and Shir Gial Shas Bakula, Head Lama Tapuk Ganpa, Tehsil Leh, Ladakh and the Prime Minister of India." 13(16)-Pt., 1949.

his daughter, Indira, and Sheikh Abdullah flew to Ladakh in July 1949, where Bakula greeted them with great fanfare.[17] Nehru, in turn, encouraged the young rinpoche to take an active role in Ladakh's political life, encouragement that Bakula would take to heart in years to come.[18]

In November 1950, Bakula again visited Nehru in Delhi. He complained that "the Sheikh administration" in Kashmir continued to neglect Ladakh, as well as imposing a new ordinance prohibiting estates of more than 182 kanals of land, a huge blow to the monasteries that were by far the largest landowners in Ladakh.[19] In response Nehru wrote to Sheikh Abdullah on December 1, 1950:

My dear Shaikh Saheb, I have already [sic] written to you about Ladakh and the deputation of Lamas from there. . . . I have a growing feeling that it is of considerable importance how Ladakh is treated. *This is so not only because of Ladakh but because of the whole Kashmir problem, as well as because of developments in Tibet.* All kinds of complications might arise, if we are not careful. I would therefore earnestly request you to take this matter in hand yourself and try to remove all legitimate grievances. It is clear that these people are feeling repressed and frustrated and have a sensation of complete neglect by Government. That is a bad feeling. If this has spread or might spread generally to the Lamas in Ladakh, it will influence large numbers of people there. . . . As you will observe, *we are facing a very grave international situation and are possibly on the verge of a world war.* The future is dark from the point of view of this unhappy world of ours. In this state of affairs we have to carry all kinds of people with us to meet the dangers and perils that might arise.[20]

Nehru's bigger picture included Partition, war with Pakistan, the victory of Mao's People's Liberation Army in China, and its "peaceful

[17] NAI, External Affairs Department, 1949. "Indian Prime Minister Visit of Indian Prime Minister to Leh and arrangements for the presentation of two presents by the Indian Prime Minister to the two monastries [sic] in Ladakh. 8(19)-Pt." See also "Pandit Nehru in Ladakh," *Times of India*, July 12, 1949, p. 1, which shows Bakula Rinpoche offering a silk ceremonial scarf (*kha.btags*) to Jawaharlal Nehru upon his arrival at Leh on July 4, 1949.

[18] Bakula Rinpoche would serve in the state assembly from 1953 to 1967. He was a member of the fourth and fifth Lok Sabha from 1967 to 1977 and served as Indian ambassador to Mongolia from 1989 to 2000. See Sonam Wangchuk Shakspo, *Bakula Rinpoche: A Visionary Lama and Statesman* (New Delhi: Sonam Wangchuk Shakspo, 2008). Sonam was Bakula Rinpoche's private secretary for decades. He was kind enough to let me see the unpublished manuscript of Bakula's autobiography/biography. See also Shakspo, *Cultural History of Ladakh*, 83–95.

[19] NAI, Ministry of State (Kashmir), Secret, 19(16)-K52. Ganesan, Deputy Secretary to Govt. of India, Ministry of States, "Political Developments in Ladakh," dated April 30, 1952. "Buddhists in Ladakh; Representations from head Lama of Ladakh; General position re: Ladakh." And NAI, Ministry of States, 1951, 1-K/51/. "Defence of North-North East Border of Jammu and Kashmir certain aspects of the administration of Ladakh."

[20] NAI, Ministry of States, 1951 No. 1(33)-K. "Jammu and Kashmir. Representation from the head Lama of Ladakh against the application of the Kashmir Land Reforms Act in Ladakh. 2 Reports reg. dissatisfaction in Ladakh." My emphases.

liberation" of Tibet. The specter of Communism that had so affected the British regarding Soviet proximity to northern India had suddenly spread across nearly the entire length of India's land border.

Sheikh Abdullah responded that he would "give the matter his personal consideration,"[21] but he was preoccupied with political infighting in Kashmir and apparently paid no heed to Nehru's request. The calls from prominent Ladakhi Buddhists to involve Ladakhis in the governance of the state grew louder. A July 1951 letter from the "Buddhist inhabitants of Ladakh" to Jawaharlal Nehru explicitly addressed growing fractures within the state. "Every single act of the [Kashmir] administration has reeked of the communal poison, but it bears the label of secular nationalism prominently [sic] displayed. But though ... nationalism, internationalism, and universalism run in our very blood, we are branded as communalists. To prove ourselves as nationalists, we are evidently expected to wipe ourselves out of existence, but we have not yet learned the nationalism which equates with utter self-immolation."[22] Over against the divisive politics of Sheikh Abdullah's new government in Srinagar, the Ladakhi Buddhist leaders simultaneously invoking a nationalist inclination toward India, their internationalism as a historical crossroads of trade, and the "universalist" spirit of Buddhism.

In December 1951, Bakula Rinpoche wrote to Jawaharlal Nehru to discuss Ladakh's future in relation to Kashmir:

> For better or worse we have decided to stay in India and we remain with Kashmir, subject to certain safeguards which have been specified separately in the memorandum addressed to Sheikh Muhammad Abdullah – as long as Kashmir stays in India. This obviously [sic] means that in case the rumoured plebescite [sic] is held for the whole state and not on a regional basis and the result is in favour of Pakistan, our connection with the State will terminate and we shall automatically merge without any intervening link with India. If, however, it becomes for any reason impossible for India to directly annexe [sic] our land, then, as the last course open to them, *our people will seek political union with Tibet which in spite of our political connection with Jammu and Kashmir State for nearly the last 120 years has continued to be the great inspirer and controller of our spiritual life and which, whatever our political affiliations must be looked upon as our eternal and inalienable home.* / We fervently hope that India will not fail us at this critical juncture of our history.[23]

Ten days earlier, Bakula Rinpoche had sent a nearly identical letter to Sheikh Abdullah. In both letters, he enumerated a series of demands

---

[21] This is summarized in a letter from Ganesan to N. Gopalaswami Ayangar, dated April 1, 1952.

[22] NAI, Ministry of States, 1 (33)-K, 1950. "Buddhist Inhabitants of Ladakh" to Prime Minister of India, July 28, 1951.

[23] NAI, Ministry of State (Kashmir), Secret, 19(16)-K52. "Buddhists in Ladakh; Representations from head Lama of Ladakh; General position re: Ladakh." My emphasis.

made, he wrote, by the people of Ladakh, aimed at redressing budgetary neglect and poor administration.[24] He underscored the same in a speech before the State Assembly on May 12, 1952, lambasting the draft of the year's budget for failing to contain a single item earmarked for Ladakh. By raising the possibility of a Ladakhi reunion with Tibet, "the great inspirer and controller of [Ladakhi] spiritual life," Bakula simultaneously reinforced a growing communalism and intimated an uncertain future.

Once again, nothing materialized in response. Bakula's letters grew stronger in tone, no doubt reflecting his exasperation at this continued neglect.[25] When Minister of States Gopalswamy Ayyangar visited Jammu in April 1952, he discussed "the problem of Ladakh" with Sheikh Abdullah and other leaders in the state government and visited with Bakula Rinpoche, "who acquainted him with the grievances of the Budhist [sic] population." Ayyangar recorded that the state ministers had been greatly embarrassed by the national publicity generated from Bakula Rinpoche's speech in the State Assembly, and even professed that "they would have no objection to the area being taken over by India." But in Ayyangar's estimate, this solution was inadvisable. Instead, "the best course would be to appoint an officer deputed by the Govt. of India to be Administrator of the whole area; a system of local Advisory Councils such as was provided in the Constitution for the Assam Tribal Areas could also be set up."[26]

As the months passed and inaction in Jammu and Kashmir continued, Bakula's language became even more exasperated. Various documents

---

[24] These included (1) that Zanskar, a part of Kargil Tehsil, be transferred to Leh Tehsil, as should the villages of Darchiks and Garkon. (2) Thereafter, the district should be divided into fifteen constituencies at the rate of 5,000 people each. In short, he proposed a Provincial Constituent Assembly that would act much like the state government acted in relation to the national government. (3) He also requested earmarked seats for higher education and technical training, hoping to better provide the necessary local services with local personnel. (4) Furthermore, "the local legislature would be the only authority competent to make Laws for the province and to control its administration and naturally Executive Council would be responsible to it. But no motion or Resolution affecting the religious or social system of any community inhabiting the Province would be brought before the Legislature unless so desired by the community concerned." (5) "A governor deputed by the Centre would represent the Central Government and be the connecting link between the Province and the centre. He would exercise the same functions as the constitutional head of the State would do in the State."

[25] NAI, Ministry of State (Kashmir), Secret, 19(16)-K52. Ganesan, Deputy Secretary to Govt. of India, Ministry of States, "Political Developments in Ladakh," dated April 30, 1952. "Buddhists in Ladakh; Representations from head Lama of Ladakh; General position re: Ladakh."

[26] NAI, Ministry of State (Kashmir), Secret, 19(16)-K52. Ganesan, Deputy Secretary to Govt. of India, Ministry of States, "Political Developments in Ladakh," dated April 30, 1952.

detailed the growing animosity between the young reincarnate lama and the "*Sher-i-Kashmīr*" ("lion of Kashmir"), Sheikh Abdullah. In a July 23, 1952, "most confidential" note sent to the Minister of States, Bakula Rinpoche accused the Kashmir government of "Sinister designs on Ladakh." He expressed a host of fears pertaining to rapidly forming sectarian[27] and communal divisions. These fears might sound paranoid, but we must remember that, in the turmoil of those post-Partition years, Ladakhis of every sort could not be certain of how long their position on the periphery of India might endure. It is worth quoting at length from a section entitled "Our Future" to give a sense of these fears.

> It is clear as crystal from all this that unless India intervenes immediately, Ladakh will be lost to it one way or the other. Let India grasp this fact clearly: the existence of the Buddhist community in Ladakh is the only factor which guarantees to it the possession of this important frontier. / We shall prefer to be wiped out of existence, but we shall not permit ourselves to be hurled into the blazing hell of Pakistan. *To prize our Buddhist culture above our very lives therefore, the thought of the advent of Communism into our land is a dreadful nightmare for us but if India casts us to the wolves we shall, as we have repeatedly declared, prefer being restored to our home Tibet even under Communist regime to being tied to the chariot-wheels of Pakistan.* Our culture, our ideals can live and thrive only under the direct sunshine of India's protection and not under its shadowy long-distance guardianship exercised through the nonconducting medium of a virtually independent Islamic Kashmir. Our demand of internal autonomy is being thrown overboard. Shri Gopalaswamy Ayyanger [*sic*] had reassured me during my recent interview with him at Jammu, that India would depute an administrator to the District. But the Prime Minister of Kashmir has informed me that he has not agreed to this proposal and that India has not agreed to the direct merger of the District with itself. This is most unfortunate for us and gravely harmful to the interests of India itself. The need of the hour is the appointment of an Administrator by India. . . . To save the Frontier, India must save the Buddhists of Ladakh and to save the Buddhists of Ladakh it musttake [*sic*] over administrative control of the District without the loss of a moment.[28]

Whether these were Bakula's words or the rhetorical flourishes of an assistant or advisor, this alarmist tone had been building throughout his writings of the previous two years.[29] Employing such damning

---

[27] In addition to Buddhist–Muslim tensions, there were also tensions between the two dominant sects of Buddhists, the Gelukpas (of which Bakula Rinpoche was a high member) and the Drukpa Kagyus.

[28] NAI, Ministry of State (Kashmir), Secret, 19(16)-K52. Bakula Rinpoche to Jawaharlal Nehru. "Buddhists in Ladakh; Representations from head Lama of Ladakh; General position re: Ladakh." The italicized emphasis is mine, while the underlined emphasis at the conclusion is original to the text.

[29] Bakula Rinpoche spoke no Urdu at this time and was assisted in those very early years by numerous people, including his political assistant Sonam Wangyal, his personal

descriptions of Pakistan, while dangling the threat of joining Tibet, certainly caught the attention of Indian leaders. For Bakula, protecting the Buddhists of Ladakh was crucial to prevent the loss of "this important frontier." A District Commissioner was sent to Ladakh not long afterward.

From the perspective of Ladakh's Buddhists, it is not surprising that a kind of "reunion" with Tibet might serve as a point of leverage in talks with the government of India. In the early 1950s the Communist regime in China had yet to perpetrate the violent suppression and policy changes by which hundreds of thousands of Tibetans would be killed, imprisoned, starved through famine, or otherwise "disappeared." Bakula Rinpoche would travel to Tibet in 1954–55 as part of an official government of India visit when Nehru was vigorously promoting *"Hindī-Cīnī bhā'ī-bhā'ī"* ("Indian-Chinese brotherhood") and the Panchsheel Treaty (see below). Ladakh was a crucial piece in this diplomacy – and Nehru (who visited Ladakh again in 1952[30]), Bakula Rinpoche, and much of the reading public of India knew it. The Minister of States put the matter succinctly: as "a frontier tract contiguous to Communist-held Tibet," Ladakh was "important for strategic and security reasons."[31]

The Muslim side of the state had its own worries. In Kashmir, Sheikh Abdullah kept in regular communication with Minister for States Gopalaswami Ayyangar.[32] The two shared fears of Communist infiltration in Ladakh, with Sheikh Abdullah worrying that reports of Chinese mistreatment of the Ladakhi Muslim traders in Lhasa (the Lhasa Khaché described in Chapter 1) was a sign of things to come.

From 1949 to the beginning of 1953, correspondence censored by the Ministry of State and the Intelligence Bureau revealed an array of rumored or actual Muslim-Buddhist problems. These ranged from Muslim boycotts of archery competitions in Leh, to their apparent

secretaries Sonam Stobdan and Tashi Rabgyas, and his friend and political mentor Shridhar Kaul.

[30] "Mr. Nehru Visits Ladakh," *Times of India*, September 1, 1952, p. 5.

[31] NAI, Ministry of State (Kashmir), Secret, 19(16)-K52. "Buddhists in Ladakh; Representations from head Lama of Ladakh; General position re: Ladakh."

[32] "The second phase of Mr. Ayyangar's career opened in 1937 as Dewan of Kashmir. His connection with Kashmir extended until his last days. Few persons in India were better qualified to speak authoritatively when the invasion of the State by Pakistan took place, raising an international problem. At Lake Success, Geneva, and elsewhere he expounded India's cause with a clarity and comprehension. Mr. Ayyangar had assumed office as Dewan during a difficult period. The attempt of the Kashmir Committee to overthrow the Maharaja had culminated in an uprising that took a communal turn. Sheikh Abdullah assumed leadership of the Muslim League (later National Conference) in 1932." From www.thehindu.com/thehindu/2003/02/10/stories/2003021001500800.htm. From 1947 to 1948, Ayyangar served as minister without portfolio in the first cabinet under Jawaharlal Nehru. This was followed by his sojourn as minister of railways and transport from 1948 to 1952, and finally, he served as defence minister from 1952 to 1953.

destruction of Buddhist *ma. ṇi* walls. It is worth noting that in most of these letters these events were described in the language of rumor, not eyewitness accounts (e.g., "it is said that a group of Muslims"). But not all rumors reflected a purely antagonistic view of communal relations. In a rather condescending letter that was censored by the Ministry of State, the English missionary Norman Driver reported: "The Buddhists and Shia Mohammedans make an agreement about the future of Ladakh ... [to the effect] that if the Communists come and take over Ladakh then the Buddhists will protect the Shias from any harm. Should Ladakh go to Pakistan then the Shias will protect the Buddhists."

7.2   Geopolitics and Nationalism

Like the narrative of the nation at large, the story of Ladakh's first years of independence is often cast as a struggle among a handful of political actors à la Carlyle's "Great Men" of history. By framing the story as simply a rivalry between Sheikh Abdullah and Bakula Rinpoche – or even between federal, state, and regional political parties more broadly – historians overlook Partition's broader impact on Ladakh on the one hand and the region's rise to a position of great geopolitical importance on the other. With Partition and the Chinese invasion of Tibet, Ladakhis suddenly found their identities refracted through three political categories: Pakistan, India, and China. This political – and spatial – tension combined with longer and less noticeable trends spanning the decades before independence. The effect was a paradoxical one: Ladakh was simultaneously made more consequential to the political considerations of India and its neighbors, just as it found itself economically isolated.

Although Ladakh's Central Asian trade saw a dramatic surge following the Russian Revolution of 1917, it had steadily declined since the late 1920s (see Table 3.1). By 1940, the Resident in Kashmir had to conclude: "The Central Asian trade today is dead and not likely to revive in present world conditions."[33] An administrator in the External Affairs Department agreed: "The Central Asian trade, which is the fons et origo of the Treaty Road and the British Joint Commissioner arrangements, is, however, not at present a living issue, and it is difficult to forecast when it may revive."[34] This spelled a problem. "Due to its remoteness," Ladakh was "difficult enough to observe," the Resident

---

[33] NAI, External Affairs Department, 798-X, 1940. "Ladakh Affairs."
[34] NAI, External Affairs Department, 798-X, 1940. W. R. Hay (external affairs) to Fraser (Resident in Kashmir), dated August 21, 1940. "Ladakh Affairs."

feared; "with no contact at all it would remain a dangerous back door into India." The problem resurrected the old question of whether the British government of India should take over direct control of Ladakh in order to more closely oversee the frontier. It also raised the question of the role of the British Joint Commissioners in Leh.

Matters did not improve after independence. Bakula Rinpoche bemoaned the impact of the end of the Central Asian trade on Ladakh: "Due to the discontinuance and stoppage of caravan from Sikyang [sic]," he wrote, "wide spread [sic] unemployment had taken place, at the same-time [sic] the prices of article [sic] of daily consumption had gone very high." Since a "large number of people from Ladakh had trade connec-tions with Tibet," Bakula continued, "now due to the communists chines [sic] insertion in Tibet, it will be stopped also. In view of the rapid deterioration in economic conditions in Ladakh if no steps are being taken to give productive work a critical situation might develop."[35] In fact, trade had dwindled as a result of expanded infrastructure in Soviet Central Asia and a decline in demand for Central Asian goods in northern India. Hashish was being produced in high volume farther south of Ladakh in Kullu. Tea from north and northeast India had replaced Chinese "brick tea." Numerous attempts to mine precious stones and metals had yielded few results. And pashmina had become less fashionable.[36] The expansion of trade routes between Bengal and central Tibet and enhanced infrastructure across India further reduced demand for the high-cost items that had to slowly make their way southward from Central Asia or westward across the Tibetan Plateau. The decline in trade was also visible in the steady decline in the size of the annual Chaba and triennial Lopchak missions. The last Lopchak caravan to Lhasa departed Leh in 1950. It comprised only four traders.[37]

Besides trade the Indian government continued British policies of building information networks along the frontier. It reinforced British military posts across the region, developing its own "forward policy" in mirror of Britain's. The post-1947 government also quickly took an interest in the major trans-frontier roads in the northwestern Himalaya. Police check posts and a wireless station were established along the route of the Hindustan–Tibet Road, to provide better security along

---

[35] NAI, Ministry of States, 1951, 1-K/51. From Bakula, Head Lama of Ladakh, and Sonam Wangial, Representative for zamindars of Ladakh, to the Secretary for States Affairs.
[36] Zutshi, "Designed for Eternity."
[37] NAI, Ministry of States, 1951, No. 1(35)-K. "Arrival of the Choba Mission from Tibet to Leh"; Central Intelligence Agency, Information Report, "Ladakh (Kashmir)-Tibet Trade/Proposed Organization of 1950 Lobchag Mission."

the frontier "in view of recent developments in Tibet."[38] The communication afforded by the Hindustan–Tibet Road and the wireless stations
connecting the border posts near the Shipki pass into Tibet would help
"prevent the infiltration of undesirable elements into India from the
border of Tibet and China."[39] The terminus of the Hindustan–Tibet
Road remained one of the "chief means of contact between India and
Tibet," even if there were "many other tracks through which contact is
made with Tibet."[40]

The new Indian government knew that not all of this trade needed to
be highly regulated. As the deputy secretary of Home Affairs acknowledged, in light of "the fact that trade has been going on for over 2,000
years over the long Indo-Tibetan border and of the inconvenience which
is likely to be caused to Tibetans if they are required to obtain passports,
it has been decided that a passport system between India and Tibet
should not be strictly enforced."[41] Still, a "system of permits for entry
and stay and stay in India for Tibetans" would be introduced.

Movement across the frontier in Ladakh was excluded from these new
provisions, however. The relaxed permit system would "not be applicable
to Tibetans wishing to enter India via Ladakh." Since the entry "of such
persons in Ladakh" would "create problems of maintenance and accom-
modation" and would "not be free from security risk," it was decided that
"no person should at all be allowed to enter India by the Ladakh route."
To effect this restriction, wireless posts were established in 1951 at
Demchok, in eastern Ladakh on the route to Gartok and Lhasa, and at
Shyok in northern Ladakh along the old Treaty Road. The addition of
two wireless operators, twelve constables, two subinspectors, and an
inspector bolstered these military posts, which had been established
prior to independence along the two main routes across Ladakh.[42]

Most importantly, the government of India slowly came to perceive the
borderlessness they had inherited in the north as a problem. In 1950, the
Ministry of Defence and the Ministry of States together took steps to
correct those borderless maps. First, they established a committee "to

---

[38] NAI, Ministry of States, 17(34)-D, 1950. V. P. Menon from E. P. Moon, Chief
Commissioner Himachal Pradesh. "Security measures on the Indo-Tibetan Border in
Chini."
[39] NAI, Ministry of States, 17(34)-D, 1950. E. P. Moon to deputy sec. to Home Affairs.
"Security measures on the Indo-Tibetan Border in Chini."
[40] NAI.
[41] NAI. Secret. From Home Affairs to All State Governments and the Regional
Commissioners, dated December 26, 1950. Signed by Fateh Singh, Deputy Secretary
to the Government of India.
[42] NAI, Ministry of States, 17(34)-D. Secret. Ministry of Home Affairs to Principal
Secretary to the Government of J&K, January 6, 1951.

survey the whole field of defence of the North and North Eastern border from Ladakh to the Indo-Burma border."[43] Next, local government officials across the Himalaya were assigned to uncover "all administrative problems which have a bearing on the contentment and loyalty of the people inhabiting the border areas" and to determine "the arrangements which may be necessary in regard to Nepal, Bhutan and Sikkim."

The national committee comprised the Deputy Minister of Defence, top officials from the (renamed) Ministry of External Affairs, the Deputy Director of the Intelligence Bureau, and top military officials. They prepared "a questionnaire on the basis of their terms of reference for obtaining the views of and information from State Governments and other authorities concerned." The questionnaire led off with a series of questions regarding the location of the "existing boundaries with Tibet and Burma":[44] "Where are the existing boundaries with Tibet and Burma?" "Do you know of any boundary disputes?" "Is the boundary fixed by any agreement or is it customary?" "Is it defined or demarcated?"

The Jammu and Kashmir officials for Ladakh began their answers as follows:

Tibet is to the east of the Frontier District of Ladakh of the J&K State. The eastern boundary runs from Damchok in the south east-32.5 0 latitude and onwards to Changchenmo valley 34.5 0. Beyond that comes the Karakaram range. The regions of North above that are unexplored. The boundary is not fixed by any agreement nor is it defined or demarcated but the existing boundary, as it seems to be well understood on both sides. Under Art: 2 of the Treaty of 16th March, 1846, the eastern boundary was to be laid down by a commission to be appointed by the then British Government and the Ruler of the State and was to be defined in a separate Engagement after survey. This survey has not taken place. The boundary is therefore only customary. There is, however, a village inside Tibet known as Mensar which is under the sovereignty of the J&K State. The revenue of this village amounts to about Rs. 278/12/- and this revenue is payable to the State. This place is 8 stages from Damchok, the farthest south eastern point of the Frontier.[45]

This response glossed over a century's worth of British attempts to establish a suitable boundary, from 1846 to 1947. It also ignored the region's much more recent past, i.e., the decade-long dispute over Dokpo Karpo in the 1920s and the claims by western Tibetan officials that seminomads like Lha.rgyal ought to pay taxes. As for the second question regarding any known boundary disputes, the official replied simply that "there have been no boundary disputes so far."[46] After various other questions regarding the land, airfields near the border regions, the

[43] NAI, Ministry of States, 1951, 1-K/51.   [44] NAI.   [45] NAI.
[46] NAI, Ministry of States, 1951, 1-K/51.

"inhabitants of the borders," whether they have "any affinities, with any tribes on the other side of the border," and whether they were "primitive races," the survey concluded with "What is the extent of communist influence, if any?" The official again noted simply that there was none.

Addressing this last concern, the Ministry of States and the Army General Staff devised strategies to "draw" Ladakh closer to India.[47] Similar to strategies employed in the eastern Himalaya, these included supporting the suggestions made by Bakula Rinpoche and organizing a center for religious education in Leh, obviating the need for Ladakhi Buddhist monks to go to Tibet for education.[48] "The continuation of the religious education and the Lamas at LHASA is not desirable as the Communists are adept in indoctrinating personnel with their ideology." Furthermore, "the Lamas should be encouraged to visit their holy places in INDIA, as opposed to those in TIBET." Finally, the "construction of a 15-Cwt [hundredweight] road between LEH and KARGIL" would provide the military with a better means of moving personnel and materiel, as well as providing Ladakhis with smoother internal "communication." This strategy would help address the rumors that traders arriving from Western Tibet were "carrying out propaganda to enhance the reputation of the CHINESE Communists, who are now in effective occupation of TIBET."[49] This propaganda apparently included a text in Bodhi script of the coerced "Seventeen Point Agreement for the Peaceful Liberation of Tibet," signed in 1951, affirming Chinese sovereignty over Tibet.

7.3   Conclusion: The (Postcolonial) Frontier Complex

By the late 1950s, optimism in India over the Panchsheel ("five virtues") Treaty and overtures to promote Sino-Indian brotherhood ("*Hindī-Cīnī bhā'ī- bhā'ī*") had faded.[50] The 1954 treaty that asserted mutual respect between China and India on issues of territorial integrity and sovereignty wrongly assumed that the two sides shared the same idea about those territories. That same year the government of India revised its official maps that showed "undemarcated" or "undefined" borders in

---

[47] NAI, Ministry of States, 1952, 19(12) K/ 52 (Secret).
[48] For an account of the strategies India and China employed in the eastern Himalaya to court local populations, see Réchard, *Shadow States*.
[49] NAI.
[50] Literally translated as "Indian-Chinese brother-brother," the term was used to refer to the Indian government's post-independence assertion of a long-standing historical connection and growing brotherhood between the two countries, underscored by the 1954 Panchsheel Treaty.

Ladakh to draw a definite border, a composite of the Johnson Line of 1865 and the 1899 Macartney–MacDonald Line, based on no additional surveying or demarcation.[51] This was, in Jawaharlal Nehru's estimate, the simplest way of dealing with the continued borderlessness inherited from the British across much of the Himalaya.[52] But when Bakula Rinpoche visited Western Tibet in the summer of 1957, he reported back that the Chinese military had been constructing a road across the uninhabited Aksai Chin plateau, connecting Xinjiang and Tibet. Sino-Indian relations were made even worse when, in 1959, India received the Dalai Lama, who had fled an uprising in Lhasa and was subsequently followed into exile by nearly 100,000 Tibetans. Then, a series of incidents between Indian and Chinese soldiers and officials in the northwestern and northeastern Himalaya began to push Indian public opinion against China. In 1960, Nehru and his Chinese counterpart Zhou Enlai held meetings in an attempt to de-escalate tensions, but these ended when China and India failed to agree on the major watershed that defined the boundary in the western sector. Indian claims clung to the major watersheds of the Himalaya, while China's did not.[53] War broke out in October 1962.[54]

The Henderson Brooks-Bhagat Report written after the war noted that the Army General Staff had failed to apprise the government of the inability to effectively support a "forward policy" in Ladakh and the North-East Frontier Agency (NEFA), a policy largely inherited from the British. This top-secret report, one that the Indian government still refuses to release, suggested that the war was hardly a case of a pure Chinese aggression.[55] The month-long war ended with a Chinese unilateral cease-fire and the establishment of the "Line of Actual Control" (LAC) that more or less exists today. China won the war on the ground, but it undoubtedly lost in the fight for world opinion.

Two months after the war's end, on Republic Day 1963, Lata Mangeshkar brought Nehru and many others to tears singing for

---

[51] Lamb, *The Sino-Indian Border in Ladakh*, 70.   [52] Maxwell, *India's China War*, xii.

[53] See Woodman, *Himalayan Frontiers*.

[54] It is well beyond the scope of this book to do justice to the complex history leading up to the Sino-Indian War. See, for instance, Lamb, *The China-India Border*; Alastair Lamb, *Asian Frontiers: Studies in a Continuing Problem* (New York: Frederick A. Raeger, 1968) and *The Sino-Indian Border in Ladakh* (Canberra: Australian National University Press, 1973); Fisher, Rose, and Huttenback, *Himalayan Battleground*; Woodman, *Himalayan Frontiers*; Maxwell, *India's China War*; John Lall, *Aksaichin and Sino-Indian Conflict* (Ahmedabad: Allied, 1989); Guyot-Réchard, *Shadow States*.

[55] The first volume of the report was recently published on the personal website of the Australian journalist Neville Maxwell, who had used much of the leaked document to write his 1970 book, *India's China War*.

the first time "Aye Mere Watan Ke Lōgon" ("Oh, People of My Country"):

When the Himalaya was injured and our freedom was threatened, they fought right to the end and then they laid down their bodies ... some were Sikh, some Jath, and some Maratha, some were Gurkhas and some Madrasi. But each brave man who died on the border was an Indian, the blood shed on the mountains, that blood was Indian.[56]

The mountainous Himalayan border (*sarhad*) was made Indian by the spilling of blood on it. The border was now something to give one's life for. This national consecration of the frontline of India added to policies that sought to establish a fixed and inviolable sense of national territory. A year earlier, for instance, as India annexed the Portuguese colony of Goa, Nehru had "made it a crime to question the territorial integrity of India."[57]

The Sino-Indian War of 1962 marked the first time that a border was effectively established on the ground in the northwestern (as well as the northeastern) Himalaya.[58] This "Line of Actual Control" (LAC) – distinguished from the "Line of Control" (LOC) to the west, which ran through Pakistan- and Indian-administered Kashmir – has been a source of tension ever since. In summer 2017, a months-long standoff at the Doklam plateau in the Central Himalaya and a particularly violent clash between Chinese and Indian soldiers along the banks of Pangong Lake in Ladakh threatened to escalate into a border war between these two nuclear powers—a pattern repeated on a larger and deadlier scale in the late spring and summer of 2020. Uncertain borderlines and the insistence on territorial inviolability were once again to blame. The power held by these spatial-political ideas radiates far beyond the sparsely populated and mountainous regions involved. The Himalaya continues to play a twofold role, both as a defensive wall and a potentially dangerous conduit at the center of a decades-long Sino-Indian standoff. Indian representations of the border dispute often paint China as the aggressor, even while acknowledging possibilities of reconciliation between the two countries.

---

[56] "*jab ghāyal huā himālaya, khatre men paḍī āzādī, Jab tak thī sāns laḍe woh, phir apnī lāsh bichha dī, ... koī Sikh koī Jāṭ Maraṭha, koi Gurkha koī Madarāsī, sarhad par marnevāla har vīr thā bhāratvāsī, jo khūn gīrā parvat par, wah khūn thā Hindustānī.*" My translation.

[57] Pankaj Mishra, "India at 70, and the Passing of Another Illusion," *New York Times*, August 11, 2017.

[58] For the history of the northeastern Himalayan border and the McMahon Line, see Lamb, *The McMahon Line*, vol. 2.

Epilogue

By the time of independence in 1947, the Himalayan region had been a vast laboratory for border making for nearly a century. But the experiments often yielded unexpected and unsatisfactory results. Instead of generating solutions to transform a vague frontier into a clear and legible border, the complex of border-making practices and ideas developed by colonial administrators and experts frequently failed to account for the dynamism of the Himalayas themselves and the people who moved through this vast complex of mountains. Their geological complexity challenged geographers' assumptions that watersheds neatly aligned with mountain ranges, and their scale challenged surveyors' ability to comprehensively record them. Like the complex perpendicular spurs running off the central Himalayan range, political space failed to follow neatly mapped borderlines. And the historical movement of peoples, animals, and goods challenged the colonial state's ability to regulate movement at its territorial edges. Although the precolonial modes of seeing space outlined in the first chapter did not disappear, they became detached from and subordinated to the political view of Ladakh as a single, solid, bounded territory – a territory now appended to the periphery of a massive state, not a historical entrepôt connecting vast swathes of people.

While the British Empire approached its frontiers as spaces to manage in different ways, the Indian nation-state's insistence on an absolute, sovereign space precluded any territorial ambiguity. Yet even after war in 1962 produced the first effective borderlines in the Himalaya, they remained porous and overlapping, and among the inhabitants there the Indian and Chinese "shadow states" vied for approval.[1] But in the desolate Aksai Chin, "where not even a blade of grass grows," the fight

---

[1] Guyot-Réchard, *Shadow States*. Deriving her title from the Westminster political system's use of an opposing "shadow cabinet" offering a "viable *alternative* political project," Guyot-Réchard argues that in the eastern Himalaya, "China and India see themselves as each other's 'shadow state'."

remained first and foremost about a line on a map representing a region that few had ever set foot on.[2]

Unlike these newly minted postcolonial "lines of control," other sorts of border points have long been accepted in the Himalaya. Typically located on established trade and pilgrimage routes, these points signaled seasonal customs duties to be paid or *corvée* labor to be given. A complete borderline through such mountainous country came into political play only when maps and geographically based logics began to hold greater authority as tools of territorial control. This authority can be seen in the evolving colonial concept of the ideal border – a concept based on "natural" principles, implemented by scientifically sound practices, and represented on increasingly classified maps, as well as in systematic manuals of governance such as the district-level gazetteers. Yet these geographical principles and practices ultimately produced more problems than solutions. No proposed line succeeded in establishing a border until the unilateral Chinese cease-fire on November 21, 1962.

The vast space of the uninhabited and inhospitable Aksai Chin was thus anything but empty. It became an intimate part of the spatial self-conception of India, though it has become a specific *place* only to the unfortunate soldiers tasked with maintaining a presence there. In this sense, then, the region remains a utopia (literally: "no place"), a spatial idea off-limits to all but a few military personnel but highly visible in the geospatial imaginary of India.

Rendered on maps that no longer showed indeterminate borderlessness, the region that once formed the center of a vast cultural and commercial network had become, at the end of 1962, a borderland by virtue of an imposed de facto borderline. Despite repeated attempts to articulate a precise, scientific rationale based on the Indus watershed, the "Line of Actual Control" reflects no particular geographical principle. No linear path had led to this outcome, only a series of ideas of how peripheral political space ought to be organized according to the natural features of the region. While rather futile in shaping the Line of Actual Control, these ideas were potent in shaping a worldview of international politics as a competition between abutting territories determined by, and dependent on, geography. It is one of the great ironies of the history of frontiers and border making: that the mountainous laboratory which seemed to offer such a clear way to define a rational and natural frontier should instead consistently fail to do so. Holdich's "finest natural combination of boundary and barrier" had proven to be anything but.[3]

---

[2] Palat, *Selected Works of Jawaharlal Nehru* 52 (September 1–30, 1959), 186.
[3] Holdich, *Political Frontiers and Boundary Making*, 280.

If the shift from empire to nation-state signals a major shift in the claims on territory, it also revealed telling continuities. By placing mountainous, sparsely populated, and increasingly peripheral spaces like Ladakh and the North-East Frontier Agency at the frontline of government policy, the Indian government was building on established imperial practices.

First, it still deemed borders to be a *sine qua non* of territory. The border, with its security risks and threats of foreign penetration, became a frontline. As the outline of the geo-body of the nascent independent state, the borders it claimed quickly became tied to swelling Indian nationalism. Unlike the managed frontiers of the British Empire, the borders of the nation-state were essential constitutive elements of the nation-state. Borders became something to die for. The violation of the geo-body of India at two remote Himalayan extremities in the Sino-Indian War had a deep impact on India's sense of nation. It is often said in India that Nehru died in 1964 of a broken heart over India's humiliating loss of territory to China.

Second, the geopolitical calculus that brought Ladakh to Nehru's attention was the product of decades of oscillation between acute concern and neglect. By the end of the nineteenth century, individual frontiers had become integrated – in policy rhetoric at least – into a single "frontier policy." But in practice the northern border of India received attention in response to particular events: some bureaucratic, others political. Administrators like the British Joint Commissioners promoted hopes of increased trade through road building, while the intelligence they collected generated fears of a too-porous frontier. Repositories of colonial knowledge like the gazetteers raised concerns about preexisting political relations and the problems associated with tribute. Finally, the trans-frontier movement of people gave regular reminders of how incomplete and inadequate were the measures to control the frontier.

Much of this continued after independence. Gazetteers continued to be one of the principal information tools of district- and state-level governance. Border roads became so explicitly tied to security concerns that they are now exclusively managed by a branch of the Indian Ministry of Defense: the Border Roads Organization. Border maps are still highly regulated. Thus, for decades India has used practices inherited from the colonial era as the basis of its approach to its borders.

Following the People's Republic of China's consolidation of control in Tibet in the 1950s, pressure mounted on both countries to define and occupy the inherited frontier. Since 1962, both India and China have invested huge military resources to assure that this desolate region, once only crossed by traders and pilgrims, is now occupied by thousands of soldiers facing off across a line whose only warrant lies in vague colonial descriptions from a series of equally vague maps. Today, taken as a fractured whole, Ladakh and the former state of Jammu and Kashmir represent one of the most militarized spaces in the world – "the vulnerable neck and head of India," as one political commentator recently put it.[4] This body metaphor is particularly telling considering how prominently maps have come to represent the geo-body of nations and how frequently Partition is described in the language of amputation.

At the regional level, the religiously based communalism that emerged in Ladakh after 1947, and that has washed over the subcontinent in subsequent decades, has become a cornerstone of Ladakhi politics. By 1990, this tension had boiled over into open rioting. At the "National Convention on the Ladakh Issue in New Delhi" in March of that year, Thupstan Chhewang, the president of the Ladakhi Buddhist Association, tried to explain why: "The State of Jammu and Kashmir, the territorial limits of which never formed a natural geopolitical entity in its real sense, still suffers from geopolitical crisis and disorder." He invoked communal identity as well as the narrative of a fractured "crossroads of High Asia": "In the last fortytwo [sic] years of Independence we, the people of Ladakh, not only have suffered rampant Kashmiri political domination but also strained under [the] severe drive of separatism. Besides, the four major wars waged by both Pakistan and China, completely shattered our indigenous economic and social strength."[5]

This posed a potent revision to the post-independence history of the region. The long, slow erosion of Central Asian trade that preceded independence and the attempts by the colonial government to regulate and restrict trans-frontier movement were overlooked in favor of a more cataclysmic, contemporary, and patriotic narrative. In this revision, Ladakh's isolation was the result of aggressive wars fought by China and Pakistan against India. The British imperial legacies undergirding those conflicts were ignored. The one imperial legacy that Ladakhi politicians still invoked was that of continued subjugation under a foreign conqueror. Now that conqueror was not British but the predominantly Kashmiri Muslim government that replaced the Hindu Dogra dynasty which had ruled over Ladakh, under the British, for a century prior to independence.

"In modern times," Thupstan Chhewang elaborated, Ladakh was like India and Kashmir like the British in the imperial era:

---

[4] Saba Naqvi, "One Point Five/Two: Jharkhand Has Been Mined, Jammu-Kashmir Is Still a Prospect," *Outlook*, January 12, 2015, 18.

[5] NMML, Thupstan Chhewang, President, Buddhist Association, "National Convention on the Ladakh Issue," New Delhi, March 18, 1990.

when the whole subcontinent has passed through the process of decolonization to enjoy the fruits of national independence, we, the people of Ladakh and our land still continue to be left under the old concept of colonial administrative structure, which suited the imperial interests and feudal rulers, under the name of the pseudo-State of Jammu and Kashmir. Gandhiji and other Indian national leaders emancipated the Indian masses from the oppressive alien domination, exploitation, feudal and colonial rule. But we, the people of Ladakh, with a distinct identity of our own have been pushed under an oppressive political domination of Kashmiris, and denied the fruits of freedom and national independence.

The dissatisfaction expressed by Chhewang was addressed on August 5, 2019, when the Indian government led by Narendra Modi revoked the special constitutional status of Jammu and Kashmir, allowing Ladakh to become a union territory on October 31, 2019.[6] The bifurcation of the state of Jammu and Kashmir pleased many in Ladakh's Buddhist community, who had long advocated for greater autonomy from the state government. Now administered on behalf of the central government without an elected assembly, the Modi government's decision also unwittingly achieved the direct rule of the region long desired by imperial frontier experts. What replacing Srinagar with New Delhi will mean for the people of Ladakh remains uncertain.

Along with the shadow of imperial political subjugation, Ladakh has become a part of a spatial idea of India rooted in a colonial-era frontier complex. The circulation of its maps remains highly restricted, if not outright prohibited. Frontier roads have been taken over by the military and are seen as key weapons in the arsenal to combat Chinese road building in Tibet and Xinjiang. In government and military rhetoric, borders are still "the razor's edge on which hang suspended the modern issues of war or peace, of life or death to nations."[7] To take Curzon's rather strange metaphor seriously for a moment, it is worth asking whether anything can actually remain suspended on a razor. Rather, a border's razor-like quality might rest on its potential to sever and divide – and, in so doing, to isolate space. The ability to impose a line of control remains among the strongest weapons available in the political arsenal of the modern state.

---

[6] Niha Masih, "India Revokes Special Status of Kashmir, Putting Tense Region on Edge," *The Washington Post*, August 5, 2019.
[7] Curzon, *Frontiers*, 7.

Archives

India

Centre for Research on Ladakh (CRL)
Jammu & Kashmir State Archives – Jammu Branch (JKSA-J)
Jammu & Kashmir State Archives – Leh Branch (JKSA-L)
Jammu & Kashmir State Archives – Srinagar Branch (JKSA-S)
Himachal Pradesh State Archives – Shimla Branch (HPSA-S)
Himalayan Club Library, India International Centre Library, Delhi (HCL)
Indian Institute for Advanced Study Library, Shimla (IIAS)
National Archives of India (NAI)
Nehru Memorial Museum and Library, Delhi (NMML)

United Kingdom

India Office Records, British Library, London (IOR)
National Archives of the United Kingdom (NAUK)
Royal Geographical Society, London (RGS)

United States

Berthold Laufer Collection, Field Museum, Chicago

Bibliography

Addy, Premen. *Tibet on the Imperial Chessboard: The Making of British Policy towards Lhasa, 1899–1925.* Calcutta: Academic, 1984.

Aggarwal, Ravina. "From Mixed Strains of Barley Grain: Person and Place in a Ladakhi Village." Dissertation, Indiana University, 1994.

"From Utopia to Heterotopia: Toward an Anthropology of Ladakh." In *Recent Research on Ladakh 6*, edited by Henry Osmaston and Nawang Tsering, 21–28. Bristol, UK: University of Bristol, 1997.

Ahmed, Manan. "Adam's Mirror: The Frontier in the Imperial Imagination." *Economic and Political Weekly* 46, no. 13 (2011): 60–65.

Aitchison, C. U., ed. *A Collection of Treaties, Engagements, and Sanads, Relating to India and Neighbouring Countries.* Vol. 9. Calcutta: Office of the Superintendent of the Government Printing, India, 1892.

ed. *A Collection of Treaties, Engagements, and Sunnuds, Relating to India and Neighbouring Countries.* Vol. 2. Calcutta: Bengal Printing Company, 1863.

Alam, Aniket. *Becoming India: Western Himalayas under British Rule.* Delhi: Foundation Books, 2008.

Alam, Muzaffar. "Trade, State Policy and Regional Change: Aspects of Mughal–Uzbek Commercial Relations, C. 1550–1750." *Journal of the Economic and Social History of the Orient* 37, no. 3 (1994): 202–27.

Alavi, Seema. "'Fugitive Mullahs and Outlawed Fanatics': Indian Muslims in Nineteenth Century Trans-Asiatic Imperial Rivalries." *Modern Asian Studies* 45, no. 6 (2011): 1337–82.

Albritton Jonsson, Fredrik. *Enlightenment's Frontier: The Scottish Highlands and the Origins of Environmentalism.* New Haven, CT: Yale University Press, 2013.

Alder, G. J. *British India's Northern Frontier: A Study of Imperial Policy.* London: Longmans, Green, 1963.

"Standing Alone: William Moorcroft Plays the Great Game, 1808–1825." *International History Review* 2, no. 2 (1980): 172–215.

Amato, Joseph A. *On Foot: A History of Walking.* New York: New York University Press, 2004.

Anderson, Benedict. *Imagined Communities: Reflections on the Origin and Spread of Nationalism.* London: Verso, 1983.

Army Headquarters, India, Chief of Staff's Division. *A Study of the Existing Strategical Conditions on the North-West Frontier.* Simla: Government Central Branch Press, 1909.

Arnold, David. *Colonizing the Body.* Berkeley: University of California Press, 1993.

Atkinson, Edwin T. *The Himalayan Districts of the North-Western Provinces of India.* Allahabad: North-western Provinces' Government Press, 1882.

Atwill, David G. "Boundaries of Belonging: Sino-Indian Relations and the 1960 Tibetan Muslim Incident." *The Journal of Asian Studies* 75, no. 3 (2016): 595–620.

Islamic Shangri-La: Inter-Asian Relations and Lhasa's Muslim Communities, 1600 to 1960. Oakland: University of California Press, 2018.

Ballantyne, Tony. "Colonial Knowledge." In *The British Empire: Themes and Perspectives*, edited by Sarah Stockwell, 177–97. Malden, MA: Blackwell, 2008.

Banerji, Arup. *Old Routes: North Indian Nomads and Bankers in Afghan, Uzbek and Russian Lands.* Gurgaon: Three Essays Collective, 2011.

Barbier, Edward B. *Scarcity and Frontiers: How Economies Have Developed through Natural Resource Exploitation.* Cambridge: Cambridge University Press, 2011.

Barrow, Ian J. *Making History, Drawing Territory: British Mapping in India, c. 1756–1905.* New Delhi: Oxford University Press, 2003.

Baud, Michiel, and Willem van Schendel. "Toward a Comparative History of Borderlands." *Journal of World History* 8, no. 2 (1997): 211–42.

Bayly, C. A. *Empire and Information: Intelligence Gathering and Social Communication in India, 1780–1870.* Cambridge: Cambridge University Press, 1996.

The Birth of the Modern World, 1780–1914. Oxford: Blackwell, 2004.

Bayly, Martin J. *Taming the Imperial Imagination: Colonial Knowledge, International Relations, and the Anglo-Afghan Encounter, 1808–1878.* Cambridge: Cambridge University Press, 2016.

Bell, Charles. *Portrait of the Dalai Lama.* London: Collins, 1946.

Benton, Lauren A. *A Search for Sovereignty: Law and Geography in European Empires, 1400–1900.* Cambridge: Cambridge University Press, 2010.

Bernier, François. *Voyages de François Bernier, Contenant la Description des États du Grand Mogol, de l'Indoustan, du Royaume de Cachemire, etc.* Vol. 1. Paris: Imprimé aux frais du gouvernement, 1830.

Beverley, Eric Lewis. *Hyderabad, British India, and the World: Muslim Networks and Minor Sovereignty, c. 1850–1950.* Cambridge: Cambridge University Press, 2015.

Bhattacharya, Neeladri. "Predicaments of Mobility: Peddlers and Itinerants in Nineteenth Century Northwestern India." In *Society and Circulation: Mobile People and Itinerant Cultures in South Asia, 1750–1950*, edited by Claude Markovits, Jacques Pouchepadass, and Sanjay Subrahmanyam, 163–214. Delhi: Permanent Black, 2003.

Bishop, Peter. *The Myth of Shangri-La: Tibet, Travel Writing and the Western Creation of Sacred Landscape.* Berkeley: University of California Press, 1989.

Blouet, Brian W. *Geopolitics and Globalization in the Twentieth Century.* London: Reaktion, 2001.

Bray, John. "Corvée Transport Labour in 19th and Early 20th Century Ladakh: A Study in Continuity and Change." In *Modern Ladakh: Anthropological Perspectives on Continuity and Change*, edited by Martijn van Beek and

Fernanda Pirie, 43–66. Brill's Tibetan Studies Library 20. Leiden: Brill, 2008.

"Dr Henry Cayley in Ladakh: Medicine, Trade and Diplomacy on India's Northern Frontier." In *Tibetan and Himalayan Healing – An Anthology for Anthony Aris*, edited by Charles Ramble and Ulrike Roesler, 81–95. Kathmandu: Vajra Books, 2015.

"Introduction: Locating Ladakhi History." In *Ladakhi Histories: Local and Regional Perspectives*, edited by John Bray, 1–30. Brill's Tibetan Studies Library 9. Leiden: Brill, 2005.

"Ladakh's Lopchak Missions to Lhasa: Gift Exchange, Diplomatic Ritual, and the Politics of Ambiguity." In *Commerce and Communities: Social Status and the Exchange of Goods in Tibetan Societies*, edited by Jeannine Bischoff and Alice Travers. Berlin: EB, 2018.

"The Lapchak Mission from Leh to Lhasa in British Indian Foreign Policy." *Tibet Journal* 15, no. 4 (1990): 75–96.

Brewer, John. *The Sinews of Power: War, Money and the English State, 1688–1783.* Cambridge, MA: Harvard University Press, 1988.

Brooke, Richard. *The General Gazetteer, or, Compendious Geographical Dictionary Containing a Description of All the Empires Kingdoms, States, Republics, Provinces, Cities, Chief Towns, Forts, Fortresses, Castles, Citadels, Seas, Harbours, Bays, Rivers, Lakes, Mountains, Capes, and Promontories in the Known World; Together with the Government, Policy, Customs, Manners, and Religion of the Inhabitants; the Extent, Bounds, and Natural Productions of Each Country; and the Trade, Manufactures, and Curiosities of the Cities and Towns; Their Longitude, Latitude, Bearing and Distances in English Miles from Remarkable Places; as Also, the Sieges They Have Undergone, and the Battles That Have Been Fought near Them, down to This Present Year: Including, an Authentic Account of the Counties, Cities and Market-Towns in England and Wales; as Also the Villages with Fairs, the Days on Which They Are Kept According to the New Stile; as Well as the Cattle, Goods and Merchandises That Are Sold Thereat.* London: J. Newbery, 1762.

Brown, Wendy. *Walled States, Waning Sovereignty.* New York: Zone Books, 2010.

Browning, Robert. "Bishop Blougram's Apology." In *Browning's Men and Women, 1855*, 141. Oxford: Clarendon Press, 1911.

Brzezinski, Zbigniew. *The Grand Chessboard: American Primacy and Its Geostrategic Imperatives.* New York: Basic Books, 1997.

Buchan, John. *A Book of Escapes and Hurried Journeys.* Boston: Houghton Mifflin, 1923.

Burnett, D. Graham. *Masters of All They Surveyed: Exploration, Geography, and a British El Dorado.* Chicago: University of Chicago Press, 2000.

Candler, Edmund. *The Unveiling of Lhasa.* London: Arnold, 1905.

Caroe, Olaf. *The Pathans: 550 B.C.–A.D. 1957.* London: Macmillan, 1958.

Soviet Empire: The Turks of Central Asia and Stalinism. London: Macmillan, 1953.

Carrington, Michael. "Officers, Gentlemen and Thieves: The Looting of Monasteries during the 1903/4 Younghusband Mission to Tibet." *Modern Asian Studies* 37, no. 1 (2003): 81–109.

Carroll, Patrick. *Science, Culture and Modern State Formation*. Berkeley: University of California Press, 2006.

Casey, Edward S. *The Fate of Place: A Philosophical History*. Berkeley: University of California Press, 2013.

Cederlof, Gunnel. *Founding an Empire on India's North-Eastern Frontiers, 1790–1840: Climate, Commerce, Polity*. Oxford: Oxford University Press, 2014.

Central Intelligence Agency. "Information Report, Ladakh (Kashmir)–Tibet Trade/Proposed Organization of 1950 Lobchag Mission." November 7, 1952. www.cia.gov/library/readingroom/docs/CIA-RDP82-00047R000200 130008-6.pdf.

Certeau, Michel de. *The Practice of Everyday Life*. Berkeley: University of California Press, 1984.

Chakrabarty, Dipesh. "The Birth of Academic Historical Writing in India." In *The Oxford History of Historical Writing: Vol. 4. 1800–1945*, 520–36. Oxford: Oxford University Press, 2011.

Charak, Sukhdev Singh, trans. *Gulabnama of Diwan Kirpa Ram: A History of Maharaja Gulab Singh of Jammu and Kashmir*. New Delhi: Light and Life, 1977.

Chatterji, Joya. *Bengal Divided: Hindu Communalism and Partition, 1932–1947*. Cambridge: Cambridge University Press, 1994.

"The Fashioning of a Frontier: The Radcliffe Line and Bengal's Border Landscape, 1947–52." *Modern Asian Studies* 33, no. 1 (1999): 185–242.

Ch'en, Jerome. *Yuan Shih-k'ai*. Stanford: Stanford University Press, 1972.

Chester, Lucy. "The 1947 Partition: Drawing the Indo-Pakistani Boundary." *American Diplomacy* 7, no. 1 (2002).

Cohn, Bernard S. *An Anthropologist among the Historians and Other Essays*. Delhi: Oxford University Press, 1987.

Colonialism and Its Forms of Knowledge: The British in India. Princeton, NJ: Princeton University Press, 1996.

"Regions Subjective and Objective: Their Relation to the Study of Modern Indian History and Society." In *An Anthropologist among the Historians and Other Essays*, 100–135. New Delhi: Oxford University Press, 1987.

Crook, John H. "The History of Zangskar." In *Himalayan Buddhist Villages*, 435–74. Bristol, UK: University of Bristol, 1994.

Cruttwell, Clement. *A Gazetteer of France: Containing Every City, Town, and Village in That Extensive Country … / Illustrated with a Map Divided into Departments*. London: Printed for G. G. J. and J. Robinson, 1793.

Cunningham, Alexander. *Ladák, Physical, Statistical, and Historical; with Notices of the Surrounding Countries*. London: W. H. Allen, 1854.

Curzon, George N. *Frontiers*. Oxford: Clarendon Press, 1908.

"The 'Scientific Frontier' an Accomplished Fact." *Nineteenth Century* 23, no. 136 (1888): 900–917.

Dalrymple, William. *White Mughals: Love and Betrayal in Eighteenth-Century India*. London: Viking, 2002.

Das, Sarat Chandra. *Indian Pandits in the Land of Snow*. Calcutta: Baptist Mission Press, 1893.

Daston, Lorraine, and Peter Galison. *Objectivity*. New York: Zone Books, 2007.

Datta, C. L. *Ladakh and Western Himalayan Politics: 1819–1848. The Dogra Conquest of Ladakh, Baltistan and West Tibet and Reactions of Other Powers.* New Delhi: Mushiram Manoharlal, 1973.

Debarbieux, Bernard, and Gilles Rudaz. *The Mountain: A Political History from the Enlightenment to the Present.* Chicago: University of Chicago Press, 2015.

Demenge, Jonathan. "The Political Ecology of Road Construction in Ladakh." University of Sussex, 2011.

Description de L'Egypte, Ou Recueil des Observations et des Recherches Qui Ont Été Faites en Egypte Pendant l'Expédition de l'Armée Française. 36 vols. Paris, 1821.

Desideri, Ippolito. *An Account of Tibet: The Travels of Ippolito Desideri of Pistoia.* Edited by Filippo de Filippi. London: George Routledge & Sons, 1937.

Dhondup, K. *The Water-Bird and Other Years: A History of the Thirteenth Dalai Lama and After.* New Delhi: Rangwang, 1986.

Diener, Alexander C., and Joshua Hagen, eds. *Borderlines and Borderlands: Political Oddities at the Edge of the Nation-State.* Plymouth, UK: Rowman & Littlefield, 2010.

Dirks, Nicholas B. *Castes of Mind: Colonialism and the Making of Modern India.* Princeton, NJ: Princeton University Press, 2011.

Dodds, Klaus, and James Sidaway. "Halford Mackinder and the 'Geographical Pivot of History': A Centennial Retrospective." *The Geographical Journal* 170, no. 4 (2004): 292–97.

Dowman, Keith, and Sonam Paljor, trans. *The Divine Madman: The Sublime Life and Songs of Drukpa Kunley.* Varanasi: Pilgrims, 2000.

Drage, Geoffrey. *Russian Affairs.* 2nd ed. London: John Murray, 1904.

Drew, Frederic. *The Jummoo and Kashmir Territories: A Geographical Account.* London: E. Stanford, 1875.

Dzuvichu, Lipokmar. "Roads and the Raj: The Politics of Road Building in Colonial Naga Hills, 1860s–1910s." *Indian Economic and Social History Review* 50, no. 473 (2013): 473–94.

Eck, Diana L. *India: A Sacred Geography.* New York: Harmony Books, 2012.

Edney, Matthew H. *Mapping an Empire: The Geographical Construction of British India, 1765–1843.* Chicago: University of Chicago Press, 1997.

Elden, Stuart. "Territory without Borders." *Harvard International Review*, 2011. http://hir.harvard.edu/article/?a=2843.

The Birth of Territory. Chicago: University of Chicago Press, 2015.

Elias, Ney, ed. *The Tarikh-i-Rashidi of Mirza Muhammad Haider, Dughlát: A History of the Moghuls of Central Asia.* Translated by E. Denison Ross. London: Sampson Low, Marston, 1895.

Elphinstone, Mountstuart. *An Account of the Kingdom of Caubul, and Its Dependencies in Persia, Tartary, and India; Comprising a View of the Afghaun Nation, and a History of the Doorauneeo Monarchy.* 2 vols. London: Longman, Hurst, Rees, Orme, and Brown, 1815.

Emmett, Robert C. "The Gazetteers of India: Their Origins and Development during the Nineteenth Century." MA thesis, University of Chicago, 1976.

Epperson, Bruce D. *Roads through the Everglades: The Building of the Ingraham Highway, the Tamiami Trail and Conners Highway, 1914–1931.* Jefferson, NC: McFarland, 2016.

Farwell, Byron. *Queen Victoria's Little Wars*. New York: Harper & Row, 1972.

Febvre, Lucien. "Frontière: The Word and the Concept." In *A New Kind of History: From the Writings of Lucien Febvre*, edited by Peter Burke, 208–18. New York: Harper Torchbooks, 1973.

Fisher, Margaret W., Leo E. Rose, and Robert A. Huttenback. *Himalayan Battleground: Sino-Indian Rivalry in Ladakh*. New York: Praeger, 1963.

Foucault, Michel. "Des Espace Autres" [Of Other Spaces]. *Architecture, Mouvement, Continuité* 5 (1984): 46–49.

Les Mots et les choses: une archeology des sciences humaines. Paris: Gallimard, 1966.

Security, Territory, Population: Lectures at the Collège de France, 1977–78. Translated by Graham Burchell. New York: Picador, 2007.

The Archaeology of Knowledge. New York: Harper Torchbooks, 1972.

Francke, August Hermann, trans. and ed. "La.dwags rGyal.rabs." In *Antiquities of Indian Tibet*, vol. 2, 19–59. Calcutta: Superintendent Government Printing, India, 1914.

French, Patrick. *Younghusband: The Last Great Imperial Adventurer*. London: HarperCollins, 1994.

Freshfield, Douglas W. "The Roads to Tibet." *The Geographical Journal* 23, no. 1 (1904): 79–91.

"Tibet. I. Notes from Tibet." *The Geographical Journal* 23, no. 3 (1904): 361–66.

"Frontiers in Theory and Practice." *The Geographical Journal* 49, no. 1 (1917): 58–61.

Fuoli, Francesca. "Incorporating North-Western Afghanistan into the British Empire: Experiments in Indirect Rule through the Making of an Imperial Frontier, 1884–87." *Afghanistan* 1, no. 1 (2018): 4–25.

Gardner, Kyle. "Elphinstone, Geography, and the Specter of Afghanistan in the Himalaya." In *Mountstuart Elphinstone in South Asia: Pioneer of British Colonial Rule*, 205–21. London: Hurst, 2018.

"Moving Watersheds, Borderless Maps, and Imperial Geography in India's Northwestern Himalaya." *The Historical Journal* 62, no. 1 (2019): 149–70.

"Review of Kailas Histories: Renunciate Traditions and the Construction of Himalayan Sacred Geography, by Alex McKay." *Bulletin of the School of Oriental and African Studies* 79, no. 3 (2016): 677–79.

"The Ready Materials for Another World: Frontier, Security, and the Hindustan-Tibet Road in the Nineteenth Century Northwestern Himalaya." *Himalaya, the Journal of the Association for Nepal and Himalayan Studies* 33, nos. 1–2 (2013): 71–84.

Gill, Bir Good. "The Venture of the Central Asian Trading Company in Eastern Turkistan, 1874–5." *Asian Affairs* 31, no. 2 (2000): 181–88.

Gilmartin, David. *Blood and Water: The Indus River Basin in Modern History*. Berkeley: University of California Press, 2015.

"Scientific Empire and Imperial Science: Colonialism and Irrigation Technology in the Indus Basin." *The Journal of Asian Studies* 53, no. 4 (1994): 1127–49.

Gommans, Jos. "The Silent Frontier of South Asia, c. AD 1100–1800." *Journal of World History* 9, no. 1 (1998): 1–23.

Grove, Richard H. *Green Imperialism: Colonial Expansion, Tropical Island Edens, and the Origins of Environmentalism, 1600–1860*. Cambridge: Cambridge University Press, 1995.

Guha, Ramachandra. *The Unquiet Woods: Ecological Change and Peasant Resistance in the Himalaya*. Berkeley: University of California Press, 2000.

Guldi, Jo. *Roads to Power: How Britain Invented the Infrastructure State*. Cambridge, MA: Harvard University Press, 2012.

Gurung, Shaurya Karanbir. "India and China Need to Demarcate LAC." *The Economic Times*, September 6, 2017. http://economictimes.indiatimes.com/news/defence/india-and-china-need-to-demarcate-lac/articleshow/6038345 1.cms.

Gutschow, Kim. "'Lords of the Fort,' 'Lords of the Water,' and 'No Lords at All': The Politics of Irrigation in Three Tibetan Societies." In *Recent Research on Ladakh 6*, edited by Henry Osmaston and Nawang Tsering, 105–15. Bristol, UK: University of Bristol, 1997.

Guyot-Réchard, Bérénice. *Shadow States: India, China and the Himalayas, 1910–1962*. Cambridge: Cambridge University Press, 2017.

"Tour Diaries and Itinerant Governance in the Eastern Himalayas, 1909–1962." *The Historical Journal* 60, no. 4 (2017): 1023–46.

Gyatso, Janet. "Down with the Demoness: Reflections on a Feminine Ground in Tibet." *Tibet Journal* 12, no. 4 (1987): 38–53.

Hamilton, Walter. *The East India Gazetteer; Containing Particular Descriptions of the Empires, Kingdoms, Principalities, Provinces, Cities, Towns, Districts, Fortresses, Harbours, Rivers, Lakes, &c. of Hindostan, and the Adjacent Countries, India beyond the Ganges, and the Eastern Archipelago; Together with Sketches of the Manners, Customs, Institutions, Agriculture, Commerce, Manufactures, Revenues, Population, Castes, Religion, History, &c. of Their Various Inhabitants*. London: J. Murray, 1815.

Hanna, Henry Bathurst. *India's Scientific Frontier: Where Is It? What Is It?* Westminster: Archibald Constable, 1895.

Hansen, Valerie. *The Silk Road: A New History*. New York: Oxford University Press, 2012.

Harley, J. B. "Deconstructing the Map." In *The New Nature of Maps: Essays in the History of Cartography*, edited by Paul Laxton, 150–68. Baltimore: Johns Hopkins University Press, 2001.

Hedin, Sven. *Trans-Himalaya: Discoveries and Adventures in Tibet*. 3 vols. New York: Macmillan, 1909.

Heesterman, J. C. *The Inner Conflict of Tradition: Essays in Indian Ritual, Kingship, and Society*. Chicago: University of Chicago Press, 1985.

Heidegger, Martin. "Building, Dwelling, Thinking." In *Basic Writings: From "Being and Time" (1927) to "The Task of Thinking" (1964)*, 347–63. San Francisco: Harper, 1993.

Herbert, J. D. "An Account of a Tour Made to Lay down the Course and Levels of the River Sutlej or Satudra, as Far as Traceable within the Limits of the British Authority, Performed in 1819." *Asiatic Researches* 18 (1819): 227–58.

Hevia, James. *Imperial Security State: British Colonial Knowledge and Empire-Building in Asia*. Cambridge: Cambridge University Press, 2012.

Hevia, James L. *Cherishing Men from Afar: Qing Guest Ritual and the Macartney Embassy of 1793.* Durham, NC: Duke University Press, 1995.

English Lessons: The Pedagogy of Imperialism in Nineteenth-Century China. Durham, NC: Duke University Press, 2003.

"Tributary Systems." In *The Encyclopedia of Empire,* edited by N. Dalziel and J. M. MacKenzie. Hoboken, NJ: John Wiley, 2016. doi:10.1002/9781118455074.wbeoe062.

Hinsley, F. H. *Sovereignty.* New York: Cambridge University Press, 1966.

Holdich, Thomas H. "African Boundaries, and the Application of Indian Systems of Geographical Survey to Africa." *Proceedings of the Royal Geographical Society and Monthly Record of Geography* 13, no. 10 (1891): 596–607.

India. The Regions of the World. London: Frowde, 1904.

Political Frontiers and Boundary Making. London: Macmillan, 1916. http://pi.lib.uchicago.edu/1001/cat/bib/2032580.

"Some Aspects of Political Geography." *The Geographical Journal* 34, no. 6 (1909): 593–607.

The Indian Borderland, 1880–1900. London: Methuen, 1901.

"The Use of Practical Geography Illustrated by Recent Frontier Operations." *The Geographical Journal* 13, no. 5 (1899): 465–77.

Tibet, the Mysterious. New York: F. A. Stokes, 1906.

Hopkins, B. D. *Ruling the "Savage" Periphery: Frontier Governance and the Making of the Modern World.* Cambridge, MA: Harvard University Press, 2020.

"The Bounds of Identity: The Goldsmid Mission and the Delineation of the Perso–Afghan Border in the Nineteenth Century." *Journal of Global History* 2, no. 2 (2007): 233–54.

The Making of Modern Afghanistan. New York: Palgrave Macmillan, 2008.

Hopkirk, Peter. *The Great Game: On Secret Service in High Asia.* Oxford: Oxford University Press, 1991.

Huber, Toni. *The Holy Land Reborn: Pilgrimage and the Tibetan Buddhist Reinvention of Buddhist India.* Chicago: University of Chicago Press, 2008.

Humboldt, Alexander von. *Asie Centrale: Recherches sur Les Chaines des Montagnes et la Climatologie Comparée.* 3 vols. Paris: Gide, 1843.

Hunter, William Wilson. *Heads of Information Required for the Imperial Gazetteer of India, with Rules for the Spelling of Indian Proper Names.* Simla: Government Central Press, 1871.

The Imperial Gazetteer of India. Vol. 1. London: Trübner, 1881.

Huntington, Ellsworth. *Climate and Civilization.* New York: Harper, 1915.

The Character of Races as Influenced by Physical Environment, Natural Selection and Historical Development. New York: C. Scribner's Sons, 1924.

The Pulse of Asia, a Journey in Central Asia Illustrating the Geographic Basis of History. Boston: Houghton, Mifflin, 1919.

Huntington, Ellsworth, and Sumner Cushing. *Principles of Human Geography.* New York: John Wiley, 1934.

Ibbetson, Denzil. *Gazetteer of the Gújrát District, 1883–84, Compiled and Published under the Authority of the Punjab Government.* Lahore: Arya Press, 1884.

Ilāhābādī, Akbar. *Kulliyyāt-i Akbar Illāhābādī.* Edited by Aḥmad Maḥfūẓ. Vol. 1. Na'i Dihlī: Qaumī kaunsil barā'e furogẖ-i Urdū zabān, 2002.

Imy, Kate. "Kidnapping and a 'Confirmed Sodomite': An Intimate Enemy on the Northwest Frontier of India, 1915–1925." *Twentieth Century British History* 28, no. 1 (2017): 29–56.

Intelligence Branch. *Gazetteer of Kashmír and Ladák, Together with Routes in the Territories of the Maharaja of Jamú and Kashmír. Compiled (for Political and Military Reference) under the Direction of the Quarter Master General in India in the Intelligence Branch.* Calcutta: Superintendent of Government Printing, India, 1890.

Iqbal, Muhammad. "Hamāla." 1901. http://iqbalurdu.blogspot.com/2011/02/h amala-bang-e-dra-1.html.

Isaac, Rhys. *The Transformation of Virginia, 1740–1790.* Williamsburg, VA: University of North Carolina Press, 1982.

Ishikawa, Noboru. *Between Frontiers: Nation and Identity in a Southeast Asian Borderland.* Athens: Ohio University Press, 2010.

Ispahani, Mahnaz Z. *Roads and Rivals: The Political Uses of Access in the Borderlands of Asia.* Ithaca, NY: Cornell University Press, 1989.

Jacquemont, Victor. *Letters from India; Describing a Journey in the British Dominions of India, Tibet, Lahore, and Cashmeer, during the Years 1828, 1829, 1830, 1831. Undertaken by Order of the French Government.* 2 vols. London: Edward Churton, 1834.

Johnson, Robert. *Spying for Empire: The Great Game in Central and South Asia, 1757–1947.* St. Paul, MN: Greenhill Books, 2006.

Jones, Stephen B. *Boundary-Making: A Handbook for Statesmen, Treaty Editors and Boundary Commissioners.* Washington, DC: Carnegie Endowment for International Peace, 1945.

Kanwar, Pamela. *Imperial Simla: The Political Culture of the Raj.* Delhi: Oxford University Press, 1990.

Kapadia, Harish. *Spiti: Adventures in the Trans-Himalaya.* New Delhi: Indus, 1996.

Kaplan, Robert D. *The Revenge of Geography: What the Map Tells Us about Coming Conflicts and the Battle against Fate.* New York: Random House, 2012.

Kaplanian, Patrick. "L'homme dans le monde surnaturel du Ladakh." In *Recent Research on Ladakh 4 & 5*, edited by Henry Osmaston and Philip Denwood, 101–8. Delhi: Motilal Banarsidas, 1995.

Kennedy, Dane. *The Magic Mountains: Hill Stations and the British Raj.* Berkeley: University of California Press, 1996.

Kennion, R. L. *Sport and Life in the Further Himalaya.* Edinburgh: William Blackwood and Sons, 1910.

Khan Lakhnavi, Hashmattulah. *Tārīkh-i-Jammūn.* Anarkali, Lahore: Maktaba Asha't Adab, 1968.

Khan, Yasmin. *The Great Partition: The Making of India and Pakistan.* New Delhi: Penguin, 2007.

Kim, Hodong. *Holy War in China: The Muslim Rebellion and State in Chinese Central Asia, 1864–1877.* Stanford, CA: Stanford University Press, 2004.

Kipling, Rudyard. *Kim.* London: Macmillan, 1901.

    Plain Tales from the Hills. 1888. Reprint, Oxford: Oxford University Press, 2001.

Koselleck, Reinhardt. *Futures Past: On the Semantics of Historical Time*. New York: Columbia University Press, 2004.

Kuhn, Thomas S. *The Structure of Scientific Revolutions*. 2nd ed. Chicago: University of Chicago Press, 1970.

Lacoste, Yves. *La géographie, ça sert, d'abord, à faire la guerre*. Paris: F. Maspero, 1982.

Lall, John. *Aksaichin and Sino-Indian Conflict*. Ahmedabad: Allied, 1989.

Lamb, Alastair. *Asian Frontiers: Studies in a Continuing Problem*. New York: Frederick A. Raeger, 1968.

    Britain and Chinese Central Asia. London: Routledge and Kegan Paul, 1960.

    The China–India Border: The Origins of the Disputed Boundaries. London: Oxford University Press, 1964.

    The McMahon Line: A Study in the Relations between India, China and Tibet, 1904 to 1914: Vol. 2. Hardinge, McMahon and the Simla Conference. London: Routledge and Kegan Paul, 1966.

    The Sino-Indian Border in Ladakh. Canberra: Australian National University Press, 1973.

Landon, Perceval. *The Opening of Tibet; an Account of Lhasa and the Country and People of Central Tibet and of the Progress of the Mission Sent There by the English Government in the Year 1903–4; Written, with the Help of All the Principal Persons of the Mission*. New York: Doubleday, 1905.

Lawrence, Walter. "The British Mission to Tibet." *The North American Review* 178, no. 571 (1904): 869–81.

Leake, Elisabeth. *The Defiant Border: The Afghan–Pakistan Borderlands in the Era of Decolonization, 1936–1965*. New York: Cambridge University Press, 2017.

Lefebvre, Henri. *The Production of Space*. Translated by Donald Nicholson-Smith. Oxford: Blackwell, 1991.

Legislative Assembly. *The Proceedings before the Judicial Committee of Her Majesty's Imperial Privy Council on the Special Case Respecting the Westerly Boundary of Ontario . . .* Toronto: Warwick, 1889.

Leonard, Zak. "Muslim Fanaticism as Ambiguous Trope: A Study in Polemical Mutation." In *Mountstuart Elphinstone in South Asia: Pioneer of British Colonial Rule*, 91–116. London: Hurst, 2019.

Lloyd, William, and Alexander Gerard. *Narrative of a Journey from Caunpoor to the Boorendo Pass in the Himalaya Mountains*. 2 vols. London: J. Madden, 1840.

Ludden, David. "The Process of Empire: Frontiers and Borderlands." In *Tributary Empires in Global History*, edited by C. A. Bayly and P. F. Bang, 132–50. London: Palgrave Macmillan, 2011.

Lyall, Alfred. "Frontiers and Protectorates." *Nineteenth Century: A Monthly Review* 30, no. 174 (1891): 312–28.

Macdonald, Robert H. *The Language of Empire: Myths and Metaphors of Popular Imperialism, 1880–1918*. Manchester, UK: Manchester University Press, 1994.

Mackinder, Halford J. "The Geographical Pivot of History." *The Geographical Journal* 23, no. 4 (1904): 421–37.

Mahan, Alfred Thayer. *The Influence of Sea Power upon History, 1660–1783*. Boston: Little, Brown, 1890.

The Problem of Asia and Its Effect upon International Policies. Boston: Little, Brown, 1900.

Maier, Charles. "Consigning the Twentieth Century to History: Alternative Narratives for the Modern Era." *The American Historical Review* 105 (June 2000): 807–31.

Once within Borders: Territories of Power, Wealth, and Belonging since 1500. Cambridge, MA: Harvard University Press, 2016.

Mallampalli, Chandra. *A Muslim Conspiracy in British India? Politics and Paranoia in the Early Nineteenth Century Deccan.* Cambridge: Cambridge University Press, 2017.

Marshall, Peter James, and G. Williams. *The Great Map of Mankind: British Perceptions of the World in the Age of Enlightenment.* London: Dent, 1982.

Martin, Dan. *Tibetan Histories: A Bibliography of Tibetan-Language Historical Works.* London: Serindia, 1997.

Maxwell, Neville. *India's China War.* New Delhi: Natraj, 2015.

McClintock, Anne. *Imperial Leather: Race, Gender and Sexuality in the Colonial Contest.* New York: Routledge, 1995.

McGranahan, Carole. "Empire and the Status of Tibet: British, Chinese, and Tibetan Negotiations, 1913 – 1934." In *The History of Tibet: Vol. 3. The Modern Period: 1895–1959, the Encounter with Modernity,* edited by Alex McKay, 267–95. London: RoutledgeCurzon, 2003.

"Empire Out of Bounds: Tibet in the Era of Decolonization." In *Imperial Formations,* edited by Ann Laura Stoler, Carole McGranahan, and Peter C. Perdue, 173–209. Santa Fe, NM: School for Advanced Research Press, 2007.

McKay, Alex. *Kailas Histories: Renunciate Traditions and the Construction of Himalayan Sacred Geography.* Leiden: Brill, 2015.

Tibet and the British Raj: The Frontier Cadre, 1904–1947. Richmond, UK: Curzon, 1997.

"'Tracing Lines upon the Unknown Areas of the Earth': Reflections on Frederick Jackson Turner and the Indo-Tibetan Frontier." In *Fringes of Empire,* edited by Sameetah Agha and Elizabeth Kolsky, 69–93. New Delhi: Oxford University Press, 2009.

McMahon, A. H. "International Boundaries." *Journal of the Royal Society of Arts* 84, no. 4330 (1935): 2–16.

Megoran, Nick. *Nationalism in Central Asia: A Biography of the Uzbekistan–Kyrgyzstan Boundary.* Pittsburgh: University of Pittsburgh Press, 2017.

Mehra, Parshotam. *An "Agreed" Frontier: Ladakh and India's Northernmost Borders, 1846–1947.* New Delhi: Oxford University Press, 1992.

Menon, Ritu. *Borders and Boundaries: Women in India's Partition.* New Delhi: Kali for Women, 1998.

Menon, V. P. *Integration of the Indian States.* New Delhi: Orient BlackSwan, 2014.

Metcalf, Tom, and Barbara Metcalf. *A Concise History of Modern India.* Cambridge: Cambridge University Press, 2001.

Mezzadra, Sandro, and Brett Neilson. *Border as Method, or, the Multiplication of Labor.* Durham, NC: Duke University Press, 2013.

Mignolo, Walter. *Local Histories/Global Designs: Coloniality, Subaltern Knowledges, and Border Thinking*. Princeton, NJ: Princeton University Press, 2012.

Mills, Martin. "The Religion of Locality: Local Area Gods and the Characterisation of Tibetan Buddhism." In *Recent Research on Ladakh 7*, edited by Thierry Dodin and Hans Rather, 309–28. Bonn, Germany: Ulmer Kulturanthroplogische Schriften, 1997.

Millward, James. *Eurasian Crossroads: A History of Xinjiang*. New York: Columbia University Press, 2008.

Mishra, Pankaj. "India at 70, and the Passing of Another Illusion." *New York Times*, August 11, 2017. www.nytimes.com/2017/08/11/opinion/india-70-partition-pankaj-mishra.html.

Mitchell, Timothy. *Colonizing Egypt*. Berkeley: University of California Press, 1991.

Mohamad, Chaudhri. *Preliminary Report of Ladakh Settlement*. Jammu: Ranbir Prakesh Press, 1908.

Mohammed, Jigar. "Mughal Sources on Medieval Ladakh, Baltistan and Western Tibet." In *Ladakhi Histories: Local and Regional Perspectives*, edited by John Bray, 147–60. Leiden: Brill, 2005.

Moorcroft, William. "A Journey to Lake Manasarovara in Undes, a Province of Little Tibet." *Asiatic Researches; or, Transactions of the Society, Instituted in Bengal* 12 (1816): 380–536.

Moorcroft, William, and George Trebeck. *Travels in the Himalayan Provinces of Hindustan and the Panjab; in Ladakh and Kashmir; in Peshawar, Kabul, Kunduz, and Bokhara; from 1819 to 1825*. Edited by Horace Hayman Wilson. 2 vols. London: John Murray, 1841.

Moran, Arik, and Catherine Warner. "Charting Himalayan Histories." *Himalaya, the Journal of the Association for Nepal and Himalayan Studies* 35, no. 2 (2016): 32–40.

Moran, Joe. *On Roads: A Hidden History*. London: Profile Books, 2009.

Moreman, T. R. "The Arms Trade and the North-West Frontier Pathan Tribes, 1890–1914." *The Journal of Imperial and Commonwealth History* 22, no. 2 (2008): 187–216.

Morgan, Gerald. *Ney Elias: Explorer and Envoy Extraordinary in High Asia*. London: George Allen and Unwin, 1971.

Mosca, Matthew. *From Frontier Policy to Foreign Policy: The Question of India and the Transformation of Geopolitics in Qing China*. Stanford, CA: Stanford University Press, 2013.

"Kashmiri Merchants and Qing Intelligence Networks in the Himalayas: The Ahmed Ali Case of 1830." In *Asia Inside Out: Connected Places*, edited by Peter C. Perdue and Helen F. Siu, 219–42. Cambridge, MA: Harvard University Press, 2015.

Muhammad, Ghulam. *Récit d'un Voyageur Musulman au Tibet*. Translated by M. Gaborieau. Paris: Librairie C. Klincksieck, 1973.

Nail, Thomas. *Theory of the Border*. Oxford: Oxford University Press, 2016.

Nandy, Ashis. *The Intimate Enemy: Loss and Recovery of Self under Colonialism*. New Delhi: Oxford University Press, 2005.

Naqvi, Saba. "One Point Five/Two: Jharkhand Has Been Mined, Jammu-Kashmir Is Still a Prospect." *Outlook*, January 12, 2015.

Nebesky-Wojkowitz, Rene de. *Oracles and Demons of Tibet: The Cult and Iconography of the Tibetan Protective Deities.* Delhi: Book Faith India, 1996.

Needham, F. J., and H. J. Elwes. "The Roads to Tibet." *The Geographical Journal* 23, no. 3 (1904): 397–400.

Neyroud, Michel. "Organisation de l'espace, Isolement et Changement dans le Domaine Transhimalayen: Le Zanskar." *L'Espace géographique* 14, no. 4 (1985): 271–84.

Pachauri, S. K. "British Perceptions of Relations with Maharaja Ranjit Singh." In *Maharaja Ranjit Singh: Ruler and Warrior,* edited by T. R. Sharma. Chandigarh: Panjab University Publication Bureau, 2005.

Palat, Madhavan K., ed. *Selected Works of Jawaharlal Nehru.* Vol. 52, Second Series. New Delhi: Jawaharlal Nehru Memorial Fund, 1984.

Pandey, Avaneesh. "India Bans Al Jazeera for 5 Days Over 'Incorrect' Kashmir Map." *International Business Times,* April 23, 2015.

Panikkar, K. M. *The Founding of the Kashmir State: A Biography of Maharajah Gulab Singh, 1792–1858.* London: George Allen and Unwin, 1953.

Patterson, Maureen L. P. *South Asian Civilizations: A Bibliographic Synthesis.* Chicago: University of Chicago Press, 1981.

Paul, A. W. "The Roads to Tibet." *The Geographical Journal* 23, no. 4 (1904): 528–29.

Perdue, Peter C. *China Marches West: The Qing Conquest of Central Eurasia.* Cambridge, MA: Harvard University Press, 2005.

Petech, Luciano. *Kingdom of Ladakh: C. 950–1842 A.D.* Serie Orientale Roma 51. Rome: Istituto italiano per il Medio ed Estremo Oriente, 1977.

Phuntsog, Sonam. "Sacrificial Offerings to Local Deities in Ladakh." In *Recent Research on Ladakh 6,* edited by Henry Osmaston and Nawang Tsering, 213–14. Bristol, UK: University of Bristol, 1997.

Pomeranz, Kenneth. "Asia's Unstable Water Tower: The Politics, Economics, and Ecology of Himalayan Water Projects." *Asia Policy* 16 (July 2013): 1–10.

Pommaret, Françoise. "Yul and Yul Lha: The Territory and Its Deity in Bhutan." *Bulletin of Tibetology* 40, no. 1 (2004): 39–67.

Pumpelly, Raphael, ed. *Explorations in Turkestan, with an Account of the Basin of Eastern Persia and Sistan. Expedition of 1903, under the Direction of Raphael Pumpelly.* Washington, DC: Carnegie Institution of Washington, 1905.

Rai, Mridu. *Hindu Ruler, Muslim Subject: Islam, Rights, and the History of Kashmir.* Princeton, NJ: Princeton University Press, 2004.

Raj, Kapil. "La Construction de l'empire de La Géographie: L'odyssée des Arpenteurs de Sa Très Gracieuse Majesté, la Reine Victoria, en Asie Centrale." *Annales: Histoire, Sciences Sociales* 52, no. 5 (1997): 1153–80.

Relocating Modern Science: Circulation and the Construction of Knowledge in South Asia and Europe, 1650–1900. New York: Palgrave Macmillan, 2007.

Rajan, Chandra, trans. *The Complete Works of Kālidāsa: Poems.* Vol. 1. New Delhi: Sahitya Akademi, 2005.

Ramaswamy, Sumathi. "Visualising India's Geo-Body: Globes, Maps, Bodyscapes." *Contributions to Indian Sociology* 36, nos. 1–2 (2002): 151–89.

Ray, Nisith Ranjan. *Himalaya Frontier in Historical Perspective.* Calcutta: Institute of Historical Studies, 1986.

Reeves, Madeleine. *Border Work: Spatial Lives of the State in Rural Central Asia.* Ithaca, NY: Cornell University Press, 2014.

Rizvi, Janet. *Ladakh: Crossroads of High Asia.* New Delhi: Oxford University Press, 1999.

Trans-Himalayan Caravans: Merchant Princes and Peasant Traders in Ladakh. New Delhi: Oxford University Press, 1999.

Rushdie, Salman. *Midnight's Children.* New York: Alfred A. Knopf, 1981.

Sahlins, Peter. *Boundaries: The Making of France and Spain in the Pyrenees.* Berkeley: University of California Press, 1989.

Said, Edward W. "Invention, Memory, and Place." In *Landscape and Power,* edited by W. J. T. Mitchell, 242–61. Chicago: University of Chicago Press, 2005.

Sauer, Carl O. "The Morphology of Landscape." *University of California Publications in Geography* 2, no. 2 (1925): 19–53.

Schendel, Willem van. "Stateless in South Asia: The Making of the India-Bangladesh Enclaves." *The Journal of Asian Studies* 61, no. 1 (2002): 115–47.

The Bengal Borderland: Beyond State and Nation in South Asia. London: Anthem Press, 2003.

Schofield, Victoria. *Afghan Frontier: Feuding and Fighting in Central Asia.* New York: Tauris Parke, 2003.

Scholberg, Henry. *The District Gazetteers of British India: A Bibliography.* Zug, Switzerland: Inter Documentation, 1970.

Schwieger, Peter. "Power and Territory in the Kingdom of Ladakh." In *Recent Research on Ladakh 7,* edited by Thierry Dodin and Heinz Rather, 427–34. Ulm: Universität Ulm, 1997.

Scott, James C. *Against the Grain: A Deep History of the Earliest States.* New Haven, CT: Yale University Press, 2017.

Seeing Like a State: How Certain Schemes to Improve the Human Condition Have Failed. New Haven, CT: Yale University Press, 1998.

The Art of Not Being Governed: An Anarchist History of Upland Southeast Asia. New Haven, CT: Yale University Press, 2009.

Sewell, William H. *The Logics of History.* Chicago: Chicago University Press, 2005.

Shakabpa, Tsepon W. D. *Tibet: A Political History.* New Haven, CT: Yale University Press, 1967.

Shakspo, Nawang Tsering. *A Cultural History of Ladakh.* Edited by Kyle Gardner. New Delhi: Centre for Research on Ladakh, 2010.

Shakspo, Sonam Wangchuk. *Bakula Rinpoche: A Visionary Lama and Statesman.* New Delhi: Sonam Wangchuk Shakspo, 2008.

Shaw, Robert. *Visits to High Tartary, Yarkand, and Kashgar (Formerly Chinese Tartary) and Return Journey over the Karakoram Pass.* London: J. Murray, 1871.

Sheikh, Abdul Ghani. *Reflections on Ladakh, Tibet and Central Asia.* Leh, Ladakh: Yasmin House, 2010.

Shneiderman, Sara. "Are the Central Himalayas in Zomia? Some Scholarly and Political Considerations across Time and Space." *Journal of Global History* 5 (2010): 289–312.

Simpson, Thomas. "Bordering and Frontier-Making in Nineteenth-Century British India." *The Historical Journal* 58, no. 2 (2015): 513–42.

"Modern Mountains from the Enlightenment to the Anthropocene." *The Historical Journal* 62, no. 2 (2018): 553–81.

Smadja, Joëlle, ed. *Reading Himalayan Landscapes over Time: Environmental Perception, Knowledge and Practice in Nepal and Ladakh*. Paris: Centre National de la Recherche Scientifique, 2003.

Smail, Daniel Lord. *Imaginary Cartographies: Possession and Identity in Late Medieval Marseille*. Ithaca, NY: Cornell University Press, 1999.

Spence, Jonathan D. *The Search for Modern China*. 2nd ed. New York: W. W. Norton, 1999.

Spengen, Wim van. *Tibetan Border Worlds: A Geohistorical Analysis of Trade and Traders*. London: Kegan Paul International, 2000.

Stratchey, Richard. "On the Snow-Line in the Himalaya." *Journal of the Asiatic Society*, April 1849.

Streets-Salter, Heather. *Martial Races: The Military, Race and Masculinity in British Imperial Culture, 1857–1914*. Manchester, UK: Manchester University Press, 2004.

Teltscher, Kate. *The High Road to China: George Bogle, the Panchen Lama and the First British Expedition to Tibet*. London: Bloomsbury, 2006.

Tinkler, Keith J. *A Short History of Geomorphology*. Totowa, NJ: Barnes and Noble, 1985.

Tod, James. *Annals and Antiquities of Rajast'han*. 2 vols. London: George Routledge, 1914.

Trotter, Henry. *Account of the Survey Operations in Connection with the Mission to Yarkand and Kashghar in 1873–74 . . ..*. Calcutta: Foreign Department Press, 1875.

Ts'e.brtan, dGe.rgan bSod.nams. *BLa.Dwags* [sic] *Rgyal.Rabs 'chi.Med Gter* [The Immortal Treasury of the Royal Chronicles of Ladakh]. Edited by sKyabs.ldan dGe.rgan. New Delhi, 1976.

Tuan, Yi-Fu. *Space and Place: The Perspective of Experience*. Minneapolis: University of Minnesota Press, 1977.

   Topophilia: A Study of Environmental Perception, Attitudes, and Values. Englewood Cliffs, NJ: Prentice Hall, 1974.

Turner, Frederick Jackson. "The Significance of the Frontier in American History." In *The Frontier in American History*, 1–38. New York: Henry Holt, 1920.

Twiss, Travers. *The Oregon Question Examined, in Respect to the Facts and the Law of Nations*. London: Longman, Brown, Green, and Longmans, 1846.

United Kingdom, House of Commons. "Minutes and Correspondence in Reference to the Project of the Hindostan and Thibet Road, with Reports of Major Kennedy and Lieutenant Briggs Relating Thereto; and, an Account of the Expenditure Incurred in the Construction of the New Road between Kalha and Dugshai." Sessional Papers, 1857 East India (roads), February 2, 1857.

Vattel, Emer de. *Droit des gens; ou, Principes de la loi naturelle appliqués à la conduite et aux affaires des nations et des souverains*. Washington, DC: Carnegie Institution of Washington, 1916.

Wacker, Corinne. "Can Irrigation Systems Disclose the History of the Villages of Ladakh? The Example of Tagmachig." In *Recent Research on Ladakh 2007*, edited by John Bray and Nawang Tsering Shakspo, 205–16. Leh: J&K Academy of Art, Culture, and Languages, 2007.

Waddell, L. A. "Map of Lhasa and Its Environs." *The Geographical Journal* 23, no. 3 (1904): 366.

Waller, Derek. *The Pundits: British Exploration of Tibet and Central Asia.* Lexington: University of Kentucky Press, 1990.

Wheaton, Henry. *Elements of International Law.* 3rd ed. Philadelphia: Lea and Blanchard, 1846.

Whitfield, Susan, and Ursula Sims-Williams. *The Silk Road: Trade, Travel, War, and Faith.* London: British Library, 2004.

Williams, Raymond. *The Country and the City.* New York: Oxford University Press, 1975.

Winichakul, Thongchai. *Siam Mapped: A History of the Geo-Body of a Nation.* Honolulu: University of Hawai'i Press, 1994.

Wink, André. "From the Mediterranean to the Indian Ocean: Medieval History in Geographic Perspective." *Comparative Studies in Society and History* 44 (2002): 416–45.

Wood, Denis. *The Power of Maps.* New York: Guilford Press, 1992.

Wood, Denis, and John Fels. *The Natures of Maps: Cartographic Constructions of the Natural World.* Chicago: University of Chicago Press, 2008.

Woodman, Dorothy. *Himalayan Frontiers: A Political Review of British, Chinese, Indian, and Russian Rivalries.* London: Barrie and Rockliff, 1969.

Wulf, Andrea. *The Invention of Nature: Alexander von Humboldt's New World.* New York: Vintage, 2015.

Yapp, Malcolm. "The Legend of the Great Game." *Proceedings of the British Academy* 111 (2001): 179–98.

Young, H. A. *The East India Company's Arsenals and Manufactories.* Oxford: Clarendon Press, 1937.

Younghusband, Francis E. "Journeys in the Pamirs and Adjacent Countries." *Proceedings of the Royal Geographical Society and Monthly Record of Geography* 14, no. 4 (1892): 205–34.

The Heart of a Continent: A Narrative of Travels in Manchuria, across the Gobi Desert, through the Himalayas, the Pamirs, and Chitral, 1884–1894. 3rd ed. New York: Scribner, 1896.

Zamindar, Vazira Fazila-Yacoobali. *The Long Partition and the Making of Modern South Asia: Refugees, Boundaries, Histories.* New York: Columbia University Press, 2007.

Zimmerman, Francis. *The Jungle and the Aroma of Meats: An Ecological Theme in Hindu Medicine.* Berkeley: University of California Press, 1987.

Zutshi, Chitralekha. "Designed for Eternity: Kashmiri Shawls, Empire, and Cultures of Production and Consumption in Mid-Victorian Britain." *Journal of British Studies* 48, no. 2 (2009): 420–40.

Kashmir's Contested Pasts: Narratives, Sacred Geographies, and the Historical Imagination. New Delhi: Oxford University Press, 2014.

Languages of Belonging: Islam, Regional Identity, and the Making of Kashmir. New York: Oxford University Press, 2004.

Index

Printed by Printforce, the Netherlands